India's Ancient Past

This book provides a comprehensive and accessible account of the history of early India. Beginning with a discussion on frameworks of the writing of history—approaches, sources, and significance—the book sheds light on the origins and growth of civilizations, empires, and religions. It covers the geographical, ecological, and linguistic backgrounds, and looks at specific cultures of the Neolithic, Chalcolithic, and Vedic periods, as well as at the Harappan civilization. The author discusses the rise of Jainism and Buddhism, Magadha and the beginning of territorial states, and the period of Mauryas, Central Asian countries, Satvahanas, Guptas, and Harshavardhana. He highlights important phenomena such as the varna system, urbanization, commerce and trade, developments in science and philosophy, and cultural legacy. He also examines the process of transition from Ancient to Medieval India and addresses topical issues such as the origin of the Aryan culture.

This engaging and lucid text, by one of the best-known scholars of ancient India, will be indispensable for students and teachers of ancient Indian history.

R. S. Sharma is Emeritus Professor, Department of History, University of Patna. He is also the Founder Chairman of Indian Council of Historical Research, New Delhi.

India's Ancient Past

R.S. Sharma

OXFORD
UNIVERSITY PRESS

OXFORD
UNIVERSITY PRESS

Oxford University Press is a department of the University of Oxford. It furthers the University's objective of excellence in research, scholarship, and education by publishing worldwide. Oxford is a registered trademark of Oxford University Press in the UK and in certain other countries.

Published in India by
Oxford University Press
22 Workspace, 2nd Floor, 1/22 Asaf Ali Road, New Delhi 110002

First Edition published in 2005
Reprint 2023

ISBN-13 (print edition): 978-93-5497-752-7
ISBN-10 (print edition): 93-5497-752-9

ISBN-13 (eBook): 978-0-19-908786-0
ISBN-10 (eBook): 0-19-908786-5

Cover image: Archer-type gold Dinara of Chandragupta II © Amit Vyas

Typeset by Le Studio Graphique, Gurgaon 122 001
Printed in India by Nutech Print Services - India

Preface

The present book is based on a good portion of my *Ancient India*, which was first published by the National Council of Educational Research and Training in 1977, but the obscurantist elements got it withdrawn from circulation by the same body in 1978. The book was restored in 1980, and several lacs were printed for school students. However, when in 2001 the NCERT published it, some passages were removed without the author's consent. Finally in 2002 the NCERT withdrew the book because of extreme conservatism. When the Oxford University Press approached me for publication, I decided to get the revised copy of the existing edition published by them. I substantially revised the book and added four new chapters to it. In doing so I took account of new ideas and materials available to me.

The book covers Indian history from the beginning to the 7th century AD. Since it is mainly meant for undergraduates and general readers, I have used non-English words without diacritics. I have also avoided chapter-wise references, but an up-to-date chapter-wise bibliography has been provided at the end of the book for the materials I have used. I will feel happy if the book retains its old popularity.

Patna
July 2005

R.S. Sharma
(RAM SHARAN SHARMA)

Acknowledgements

In preparing *India's Ancient Past* I have received helps from several quarters. Sita Ram Roy has prepared the chronology and also suggested some improvements in the text. The index has been mainly prepared by Anjani Kumar who has also compiled the bibliography. In addition to these two persons, Angaraj Choudhary, Arundhati Banerji, Chandraprakash Narayan Singh, K.K. Mandal, Parvej Akhtar, Prachi Sharma, Rajeshwar Prasad, R.L. Shukla, Sarjun Prasad, and Surendra Gopal, have helped me in different ways. I thank all of them. Nitasha Devasar, Aparajita Basu, and Shashank Sinha of the OUP have helped me in the publication of the book. They deserve my sincere thanks.

Contents

Plates

Between Pages 212–213

Maps

1

The Significance of Ancient Indian History

The study of ancient Indian history is important for several reasons. It tells us how, when, and where people developed the earliest cultures in India, how they began undertaking agriculture and stock raising which made life secure and settled. It shows how the ancient Indians discovered and utilized natural resources, and how they created the means for their livelihood. We get an idea of how the ancient inhabitants made arrangements for food, shelter, and transport, and learn how they took to farming, spinning, weaving, metalworking, and the like, how they cleared forests, founded villages, cities, and eventually large kingdoms.

People are not considered civilized unless they know how to write. The different forms of writing prevalent in India today are all derived from the ancient scripts. This is also true of the languages that we speak today. The languages we use have roots in ancient times, and have developed through the ages.

Unity in Diversity

Ancient Indian history is interesting because many races and tribes intermingled in early India. The pre-Aryans, the Indo-Aryans, the Greeks, the Scythians, the Hunas, the Turks, and others made India their home. Each ethnic group contributed its mite to the evolution of the Indian social system, art and architecture, language and literature. All these peoples and their cultural traits commingled so inextricably that currently they can be clearly identified in their original form.

A remarkable feature of ancient Indian culture has been the commingling of cultural elements from the north and south, and from the east and west. The Aryan elements are equated with the Vedic and Puranic culture of the north and the pre-Aryan with the Dravidian and Tamil culture of the south. However, many Munda, Dravidian and other non-Sanskritic terms occur in the Vedic texts ascribed to 1500–500 BC. They indicate ideas, institutions, products, and settlements associated with peninsular and non-Vedic India. Similarly, many Pali and Sanskrit terms, signifying ideas and institutions, developed in the Gangetic plains, appear in the earliest Tamil texts called the Sangam literature which is roughly used for the period 300 BC–AD 600. The eastern region inhabited by the pre-Aryan tribals made its own contribution. The people of this area spoke the Munda or Kolarian languages. Several terms that signify the use of cotton, navigation, digging stick, etc., in the Indo-Aryan languages have been traced to the Munda languages by linguists. Although there are many Munda pockets in Chhotanagpur plateau, the remnants of Munda culture in the Indo-Aryan culture are fairly strong. Many Dravidian terms too are to be found in the Indo-Aryan languages. It is held that changes in the phonetics and vocabulary of the Vedic language can be explained as much on the basis of the Dravidian influence as that of the Munda.

India has since ancient times been a land of several religions. Ancient India saw the birth of Brahmanism or Hinduism, Jainism, and Buddhism, but all these cultures and religions intermingled and interacted. Thus, though Indians speak different languages, practise different religions, and observe different social customs, they follow certain common styles of life. Our country shows a deep underlying unity despite great diversity.

The ancients strove for unity. The Indian subcontinent was geographically well defined and its geographical unity was supplemented by cultural integration. Though there existed many states, languages, cultures, and communities, gradually people developed territorial identity. The states or territorial units, called *janapadas*, were named after different tribes. However, the country as a whole came to be named Aryavarta after the dominant cultural community called the Aryans. Aryavarta denoted northern and central India and extended from the eastern to the western sea coasts. The other name by which India was better known was Bharatavarsha or the land of the Bharatas. Bharata, in the sense of tribe or family, figures in the *Rig Veda* and *Mahabharata*, but the name Bharatavarsha occurs in the *Mahabharata* and post-Gupta Sanskrit texts. This name was applied to one of the nine divisions of the earth, and in the post-Gupta period it denoted India. The term Bharati or an inhabitant of India occurs in post-Gupta texts.

Iranian inscriptions are important for the origin of the term Hindu. The term Hindu occurs in the inscriptions of fifth–sixth centuries BC. It is derived from the Sanskrit term Sindhu. Linguistically s becomes h in Iranian. The Iranian inscriptions first mention Hindu as a district on the Indus. Therefore, in the earliest stage, the term Hindu means a territorial unit. It neither indicates a religion nor a community.

Our ancient poets, philosophers, and writers viewed the country as an integral unit. They spoke of the land stretching from the Himalayas to the sea as the proper domain of a single, universal monarch. The kings who tried to establish their authority from the Himalayas to Cape Comorin and from the valley of the Brahmputra in the east to the land beyond the Indus in the west were universally praised. They were called Chakravartis. This form of political unity was attained at least twice in ancient times. In the third century BC Ashoka extended his empire over the whole of India barring the extreme south. His inscriptions are scattered across a major part of the Indo-Pakistan subcontinent, and even in Afghanistan. Again, in the fourth century AD, Samudragupta carried his victorious arms from the Ganga to the borders of the Tamil land. In the seventh century, the Chalukya king, Pulakeshin defeated Harshavardhana who was called the lord of the whole of north India. Despite the lack of political unity, political formations all over India assumed more or less a single form. The idea that India constituted one single geographical unit persisted in the minds of the conquerors and cultural leaders. The unity of India was also recognized by foreigners. They first came into contact with the people living on the Sindhu or the Indus, and so they named the entire country after this river. The word Hind or Hindu is derived from the Sanskrit term Sindhu, and on the same basis, the country became known as 'India' which is very close to the Greek term for it. India came to be called 'Hind' in the Persian and Arabic languages. In post-Kushan times, the Iranian rulers conquered the Sindh area and named it Hindustan.

We find continuing efforts to establish linguistic and cultural unity in India. In the third century BC Prakrit served as the lingua franca across the major part of India. Ashoka's inscriptions were inscribed in the Prakrit language mainly in Brahmi script. Later, Sanskrit acquired the same position and served as the state language in the remotest parts of India. This process was conspicuous during the Gupta period in the fourth century. Although

India witnessed the rise of numerous small states during the post-Gupta period, the official documents were written in Sanskrit.

Another notable fact is that the ancient epics, the *Ramayana* and the *Mahabharata*, were studied with the same zeal and devotion in the land of the Tamils as in the intellectual circles of Banaras and Taxila. Originally composed in Sanskrit, various versions of these epics were produced in different local languages. However, whatever the form in which Indian cultural values and ideas were expressed, the substance remained largely the same throughout India.

Indian history is especially worthy of our attention because of a peculiar type of social system which developed in India. In north India, the varna/caste system developed which eventually spread throughout the country, and influenced even the Christians and the Muslims. Even converts to Christianity and Islam continued to follow some of their old caste practices of Hinduism.

The Relevance of the Past to the Present

The study of India's past assumes special significance in the context of the problems we currently face. Some people clamour for the restoration of ancient culture and civilization, and a substantial number are sentimentally swayed by what they consider to be the past glories of India. This is different from a concern for the preservation of ancient heritage in art and architecture. What they really want to bring back is the old pattern of society and culture. This demands a clear and correct understanding of the past. There is no doubt that Indians of old made remarkable progress in a variety of fields, but these advances alone cannot enable us to compete with the achievements of modern science and technology. We cannot ignore the fact that ancient Indian society was marked by gross social injustice. The lower orders, particularly the shudras and untouchables, were encumbered with disabilities which are shocking to the modern mind. Similarly, law and custom discriminate against women in favour of men. The restoration of the old way of life will naturally revive and strengthen all these inequities. The success of the ancients in surmounting the difficulties presented by nature and human factors can build our hope and confidence in the future but any attempt to bring back the past will mean a perpetuation of the social inequity that afflicted India. All this makes it essential for us to understand what the past means.

We have many survivals of ancient, medieval, and later times persisting in the present. The old norms, values, social customs, and ritualistic practices are so deeply ingrained in the minds of the people that they cannot easily themselves get rid of them. Unfortunately, these survivals inhibit the development of the individual and the country, and were deliberately fostered in colonial times. India cannot develop rapidly unless such vestiges of the past are eradicated from its society. The caste system and sectarianism hinder the democratic integration and development of India. Caste barriers and prejudices do not allow even educated individuals to appreciate the dignity of manual labour and hamper our unification for a common cause. Though women have been enfranchised, their age-old social subordination prevents them from playing their due role in society, and this is true too of the lower orders of society. Studying the ancient past helps us to deeply examine the roots of these prejudices and discover the causes that sustain the caste system, subordinate women, and promote narrow religious sectarianism. The study of ancient Indian history is, therefore, relevant not only to those who want to understand the true nature of the past but also to those who seek to understand the nature of the obstacles that hamper India's progress as a nation.

Chronology

1500–500 BC	Dravidian and non-Sanskritic terms found in Vedic texts.
300 BC–AD 600	Sangam literature.
3 C BC	Prakrit as the lingua franca.
AD 4 C onwards	Sanskrit as the state language.

2

Modern Historians of Ancient India

Colonialist Views and their Contribution

Although educated Indians retained their traditional history in the form of handwritten epics, Puranas, and semi-biographical works, modern research in the history of ancient India began only in the second half of the eighteenth century to serve the needs of the British colonial administration. When Bengal and Bihar fell under the rule of the East India Company in 1765, they found it difficult to administer the Hindu law of inheritance. Therefore, in 1776, the *Manu Smriti*, (the law-book of Manu), which was considered authoritative, was translated into English as *A Code of Gentoo Laws*. Pandits were associated with British judges to administer Hindu civil law and *maulvis* to administer that of Muslims. The initial efforts to understand ancient laws and customs, which continued largely until the eighteenth century, culminated in the establishment in Calcutta in 1784 of the Asiatic Society of Bengal. It was set up by a civil servant of the East India Company, Sir William Jones (1746–94). He was the first to suggest that Sanskrit, Latin, and Greek belonged to the same family of languages. He also translated the play known as the *Abhijnanashakuntalam* into English in 1789; the *Bhagvadgita*, the most popular Hindu religious text was translated into English by Wilkins in 1785. The Bombay Asiatic Society was set up in 1804, and the Asiatic Society of Great Britain was set up in London in 1823. William Jones emphasized that originally the European languages were very similar to Sanskrit and the Iranian language. This enthused European countries such as Germany, France, and Russia, to foster Indological studies. During the first half of the nineteenth century, chairs in Sanskrit were established in the UK and several other European countries.

The greatest impetus to Indological studies was given by the German-born scholar F. Max Mueller (1823–1902), who was largely based in England. The Revolt of 1857 caused Britain to realize that it badly needed a deeper knowledge of the manners and social systems of an alien people over whom it ruled. Similarly, the Christian missionaries sought to uncover the vulnerabilities in the Hindu religion to win converts and strengthen the British empire. To meet these needs, ancient scriptures were translated on a massive scale under the editorship of Max Mueller. Altogether fifty volumes, some in several parts, were published under the Sacred Books of the East series. Although a few Chinese and Iranian texts were included, ancient Indian texts were predominant.

In the introductions to these volumes and the books based on them, Max Mueller and other Western scholars made certain generalizations about the nature of ancient Indian history and society. They stated that the ancient Indians lacked a sense of history, especially of the element of time and chronology. They added that Indians were accustomed to despotic rule, and also natives were so engrossed in the problems of spiritualism or of the next world that they felt no concern about the problems of this world. The Western scholars stressed that Indians had experienced neither a sense of nationhood nor any form of self-government.

Many of these generalizations were made in the *Early History of India* by Vincent Arthur Smith (1843–1920), who wrote in 1904 the first systematic history of ancient India. His book, which was based on an in-depth study of the available sources gave primacy to political history. It served as a textbook for nearly fifty years and is still used by scholars. Smith's approach to history was pro-imperialist. As a loyal member of the Indian Civil Service, he emphasized the role of foreigners in ancient India. Alexander's invasion accounted for almost one-third of his book. India was presented as a land of despotism which had not experienced political unity until the establishment of British rule. He observes: 'Autocracy is substantially the only form of government with which the historian of India is concerned'.

In sum, British interpretations of Indian history served to denigrate the Indian character and achievements, and justify colonial rule. A few of these observations appeared to have some validity. Thus, in comparison to the Chinese, Indians did not show any strong sense of chronology although in the earlier stage, important events were dated with reference to the death of Gautama Buddha. However, generalizations made by colonialist historians were by and large either false or grossly exaggerated, but served as good propaganda material for the perpetuation of the despotic British rule. Their emphasis on the Indian tradition of one-man rule could justify the system which vested all powers in the hands of the viceroy. Similarly, if Indians were obsessed with the problems of the next world, the British colonial masters had no option but to look after their life in this world. Without any experience of self-rule in the past, how could the natives manage their affairs in the present? At the heart of all such generalizations lay the need to demonstrate that Indians were incapable of governing themselves.

Nationalist Approach and its Contribution

All this naturally came as a great challenge to Indian scholars, particularly to those who had received Western education. They were upset by the colonialist distortions of their past history and at the same time distressed by the contrast between the decaying feudal society of India and the progressive capitalist society of Britain. A band of scholars took upon themselves not only the mission to reform Indian society, but also to reconstruct ancient Indian history in such a way as to make a case for social reforms and, more importantly, for self-government. In doing so, most historians were guided by the nationalist ideas of Hindu revivalism, but there was no dearth of scholars who adopted a rationalist and objective approach. To the second category belongs Rajendra Lal Mitra (1822–91), who published some Vedic texts and wrote a book entitled *Indo-Aryans*. A great lover of ancient heritage, he took a rational view of ancient society and produced a forceful tract to show that in ancient times people ate beef. Others sought to prove that in spite of its peculiarities, the caste system was not basically different from the class system based on division of labour found in Europe's pre-industrial and ancient societies.

In Maharashtra, Ramakrishna Gopal Bhandarkar (1837–1925) and Vishwanath Kashinath Rajwade (1869–1926) emerged as two great dedicated scholars who pieced together varied sources to reconstruct the social and political history of India. R.G. Bhandarkar reconstructed the political history of the Satavahanas of the Deccan and the history of Vaishnavism and other sects. A great social reformer, through his researches he advocated widow remarriage and castigated the evils of the caste system and child marriage. With his unadulterated passion for research, V.K. Rajwade journeyed from village to village in Maharashtra in search of Sanskrit manuscripts and sources of Maratha history; the sources were eventually published in twenty-two volumes. He did not write much, but the history of the institution of marriage that he wrote in Marathi in 1926 will continue to be a classic because of its solid base in Vedic and other texts, and also because of the author's insight into the stages in the evolution of marriage in India. Pandurang Vaman Kane (1880–1972), a great Sanskritist wedded to social reform, continued the earlier tradition of scholarship. His monumental work entitled the *History of the Dharmasastra*, published in five volumes in the twentieth century, is an encyclopaedia of ancient social laws and customs. That enables us to study the social processes in ancient India.

The Indian scholars diligently studied polity and political history to demonstrate that India did have a political history and that the Indians possessed expertise in administration. Here due credit should be given to Devdatta Ramakrishna Bhandarkar (1875–1950), an epigraphist, who published books on Ashoka and on ancient Indian political institutions. More valuable work was done by Hemachandra Raychaudhuri (1892–1957), who reconstructed the history of ancient India from the time of the Bharata (Mahabharata) war, that is, tenth century BC to the end of the Gupta empire. As a teacher of European history, he adopted some of the methods and comparative insights in writing this book. Although he did not discuss the problem of periodization, his history of ancient India stopped with the sixth century AD. Though he recognized the contribution of V.A. Smith to the reconstruction of early Indian history, yet Raychaudhuri criticized the British scholar at many points. His writings are marked by impeccable scholarship but show a streak of militant Brahmanism when he criticizes Ashoka's policy of peace. A stronger element of Hindu revivalism appears in the writings of R.C. Majumdar (1888–1980), who was a prolific writer and the general editor of the multi-volume publication *History and Culture of the Indian People.*

Most writers on early Indian history did not give adequate attention to south India. Even K.A. Nilakanta Sastri (1892–1975), the great historian from south India, followed the same approach in his *A History of Ancient India*, but this was more than rectified in his *A History of South India*. His style is terse but his writing lucid. In the presentation of facts he is as dependable as Raychaudhuri. However, his general observations on the nature of polity and society in south India are questioned by several scholars. Nilakanta Sastri emphasized the cultural supremacy of the brahmanas and also highlighted the harmony that prevailed in early Indian society. Under his leadership several research monographs were produced on the dynastic history of south India.

Until 1960, political history attracted the largest number of Indian scholars, who also glorified the histories of their respective regions on dynastic lines. Those who wrote history at a pan-India level were inspired by the ideas of nationalism. In contrast to the book of V.A. Smith, who devoted almost a third of the total space to Alexander's invasion, Indian scholars gave this subject much less importance. On the other hand, they stressed the importance of the dialogue of Porus with Alexander and Chandragupta Maurya's liberation of north-western India from Seleucus. Some scholars, such as K.P. Jayaswal (1881–1937) and A.S. Altekar (1898–1959), overplayed the role of the indigenous ruling dynasties in liberating India from the rule of the Shakas and Kushans, little realizing that Central Asians and others became an intrinsic part of India's life and did not exploit Indian resources for their original homeland.

However, the greatest merit of K.P. Jayaswal lay in exploding the myth of Indian despotism. As early as 1910–12, he wrote several articles to show that republics existed in ancient times and enjoyed a measure of self-government. His findings finally appeared in *Hindu Polity* in 1924. Although Jayaswal is charged with projecting modern nationalist ideas into ancient institutions, and the nature of the republican government presented by him is attacked by many writers including U.N. Ghoshal (1886–1969), his basic thesis regarding the practice of the republican experiment is widely accepted, and his pioneer work *Hindu Polity*, now in its sixth edition, is considered a classic.

Move Towards Non-Political History

British historian, A.L. Basham (1914–86), a Sanskritist by training, questioned the wisdom of looking at ancient India from the modern point of view. His earlier writings show his deep interest in the materialist philosophy of some heterodox sects. Later he believed that the past should be read out of curiosity and pleasure. His book, *The Wonder That Was India* (1951), is a sympathetic survey of the various facets of ancient Indian culture and civilization free from the prejudices that plague the writings of V.A. Smith and many other British writers.

Basham's book marks a great shift from political to non-political history. The same shift is evident in D.D. Kosambi's (1907–66) book, *An*

Introduction to the Study of Indian History (1957), later popularized in *The Civilisation of Ancient India in Historical Outline* (1965). Kosambi blazed a new trail in Indian history. His treatment follows a materialist interpretation of history, which is derived from the writings of Karl Marx. He presents the history of ancient Indian society, economy, and culture as an integral part of the development of the forces and relations of production. His was the first survey volume to show the stages of social and economic development in terms of tribal and class processes. He was criticized by many scholars, including Basham, but his book continues to be widely read.

Over the past forty years there has been a sea change in the methods and orientation of those who work on ancient India. They lay greater stress on social, economic, and cultural processes, and try to relate them to political developments. They take account of the stratification of the texts and compare their conventional nature with archaeological and anthropological evidence. All this bodes well for the future of historical studies. Western writers no longer insist that all cultural elements came to India from outside. Some of them, however, hold that religious ideas, rituals, caste, kinship, and tradition are the central forces in Indian history. They also underscore various divisive features which made for stagnation, and are more concerned about the problem of stability and continuity. They seem to be fascinated by old, exotic elements and want to preserve them forever. Such an approach implies that Indian society has not changed and cannot be changed; that stagnation is an integral part of the Indian character. Thus, the chauvinists and sophisticated colonialists use the study of India's past to prevent its progress. A few Indian writers magnify the role of religion, and believe that everything good and great originated in their country.

Communal Approach

Since 1980 some Indian writers and their Western counterparts have adopted an aggressive and irrational approach to the study of ancient India. They identify it with Hinduism. Under British rule, colonialist historians deliberately denigrated India's achievements and attributed important elements of Indian culture to external influence. Indian historians underlined India's contribution to world culture. Hence, in the interpretation of history, there was a continuing struggle between colonialism and nationalism. Now the situation has undergone a change. The struggle now is between communalism and irrationalism, on the one hand, and rationalism and professionalism, on the other. Though most writers are rational and professional, some have become communal and irrational. The latter overplay myths and legends, arguing for the existence of Rama's Ayodhya without historical evidence. They censure all critical studies of the brahmanical social structure and even support the caste system by ignoring the social inequity stressed by Manu.

Those who once attributed the Painted Grey Ware to the Vedic people and looked for it outside India now declare the Indo-Aryans to be indigenous Indians. They argue that the Muslims and Christians who came from outside are foreigners. Such generalizations need to be dispassionately examined on the basis of a rational reading of the sources. In the context of religion, neither Hindu nor Hindu dharma is known to any ancient Sanskrit text nor to any other ancient source. The communal writers go on harping on Hindu and Hindutva. Under the circumstances, historians wedded to objective and scientific criteria have to be alert and adhere to reason and long established historical standards.

Chronology

(AD)	
Second half of the eighteenth century	Modern research in the history of ancient India.
1765	Bihar and Bengal came under the rule of the East India Company.
1776	*Manusmriti* tr. as *Code of Gentoo Laws.*
1784	Asiatic Society of Bengal founded in Calcutta.
1785	*Bhagvadgita* tr. into English.
1804	Bombay Asiatic Society founded.
1823	Asiatic Society of Great Britain set up in London.
First half of the 19 C	Chairs in Sanskrit established in England and several other European countries.
1904	*Early History of India* by V.A. Smith.
1924	*Hindu Polity* by K.P. Jayaswal.
1926	*The History of the Institution of Marriage* (in Marathi) by V.K. Rajwade.
1951	*The Wonder That Was India* by A.L. Basham.

1957	*An Introduction to the Study of Indian History* by D.D. Kosambi.
1965	*The Civilization of Ancient India in Historical Outline* by D.D. Kosambi.
1837–1925	R.G. Bhandarkar.
1869–1926	V.K. Rajawade.
1875–1950	D.R. Bhandarkar.
1880–1972	P.V. Kane.
1881–1937	K.P. Jayaswal.
1886–1969	U.N. Ghoshal.
1888–1980	R.C. Majumdar.
1892–1957	H.C. Raychaudhuri.
1892–1975	K.A. Nilakanta Sastri.
1898–1959	A.S. Altekar.
1907–66	D.D. Kosambi.
1914–86	A.L. Basham.

3

Nature of Sources and Historical Construction

Material Remains

The methods of archaeology help us to recover the material remains of the past, relating to ancient, medieval, and modern periods of our history. In India and many other countries, archaeology is used to study prehistory and ancient history. Prehistory is concerned with the period for which there are no written sources, and history is basically based on written material. Prehistoric sites differ from historical sites in several respects. Generally they are not in the form of prominent habitation remains, but principally of fossils of humans, plants, and animals. They are found on the hill slopes of plateaus and mountains, and on the banks of nearby rivers with terraces, and comprise sundry fauna and flora. More importantly, numerous stone tools from the Stone Age have been found at these sites. The remains of tools, plants, animals, and humans from the pre-ice age indicate the climatic conditions that prevailed at the time. Although writing was known in India by the middle of the third millennium BC in the Indus culture, it has not so far been deciphered. Thus, though the Harappans knew how to write, their culture is placed in the proto-historic phase. The same is the case with the Chalcolithic or copper–Stone Age cultures which had no writing. Decipherable writing was known in India only in the third century BC with the Ashokan inscriptions providing solid evidence for historical reconstruction from that time. However, despite the critical use of Vedic and post-Vedic literary sources for history in pre-Ashokan times, archaeology remains a very important source for historians.

The ancient Indians left innumerable material remains. The stone temples in south India and the brick monasteries in eastern India still stand to remind us of the great building activities of the past. However, the major part of these remains lies buried in mounds scattered all over India. (A mound is an elevated portion of land covering the remains of old habitations.) It may be of different types: single-culture, major-culture, and multi-culture. Single-culture mounds represent only one culture throughout. Some mounds represent only the Painted Grey Ware (PGW) culture, others Satavahana culture, and yet others that of the Kushans. In major-culture mounds, one culture is dominant and the others are of secondary importance. Multi-culture mounds represent several important cultures in succession which occasionally overlap with one another. As is the case with the *Ramayana* and *Mahabharata*, an excavated mound can be used to understand successive layers of the material and other aspects of a culture.

A mound can be excavated vertically or horizontally. Vertical excavation means lengthwise digging to uncover the period-wise sequence of cultures; it is generally confined to a part of the site. Horizontal excavation entails digging the mound as a whole or a major part of it. The method may enable the excavator to obtain a complete idea of the site culture in a particular period.

As most sites have been dug vertically, they provide a good chronological sequence of material culture. Horizontal diggings, being very expensive, are very few in number, with the result that the excavations do not give us a full or even adequate picture of material life in many phases of ancient Indian history.

Even in those mounds which have been excavated, the ancient remains have been preserved in varying proportions. In the dry arid climate of western UP, Rajasthan, and north-western India, antiquities are found in a better state of preservation, but in the moist and humid climate of the mid-Gangetic plains and in the deltaic regions even iron implements suffered corrosion and mud structures become difficult to detect. Only the burnt brick structures or stone structures of the Gangetic plains are well preserved.

Excavations have brought to light the villages that people established around 6000 BC in Baluchistan. They also tell us about the material culture which was developed in the Gangetic plains in the second millennium BC. They show the layout of the settlements in which people lived, the types of pottery they used, the form of house in which they dwelt, the kind of cereals they ate, and the type of tools and implements they used. Some people in south India buried in graves, along with the dead, their tools, weapons, pottery, and other belongings, and these were encircled by large pieces of stone. These structures are called megaliths, although some megaliths do not fall in this category. By digging them we learn of the life people lived in the Deccan from the Iron Age onwards. The science that enables us to systematically dig the successive layers of old mounds, and to form an idea of the material life of the people is called archaeology.

Their dates are fixed by various methods. Of them, radiocarbon dating is the most important. Radiocarbon or Carbon 14 (C^{14}) is a radioactive carbon (isotope) which is present in all living objects. It decays, like all radioactive substances, at a uniform rate. When an object is living, the process of decay of C^{14} is neutralized by absorption of C^{14} through air and food. However, when an object ceases to be alive, its C^{14} content continues to decay at a uniform rate but ceases to absorb C^{14} from air and food. By measuring the loss of C^{14} content in an ancient object, its age can be determined. This is because, as stated earlier, the decay of C^{14} takes place at a uniform rate. It is known that the half-life of C^{14} is 5568 years. The half-life of a radioactive material is defined as the period during which half the radioactive content in an object disappears. Thus, the C^{14} content in an object that ceased to live 5568 years ago would be half of what it was when it was living, and in an object which ceased to live 11,136 years ago, its C^{14} content would be one-fourth of that it had been when it was living. But no antiquity older than 70,000 years can be dated by this method.

The history of climate and vegetation is known through an examination of plant residues, and especially through pollen analysis. On this basis it is suggested that agriculture was practised in Rajasthan and Kashmir around 7000–6000 BC. The nature and components of metal artefacts are analysed scientifically, and consequently the mines from which the metals were obtained are located and the stages in the development of metal technology identified. An examination of animal bones shows whether the animals were domesticated, and also indicates the uses to which they were put.

I may add that archaeology provides a kind of soil archive which contains various material remains. However, for a total study of prehistory extending roughly up to 3000 BC or so, it is necessary to get an idea of the history of the soil, rocks, etc. This is provided by geological studies. Similarly, the world of plants and animals keeps on changing though at a slow pace. Their history is provided by biological studies. Human history cannot be understood without an idea of the continuing interaction between soils, plants, and animals, on the one hand, and humans, on the other. Geological and biological advances enable us to understand not only prehistory but also history. Taken together with archaeological remains, geological and biological studies act as important sources for the study of over 98 per cent of the total time scale of history starting with the origin of the earth.

Coins

Although a large number of coins and inscriptions have been found on the surface, many of them have been unearthed by digging. The study of coins is called numismatics. Ancient Indian currency was not issued in the form of paper, as is the case nowadays, but as metal coins. Ancient coins were made of metal—copper, silver, gold, and lead. Coin moulds made of burnt clay have been discovered in large numbers. Most of them relate to the Kushan period, that is, the first three Christian centuries. The use of such moulds in the post-Gupta period virtually disappeared.

As there was nothing like the modern banking system in ancient times, people stored money in earthenware and also in brass vessels, and maintained them as precious hoards on which they could fall back in time of need. Many of these hoards, containing not only Indian coins but also those minted abroad, such as in the Roman empire, have been discovered in different parts of India. They are preserved mostly in museums in Kolkata, Patna, Lucknow, Delhi, Jaipur, Mumbai, and Chennai. There are many Indian coins in the museums of Nepal, Bangladesh, Pakistan, and Afghanistan. As Britain ruled over India for a long time, British officials succeeded in transferring many of the Indian coins to private and public collections in Britain. Coins of the major dynasties have been catalogued and published. We have catalogues of the coins in the Indian Museum at Kolkata, of Indian coins in the British Museum in London, and so on. None the less, there are a large number of coins that have yet to be catalogued and published.

Our earliest coins contain a few symbols, but the later coins depict the figures of kings, and divinities, and also mention their names and dates. The areas where they are found indicate the region of their circulation. This has enabled us to reconstruct the history of several ruling dynasties, especially of the Indo-Greeks who came to India from north Afghanistan and ruled here in the second and first centuries BC.

As coins were used for various purposes such as donations, a mode of payment, and a medium of exchange, they throw considerable light on economic history. Some coins were issued by guilds of merchants and goldsmiths with the permission of the rulers. This shows that crafts and commerce had become important. Coins helped transactions on a large scale and contributed to trade. The largest number of Indian coins date to the post-Maurya period. These were made of lead, potin, copper, bronze, silver, and gold. The Guptas issued the largest number of gold coins. All this indicates that trade and commerce flourished, especially in post-Maurya and a good part of the Gupta period. However, only a few coins belonging to the post-Gupta period have been found, which indicates a decline of trade and commerce in that period.

Coins also portray kings and gods, and contain religious symbols and legends, all of which throw light on the art and religion of the time.

Cowries were also used as coins, though their purchasing power was low. They appear in substantial numbers in post-Gupta times, but may have been used earlier.

Inscriptions

Far more important than coins are inscriptions. Their study is called epigraphy, and the study of the old writing used in inscriptions and other old records is called palaeography. Inscriptions were carved on seals, stone pillars, rocks, copperplates, temple walls, wooden tablets, and bricks or images.

In India as a whole, the earliest inscriptions were recorded on stone. However, in the early centuries of the Christian era, copperplate began to be used for this purpose. Even then the practice of engraving inscriptions on stone continued on a large scale in south India. We have also in that region a large number of inscriptions recorded on the walls of temples to serve as permanent records.

Like coins, inscriptions are preserved in various museums of the country, but the largest number may be found in the office of the chief epigraphist at Mysore. The earliest inscriptions were written in Prakrit in the third century BC. Sanskrit was adopted as an epigraphic medium in the second century AD and its use became widespread in the fourth and fifth centuries, but even then Prakrit continued to be used. Inscriptions began to be composed in regional languages in the ninth and tenth centuries. Most inscriptions bearing on the history of the Maurya, post-Maurya, and Gupta periods have been published in a series of collections called *Corpus Inscriptionum Indicarum*, but not many inscriptions of the post-Gupta period figure in such systematic compilations. In the case of south India, topographical lists of inscriptions have been published. Still, over 50,000 inscriptions, mostly of south India, await publication.

The Harappan inscriptions, which await decipherment, seem to have been written in a pictographic script in which ideas and objects were expressed in the form of pictures. Most Ashokan inscriptions were engraved in the Brahmi script, which was written from left to right, but some were also incised in the Kharoshthi script which was written from right to left. However, the Brahmi script prevailed virtually all over India except for the north-western part. Greek and Aramaic scripts were employed in writing Ashokan inscriptions in Pakistan and Afghanistan, but Brahmi continues to be the main script till the end of Gupta times. An epigraphist can decipher most Indian inscriptions up to about the seventh century if he has mastered Brahmi and its variations, but subsequently we notice strong regional variations in this script.

Inscriptions found on the seals of Harappa belonging to about 2500 BC are considered symbolic by some scholars. For Indian history, the earliest deciphered inscriptions are Iranian. They belong to the sixth–fifth centuries BC and are found in Iran. They appear in Old-Indo-Iranian and also in Semitic languages in the cuneiform script. They speak of the Iranian conquest of the Hindu or Sindhu area. Of course, in India the earliest deciphered are Ashokan inscriptions. They are generally written in Brahmi script and Prakrit language in the third century BC. They throw light on Maurya history and Ashoka's achievements. In the fourteenth century AD two Ashokan pillar inscriptions were found by Firoz Shah Tughlaq, one in Meerut and another at a place called Topra in Haryana. He brought them to Delhi and asked the pandits of his empire to decipher the inscriptions, but they failed to do so. The same difficulty was faced by the British when in the last quarter of the eighteenth century they discovered Ashokan inscriptions. These epigraphs were first deciphered in 1837 by James Prinsep, a civil servant in the employ of the East India Company in Bengal.

We have various types of inscriptions. Some convey royal orders and decisions regarding social, religious, and administrative matters to officials and the people in general. Ashokan inscriptions belong to this category. Others are votive records of the followers of Buddhism, Jainism, Vaishnavism, Shaivism, and the like. They appear on pillars, tablets, temples, or images as marks of devotion. Yet other types eulogize the attributes and achievements of kings and conquerors, and ignore their defeats or weaknesses. To this category belongs the Allahabad Pillar inscription of Samudragupta. Finally, we have many donative records which refer especially to gifts of money, cattle, land, etc., mainly for religious purposes, made not only by kings and princes but also by artisans and merchants.

Inscriptions recording land grants, made mainly by chiefs and princes, are very important for the study of the land system and administration in ancient India. These were mostly engraved on copperplates. They record grants of lands, revenues, and villages made to monks, priests, temples, monasteries, vassals, and officials. They were written in all languages, including Prakrit, Sanskrit, Tamil, and Telugu.

Literary Sources

Although the ancient Indians knew how to write as early as 2500 BC, our most ancient manuscripts are not older than the AD fourth century and are found in Central Asia. In India, they were written on birch bark and palm leaves, but in Central Asia, where the Prakrit language had spread from India, manuscripts were also written on sheep leather and wooden tablets. These writings are called inscriptions, but they are as good as manuscripts. When printing was not known, manuscripts were very highly valued. Although old Sanskrit manuscripts are found all over India, they mostly relate to south India, Kashmir, and Nepal. Currently, inscriptions are largely preserved in museums, and manuscripts in libraries.

Most ancient books contain religious themes. Hindu religious literature includes the Vedas, the *Ramayana* and the *Mahabharata*, the Puranas, and the like. They throw considerable light on the social and cultural conditions of ancient times, but it is difficult to use them in the context of time and place. The *Rig Veda* may be assigned to *c.* 1500–1000 BC, though such collections as the *Atharva Veda, Yajur Veda*, the Brahmanas, Aranyakas, and the Upanishads date roughly to 1000–500 BC. Almost every Vedic text contains interpolations, which generally appear at the beginning or the end and seldom in the middle. The *Rig Veda* mainly comprises prayers, whereas the later Vedic texts comprise prayers as well as rituals, magic, and mythological stories. However, the Upanishads contain philosophical speculations.

In order to understand the Vedic texts it was necessary to study the Vedangas or the limbs of the Veda. These supplements of the Veda comprised phonetics (*shiksha*), ritual (*kalpa*), grammar (*vyakarana*), etymology (*nirukta*), metrics (*chhanda*), and astronomy (*jyotisha*), and much literature grew around each of these subjects. They were written in the form of precepts in prose. A precept was called a *sutra* because of its brevity. The most famous example of this writing is the grammar of Panini written around 450 BC. While illustrating the rules of grammar, Panini casts invaluable light on the society, economy, and culture of his times.

The two epics and the major Puranas seem to have been finally compiled by *c*. AD 400. Of the epics, the *Mahabharata* attributed to Vyasa is older and possibly reflects the state of affairs from the tenth century BC to AD fourth century. Originally, it consisted of 8800 verses and was called *Jaya* or a collection dealing with victory. These were increased to 24,000 and came to be known as *Bharata* because it contains the stories of the descendants of one of the earliest Vedic tribes called Bharata. The final compilation increased the verses to 100,000 which came to be known as the *Mahabharata* or the *Shatasahasri Samhita*. It contains narrative, descriptive, and didactic material. The main narrative which relates to the Kaurava–Pandava conflict may relate to the later Vedic period, the descriptive portion might be of the post-Vedic period, and the didactic portion generally relates to the post-Maurya and Gupta periods. Similarly, the *Ramayana* of Valmiki originally consisted of 6000 verses which were raised to 12,000, and eventually to 24,000. Although this epic appears to be more unified than the *Mahabharata*, it too has its didactic parts which were subsequently added. The *Ramayana* composition started in the fifth century BC. After that, it passed through as many as five stages, and the fifth stage seems to have been as late as the twelfth century AD. As a whole, the text seems to have been composed later than the *Mahabharata*.

In the post-Vedic period we have a large corpus of ritual literature. Grand public sacrifices to be made by princes and men of substance belonging to the three higher varnas are set out in the Shrautasutras, which provide for several ostentatious royal coronation ceremonies. Similarly, domestic rituals connected with birth, naming, sacred thread investiture, marriage, funerals, etc. are prescribed in the Grihyasutras. Both the Shrautasutras and the Grihyasutras relate to *c*. 600–300 BC. Mention may also be made of the Sulvasutras, which prescribe various kinds of measurements for the construction of sacrificial altars. They mark the beginnings of the study of geometry and mathematics.

The religious books of the Jainas and the Buddhists refer to historical persons and incidents. The earliest Buddhist texts were written in Pali, which was spoken in Magadha or south Bihar, and was basically a form of Prakrit. They were finally compiled in the first century BC in Sri Lanka, but the canonical portions reflect the state of affairs in India in the age of the Buddha. They tell us not only about the life of the Buddha but also about some of his royal contemporaries who ruled over Magadha, north Bihar, and eastern UP. The most important and interesting portion of the non-canonical literature is provided by the stories of the previous births of Gautama Buddha. It was believed that before he was actually born as Gautama, the Buddha passed through over 550 births, in many cases in the form of animals. Each birth story is called a Jataka, which is a folk tale. The Jatakas throw invaluable light on the social and economic conditions of the period between the fifth and second century BC. They also make incidental references to political events in the age of the Buddha.

The Jaina texts were written in Prakrit and were eventually compiled in AD sixth century in Valabhi in Gujarat. They, however, contain many passages that help us to reconstruct the political history of eastern UP and Bihar in the age of Mahavira. The Jaina texts refer repeatedly to trade and traders.

We also have a large body of secular literature. To this class belong the law-books, called the Dharmasutras and Smritis, which, together with their commentaries, are called Dharmashastras. The Dharmasutras were compiled in 500–200 BC and the principal Smritis were codified in the first six centuries of the Christian era. They prescribe the duties to be performed by the different varnas as well as by kings and their officials. They set out the rules for marriage together with the laws according to which property is to be held, sold, and inherited. They also prescribe punishments for persons guilty of theft, assault, murder, adultery, and the like.

An important law-book is the *Arthashastra* of Kautilya. The text is divided into fifteen books, of which Books II and III may be regarded as being of an earlier date, and seem to have been the work of different hands. This text was put in its final form in the beginning of the Christian era, but its earliest portions reflect the state of society and economy in the age of the Mauryas. It provides rich material for the study of ancient Indian polity and economy.

Of the non-religious texts, the grammatical works are very important for historical construction. They begin with the *Astadhyayi* of Panini. Panini lived in the north-western part of the subcontinent. He is not mentioned in the Pali texts which principally represent Bihar and UP. Panini is dated to around 450 BC by V.S. Agrawala, who has written about Panini's India in both Hindi and English. In his view, no other text provides as much information about the *janapadas* or territorial states of pre-Mauryan times as Panini's does. Patanjali's commentary on Panini, dated 150 BC, supplies valuable information about post-Maurya times.

We also have the works of Bhasa, Sudraka, Kalidasa, and Banabhatta. Apart from their literary value, they mirror the conditions of the times to which the writers belonged. The works of Kalidasa comprise *kavyas* and dramas, the most famous of which is *Abhijnanashakuntalam*. Besides being great creative compositions, they provide us with glimpses of the social and cultural life of the Guptas.

In addition to Sanskrit sources, we have some of the earliest Tamil texts in the corpus of Sangam literature. This literature was produced over a period of three to four centuries by poets who assembled in colleges patronized by chiefs and kings. Such colleges were called Sangam, and the literature produced in these assemblies was known as Sangam literature. The compilation of the corpus is attributed to the first four Christian centuries, although they were really completed by the sixth century.

The Sangam literature comprises about 30,000 lines of poetry arranged in eight anthologies called Ettuttokai. The poems are collected in groups of hundreds such as *Purananuru* (The Four Hundred of the Exterior). There are two main goups *Patinenkil Kannakku* (The Eighteen Lower Collections) and *Pattuppattu* (The Ten Songs). The former is generally assumed to be older than the latter, and hence is considered to be of great historical importance. The Sangam texts have several layers, but at present these cannot be established on the basis of style and content, but, as shown later, they can be detected on the basis of stages in social evolution.

The Sangam texts are different from the Vedic texts, particularly the *Rig Veda*. They do not constitute religious literature. The short and long poems were composed by numerous poets in praise of various heroes and heroines and are thus secular in nature. They are not primitive songs, but literature of high quality. Many poems mention a warrior or a chief or a king by name and describe in detail his military exploits. The gifts made by him to bards and warriors are celebrated. These poems may have been recited in the courts. They are compared with the heroic poetry of the Homeric age, for they represent a heroic age of warriors and battles. It is difficult to use these texts for historical purposes. Perhaps the proper names, titles, dynasties, territories, wars, and the like mentioned in the poems are partly real. Some of the Chera kings mentioned in the Sangam texts also appear as donors in inscriptions of the first and second centuries.

The Sangam texts refer to many settlements, including Kaveripattanam whose flourishing existence has now been archaeologically corroborated. They also speak of the Yavanas coming in their own vessels, purchasing pepper with gold, and supplying wine and women slaves to the natives. This trade is known not only from Latin and Greek writings but also from the archaeological record. The Sangam literature is a major source of our information for the social, economic, and political life of the people living in deltaic Tamil Nadu in the early Christian centuries. What it says about trade and commerce is confirmed by foreign accounts and archaeological finds.

Foreign Accounts

Indigenous literature can be supplemented by foreign accounts. To India came Greek, Roman, and Chinese visitors, either as travellers or religious converts, and they left behind accounts of the things that they saw. It is remarkable that Alexander's invasion finds no mention in Indian sources, and it is entirely on the basis of the Greek sources that we have to reconstruct the history of his Indian exploits.

The Greek writers mention Sandrokottas, a contemporary of Alexander the Great, who invaded India in 326 BC. Prince Sandrokottas is identified with Chandragupta Maurya, whose date of accession is fixed at 322 BC. This identification has served as the sheet anchor in ancient Indian chronology. The *Indika* of Megasthenes, who came to the court of Chandragupta Maurya, has been preserved only in fragments quoted by subsequent classical writers. These fragments, when read together, furnish valuable information not only about the system of Maurya administration but also about social classes and economic activities in the Maurya period. The *Indika* is not free from credulity and exaggerations, which is true of many other ancient accounts.

Greek and Roman accounts of the first and second centuries mention many Indian ports and enumerate items of trade between India and the Roman empire. The *Periplus of the Erythrean Sea* and Ptolemy's *Geography*, both written in Greek, provide valuable data for the study of ancient geography and commerce. The date ascribed to the first ranges between AD 80 and 115, whereas the second is attributed to about AD 150. The

Periplus of the Erythrean Sea, which was written by an anonymous author, describes the Roman trade in the Red Sea, Persian Gulf, and the Indian Ocean. Pliny's *Naturalis Historia,* which relates to the first century, was written in Latin, and tells us about trade between India and Italy.

The last Graeco-Roman scholar who wrote on India was called Kosmos Indikopleustes. He hailed from Alexandria, a centre of Hellenistic culture in Egypt. Around 550 he wrote the *Christian Topography* which mentions Christians in India and Sri Lanka and also refers to horse trade.

Of the Chinese travellers, mention may be made of Fa-hsien and Hsuan Tsang. Both of them were Buddhists, and came to this country to visit the Buddhist shrines and to study Buddhism. The first came in the beginning of the fifth century and the second in the second quarter of the seventh century. Fa-hsien describes the social, religious, and economic conditions in India in the age of the Guptas, and Hsuan Tsang presents a similar account of India in the age of Harsha.

Village Study

Relics of communal sharing in feasts, festivals, and pujas throw light on the egalitarian character of ancient tribal society. Loyalty to the clan and caste persists to this day. Survivals of rituals give us an idea of ancient sects and also of the institutions of marriage and family. High caste people do not milk the cow and never take to the plough. Their contempt for manual labour promotes untouchability. Strong traces of inequality are not confined to castes alone but also colour the relationship between man and woman. Till the 1930s even the sati system prevailed in rural parts of Bihar. Thus social inequalities, which prevail despite universal suffrage, indicate the nature of ancient Indian society. Rural rituals and caste prejudices illustrate many of the Dharmashastra rules governing our ancient polity and society.

Natural Sciences

The use of the findings of social sciences started about thirty years ago for the historical construction of ancient India. Recently the use of natural sciences has begun. Evidence from chemistry, geology, and biology has become relevant to the study of ancient India.

Historical Sense

Ancient Indians are charged with a lack of sense of history. It is evident that they did not write history in the manner it is done today, nor did they write it in the way the Greeks did. We have a sort of history in the Puranas, which are eighteen in number (eighteen was a conventional term). Though encyclopaedic in content, the Puranas provide dynastic history up to the beginning of Gupta rule. They mention the places where the events took place and sometimes discuss their causes and effects. Statements about events are made in the future tense, although they were recorded much after the events had occurred. The authors of the Puranas were not unaware of the idea of change, which is the essence of history. The Puranas speak of four ages called *krita, treta, dvapara*, and *kali*. Each succeeding age is depicted as worse than the preceding one, and as one age slides into the other, moral values and social institutions degenerate. The importance of time and place, vital elements in history, is indicated. It is said that *dharma* becomes *adharma* and vice versa in accordance with changes in time and place. Several eras, according to which events were recorded, were started in ancient India. Vikrama Samvat began in 57–8 BC, Shaka Samvat in AD 78, and the Gupta era in AD 319. Inscriptions record events in the context of time and place. During the third century BC Ashokan inscriptions demonstrate considerable historical sense. Ashoka ruled for thirty-seven years. His inscriptions record events that happened from the eighth to the twenty-seventh regnal year. To date, events relating to only nine regnal years figure in the inscriptions that have been discovered. Future discoveries may throw light on events relating to the remaining years of his reign. Similarly, in the first century BC Kharavela of Kalinga records a large number of events in his life year by year in the Hathigumpha inscription.

Indians display a considerable historical sense in biographical writings, a good example of which is the composition of the *Harshacharita* by Banabhatta in the seventh century. It is a semi-biographical work written in an ornate style which became the despair of later imitators. It describes the early career of Harshavardhana. Although highly exaggerated, it gives an excellent idea of court life under Harsha and the social and religious life in his age. Later, several other *charita*s or biographies were written. Sandhyakara Nandi's *Ramacharita* (twelfth century) narrates the story of the conflict between the Kaivarta peasants and the Pala prince Ramapala, resulting in the latter's victory. Bilhana's *Vikramankadevacharita* recounts the achievements of his patron, Vikramaditya VI (1076–1127), the Chalukya king of Kalyan. Even the biographies (*charita*) of some merchants of Gujarat were written in AD twelfth–thirteenth centuries. Similar historical works may have been written in south India, but thus far only one such account has been discovered. This is called *Mushika Vamsha* and was written by Atula in the eleventh century. It is an account of the dynasty of the Mushikas which ruled in northern Kerala. However, the best example of the earliest historical writing is provided by the *Rajatarangini* or *The Stream of Kings* written by Kalhana in the twelfth century. It is a string of biographies of the kings of Kashmir, and can be considered to be the first work to possess several characteristics of historical writing as it is understood today.

Constructing History

So far numerous sites, prehistoric, proto-historic, and historical, have been excavated and explored, but the results do not find a place in the mainstream of ancient Indian history. The stages of social evolution in India cannot be properly comprehended without taking into account the results of prehistoric and proto-historic archaeology, not to speak of historical archaeology. Although nearly 200 sites relating to the ancient historical period have been excavated, yet their relevance to the study of the social, economic, and cultural trends in ancient times has not been adequately discussed in survey studies. This needs to be done both in the context of the rural and urban aspects of ancient India. So far the significance of largely Buddhist and some brahmanical sites has been highlighted, but religious history needs to be seen in relation to social and economic developments.

Ancient history has so far been constructed principally on the basis of literary sources, foreign and indigenous. Coins and inscriptions play some part, but the texts receive greater weightage. Now new methods must be adopted. Historical knowledge keeps growing. We have to be more critical about the dates and contents of the texts. This may be done if we examine the texts in the context of archaeological evidence. Initially, archaeologists were inspired by written texts, and several sites mentioned in the brahmanical and Buddhist texts were excavated. This immensely enriched historical information, though the digging results did not always confirm the contents of the texts. Though full-length reports of many excavated sites are yet to be published, it is advisable to examine the texts in the context of archaeological findings. For the study of the age of the *Rig Veda* we have to take into account of the Gandhara grave culture in which the horse was used and the dead were cremated in the second millennium BC. We have to establish a co-relation between the later Vedic age, on the one hand, and the Painted Grey Ware and other types of archaeological finds, on the other. Similarly, early Pali texts have to be related to the Northern Black Polished Ware (NBPW) archaeology. Besides, the information derived from the Sangam texts needs to be co-related with that inferred from inscriptions and early Megalithic archaeology in peninsular India.

Archaeological evidence should be considered far more important than the long family trees found in the Puranas. The Puranic tradition could be used to date Rama of Ayodhya to around 2000 BC, but diggings and extensive explorations in Ayodhya do not show any settlement around that date. Similarly, although Krishna plays an important role in the *Mahabharata,* the earliest inscriptions and sculptural pieces from Mathura between 200 BC and AD 300 do not attest to his presence. Given such difficulties, the ideas of an epic age based on the *Ramayana* and the *Mahabharata* must be discarded, although in the past it formed a chapter in most survey volumes on ancient India. Of course, several stages of social evolution in both the *Ramayana* and the *Mahabharata* can be detected. This is so because the epics do not belong to a single phase of social evolution; we may recall that they have undergone several editions. Further, on the basis of literary traditions and epigraphic material, Vardhamana Mahavira and Gautama Buddha are generally dated to the sixth century BC, but the cities they visited are archaeologically not older than 400 BC and therefore the tradition-based dates of these great personalities need to be reconsidered.

On chronological and rational grounds, archaeology, inscriptions, and coins are more important than texts. However, the grammatical works of Panini and Patanjali have almost fixed dates, and they are comparatively free from myths and legends and are therefore as important as coins, inscriptions, and the results of excavations.

Many inscriptions have to date been dismissed on the ground that they are of little historical value. 'Historical value' is taken to mean information necessary to reconstruct political history. However, a royal inscription contains exaggerations. The term hundreds of thousands seems to be a cliché in Ashokan inscriptions. It is applied to people and animals, and raises doubts about the number of the people killed in the Kalinga war and those brought to Pataliputra. There are exaggerations too in the inscriptions of Samudragupta and King Chandra. Despite these exaggerations, in comparison to Puranic traditions, inscriptions are certainly more reliable. Thus, though the Puranas are used to push back the origin of the Satavahanas, the inscriptions place it in the first century BC. Inscriptions may indicate the regnal period of a king, his conquest, and its extent, but they also reveal trends in the development of polity, society, economy, and religion. This study, therefore, does not use inscriptions merely for political or religious history. Epigraphic land grants are valued not for the family trees and lists of conquest, but more importantly for the rise of new states and changes in the social and agrarian structure, particularly in post-Gupta times. Similarly, coins need to be used not only for the reconstruction of the history of the Indo-Greeks, Shakas, Satavahanas, and Kushans, but also for the history of trade and urban life.

In sum, a careful collection of the material derived from texts, coins, inscriptions, archaeology, etc., is essential for historical reconstruction. We have seen that this raises the problem of the relative importance of the sources. Thus, coins, inscriptions, and archaeology are considered more important than mythologies found in the epics and Puranas. Mythologies may support dominant norms, validate social mores, and justify the privileges and disabilities of people organized in castes and other social groups, but the events described in them cannot be taken to be true. Past practices can also be explained with the help of some ancient survivals in our own times. Familiarity with village life and the insights derived from the study of primitive people are valuable assets in the construction of ancient history. A sound historical reconstruction cannot ignore developments in other ancient societies. A comparative view may remove the obsession with the idea of the 'rare' or 'unique' in ancient India and may bring out those trends that ancient India shares with the past societies of the other countries. We may also use the results of human genetic research to learn about Indian connection with peoples in other parts of the world. A scientific study of heredity and generationwise inherited traits indicate ethnic mixture, dispersal of population, and dissemination of culture.

Chronology

(BC)	
3 M	Writing enters the Indus culture.
1500–1000	*Rig Veda.*

1000–500	*Yajur Veda, Atharva Veda,* the Brahmanas, Aranyakas, and the Upanishads.
600–300	Shrautasutras and Grihyasutras.
6 C	Mahavira and the Buddha as per literature.
500–200	Dharmasutras.
450	Grammar of Panini.
5 C	Mahavira and the Buddha in the context of archaeology.
326	Alexander's invasion.
322	Accession of Chandragupta Maurya.
3 C	Decipherable writing in India.
57–8	Vikrama Samvat.
1 C	Hathigumpha inscription of Kharavela of Kalinga.
1 C	The earliest Pali Buddhist texts compiled in Sri Lanka.
(AD)	
1 C	The *Arthashastra* of Kautilya finally compiled.
78	Start of Shaka Samvat.
80–115	The *Periplus of the Erythrean Sea.*
150	Ptolemy's *Geography.*
319	Start of the Gupta era.
400	*Mahabharata*, *Ramayana*, and major Puranas finally compiled.
4 C	Earliest Indian manuscript found in Central Asia.
5 C	Fa-hsien comes to India.
6 C	The Prakrit Jaina texts finally compiled in Valabhi.
7 C	Hsuan Tsang's visit. *Harshacharita* by Banabhatta.
11 C	*Mushika Vamsha* by Atula.
11–12 C	*Vikramankadevacharita* by Bilhana.
12 C	*Ramacharita* by Sandhyakara Nandi.
	Rajatarangini by Kalhana.
1837	Ashokan inscriptions first deciphered by James Prinsep.

4

Geographical Setting

Emergence of India

The Indian subcontinent emerged as a separate geographical unit some 40 million years ago. Originally peninsular India, together with Antarctica, Africa, Arabia, and South America, is considered to have been a part of the southern super-continent called Gondwanaland. Earlier, Gondwanaland, together with the northern super-continent Laurisia, comprising North America, Greenland, Europe, and most of Asia north of the Himalayas, formed a single land mass called Pangaea. Then Gondwanaland and Laurisia became separate units. Due to tectonic movements different parts began to break away from Gondwanaland, giving rise to separate geographical units including peninsular India. This process began around 225 million years ago, and 40 million years ago India became a separate unit. India moved north to join the Eurasian continent sometime between 58 and 37 million years ago. In comparison to earlier dates, India's Himalayan boundary is very young. The uplift of the Himalayas took place in four phases. The last and the final uplift took place in the Pleistocene epoch, that is, in *c*. 2 million–12000 BC. The Himalayas played an important part in forming the Indo-Gangetic plains through its rivers which brought down alluvial deposits in the Pleistocene epoch. The Indian subcontinent is as large in area as Europe without Russia, with a total area of 4,202,500 sq. km. The subcontinent is divided into five countries: India, Bangladesh, Nepal, Bhutan, and Pakistan. India has nearly 1000,000,000 people. It comprises twenty-eight states and seven union territories, including the National Capital Territory of Delhi. Some of its states are larger than many European countries.

The Role of the Monsoon

The Indian subcontinent is a well-defined geographical unit and is largely situated in the tropical zone. The monsoon has played an important role in India's history. The south-west monsoon lasts between June and October and brings rain in varying degrees to major parts of the country. In ancient times, irrigation was not an important factor and rains played a crucial role in agriculture. What is known today as the *kharif* crop in north India depended primarily in ancient times on the south-west monsoon. In winter, the western disturbances bring rains to northern India where wheat, barley, and the like constitute the main crop. A part of the peninsular India, particularly the coastal areas of Tamil Nadu, gets its major rainfall from the north-east monsoon from mid-October to mid-December. Once the direction of the monsoon was discovered some time around AD first century, traders sailed with the south-west monsoon from western Asia and the Mediterranean area, and came to India and Southeast Asia. They returned westward with the arrival of the north-east monsoon. The discovery of the monsoon enabled India to carry on trade and establish cultural contacts with western Asia and the Mediterranean area as well as with Southeast Asia.

The Northern Boundaries

India is bounded by the Himalayas on the north and seas on the other three sides. The Himalayas protect the country against the cold arctic winds blowing from Siberia through Central Asia. This keeps the climate of northern India fairly warm throughout the year. As the cold is not very severe in the plains, people do not need heavy clothing and can live in the open for longer periods. Secondly, the Himalayas are sufficiently high to shield India against invasions from the north. This was specially true in pre-industrial times when communications were very difficult. However, on the north-west, the Sulaiman mountain ranges, which are a southward continuation of the Himalayas, could be crossed through the Khyber, Bolan, and Gomal passes. The Sulaiman ranges are joined southward in Baluchistan by the Kiarthar ranges which could be crossed through the Bolan pass. Through these passes, two-way traffic between India and Central Asia has continued from prehistoric times onwards. Various peoples from Iran, Afghanistan, and Central Asia came to India as invaders and immigrants, and vice versa. Even the Hindu Kush, the westward extension of the Himalayan system, did not form an insuperable barrier between the Indus and the Oxus systems. The passes facilitated trade and cultural contacts between India, on the one hand, and Central Asia and West Asia, on the other.

Nestled in the Himalayas are the valleys of Kashmir and Nepal. Surrounded on all sides by high mountains, the valley of Kashmir developed its own way of life, but could be reached through several passes. Its winter compelled some of its people to go to the plains and its summer attracted the shepherds from the plains. Economic and cultural interaction between the plains and the valley was continuing. The Pamir plateau did not prevent it from becoming a transmission centre of Buddhism to the adjacent areas of Central Asia. The valley of Nepal, smaller in size, is accessible to the people of the Gangetic plains through a number of passes. Like Kashmir, it too became a centre for the cultivation of Sanskrit; both these valleys became repositories of the largest number of Sanskrit manuscripts.

The foothills of the Himalayas lent themselves to easier clearance than the jungles on the alluvial soil of the plains. It was easy to cross rivers in these areas because of their narrower width, and hence the earliest routes skirted along the foothills of the Himalayas from the west to the east and vice versa. It was therefore natural that the earliest agricultural settlements were founded in the foothills and uplands, and trade routes followed the terai route.

Rivers

The heart of historical India is formed by its important rivers which are swollen by the tropical monsoon rains. These consist of the plains of the Indus system, the Indo-Gangetic divide, the Gangetic basin, and the Brahmaputra basin. Proceeding from west to east we find the annual rainfall gradually increasing from 25 cm to over 250 cm. The Indus vegetation based on 25 to 37 cm rainfall and possibly the western Gangetic vegetation based on 37 to 60 cm rainfall could be cleared with stone and copper implements and made fit for cultivation, but this was not possible in the case of the mid-Gangetic vegetation based on 60 to 125 cm rainfall, and certainly not in the case of the lower Gangetic and Brahmaputra vegetation based on 125 to 250 cm rainfall. The thickly forested areas, which also had hard soil, could be cleared only with the aid of iron implements which became available at a much later stage. Therefore, the natural resources of the less rainy western area were utilized first, and large-scale human settlements generally spread from west to east.

Once brought under cultivation, the Indus–Gangetic plains produced rich crops and supported successive cultures. The Indus and the western Gangetic plains principally produced wheat and barley, while the middle and lower Gangetic plains largely produced rice, which also became the staple diet in Gujarat and south of the Vindhyas. The Harappan culture originated and flourished in the Indus Valley; the Vedic culture originated in the North-West Frontier Province and the Punjab, and flourished in the western Gangetic basin; the post-Vedic culture, mainly based on the use of iron, throve in the mid-Gangetic basin. The lower Gangetic valley and north Bengal really came into focus in the age of the Guptas; and finally, the Brahmaputra valley covering Assam gained importance in early medieval times. Powerful rulers fought for the possession of these plains and valleys, and the Ganga–Yamuna doab in particular proved to be the most coveted and contested area.

The rivers served as arteries of commerce and communications. In ancient times it was difficult to build roads, and so men and material were moved by boat. The river routes, therefore, well-served military and commercial transport. Evidently the stone pillars built by Ashoka were transported to different parts of the country by boat. The importance of rivers for communications continued till the days of the East India Company. Besides, the rivers inundated the neighbouring areas and made them fertile; they also supplied water to the canals cut from them. However, they caused heavy floods which periodically inundated and destroyed towns and villages in the northern plains, and therefore many ancient buildings were totally washed away and destroyed. Nevertheless, important towns and capitals, such as Hastinapur, Prayag, Varanasi, and Pataliputra were situated on the banks of the rivers. In modern times, urban sites are located at railway and road junctions or in industrial or mining zones, but in pre-industrial times towns were mostly situated on river banks and junctions.

Above all, it was the rivers that demarcated political and cultural boundaries, which were also formed by mountains. Thus, in the eastern part of the Indian peninsula, the area known as Kalinga, covering the coastal belt of Orissa, was situated between the Mahanadi to the north and the Godavari to the south. Similarly, Andhra Pradesh largely lay between the Godavari to the north and the Krishna to the south. The deltaic plains formed by these two rivers at their mouths shot into prominence by the beginning of the Christian era when they became studded with towns and ports under the Satavahanas and their successors. Finally, a major part of Tamil Nadu was situated between the Krishna to the north and the Kaveri to the south. The Kaveri valley extended in the south roughly to the Vaigai river, and in the north to the south Pennar river. It formed a distinct geographical zone and became the seat of the Chola power a little before the beginning of the Christian era. This area was different from north Tamil Nadu, which consisted of uplands and came into prominence under the Pallavas in the fourth–sixth centuries. The eastern part of the peninsula is bounded by the Coromandel coast. Although the coastline is flanked by the Eastern Ghats or steps, the ghats are not very high and have several openings caused by the eastward flow of the rivers into the Bay of Bengal. Thus communication between the eastern coast, on the one hand, and other parts of Andhra and Tamil Nadu, on the other, was not difficult in ancient times. The port cities of Arikamedu (modern name), Mahabalipuram, and Kaveripattanam were situated on the Coromandel coast.

The western part of the peninsula does not have such distinct regional units. We can, however, locate Maharashtra between the Tapi (or Damanganga) to the north and the Bhima to the south. The area covered by Karnataka seems to have been situated between the Bhima and the upper regions of the Krishna to the north and the Tungabhadra to the south. For a long time, the Tungabhadra provided a natural frontier between the warring powers to its north and south. Just as the Chalukyas of Badami and the Rashtrakutas found it difficult to extend their sway to the south of the Tungabhadra, so also the Pallavas and Cholas found it difficult to extend their authority to its north. The coastal area in the extreme south-west of the peninsula was covered by the modern state of Kerala. The sea coast along the western part of the peninsula is called the Malabar coast. Although the coast came to have several ports and small kingdoms, communications between the coast and the adjoining areas of Maharashtra, Karnataka, and Kerala were rendered difficult by the Western Ghats with difficult passes to cross.

In between the Indus and the Gangetic systems to the north and the Vindhya mountains to the south lies a vast stretch of land which is divided into two units by the Aravalli mountains. The area west of the Aravallis is covered by the Thar desert, although a part of Rajasthan also lies in this region. The vast expanse of the desert made human settlements impossible in ancient times. However, a few fertile oases scattered in the desert were settled, and from early times it has been possible to cross the desert on camels. The south-eastern portion of Rajasthan has been a comparatively fertile area since ancient times, and because of the existence of the Khetri copper mines in this region, it came to be settled in the Chalcolithic period.

Rajasthan shades off into the fertile plains of Gujarat, which are irrigated by the waters of the Narmada, Tapi, Mahi, and Sabarmati. Situated at the end of the north-western portion of the Deccan plateau, Gujarat includes the less rainy Kathiawar peninsula. The coastal area of this state is fairly indented, and therefore suitable for the establishment of several harbours. Therefore, since ancient times, Gujarat has been famous for its coastal and foreign trade, and its people have proved to be enterprising traders.

South of the Ganga–Yamuna doab, and bounded by the Chambal river to the west, the Son river on the east, and the Vindhya mountains and the Narmada river to the south, lies the state of Madhya Pradesh. Its northern part consists of fertile plains. At present, MP is the largest state in the country, and can be broadly divided into two parts, eastern and western. The eastern part, mostly covered by the Vindhyas, became historically important in Gupta times in the fourth and fifth centuries. However, western MP includes Malwa, which has been the scene of historical activities from the sixth century BC onwards. Malwa served as an important hinterland for the Gujarat ports, and many wars were fought between the Deccan and the northern powers for the possession of Malwa and Gujarat. The Shakas and the Satavahanas fought for the possession of this key area in the first and second centuries, and the Marathas and the Rajputs in the eighteenth century.

Natural Frontiers and Cultural Contacts

Each of the areas bounded by rivers, in some cases by mountains, and sometimes with deltas and plateaus, constituted a political and administrative unit in which different ruling dynasties rose and fell. On account of difficult communications in a vast country and the defensibility of the natural frontiers, it was not easy for the ruling class of one region to establish its control over all the other regions. Gradually every region grew into a distinct cultural unit with its own style of life and language. However, in northern and western India, most languages were derived from the same Indo-Aryan stock, and hence had many elements in common. What is also important is that virtually throughout India Sanskrit came to be cultivated and understood.

The Vindhya mountains cut right across India from west to east and formed a boundary between north and south India. The speakers of the Dravidian languages lived south of the Vindhyas, and of the Indo-Aryan languages north of them. In between lived tribal peoples in the Vindhya regions where they are still found. The coastal areas along the Eastern and Western Ghats attracted settlers and traders, and the south was engaged in flourishing foreign trade. The Vindhyas do not constitute insurmountable barriers. In ancient times, despite the difficulties of communications, people moved from north to south, and vice versa. This led to a give and take in culture and language. Repeatedly, the northern powers moved down to the south and the southern rulers moved up to the north. So too did traders, missionaries, and cultural leaders, particularly the brahmanas. This two-way traffic was continuing and helped the development of a composite culture.

Although most regions had well-defined natural frontiers, not every region possessed the resources necessary to sustain livelihoods in isolation. Therefore, from prehistoric times onwards, the common need for metals and other resources produced a network of interconnection between the different regions of the country.

Minerals and Other Resources

The exploitation of the natural resources of India has an important bearing on its history. Until human settlements developed on a large scale, given the heavy rainfall, substantial areas of the Indian plains abounded in thickly forested areas which provided game and supplied forage, fuel, and timber. In early times, when burnt bricks were not much in use, timber houses and palisades were constructed. They have been found in Pataliputra, India's first important capital. For construction and tool-making, all kinds of stones, including sandstone, are available in India. The earliest human settlements are naturally found in the hilly areas and in those river valleys that are situated between the hills. In historical times, more temples and pieces of sculpture were made of stone in the Deccan and south India than in the plains of northern India.

Copper is widely distributed in India. The richest copper mines are located in the Chhotanagpur plateau, particularly in Singhbhum district. The copper belt is about 130 km long and shows many signs of ancient workings. The earliest people who used copper implements in Bihar exploited the copper mines of Singhbhum and Hazaribagh, and many copper tools have been discovered in south Bihar and parts of MP. Rich copper deposits are also to be found in the Khetri mines in Rajasthan. These were tapped by both pre-Vedic and Vedic people, who lived in areas now covered by Pakistan, Rajasthan, Gujarat, and the Ganga–Yamuna doab. Numerous copper belts have been found in the Khetri zone, and they seem to belong to a period anterior to *c.* 1000 BC. As copper was the first metal to be used, it is invested by Hindus with great purity, and utensils made of it are used in religious rituals.

India today produces virtually no tin and this was scarce even in ancient times. There is reason to believe that it was found in Rajasthan, south MP, and Bihar, but the deposits have been virtually exhausted. As bronze is made by mixing tin with copper, we do not find many bronze objects in prehistoric times. The Harappans possibly procured some tin from Rajasthan but their main supply came from Afghanistan, and even this was limited. Hence, although the Harappa people used bronze tools, their number in comparison to those found in western Asia, Egypt, and Crete is very small, and their tools contain a smaller percentage of tin. Therefore, the major part of India had no proper Bronze Age, that is, an age in which tools and implements were largely made of bronze. Starting with the early centuries of the Christian era, India developed intimate connections with Myanmar and the Malay peninsula which had an abundance of tin. This made possible the use of bronze on a large scale, especially for statues of the gods in south India. Tin for the Bihar bronzes of Pala times was possibly obtained from Gaya, Hazaribagh, and Ranchi, for in Hazaribagh tin ores were smelted till the middle of the last century.

India has been rich in iron ores, which are found particularly in south Bihar, eastern MP, and Karnataka. Once the art of smelting using bellows (making steel) was learnt, iron could be used for war, and more usefully to clear jungles and for deep and regular cultivation. The formation of the first empire in Magadha in the sixth to fourth centuries BC owed much to the availability of iron just south of this region. The large scale use of iron made Avanti, with its capital at Ujjain, an important kingdom in the sixth and fifth centuries BC. The Satavahanas and the other dynasties that arose south of the Vindhyas may have exploited the iron ores of Andhra and Karnataka.

Andhra possesses large lead resources, which explains the large numbers of lead coins in the kingdom of the Satavahanas, who ruled over Andhra and Maharashtra in the first two centuries of the Christian era. Lead may have also been obtained from towns in Rajasthan.

The earliest coins, called punch-marked coins, were made largely of silver, although this metal is rarely found in India. However, silver mines existed in early times in the Kharagpur hills in Monghyr district, and they are mentioned as late as the reign of Akbar. This accounts for the use of the white metal in the earliest punch-marked coins found in Bihar.

Large quantities of gold dust, which were carried by river streams from the Himalayas, were collected from the deposits of river channels in the plains. These deposits are called placers. Gold is found in the Kolar goldfields of Karnataka. A very early trace of gold has been found at a new Stone Age site of around 1800 BC in Karnataka. We have no indication of its exploitation till the beginning of the second century AD. Kolar is considered to be the earliest capital of the Gangas of south Karnataka. Much of the gold used in early times was obtained from Central Asia and the Roman empire. Gold coins, therefore, came into regular use during the first five centuries of the Christian era. As the local resources were insufficient to maintain the gold currency over a long spell of time, once the supply from outside stopped, gold coins became rare.

In ancient times, India also produced a variety of precious stones, including pearls, especially in central India, Orissa, and south India. Precious stones formed an important item of trade in articles which were eagerly sought for by the Romans in the early centuries of the Christian era.

Chronology

(BP)

40 m years	Emergence of the Indian subcontinent.
2 m–1200	The last phase of the uplift of the Himalayas.

(BC)

1800	Early trace of gold in Karnataka.
1000	Earliest date of the Khetri copper belts.

(AD)

1 C	Discovery of the direction of the monsoon.

5

Ecology and Environment

In contemporary times, growing industrialization with explosive population growth in several countries has highlighted the problem of protecting the natural environs such as plants, animals, water resources, soils, and metals on a world scale. The interaction between natural environments and the human population is considered an important issue, and is described as the problem of ecology and environment.

Ecology

Ecology as a term was coined in 1869, and is a relatively new science. Till recent times it was treated as a branch of biology but is now considered an independent subject. However, it is closely connected with biology. This subject deals with interaction between various living organisms such as plants, animals, and human beings. With the emergence of humans, the need for food, shelter, and transport came to the forefront. In ancient times, humans lived on wild produce and hunting birds and animals. However, in the industrial age, the relation of humans with plants and animals has undergone a fundamental change, and now many living organisms are preserved through human efforts.

Environment and Human Advance

Environment means surroundings, both natural and man-made. Natural elements comprise soil, air, and water on which animals, plants, and people live. A man-made environment signifies food, shelter, and transport facilities such as roads, bridges, dams, and various types of structures used as dwellings.

This environment also includes rural, urban, socio-economic, cultural, and political conditions.

The environment has a direct bearing on human efforts. But it would be wrong to think of environmental determinism, for human efforts substantially affect the natural surroundings. Thus, deforestation followed by the production of cereals led to large settlements. On the other hand, changes in climate and river courses led to the desertion of some settlements and migration of populations. Though there have been no major climatic changes since 9000 BC on a world scale, there have been some important regional variations. Thus, many scholars of ancient climate hold that extreme aridity and freezing temperature prevailed in Central Asia in the third and the second millennia BC. Towards the turn of the second millennium BC it was bitterly cold. This compelled many people of south Central Asia to move towards the Indian subcontinent in search of a less cold area. This migration is attributed to the speakers of the Indo-Aryan language and the Rig Vedic people.

We cannot think of human advance in ancient times without the exploitation of natural resources. The earliest settlements in India were generally founded near lakes or rivers in hilly, plateau, or wooded areas where people could make stone and bone tools to earn a livelihood. These tools were used for hunting birds and animals, tilling the soil to grow plants and cereals, and also to prepare the sites for setting up dwellings.

Surroundings and Settlements

It was almost impossible to found large agricultural settlements in the Gangetic plains without deforestation and cultivation of the hard alluvial soil. This could be effectively done only with the use of the iron axe and iron ploughshare from about 500 BC. For this, iron mines had to be discovered and the technology for the extraction and the manufacture of iron artefacts had to be developed in various parts of the country. The hard alluvial soil of the mid-Gangetic plains, the red soil of the Vindhyan zone, and the black cotton soil of the Deccan and western India needed iron shares for effective ploughing. Today, safeguarding the natural environment is emphasized. However, despite deforestation, the doab forests continued until the sixteenth to seventeenth centuries when wild animals were hunted in this area. This ecological change was completed only in modern times. In any case, human society progressed at the cost of plants and animals.

Once human beings started growing plants and rearing animals, they multiplied both of them.

The location and size of settlements were conditioned by environmental factors, with soil and climatic conditions which determine the selection of sites. Favourable rainy zones with river, lakes, forests, hills, minerals, and fertile soils attracted many settlers. On the other hand, arid, desert areas without water resources discouraged people from settling there. The Gangetic plains formed an attractive environmental zone. Numerous settlements were established there in the post-500 BC period and quite a number in the earlier period. Many towns were established in the doab and the mid-Gangetic plains. Rivers served as transport routes like the roads and railways of today. When they flooded, they washed away forested banks and prevented the forests from re-growing there. Moreover they irrigated the land thus made available to farmers.

Changes in river courses affected the fortunes of settlements around 2500 BC. The Sarasvati, coterminous with the Ghagar–Hakara, was joined by the Yamuna and the Sutlej, and the three together contributed to the growth of the Harappan culture. However, in 1700 BC, the Sutlej, and possibly the Yamuna, moved eastward, adversely affecting post-urban Harappan settlements.

The river junctions served as sites for the early settlements. The junctions effectively cleared forests and helped human habitation. This can be said of Pataliputra, the first great city of India. This place lay on the junction of the Ganges and the Son. Not far from the town, the Gandak and the Ghagara too joined the Ganges on the north and the Punpun joined it on the south. The presence of the rivers on three sides made Pataliputra virtually a water port and helped it to become the first great state capital. Though Pataliputra was located at the junction of the Ganges and Son, later the Son shifted westward. In prehistoric times, Chirand became important because it was located on the junction of the Ganges and the Ghaghara, and sites around it seem to have been forested. This is indicated by the excavation of Neolithic tools in Chirand. Many of them are made of antler bones which suggest that deer were hunted in the nearby forest.

Although rivers were preferred sites for settlement, people also settled near lakes and tanks. We find such sites in eastern UP and northern Bihar in the second millennium BC. The practice of settling near water reservoirs continues to this day.

The Rain and Human Effort

We may recall the relevance of rainfall indicated in Chapter 4, and examine the relation between rains and human efforts. Though the Harappan culture is found in an arid, semi-desert zone, this is attributed to good rainfall. Scientists speak of adequate rainfall in the Harappan area in the third millennium BC. Once the rainfall reverted to its usual level, this adversely affected the Harappan settlements. Plant and animal remains from Inamgaon in Maharashtra suggest the onset of an extremely arid phase around 1000 BC that forced the farmers to desert their homes and take to pastoral nomadism.

Rainfall certainly helped human society in pursuing agriculture and founding settlements, but heavy rains during the tropical monsoon deterred people from regular work. Gautama Buddha used to suspend his mission of teaching Buddhism annually for four months during the rainy season and stay at such places as Rajagriha, Vaishali, and Shravasti for *varsha-vasa.* He is said to have spent twenty-six rainy seasons in Shravasti. This idea still influences some people, and no marriages are performed in the rainy season, but today, unless the institutions are closed or their workers granted leave, people have to continue work despite heavy showers.

Some other natural hazards are far more catastrophic than heavy rainfall. They include floods, hurricanes, and earthquakes. We hear of a famine leading to the migration of some Jainas, in pre-Mauryan times from Magadh to south India. However, the researchers have yet to discover the sources that mention the natural hazards causing famines and other calamities.

Ancient Attitudes Towards the Environment

In ancient India, rivers came to be regarded as divine. The *Rig Veda* depicts the Sarasvati as a goddess. However, in post-Vedic times, the Ganga emerges as the mother goddess, and the tradition persists to this day. As both earth and water sustained plants and animals, they came to be considered mothers, though there is nothing to show that plans were devised to protect either of them.

Many trees and plants, including *neem*, *pipal*, *vat*, *shami*, and *tulsi* are considered sacred. That is also the case with herbs, including grass. All these are valued because of their medicinal properties, and therefore they are preserved and worshipped. The desire to protect large and small trees is expressed in various ancient texts, and it continues to this day. At the conclusion of large sacrifices and even ordinary rituals, priests and the common worshippers wish peace and prosperity (*shanti*) to forest trees and plants in general.

More importantly, many ancient texts condemn the slaughter of animals. Gautama Buddha was the first person to stress the need to protect cows in a Pali canonical text called the *Suttanipata*. He stressed the virtue of rearing cows because in his view cattle help to grow plants and provide people with food, vitality, health and happiness. Hence his injunction that people should not kill cows. In the early Christian centuries, brahmanical texts lent religious colour to the Buddhist teaching, speaking of dire consequences in the next world for those who killed cows. Later, even the elephant came to be worshipped.

A background of ecology and environment may help the study of ancient India, and may be especially useful in the study of our prehistory. However, human society cannot advance by halting man's struggle against nature. In ancient times, this struggle was principally directed against plants and animals. Once these were brought under control, efforts were made to multiply both of them. History deals primarily with interaction between humans in terms of time and place, but it cannot be correctly constructed unless historians bear in mind the ongoing interaction between human efforts, on the one hand, and the functioning of natural forces, on the other.

Chronology

(BC)

3rd–2nd M	Extreme aridity and freezing temperature in Central Asia.
9000 onwards	No major climatic change on a world scale.
500 onwards	Wide use of iron tools in the Gangetic plains and spurt in settlements.
300	Famine and Jain migration from Magadha to south India.

(AD)

16th–17th C	Forests in the doab despite deforestation.
1869	The term 'ecology' coined.

6

The Linguistic Background

Principal Language Groups

India is a land of numerous languages. According to Grierson, the editor and compiler of *The Linguistic Survey of India*, nearly 180 languages and about 550 dialects are spoken by Indians. These languages belong to four important groups: the Austro-Asiatic, Tibeto-Burman, Dravidian, and Indo-Aryan. The Austro-Asiatic languages in India seem to be the earliest and are generally known because of Munda speech. The speakers of this language are found as far east as Australia and as far west as Madagascar near the eastern coast of Africa. They, however, have a large number of speakers in Southeast Asia. The anthropologists believe that the Austric people appeared in Australia around 40,000 BC. It is, therefore, more likely that they went from Africa to Southeast Asia and Australia via the coast of the Indian subcontinent about 50,000 years ago. By that time, language seems to have been invented. Human genetics show that, 50,000 years ago, the Africans came to the deep south in India from where they passed through the Andaman-Nicobar Islands to Indonesia and later to Australia.

Austro-Asiatic

The Austric language family is divided into two subfamilies, Austric-Asiatic spoken in the Indian subcontinent and Austronesian spoken in Australia and Southeast Asia. The Austric-Asiatic subfamily has two branches: Munda and Mon-Khmer. Mon-Khmer represents the Khasi language which is spoken in the Khasi and Jantia hills in Meghalaya in north-east India and also in the Nicobar islands. However, the Munda tongue is spoken in a much larger area. The Santhals, who constitute the largest tribal group in the subcontinent, speak it in Jharkhand, Bihar, West Bengal, and Orissa.

The forms of speech of the Mundas, Santhals, Hoes, etc., also known as the Mundari language, are prevalent in West Bengal, Jharkhand, and central India. In the Himalayas, Munda survivals are most apparent.

Tibeto-Burman

The second group of languages, that is Tibeto-Burman, is a branch of the Sino-Tibetan family. If we take account of China and other countries, the number of the speakers of this family far exceeds that of the Austric family and even of the Indo-Aryan family. This family has some 300 languages which are spoken in China, Tibet, and Myanmar (Burma). In the Indian subcontinent, Tibeto-Burman speech extends along the Himalayas from north-eastern Assam to north-east Punjab. These forms are found in the north-eastern states of India, and a large number of people in this area speak various forms of the Tibeto-Burman tongue. Various tribes use as many as 116 dialects of this language. The north-eastern states, where they are spoken, include Tripura, Sikkim, Assam, Meghalaya, Arunanchal, Nagaland, Mizoram, and Manipur. The Tibeto-Burman language also prevails in the Darjeeling area of West Bengal. Although both the Austric and the Tibeto-Burman forms of speech are much older than the Dravidian and Indo-Aryan, no literature developed in those tongues because, unlike the Indo-Aryans and the Dravidians, they did not have any form of writing. The speakers were, however, conversant with oral legends and traditions which were first recorded by Christian missionaries in the nineteenth century. It is significant that a Tibeto-Burman term called *burunji* was used by the Ahoms in medieval times in the sense of the family tree. It is likely that the Maithili term *panji* for the family tree was linked to the Tibeto-Burman term.

Dravidian

The third family of languages spoken in India is Dravidian. This form of speech covers almost the whole of south India, and is also prevalent in north-eastern Sri Lanka. Over twenty Dravidian languages are spoken in this area. The earliest form of Dravidian speech, Brahui, is found in the north-western part of the Indian subcontinent located in Pakistan. There are two views about the migration of the Dravidian speaking people, genetic and linguistic. According to the genetic view, the first major migration into India came from the Middle East around 30,000 years ago. According to the second view, the Dravidians came from Elam around 6000 years ago. It seems that the process of the dispersal of the Dravidian speakers started in about 30,000 BC and continued until 4000 BC. Scholars of linguistics attribute the origin of the Dravidian language to Elam, that is south-western Iran. This language is assigned to the fourth millennium BC, and Brahui is a later form of it. It is still spoken in Iran, Turkmenistan, and Afghanistan, and also in the states of Baluchistan and Sindh in Pakistan. It is said that the Dravidian language travelled via the Pakistan area to south India where it gave rise to Tamil, Telugu, Kannada, and Malayalam as its main branches, but Tamil is far more Dravidian than the other languages. Oraon or Kurukh, spoken in Jharkhand and central India, is also Dravidian, but is spoken mainly by members of the Oraon tribe.

Indo-Aryan

The fourth language group, Indo-Aryan belongs to the Indo-European family. According to scientists genetic signals found in the steppe, people throughout Central Asia appear in a good degree in the speakers of the Indo-Aryan languages in India and very little in Dravidian speakers. This suggests that the speakers of the language of the Indo-European family migrated to India. It is said that the eastern or Arya branch of the Indo-European family split into three sub-branches known as Indo-Iranian, Dardic, and Indo-Aryan. Iranian, also called Indo-Iranian, is spoken in Iran and the earliest specimen of it is found in the *Zend Avesta*. The Dardic language belongs to eastern Afghanistan, north Pakistan, and Kashmir, though most scholars now consider Dardic speech to be a branch of the Indo-Aryan language. Indo-Aryan is spoken by a large number of people in Pakistan, India, Bangladesh, Sri Lanka, and Nepal. Nearly 500 Indo-Aryan languages are spoken in north and central India.

The Old Indo-Aryan covers Vedic Sanskrit. The middle Indo-Aryan covers Prakrit, Pali, and Apabhramsha from about 500 BC to AD 1000. Both Prakrit and classical Sanskrit continued to develop in early medieval times, and many words appeared in Apabhramsha from AD 600. The modern Indo-Aryan regional languages such as Hindi, Bengali, Assamese, Oriya, Marathi, Gujarati, Punjabi, Sindhi, and Kashmiri developed in medieval times out of Apabhramsha, as is also the case with Nepali. Kashmiri is Dardic in origin, but it has been deeply influenced by Sanskrit and later Prakrit.

Although India has four groups of languages, their speakers do not form isolated units. In the past an ongoing interaction went on between the various linguistic groups. Consequently, words from one language group appear in another language group. The process began in Vedic times. Large numbers of Munda and Dravidian words are to be found in the *Rig Veda*. However, eventually the Indo-Aryan language superseded many tribal languages because of the socio-economic dominance of its speakers. Though the Indo-Aryan ruling groups used their own language, they could not exploit tribal resources and manpower without using the tribal dialects. This led to the mutual borrowing of words.

Ethnic Groups and Language Families

In the Indian subcontinent, each of the four language families is attributed to each one of the four ethnic groups into which the people of India are divided. These four groups are Negrito, Australoid, Mongoloid, and Caucasoid. This racial division was made in the nineteenth century and was based on the physical features of various peoples. Thus, short stature, short face, and short lips are assigned to the Negrito, who live in the Andaman and Nicobar Islands and the Nilgiri Hills of Tamil Nadu. The Negrito are also placed in Kerala and Sri Lanka. It is thought that they speak some Austric language. The Australoids too are of short stature though they are taller than the Negrito. They too have dark complexions and plenty of body hair. They live mainly in central and southern regions, though also in the Himalayan areas, and speak Austric or Munda languages. The Mongoloids are of short stature, have scanty body hair, and flat noses. They live in the sub-Himalayan and north-eastern regions and speak Tibeto-Burman languages. The Caucasoids are generally of tall stature with long faces, and show well-developed chins, fair skin, and narrow but prominent noses. They speak both the Dravidian and Indo-Aryan languages, and are not therefore linked to a single language.

It is difficult to demarcate one racial group from another, for their physical features keep changing due to climatic conditions. It is interesting that brahmanas and *chamar*s share the same physical features in some areas, and both of them speak the same language. Brahmanas mention their clan groups called *gotra*s to which they belong, but such *gotra*s are not assigned to the chamars. However, in all the bordering areas of various cultural zones, people speak two or more languages. More importantly, commingling of various peoples leads to intermixture of languages. Thus, neither do the people concerned retain their original features nor does the language retain its original character. It is, therefore, not easy to assign a particular language to any one ethnic group.

Chronology

(BC)	
50,000	Austric people come to India.
30,000	Dravidians come to India.
4,000	Brahui (Dravidian) speakers come to India.
500	Start of the Middle Indo-Aryan, covering Prakrit, Pali, and Apabhramsha languages.
(AD)	
19 C	Oral legends and traditions of Munda and Tibeto-Burman languages recorded by Christian missionaries.

7

Human Evolution: The Old Stone Age

African Ancestors of Human Beings

The earth is over 4600 million years old. The evolution of its crust shows four stages. The fourth stage is called the quaternary. It is divided into two epochs called Pleistocene (ice age) and Holocene (post-ice age). The first epoch lasted from 2 million BC to 12,000 BC, the second began in about 12,000 BC and continues to this day. Though life began on the earth around 3500 million years ago, it was confined to plants and animals for many millennia. Humans appeared on the earth in pre-Pleistocene and early Pleistocene times. Several types of humans, called hominids, lived in southern and eastern Africa about 6 million years ago. The earliest humans were not very different from apes which first developed 30 million years ago. The birth of the creature called *Australopithecus* was the most momentous step in the evolution of the human line. *Australopithecus* is a term that originated in Latin and means southern ape. This species or family possessed both ape-like and human characteristics, and originated roughly between 5.5 million and 1.5 million years ago. This creature was bipedal and pot-bellied, with a very small braincase measuring 400 cubic centimetres. The Australopithecus was marked by some elements found in other living beings called homos or human beings. Humans form part of the hominid line of evolution and Australopithecus was the last of the pre-human hominids. That is why this species is also called proto-human.

The first important *Homo* or human was *Homo habilis* found in eastern and southern Africa about 2–1.5 million years ago. *Homo habilis* means a handy or skilful man. This first real human broke stone into pieces and sharpened the latter to use as tools. Fractured pieces of stone have been found in the same places as the bones of *Homo habilis*. This creature had a lightly built braincase which measured 500–700 cubic centimetres. The second important step saw the appearance of *Homo erectus* dated to 1.8 to 1.6 million years ago. *Homo erectus* means an erect or upright man. Its skull was strongly built, its braincase measuring 800–1200 cubic centimetres.

New types of stone tools have been found with *Homo erectus.* The hand axe is considered the most distinctive. It is believed that the *Homo erectus* people discovered how to make and use fire, and this kept them warm in cold climates and protected them from wild animals. In sharp contrast to the *Homo habilis*, the *Homo erectus* travelled long distances. Their remains have been found not only in Africa but also in China, South Asia, and Southeast Asia.

The third step marked the emergence of *Homo sapiens*, which means wise man. Our own species evolved from *Homo sapiens.* It resembles the Neanderthal man found in western Germany around 230,000–30,000 years ago. It had a short body and very narrow forehead, but its braincase measured about 1200 to 1800 cubic centimetres. The race probably evolved in Europe, but the Neanderthal remains have also been found in the Near East and elsewhere in the Old World.

The full-fledged modern man called *Homo sapiens sapiens* is traceable to about 115,000 years ago in southern Africa in the late Stone Age called the Upper Palaeolithic. Compared to other hominid species, it had a large forehead and thinner bones. Modern man originally made diverse stone tools for different functions, but it is not clear whether he was anatomically equipped to speak. Till recent times it was thought that language originated around 35,000 BC but now this date has been pushed back to 50,000 BC. However, the *Homo sapiens sapiens* had a large rounded braincase of about 1200–2000 cubic centimetres in volume. This enabled the modern human to function much more effectively and enabled him to modify the environment.

The Early Man in India

Only a few fossils relating to human evolution have been discovered in the subcontinent. None the less, some of the earliest skull fossils have been found in the Siwalik hills covering India and Pakistan. These skulls appear in the Potwar plateau, in Punjab province of Pakistan, which developed on sandstone. These skulls are called Ramapithecus and Sivapithecus. They seem to possess some hominid features though they represent apes.

Ramapithecus was the female, but both belonged to the same group. A representative of this group found in Greece is dated around 10 million years ago. This may be a ground for dating Ramapithecus and Sivapithecus, but these skulls are considered *c.* 2.2 million years old. In any case, there is nothing to show that this species spread in other parts of the subcontinent. It seems that further evolution from the Siwalik category of hominids came to a dead end in the subcontinent, and this species became extinct.

Nevertheless, an almost complete hominid skull was discovered in 1982 in the middle valley of the Narmada at Hathnora in MP. This fossilized skull was called *Homo erectus* or upright human, but is now anatomically recognized as archaic *Homo sapiens.*

So far the remains of *Homo sapiens* have not been found elsewhere in the subcontinent. However, the remains of a full-fledged modern man called *Homo sapiens sapiens* have been reported from Sri Lanka. The find place is called Fa Hien, and the fossils found nearby are 34,000 years old. They represent the hunting and foraging life which is attributed to the Late Pleistocene and Early Holocene periods in Sri Lanka. Fa Hien cave seems to be the earliest Upper Palaeolithic site in the Indian subcontinent. Its artefacts are about 31,000 years old. Modern humans are considered 34,000 years old. In any case it seems that the earliest modern humans arrived in India from the South because of an early coastal migration around 50,000 years ago from Africa. They did not come from the North.

Phases in the Palaeolithic Age

The Palaeolithic Age in India is divided into three phases in accordance with the type of stone tools used by the people and also according to the nature of climatic change. The first phase is called Early or Lower Palaeolithic, the second Middle Palaeolithic, and the third Upper Palaeolithic. Until further and adequate information is available about the Bori artefacts, the first phase may be placed broadly between 600,000 and 150,000 BC, the second between 150,000 and 35,000 BC, and the third between 35,000 and 10,000 BC. However, between 35,000 and 1500 BC, tools relating to both Middle and Upper Palaeolithic ages have been found in the Deccan Plateau.

The Lower Palaeolithic or the Early Old Stone Age covers the greater part of the ice age. The Early Old Stone Age may have begun in Africa around two million years ago, but in India it is not older than 600,000 years. This date is given to Bori in Maharashtra, and this site is considered to be the earliest Lower Palaeolithic site. People use hand axes, cleavers, and choppers. The axes found in India are more or less similar to those of western Asia, Europe, and Africa. Stone tools were used largely for chopping, digging, and skinning. Early Old Stone Age sites have been found in the valley of river Son or Sohan in Punjab, now in Pakistan. Several sites have been found in Kashmir and the Thar desert. Lower Palaeolithic tools have also been found in the Belan valley in UP and in the desert area of Didwana in Rajasthan. Didwana yielded not only Lower Palaeolithic stone tools but also those of the Middle and Upper Palaeolithic ages. Chirki-Nevasa in Maharashtra has yielded as many as 2000 tools, and those have also been found at several places in the south. Nagarjunakonda in Andhra Pradesh is an important site, and the caves and rock shelters of Bhimbetka near Bhopal also show features of the Lower Palaeolithic age. The rock shelters may have served as seasonal camps for human beings. Hand axes have been found in a deposit of the time of the second Himalayan inter-glaciation, when the climate became less humid. The people of the Lower Stone Age seem to have principally been food gatherers. They took to small game hunting and lived also on fish and birds. The Early or Lower Stone Age in India may be associated with the people of the *Homo sapiens* group.

The Middle Palaeolithic industries were largely based upon flakes or small pieces of stone which have been found in different parts of India with regional variations. The principal tools comprise blades, points, borers, and scrapers, all made of flakes. The geographical horizon of the Middle Palaeolithic sites coincides roughly with that of the Lower Palaeolithic sites. The artefacts of this age are found at several places on the river Narmada, and also at several places, south of the Tungabhadra river. The Belan valley (UP), which lies at the foothills of the Vindhyas, is rich in stone tools and animal fossils including cattle and deer. These remains relate to both the Lower and Middle Stone ages.

In the Upper Palaeolithic phase we find 566 sites in India. This may be due to the general presence of grassland dotted with few trees. The climate was less humid, coinciding with the last phase of the ice age when the climate became comparatively warm. In the world context, it marks the appearance of new flint industries and men of the modern type (*Homo sapiens sapiens*). In India, we notice the use of blades and burins, which have been found in AP, Karnataka, Maharashtra, central MP, southern UP, Jharkhand and adjoining areas. Caves and rock shelters for use by human beings in the Upper Palaeolithic phase have been discovered at Bhimbetka.

45 km south of Bhopal. An Upper Palaeolithic assemblage, characterized by comparatively large flakes, blades, burins, and scrapers has also been found in the upper levels of the Gujarat sand dunes.

The Mesolithic Age: Hunters and Herders

The Upper Palaeolithic age came to an end with the end of the ice age around 10,000 BC. It may be noted that the Pleistocene marked by a succession of ice ages coincided with the Palaeolithic age in the world context and lasted from two million years ago to 12,000 BC, and when it ended, the climate became warm and rainy. Climatic changes brought about changes in fauna and flora. Humans took advantage of adequate rainfall, dense vegetation, and forest. Since then no major changes have appeared in climatic conditions.

In 9000 BC began an intermediate stage in Stone-Age culture, which is called the Mesolithic age. It intervened as a transitional phase between the Palaeolithic and the Neolithic or New Stone ages. The Mesolithic people lived on hunting, fishing, and food gathering; at a later stage they also domesticated animals. The first three occupations continued the Palaeolithic practice, whereas the last developed in the Neolithic culture. Thus the Mesolithic age marked a transitional phase in the mode of subsistence leading to animal husbandry.

The characteristic tools of the Mesolithic age are microliths or tiny tools. Mesolithic sites abound in Rajasthan, southern UP, central and eastern India, and also south of the river Krishna. Of them, Bagor in Rajasthan is very well excavated. It had a distinctive microlithic industry, and its inhabitants subsisted on hunting and pastoralism. The site remained occupied for 5000 years from the fifth millennium BC onwards. Adamgarh in MP and Bagor in Rajasthan provide the earliest evidence for the domestication of animals in the Indian part of the subcontinent; this could be around 5000 BC. The cultivation of plants around 7000–6000 BC is suggested in Rajasthan from a study of the deposits of Sambhar, the former salt lake.

So far, only a few finds of the Mesolithic age have been scientifically dated. The Mesolithic culture continued to be important roughly from 9000 to 4000 BC, and undoubtedly paved the way for the rise of the Neolithic culture.

Art in the Old Stone Age

The people of the Palaeolithic and Mesolithic ages practised painting. Prehistoric art appears at several places, but Bhimbetka in MP is a striking site. Situated in the Vindhyan range, 45 km south of Bhopal, it has over 500 painted rock shelters distributed in an area of 10 sq. km. At Bhimbetka, the rock paintings extend from the Upper Palaeolithic to the Mesolithic age and in some series even up to recent times. However, a substantial number of rock shelters are associated with the Mesolithic occupation. Many birds, animals, and human beings are painted, and obviously most of the birds and animals that figure in the paintings were hunted for subsistence. Perching birds that live on grain do not figure in the earliest group of paintings. These paintings evidently belong to the hunting/gathering economy.

Why did the Upper Palaeolithic people practise art? It is argued that they did this for the sake of art. This would, however, suggest too much sophistication at a very early stage in human history. It is also said that they took to art and ritual to overcome social conflict. This may apply to a complex social structure which suffers from sharp social differentiation, which hardly existed in the Upper Palaeolithic society. In all probability, people depicted various wild animals to ensure control over them, for hunting was their principal source of livelihood. Although we find some human male and female figures, animals of various types figure frequently. These animal painting rituals were realistic in the context of hunting. In the Harappan context, animal paintings become conventional. Animals continue to be depicted on the Harappan seals although the people largely lived on the food they grew.

Earliest Human Organization

How were humans organized socially? It is not clear whether they lived in a band or pre-band society. Bands were formed for hunting, and the maximum number of persons could be around 25. There could have been a form of alliance between various bands for mutual aid, and the number in such a large group would not have exceeded around 500. Rituals could have been conducted to ratify such an alliance. Eventually the band turned into an exogamous group called clan in the Neolithic phase. Members of a clan would always marry outside the clan, but bands established mutual aid relationships. In the Upper Palaeolithic phase, members of a band shared the fruits of hunting and food gathering in a society based on these occupations. Formation of bands and groups of bands may have been facilitated by the use of language which seems to have originated in the Upper Palaeolithic phase, and communication may have played an important role in keeping the people together.

Chronology

(BP)	
4600 m years	Age of the Earth.
3500 m years	Birth of life on earth.
30 m years	Appearance of the earliest humans (who were not very different from apes) on earth.
6 m years	Appearance of hominids on earth (southern and eastern Africa).
5.5–1.5 m years	Appearance of *Australopithecus* on earth.
2.2 m years	Skulls of Ramapithecus and Sivapithecus in the Potwar plateau in Pakistani Punjab in the Siwalik hill area.
2 m years	Lower Palaeolithic age in Africa.
2–1.5 m years	Appearance of *Homo habilis* on earth (eastern and southern Africa).
1.8–1.6 m years	Appearance of *Homo erectus* on earth. Earliest stone hand axe. Fire discovered.
230,000–30,000 m years	Appearance of *Homo sapiens* on earth.
115,000 years	Appearance of *Homo sapiens sapiens* (modern man) in southern Africa.

(BC)	
2 m–12,000	Pleistocene (ice age).
700,000	The skull of archaic *Homo sapiens* from the Narmada valley.
34,000	Fossils of *Homo sapiens sapiens* in Sri Lanka.
600,000–150,000	Lower Palaeolithic age in India.
150,000–35,000	Middle Palaeolithic age in India.

50,000	Origin of language.
35,000–10,000	Upper Palaeolithic age in India.
9000–4000	Mesolithic age culture in India.
12000 to the present	Holocene (post-ice age).
7000–6000	Start of plant cultivation in India.
5000	Earliest evidence of the domestication of animals in India.

8

The Neolithic Age: First Food Producers and Animal Keepers

Earliest Rural Settlements in Baluchistan

In the world context, the New Stone or the Neolithic age began in 9000 BC. The only known Neolithic settlement in the Indian subcontinent, attributed to 7000 BC, is in Mehrgarh, which is situated in Baluchistan, a province of Pakistan. Mehrgarh is located on the bank of the Bolan river in the Kochi plain which is called the 'bread basket' of Baluchistan. The settlement lay on the edge of the Indus plains. It is called one of the largest Neolithic settlements between the Indus and the Mediterranean. Though the earliest settlers raised domestic animals and produced cereals, they were disturbed around 5500 BC by floods. Agricultural and other activities were resumed around 5000 BC with the help of both stone and bone tools. The Neolithic people of this area produced wheat and barley from the outset. They domesticated cattle, sheep, and goats in the initial stage. Initially, goats predominated, but eventually cattle outnumbered the two other animals. Cattle rearing may have helped agriculture. Cereals were produced in substantial quantities and stored in granaries which have been discovered in different phases. Generally granaries were made of mud bricks which were used for constructing dwellings. Many mud-brick structures, which are compartmented, appear to be granaries. The period 4500–3500 BC saw considerable agricultural expansion from the Kochi plain area into the Indus plain area, and also saw progress in pottery. Up to 5000 BC, the people did not make pots but after 4500 BC, the potter's wheel was known. Pots rapidly multiplied and they began to be painted. In the dried basin of Hakra, a tributary of the Indus, forty-seven Later Neolithic settlements have been found. Evidently they paved the way for the rise of the Harappan culture.

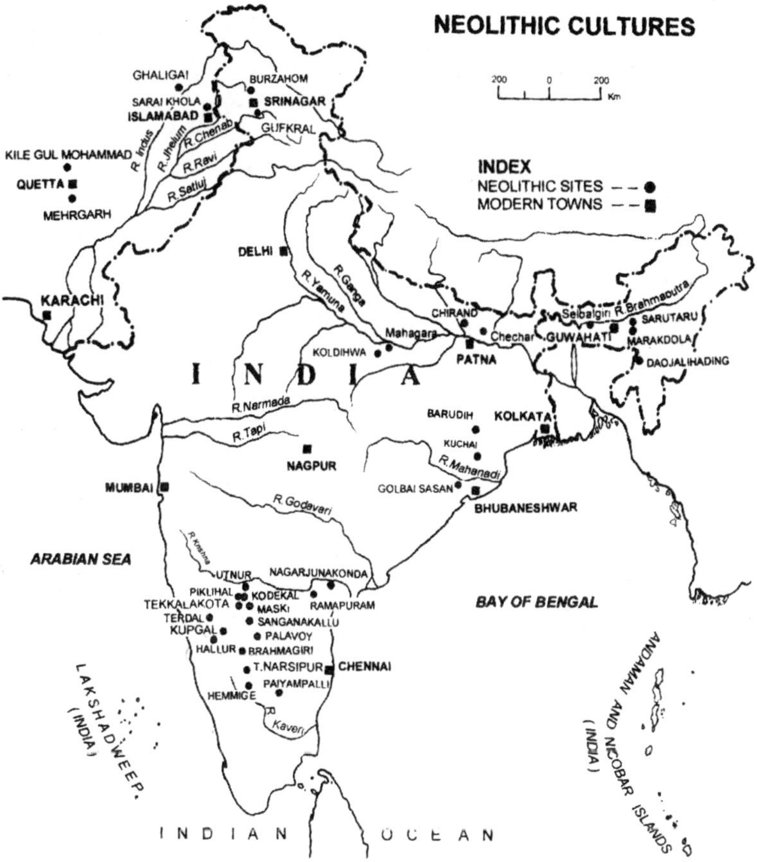

MAP 1 Neolithic Cultures. *Courtesy Archaeological Survey of India (ASI)*

Some Neolithic sites found on the northern spurs of the Vindhyas are considered as old as 5000 BC but generally Neolithic settlements found in south India are not older than 2500 BC; in some parts of southern and eastern India they are as late as 1000 BC.

The people of the Neolithic age used tools and implements of polished stone. They particularly used stone axes, which have been found in large numbers in a substantial part of the hilly tracts of India. The stone axe was put to various uses by the people, and ancient legends represent Parashurama as an important axe-wielding hero.

Based on the types of axes used by Neolithic settlers, we notice three important areas of Neolithic settlements—north-western, north-eastern, and southern. The north-western group of Neolithic tools is distinguished by rectangular axes with a curved cutting edge; the north-eastern group by polished stone axes with a rectangular butt and occasional shouldered hoes; and the southern group by axes with oval sides and pointed butt.

Use of Bone Tools in the Sites of Burzahom and Chirand

In the north-west, Kashmiri Neolithic culture was distinguished by its dwelling pits, wide range of ceramics, the variety of stone and bone tools, and the complete absence of microliths. Its most important site is Burzahom, which means 'the place of birch', situated 16 km north-west of Srinagar. The Neolithic people lived there on a lake-side in pits, and probably had a hunting and fishing economy, and seem to have been acquainted with agriculture. The people of Gufkral (literally the 'cave of the potter'), a Neolithic site, 41 km south-west of Srinagar, practised both agriculture and animal husbandry. The Neolithic people in Kashmir used not only polished tools of stone, but also numerous tools and weapons made of bone. The only other place which has yielded considerable bone implements in India is Chirand, 40 km west of Patna on the northern side of the Ganges. Made of antlers (horn of deer), these implements have been found in a late Neolithic settlement in an area with about 100 cm rainfall. The establishment of the settlement was made possible by the open land available at the junction of four rivers, the Ganges, Son, Gandak, and Ghaghra and is marked by a paucity of stone tools.

The people of Burzahom used coarse grey pottery. It is interesting that at Burzahom, domestic dogs were buried with their masters in their graves.

This practice does not seem to be evident in any other Neolithic culture in India. The earliest date for Burzahom is about 2700 BC, but the bones recovered from Chirand cannot be dated earlier than 2000 BC and possibly belong to the late Neolithic phase.

We may place the Baluchistan and Kashmir valley Neolithic settlements in the north-western group.

Another area from which Neolithic tools have been recovered is situated in the hills of Assam. Neolithic tools have also been found in the Garo hills in Meghalaya on the north-eastern frontier of India. The second group may include the settlements in the Vindhyas and the Kaimur hills; we also find a number of Neolithic settlements on the northern spurs of the Vindhyas in Mirzapur and Allahabad districts of UP. Neolithic sites such as Koldihwa and Mahagra in Allahabad district are known for the cultivation of rice in the fifth millennium BC. Senuwar in Rohtas district in the Kaimur hilly area is the most important site. Also notable is the site of Taradih close to the Bodh-Gaya temple.

The riverine site of Chirand may be included in the north-eastern group. This site forms an entity by itself because no stone is easily available in the riverine tract.

Neolithic Settlements in South India

An important group of Neolithic people lived in south India, south of the Godavari river. They usually settled on the tops of granite hills or on plateaus near the river banks. They used stone axes and also a kind of stone blades. Fire-baked earthen figurines suggest that they kept a large number of cattle, besides sheep and goats. They used stone querns for grinding corn, which shows that they were acquainted with the art of producing cereals. South India has the largest number of Neolithic settlements, because of the easy availability of stone, with over 850 settlements spread across AP, Karnataka, and Tamil Nadu.

Some of the important Neolithic sites or those with Neolithic layers that have been excavated include Maski, Brahmagiri, Hallur, Kodekal, Sanganakallu, Piklihal, and Takkalakota in Karnataka, and Paiyampalli in Tamil Nadu. Utnur is an important Neolithic site in AP. The Neolithic phase in south India seems to have covered the period from about 2400 to about 1000 BC.

The Neolithic settlers in Piklihal were cattle-herders. They domesticated cattle, sheep, goats, etc., and set up seasonal camps surrounded by cowpens made with posts and stakes in which they accumulated dung. When it was time to move, the entire camping ground was set afire and cleared for the next session of camping. Both ash mounds and habitation sites have been found in Piklihal.

Farming and Cereals

The Neolithic settlers were the earliest farming communities. They broke the ground with stone hoes and digging sticks at the end of which ring stones weighing one to half a kilogram were fixed. Besides polished tools of stone, they used microlith blades. They lived in circular or rectangular houses made of mud and reed. It is held that the primitive people living in circular houses owned property in common. In any case, these Neolithic people led a settled life and produced *ragi* and horse gram (*kulathi*), and even rice. The Neolithic people of Mehrgarh were more advanced. They produced wheat and barley, and lived in mud-brick houses.

During the Neolithic phase, several settlements became acquainted with the cultivation of cereals and the domestication of animals. So they needed pots in which they could store their food grains, and also pots for cooking, eating, and drinking. Pottery, therefore, first appears in this phase, with handmade pottery in the early stage. Later, the Neolithic people used foot wheels to make pots. It seems that the potter's wheel came to Baluchistan from western Asia and from there it spread across the subcontinent. The Neolithic pottery included black-burnished ware, grey ware, and mat-impressed ware.

Neolithic celts, axes, adzes, chisels, and the like, have also been found in the Orissa and the Chhotanagpur hill areas, but traces of Neolithic settlements are generally few in parts of MP and the tracts of the upper Deccan. These tracts lack the types of stone which easily lend themselves to grinding and polishing.

Progress in and Limitation of the Neolithic Phase

The period between 9000 and 3000 BC saw remarkable technological progress in western Asia. The people developed the arts of cultivation, weaving, pot-making, house building, stock raising, writing, and the like. This process, however, started a little late in India. The Neolithic age in the Indian subcontinent began around the seventh millennium BC. Some important crops, including wheat and barley, came to be cultivated in the subcontinent, and villages were established in this part of the world. What distinguished the Neolithic people was their use of stone celts which were edged and pointed. These celts mostly served as tilling tools such as hoes and ploughshares. They were meant for digging the ground and sowing seeds. All this meant a revolutionary change in the mode of subsistence. People no longer depended on hunting, fishing, and gathering, with cultivation and cattle husbandry providing them with food. With their tools, they also built dwellings. With new means of food and shelter, they were on the threshold of civilization.

The people of the Stone Age suffered from one great limitation. As they had to depend almost entirely on tools and weapons made of stone, they could not found settlements far away from the hilly areas. They could settle only on the slopes of the hills in rock shelters and the hilly river valleys. Also, even with great effort, they were unable to produce more than they needed for bare subsistence.

Chronology

(BC)	
9000	Neolithic age began in western Asia.
7000	Neolithic settlement in the Indian subcontinent.
5000	Neolithic sites to the north of the Vindhyas.
4500 onwards	Potter's wheel.
2700	Earliest date for Neolithic settlement in Kashmir.
2500	Earliest Neolithic settlement in south India.
2000	Earliest date for Chirand's Neolithic phase.
1000	Latest evidence of Neolithic settlements in southern and eastern India.

9

Chalcolithic Cultures

Chalcolithic Settlements

The end of the Neolithic period saw the use of metals. The metal first used was copper, and several cultures were based on the use of copper and stone implements. Such a culture is called Chalcolithic, which means the copper–stone phase. Technologically, the Chalcolithic stage is applied to the pre-Harappan phase. However, in various parts of India the Chalcolithic cultures followed the Bronze Age Harappa culture. Here we consider principally such cultures as came in the later part of the mature Harappa culture or after its end.

The Chalcolithic people mostly used stone and copper objects, but they also occasionally used low grade bronze and even iron. They were primarily rural communities spread over a wide area with hilly land and rivers. On the other hand, the Harappans used bronze and had urbanized on the basis of the produce from the flood plains in the Indus Valley. In India, settlements relating to the Chalcolithic phase are found in south-eastern Rajasthan, the western part of MP, western Maharashtra, and in southern and eastern India. In south-eastern Rajasthan, two sites, one at Ahar and the other at Gilund, have been excavated. They lie in the dry zones of the Banas valley. In western MP or Malwa, Kayatha and Eran have been excavated. Malwa-ware characteristic of the Malwa Chalcolithic culture of central and western India is considered the richest among Chalcolithic ceramics, and some of this pottery and other related cultural elements also appear in Maharashtra.

However, the most extensive excavations have taken place in western Maharashtra. Several Chalcolithic sites, such as Jorwe, Nevasa, Daimabad in Ahmadanagar district; Chandoli, Songaon, and Inamgaon in Pune district;

and also Prakash and Nasik have been excavated. They all relate to the Jorwe culture named after Jorwe, the type-site situated on the left bank of the Pravara river, a tributary of the Godavari, in Ahmadnagar district. The Jorwe culture owed much to the Malwa culture, but it also shared elements of the Neolithic culture of the south.

The Jorwe culture, *c.* 1400 to 700 BC covered modern Maharashtra except parts of Vidarbha and the coastal region of Konkan. Although the Jorwe culture was rural, some of its settlements, such as Daimabad and Inamgaon, had almost reached the urban stage. All these Maharashtra sites were located in semi-arid areas mostly on brown–black soil which had *ber* and *babul* vegetation but fell in the riverine tracts. In addition to these, we have Navdatoli situated on the Narmada. Most Chalcolithic ingredients intruded into the Neolithic sites in south India.

Several Chalcolithic sites have been found in the Vindhyan region of Allahabad district. In eastern India, besides Chirand on the Ganges, mention may be made of Pandu Rajar Dhibi in Burdwan district and Mahishdal in Birbhum district in West Bengal. Some additional sites have been excavated, notable among which are Senuar, Sonpur, and Taradih in Bihar; and Khairadih and Narhan in eastern UP.

The Chalcolithic people used tiny tools and weapons made of stone in which the stone blades and bladelets were an important element. In many places, particularly in south India, the stone blade industry flourished and stone axes continued to be used. Obviously such areas were not situated far from the hills. Certain settlements show a large number of copper objects. This seems to be the case with Ahar and Gilund, which were situated more or less in the dry zones of the Banas valley in Rajasthan. Unlike the other contemporary Chalcolithic farming cultures, Ahar virtually used no microlithic tools; stone axes or blades are virtually absent here. Objects relating to it include several flat axes, bangles, several sheets, all made of copper, although there is also a bronze sheet. Copper was locally available. The people of Ahar practised smelting and metallurgy from the very outset, and the original name of Ahar is Tambavati or a place that has copper. The Ahar culture is dated to between *c.* 2100 and 1500 BC, and Gilund is considered a regional centre of it. Gilund shows only fragments of copper, but it had a stone blade industry. Flat, rectangular copper axes have been found in Jorwe and Chandoli in Maharashtra, and copper chisels in Chandoli.

The people of the Chalcolithic phase use different types of pottery, one of which is called black-and-red and seems to have been widely prevalent

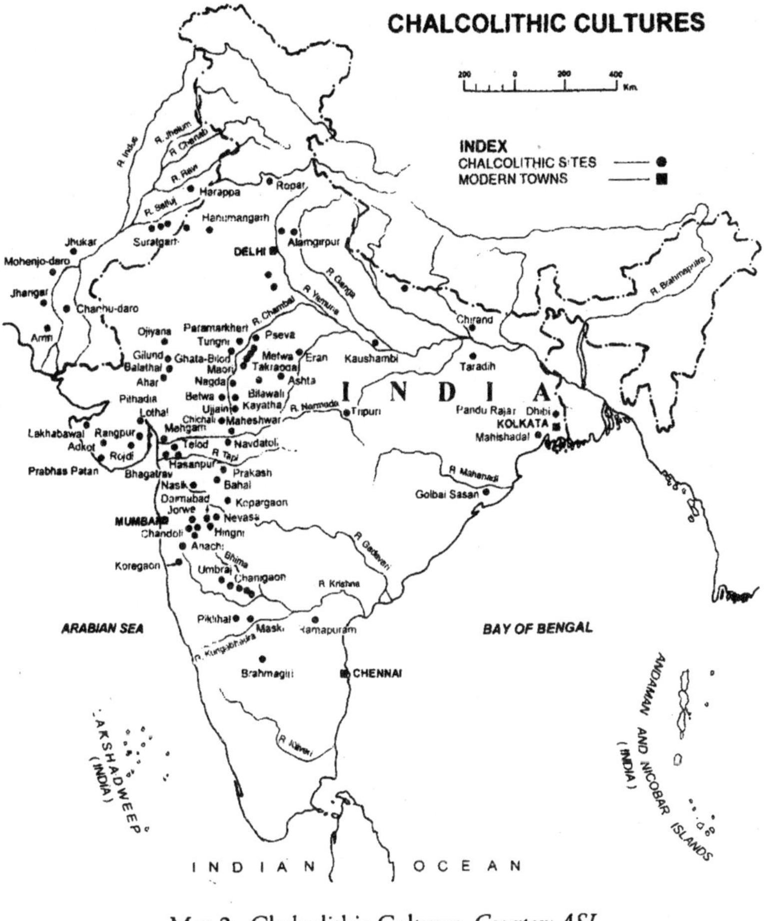

MAP 2 Chalcolithic Cultures. *Courtesy ASI*

from nearly 2000 BC onwards. It was thrown on wheel and occasionally painted with white linear designs. This is true not only of settlements in Rajasthan, MP, and Maharashtra but also of habitations found in Bihar and West Bengal. People living in Maharashtra, MP, and Bihar produced channel-spouted pots, dishes-on-stand, and bowls-on-stand. It would be wrong to think that all the people who used black-and-red pottery were of the same culture. Black-and-red-ware pottery from Maharashtra, MP, and Rajasthan was painted, but there were very few such painted pots in eastern India.

The people living in the Chalcolithic age in south-eastern Rajasthan, western MP, western Maharashtra, and elsewhere domesticated animals and practised agriculture. They reared cows, sheep, goats, pigs, and buffaloes, and hunted deer. Camel remains have also been found, but generally they were not acquainted with the horse. Some animal remains are identified as being either of the horse, donkey, or wild ass. People certainly ate beef and pork, but they did not eat pork on any considerable scale. What is remarkable is that these people produced wheat and rice, and in addition to these staple crops they also cultivated bajra. They produced several pulses such as lentil (*masur*), black gram, green gram, and grass pea. Almost all these food grains have been found at Navdatoli situated on the bank of the Narmada in Maharashtra. Perhaps at no other place in India has so many cereals been discovered as a result of excavation. The people of Navdatoli also produced *ber* and linseed. Cotton was produced in the black cotton soil of the Deccan, and *rui*, *bajra*, and several millets were cultivated in the lower Deccan. In eastern India, fish hooks have been found in Bihar and West Bengal, where we also find rice. This suggests that the Chalcolithic people in the eastern region lived on fish and rice, which is still a popular diet in that part of the country. Most settlements in the Banas valley in Rajasthan are small, but Ahar and Gilund spread over an area of nearly four hectares.

The Chalcolithic people were generally not acquainted with burnt bricks, which were seldom used, as in Gilund around 1500 BC. Occasionally their houses were made of mud-brick, but mostly these were constructed with wattle and daub, and seem to have been thatched houses. However, the people in Ahar lived in stone houses. Of the 200 Jorwe sites discovered so far, the largest is Daimabad in the Godavari valley. It is about 20 hectares in extent which could have accommodated around 4000 people. It also seems to have been fortified with a mud wall which had stone rubble bastions. Daimabad is famous for the recovery of many bronze goods, some of which were influenced by the Harappan culture.

At Inamgaon, in the earlier Chalcolithic phase in western Maharashtra, large mud houses with ovens and circular pit houses have been discovered. In the later phase (1300–1000 BC) we have a house with five rooms, four rectangular and one circular. This was located at the centre of the settlements, and may have been the house of a chief. The granary, located close to it, may have been used for storing tributes in kind. Inamgaon was a large Chalcolithic settlement with over a hundred houses and numerous grave sites. It was fortified and surrounded by a moat.

We know a good deal about the Chalcolithic arts and crafts. They were clearly expert coppersmiths and also skilful workers in stone. Tools, weapons, and bangles of copper have been unearthed. They manufactured beads of semiprecious stones such as carnelian, steatite, and quartz crystal, and the people knew the art of spinning and weaving because spindle whorls have been discovered in Malwa. Cotton flax and silk threads made of cotton silk and of *semal* silk (cotton tree) have been found in Maharashtra, indicating an expertise in the manufacture of cloth. In addition to the artisans who practised these crafts at various sites, Inamgaon had potters, smiths, ivory carvers, lime makers, and terracotta artisans.

Regional differences in social structure, cereals, pottery, etc., become apparent in the copper–stone phase. Eastern India produced rice; western India cultivated barley and wheat. Chronologically, certain settlements in Malwa and central India, such as those in Kayatha and Eran, were established early; those of western Maharashtra and eastern India at a much later date.

We are able to form some idea about the burial practices and religious cults of these people. In Maharashtra, people buried their dead in urns beneath the floor of their house in the north-to-south position. They did not use separate cemeteries for this purpose, as was the case with the Harappans. Pots and some copper objects were deposited in the graves obviously for the use of the dead in the next world.

Terracotta figures of women suggest that the Chalcolithic people venerated the mother goddess, and some unbaked nude clay figurines were also used for worship. A figure of the mother goddess, similar to that found in western Asia, has been found in Inamgaon. In Malwa and Rajasthan, stylized bull terracottas show that the bull was the symbol of a religious cult.

Both the settlement pattern and burial practices suggest the beginnings of social inequalities in Chalcolithic society. A kind of settlement hierarchy is visible in several Jorwe settlements of Maharashtra. Some of them are as large as twenty hectares, but others encompass only five hectares and even less. This would imply two-tier habitations. The difference in the size of settlements suggests that the larger settlements dominated the smaller ones. However, in both large and small settlements, the chief and his kinsmen, who lived in rectangular houses, dominated others who lived in round huts. In Inamgaon, the craftsmen lived on the western fringes, and the chief probably at the centre; this suggests social distance between the inhabitants. In the graves at Chandoli and Nevasa in western Maharashtra, some children were buried with copper-based necklaces around their necks, others had grave goods consisting only of pots. At Inamgaon, an adult was buried with pottery and some copper. In one house in Kayatha, twenty-nine copper bangles and two unique axes were found. At the same place, necklaces of semiprecious stones such as steatite and carnelian beads were found in pots. It is evident that those who possessed these objects were affluent.

Chronologically, special note may be taken of a site at Ganeshwar which is located close to the rich copper mines of the Sikar–Jhunjhunu area of the Khetri copper belt in Rajasthan. The copper objects excavated from this area include arrowheads, spearheads, fish hooks, colts, bangles, chisels, etc. Some of their shapes are similar to those discovered at Indus sites; a terracotta cake resembling the Indus type was also found. There were also many microliths that are characteristic of the Chalcolithic culture. We also find the OCP (Ochre-Coloured Pottery) which is a red-slipped ware often painted in black and largely in vase forms. As the Ganeshwar deposits are ascribed to 2800–2200 BC, they by and large predate the mature Harappan culture. Ganeshwar principally supplied copper objects to Harappa and did not receive much from it. The Ganeshwar people partly lived on agriculture and largely on hunting. Although their principal craft was the manufacture of copper objects, they were unable to urbanize. The Ganeshwar assemblage was neither urban nor a proper OCP/Copper Hoard Culture. With its microliths and other stone tools, much of the Ganeshwar culture can be considered a pre-Harappan Chalcolithic culture that contributed to the making of the mature Harappan culture.

Chronologically, there are several series of Chalcolithic settlements in India. Some are pre-Harappan, others are contemporaneous with the Harappan culture, and yet others are post-Harappan. Pre-Harappan strata on some sites in the Harappan zone are also called early Harappan in order to distinguish them from the mature urban Indus civilization. Thus, the pre-Harappan phase at Kalibangan in Rajasthan and Banawali in Haryana is distinctly Chalcolithic. So too is the case with Kot Diji in Sindh in Pakistan.

Pre-Harappan and post-Harappan Chalcolithic cultures and those coexisting with the Harappan have been found in northern, western, and central India. An example is the Kayatha culture *c.* 2000–1800 BC, which existed towards the end of the Harappan culture. It has some pre-Harappan elements in pottery, but also evidences Harappan influence. Several post-Harappan Chalcolithic cultures in these areas are influenced by the post-urban phase of the Harappan culture.

Several other Chalcolithic cultures, though younger in age than the mature Harappan culture, are not connected with the Indus civilization. The Malwa culture (1700–1200 BC) found in Navdatoli, Eran, and Nagda is considered to be non-Harappan. That is also the case with the Jorwe culture (1400–700 BC) which encompasses the whole of Maharashtra except parts of Vidarbha and Konkan. In the southern and eastern parts of India, Chalcolithic settlements existed independently of the Harappan culture. In south India, they are invariably found in continuation of the Neolithic settlements. The Chalcolithic settlements of the Vindhya region, Bihar, and West Bengal too are not related to Harappan culture.

Evidently, various types of pre-Harappan Chalcolithic cultures promoted the spread of farming communities in Sindh, Baluchistan, Rajasthan, and elsewhere, and created conditions for the rise of the urban civilization of Harappa. Mention may be made of Amri and Kot Diji in Sindh; Kalibangan and even Ganeshwar in Rajasthan. It appears that some Chalcolithic farming communities moved to the flood plains of the Indus, learnt bronze technology, and succeeded in setting up cities.

Some work has been done on the Chalcolithic sites in the mid-Gangetic valley where 138 sites have been located. Considering the area of the mid-Gangetic valley, this number is not large when we find 854 Neolithic sites in south India. Of 138 sites, only fourteen sites in UP and Bihar have been excavated so far and these show little use of copper. Though the people largely lived on agriculture, Chalcolithic settlements seem to have been confined to the river junctions and upland areas near the hills. Sizable settlements do not figure in the purely plain areas until the coming of the Iron Age. The Chalcolithic sites of the mid-Gangetic zone and those of West Bengal relate to *c.* 1500–700 BC or even later. Pandu Rajar Dhibi and Mahishdal are important sites in West Bengal. All these sites of the mid- and lower-Gangetic area used more stone tools and fewer copper ones, the latter being very sparse though some fish hooks have been found.

Chalcolithic cultures in central and western India disappeared by 1200 BC or thereabout; only the Jorwe culture continued until 700 BC. In several parts of India, the Chalcolithic black-and-red ware continued into historical times till the second century BC. However, by and large, there was a gap of about four to six centuries between the end of the Chalcolithic cultures and the rise of the early historic cultures in central and western India. In western India and western MP, the eclipse of the Chalcolithic habitations is attributed to a decline in rainfall from about 1200 BC onwards, but in West Bengal and in the mid Gangetic zone, they continued for a long time. Probably in western India, the Chalcolithic people were unable to continue for long with the digging stick in the black clayey soil area that is difficult to break in the dry season. In the red soil areas, especially in eastern India, however, the Chalcolithic phase was immediately followed, without any gap, by the iron phase which gradually transformed the people into full-fledged agriculturalists. The same is true of the Chalcolithic cultures of the mid-Gangetic plains. Similarly, at several sites in southern India, Chalcolithic culture was transformed into the Megalithic culture using iron.

Importance of the Chalcolithic Phase

Barring the alluvial plains and the thickly forested areas, traces of Chalcolithic cultures have been discovered almost all over India. In the alluvial plains of the mid-Gangetic region, several Chalcolithic sites occur, particularly near a lake or a river confluence. During this phase, people mostly founded rural settlements on river banks not far removed from the hills. As stated earlier, they used microliths and other stone tools supplemented by some copper tools. It seems that most of them knew the art of copper smelting. Almost all Chalcolithic communities used wheel-turned black-and-red pots. Considering their pre-Bronze phase of development, we find that they were the first to use painted pottery. Their pots were meant for cooking, eating, drinking, and storage. They used both the *lota* and *thali*. In south India, the Neolithic phase imperceptibly faded into the Chalcolithic, and so these cultures are called Neolithic–Chalcolithic. In other parts, especially in western Maharashtra and Rajasthan, the Chalcolithic people seem to have been colonizers. Their earliest settlements were in Malwa and central India, such as those in Kayatha and Eran; those in western Maharashtra were established later; and those in Bihar and West Bengal much later.

The Chalcolithic communities founded the first large villages in peninsular India and cultivated far more cereals than were known to the Neolithic communities. In particular, they cultivated barley, wheat, and lentil in western India, and rice in southern and eastern India. Their cereal food was supplemented by non-vegetarian food. In western India, more animal food was consumed, but fish and rice formed important elements in the diet of eastern India. More remains of structures have been found in western Maharashtra, western MP, and south-eastern Rajasthan. The settlements at Kayatha and Eran in MP, and at Inamgaon in western Maharashtra, were fortified. On the other hand, the remains of structures in Chirand and Pandu Rajar Dhibi in eastern India were poor, indicating post-holes and round houses. The burial practices were different. In Maharashtra, the dead body was placed in the north–south position, but in south India in the east–west position. There was virtually complete extended burial in western India, but fractional burial in eastern India.

Limitations of Chalcolithic Cultures

The Chalcolithic people domesticated cattle, sheep/goats, which were tethered in the courtyard. In all probability, the domesticated animals were slaughtered for food and not used for milk and dairy products. The tribal people, such as the Gonds of Bastar, believe that milk is meant only to feed young animals and, therefore, they do not milk their cattle. Consequently, the Chalcolithic people were not able to make full use of the animals. Also, the Chalcolithic people living in the black cotton soil area of central and western India did not practise cultivation on any intensive or extensive scale. Neither hoe nor plough has been found at Chalcolithic sites. Perforated stone discs alone were tied as weights to the digging sticks which could be used in slash–burn or *jhum* cultivation. It was possible to sow in the ashes with the aid of such a digging stick. Intensive and extensive cultivation on the black soil required the use of iron implements which rarely occured in the Chalcolithic culture. The Chalcolithic people living in the red soil areas of eastern India also faced the same difficulty.

The general weakness of Chalcolithic cultures is evident from the burial of a large number of children in western Maharashtra. Despite a food-producing economy, the rate of infant mortality was very high. This might be attributed to lack of nutrition, absence of medical knowledge, or outbreaks of epidemics. In any event, the Chalcolithic social and economic pattern did not promote longevity.

The copper–stone culture had an essentially rural background. During its continuance, the supply of copper was limited. Though we find copper mines in eastern India, few copper tools have been found in the Chalcolithic sites of Bihar and the neighbouring states. Some Chalcolithic people primarily used microliths or small stone tools. By itself, a tool made of copper was pliant. People were unaware of the art of mixing tin with copper and thus forging the much stronger and useful metal called bronze. Bronze tools facilitated the rise of the earliest civilizations in Crete, Egypt, Mesopotamia, and also in the Indus Valley.

The people of the Copper–Stone age could not write, nor did they live in cities as did those of the Bronze Age. All these elements of civilization figure for the first time in the Indus region of the Indian subcontinent. Although most Chalcolithic cultures existing in a major part of India were younger than the Indus Valley civilization, they did not derive any substantial benefit from the advanced technological knowledge of the Indus people.

The Copper Hoards and the Ochre-Coloured Pottery Phase

Over eighty copper hoards consisting of rings, celts, hatchets, swords, harpoons, spearheads, and human-like figures have been found in a wide area ranging from West Bengal and Orissa in the east to Gujarat and Haryana in the west, and from AP in the south to UP in the north. The largest hoard comes from Gungeria in MP comprising 424 copper tools and weapons and 102 thin sheets of silver objects. However, a substantial number of copper hoards are concentrated in the Ganga–Yamuna doab; in other areas, we encounter stray finds of copper harpoons, antennae swords, and anthropomorphic figures. These artefacts served several purposes. They were meant not only for fishing, hunting, and fighting but also for artisanal and agricultural use. They presuppose high technological skill and knowledge on the part of the coppersmith, and cannot have been the handiwork of primitive nomad artisans. In excavations at two places in western UP, some of these objects have been discovered in association with ochre-coloured pots and some mud structures. At one place, stray baked-brick fragments have also been found, as have stone tools. All this suggests that the people who used the implements of the copper hoards supplemented by some other tools led a settled life, and were among the earliest Chalcolithic agriculturalists and artisans to settle in a substantial part of the doab. Many Ochre-Coloured Pottery sites have been found in the upper portion of the doab, but stray copper hoards have been discovered in the plateau areas of Jharkhand and other regions, and many copper celts in the Khetri zone of Rajasthan.

The period covered by the Ochre-Coloured Pottery culture may roughly be placed between 2000 and 1500 BC, on the basis of a series of eight scientific datings. When the settlements of this culture disappeared, the doab did not have much habitation until about 1000 BC. We learn of some habitation by people using black-and-red ware, but their habitational deposits are so thin and the antiquities so poor in quality that we cannot form a distinct idea of their cultural equipment. In any case, in the upper part of the doab, settlement begins with the arrival of the Ochre-Coloured Pottery people. Jodhpura, on the border of Haryana and Rajasthan, evidences the thickest OCP deposits of 1.1 m. It appears, however, that at no place did these settlements last for over a century or so. They were neither large nor spread over a wide territory. Why and how these settlements came to an end is not clear. A suggestion has been made that inundation followed by water logging in an extensive area may have made the area unfit for human settlements. The present soft texture of the Ochre-Coloured Pottery is, according to some scholars, the result of its association with water for a considerable period of time.

The OCP people may have been the junior contemporaries of the Harappans, and their area was not far removed from that of the Harappans. We may, therefore, expect some give and take between the OCP people and the bronze-using Harappans.

Chronology

(BC)	
2800–2200	Date of Ganeshwar deposits (Rajasthan).
2100–1500	Ahar Chalcolithic culture (Banas valley, Rajasthan).
2000 onwards	Wide use of black-and-red ware.
2000–1800	Kayatha Chalcolithic culture (MP).
2000–1500	Ochre-Coloured Pottery culture.

1700–1200	Malwa culture found in Navdatoli, Eran, and Nagda (MP).
1500	Chalcolithic burnt bricks in Gilund (Rajasthan).
1400–700	Jorwe culture (Maharashtra).
1200	Many Chalcolithic sites in central and eastern India.
1200 onwards	The eclipse of the Chalcolithic habitations in western India.
Till 2nd C	Continuity of Chalcolithic black-and-red ware.

10

Harappan Culture: Bronze Age Urbanization in the Indus Valley

Introduction

The urban culture of the Bronze Age found in Harappa in Pakistani Punjab was a path-breaking discovery. In 1853, A. Cunningham, the British engineer who became a great excavator and explorer, noticed a Harappan seal. Though the seal showed a bull and six written letters, he did not realize its significance. Much later, in 1921, the potentiality of the site of Harappa was appreciated when an Indian archeologist, Daya Ram Sahni, started excavating it. At about the same time, R.D. Banerjee, a historian, excavated the site of Mohenjo-daro in Sindh. Both discovered pottery and other antiquities indicative of a developed civilization. Large-scale excavations were carried out at Mohenjo-daro under the general supervision of Marshall in 1931. Mackay excavated the same site in 1938. Vats excavated at Harappa in 1940. In 1946 Mortimer Wheeler excavated Harappa, and the excavation of the pre-Independence and pre-Partition period brought to light important antiquities of the Harappan culture at various sites where bronze was used.

In the post-Independence period, archaeologists from both India and Pakistan excavated the Harappan and connected sites. Suraj Bhan, M.K. Dhavalikar, J.P. Joshi, B.B. Lal, S.R. Rao, B.K. Thapar, R.S. Bisht, and others worked in Gujarat, Harayana, and Rajasthan.

In Pakistan, Kot Diji in the central Indus Valley was excavated by F.A. Khan, and great attention was paid to the Hakra and pre-Hakra cultures by M.R. Mughal. A.H. Dani excavated the Gandhara graves in the North-West Frontier Province of Pakistan. American, British, French, and Italian archaeologists also worked at several sites including Harappa.

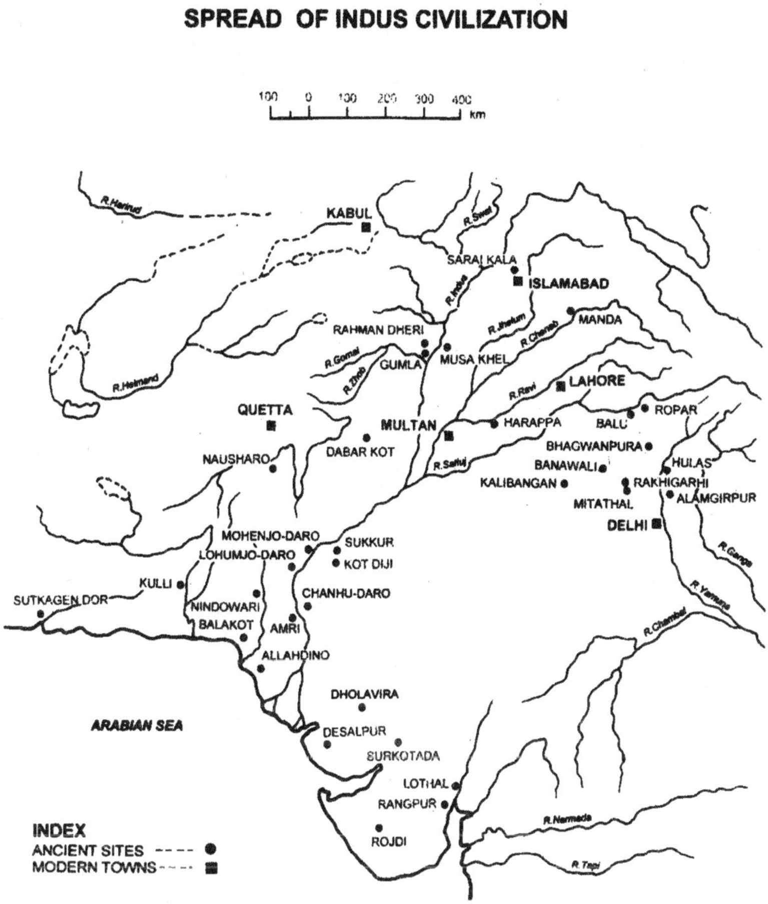

MAP 3 Spread of Indus Civilization. *Courtesy ASI*

Now we have a wealth of Harappan material, though excavations and explorations are still in progress. All scholars agree on the urban character of the Harappan culture, but opinions differ on the role of the Sarasvati identified with the Hakra–Ghaggar river and also on the identity of the people who created this culture. The problem will be considered later in this chapter.

The Indus or the Harappan culture is older than the Chalcolithic cultures that have been examined earlier, but as a bronze-using culture it is far more developed than the latter. It developed in the north-western part of the Indian subcontinent. It is called Harappan because this civilization was discovered first in 1921 at the modern site of Harappa situated in the province of Punjab in Pakistan. Many sites in Sindh formed the central zone of pre-Harappan culture. This culture developed and matured into an urban civilization that developed in Sindh and Punjab. The central zone of this mature Harappan culture lay in Sindh and Punjab, principally in the Indus Valley. From there it spread southwards and eastwards. In this way, the Harappan culture covered parts of Punjab, Haryana, Sindh, Baluchistan, Gujarat, Rajasthan, and the fringes of western UP. It extended from the Siwaliks in the north to the Arabian Sea in the south, and from the Makran coast of Baluchistan in the west to Meerut in the north-east. The area formed a triangle and accounted for about 1,299,600 sq. km which is a larger area than that of Pakistan, and certainly larger than ancient Egypt and Mesopotamia. No other culture zone in the third and second millennia BC in the world was as widespread as the Harappan.

Nearly 2800 Harappan sites have so far been identified in the subcontinent. They relate to the early, mature, and late phases of Harappan culture. Of the mature phase sites, two most important cities were Harappa in Punjab and Mohenjo-daro (literally, the mound of the dead) in Sindh, both forming parts of Pakistan. Situated at a distance of 483 km, they were linked by the Indus. A third city lay at Chanhu-daro about 130 km south of Mohenjo-daro in Sindh, and a fourth at Lothal in Gujarat at the head of the Gulf of Cambay. A fifth city lay at Kalibangan, which means black bangles, in northern Rajasthan. A sixth, called Banawali, is situated in Hissar district in Haryana. It saw two cultural phases, pre-Harappan and Harappan, similar to that of Kalibangan. To the Harappan period relate the remains of mud-brick platforms, and of streets and drains. The Harappan culture is traceable in its mature and flourishing stage to all these six places, as also to the coastal cities of Sutkagendor and Surkotada, each of which is marked by a citadel. The later Harappan phase is traceable to Rangpur and Rojdi in the Kathiawar peninsula in Gujarat. In addition, Dholavira, lying in the Kutch area of Gujarat, has Harappan fortification and all the three phases of the Harappan culture. These phases are also manifested in Rakhigarhi which is situated on the Ghaggar in Haryana and is much larger than Dholavira.

In comparative terms, Dholavira covers 50 ha but Harappa 150 ha and Rakhigarhi 250 ha. However, the largest site is Mohenjo-daro, which covers 500 ha. In ancient times, a large part of this city was completely destroyed by massive floods.

Town Planning and Structures

The Harappan culture was distinguished by its system of town planning. Both Harappa and Mohenjo-daro had a citadel or acropolis, and this was possibly occupied by members of the ruling class. Below the citadel in each city lay a lower town with brick houses, that were inhabited by the common people. The remarkable thing about the arrangement of the houses in the cities is that they followed a grid system, with roads cutting across one another virtually at right angles. Mohenjo-daro scored over Harappa in terms of structures. The monuments of the cities symbolized the ability of the ruling class to mobilize labour and collect taxes; the huge brick constructions were a means of impressing upon the common people the prestige and influence of their rulers.

The most important public place of Mohenjo-daro seems to have been the great bath, comprising the tank which is situated in the citadel mound, and is a fine example of beautiful brickwork. It measures 11.88 × 7.01 m and 2.43 m deep. Flights of steps at either end lead to the surface, and there are side rooms for changing clothes. The floor of the bath was made of burnt bricks. Water was drawn from a large well in an adjacent room, and an outlet from the corner of the bath led to a drain. It has been suggested that the great bath was primarily intended for ritual bathing, which has been so vital to any religious ceremony in India. The large tank found in Dholavira may be compared to the great bath. The Dholavira tank was probably used for the same purpose as the great bath of Mohenjo-daro.

In Mohenjo-daro, the largest building is a granary, 45.71 m long and 15.23 m wide. In the citadel of Harappa, however, we find as many as six granaries. A series of brick platforms formed the basis for two rows of six granaries. Each granary measured 15.23 × 6.09 m and lay within a few metres of the river bank. The combined floor space of the twelve units would be about 838 sq. m. It was approximately of the same area as the great granary at Mohenjo-daro. To the south of the granaries at Harappa lay working floors consisting of the rows of circular brick platforms. These were evidently meant for threshing grain, because wheat and barley were found in the crevices of the floors. Harappa also had two-roomed barracks which possibly accommodated labourers.

In the southern part of Kalibangan too, there are brick platforms, which may have been used for granaries. Thus, it would appear that granaries played an important role in Harappan cities.

The use of burnt bricks in the Harappan cities is remarkable because in the contemporary buildings of Egypt dried bricks were primarily used. We find the use of baked bricks in contemporary Mesopotamia, but they were used to a much larger extent in the Harappan cities.

The drainage system of Mohenjo-daro was very impressive. In almost all the cities, every house, large or small, had its own courtyard and bathroom. In Kalibangan many houses had their own wells. Water flowed from the house to the streets which had drains. Sometimes these drains were covered with bricks and sometimes with stone slabs. The remains of streets and drains have also been found at Banawali. Altogether, the quality of the domestic bathrooms and drains is remarkable, and the drainage system of Harappa is almost unique. Perhaps no other Bronze Age civilization paid so much attention to health and cleanliness as did the Harappan.

Agriculture

Comparatively rainless, the Indus region is not so fertile today, but the prosperous villages and towns of the past testify that it was fertile in ancient times. Today the rainfall is about 15 cm, but in the fourth century BC, one of the historians of Alexander informs us, that Sindh was a fertile part of India. In earlier times, the Indus region had more natural vegetation which contributed to rainfall. It supplied timber for baking bricks and also for construction. In course of time, the natural vegetation was destroyed by the extension of agriculture, large-scale grazing, and supply of fuel. A far more important reason for the fertility of the area seems to have been the annual inundation of the Indus, which is the longest Himalayan river. Walls made of burnt bricks raised for protection indicate that floods were an annual event. Just as the Nile created Eygpt and supported its people, so too the

Indus created Sindh and fed its people. The Indus people sowed seeds in the flood plains in November, and reaped their harvests of wheat and barley in April, before the next flood. No hoe or ploughshare has been discovered, but the furrows discovered in the pre-Harappan phase at Kalibangan indicate that the fields were ploughed in Rajasthan during the Harappan period. The Harappans probably used the wooden plough drawn by oxen, and camels may also have been used for this purpose. Stone sickles may have been used for harvesting the crops. *Gabarbands* or *nala*s enclosed by dams for storing water were a feature in parts of Baluchistan and Afghanistan, but channel or canal irrigation was probably not practised. Harappan villages, mostly situated near the flood plains, produced sufficient food grains not only for their inhabitants but also the towns people. They must have worked very hard to meet their own requirements as well as those of the artisans, merchants, and others who lived in the city and were not directly concerned with food-production activities.

The Indus people produced wheat, barley, *rai*, peas, and the like. Two types of wheat and barley were grown. A substantial quantity of barley was discovered at Banawali. In addition, sesamum and mustard were grown. However, the position seems to have been different with the Harappans at Lothal. It seems that as early as 1800 BC, the people of Lothal grew rice, the remains of which have been found. Food grains were stored in huge granaries in both Mohenjo-daro and Harappa, and possibly in Kalibangan. In all probability, cereals were received as taxes from peasants and stored in granaries for the payment of wages as well as for use during emergencies. This can be surmised from the analogy of Mesopotamian cities where wages were paid in barley. The Indus people were the earliest people to produce cotton, and because of this, the Greeks called the area Sindon which is derived from Sindh.

Domestication of Animals

Although the Harappans practised agriculture, animals were raised on a large scale. Oxen, buffaloes, goats, sheep, and pigs were domesticated. Humped bulls were favoured by the Harappans. There is evidence of dogs and cats from the outset, and asses and camels were bred and were obviously used as beasts of burden, and the latter may also have been used for ploughing. Evidence of the horse comes from a superficial level of Mohenjo-daro and from a doubtful terracotta figurine from Lothal. The remains of a horse are reported from Surkotada, situated in west Gujarat, and relate to around 2000 BC but the identity is doubtful. In any case, the Harappan culture was not horse-centred. Neither the bones of a horse nor its representations have been traced in early and mature Harappan cultures. Elephants were well known to the Harappans, who were also acquainted with the rhinoceros. The contemporary Sumerian cities in Mesopotamia produced virtually the same food grains and domesticated the same animals as did the Harappans, but the Harappans in Gujarat produced rice and domesticated elephants which was not the case with the Mesopotamians.

Technology and Crafts

The rise of towns in the Indus zone was based on agricultural surplus, the making of bronze tools, various other crafts, and widespread trade and commerce. This is known as the first urbanization in India, and the Harappan urban culture belongs to the Bronze Age. The people of Harappa used many tools and implements of stone, but they were very well acquainted with the manufacture and use of bronze. Ordinarily bronze was made by smiths by mixing tin with copper, but they occasionally also mixed arsenic with copper for this purpose. As neither tin nor copper was easily available to the Harappans, bronze tools do not abound in the region. The impurities of the ores show that copper was obtained from the Khetri copper mines of Rajasthan, although it could also be brought from Baluchistan. Tin was possibly brought with difficulty from Afghanistan, although its old workings are stated to have been found in Hazaribagh and Bastar. The bronze tools and weapons recovered from the Harappan sites contain a smaller percentage of tin. However, the kits used for the manufacture of bronze goods left by the Harappans are so numerous as to suggest that the bronze smiths constituted an important group of artisans in Harappan society. They produced not only images and utensils but also various tools and weapons such as axes, saws, knives, and spears.

Several other important crafts flourished in Harappan towns. A piece of woven cotton has been recovered from Mohenjo-daro, and textile impressions have been found on several objects. Spindle whorls were used for spinning. Weavers wove cloth of wool and cotton. Huge brick structures suggest that bricklaying was an important craft, and attest to the existence of a class of masons. The Harappans also practised boat-making. As will be shown later, seal-making and terracotta manufacturing were also important crafts. The goldsmiths made jewelleries of silver, gold, and precious stones; the first two materials may have been obtained from Afghanistan and the last from south India. The Harappans were also expert bead makers. The potter's wheel was extensively used, and the Harappans produced their characteristic glossy, gleaming pottery.

Trade and Commerce

The importance of trade in the life of the Indus people is supported not only by granaries found at Harappa, Mohenjo-daro, and Lothal but also by finds of numerous seals, a uniform script, and regulated weights and measures covering a wide area. The Harappans conducted considerable trade in stone, metal, shell, etc., within the Indus culture zone. However, their cities did not have the necessary raw material for the commodities they produced. They did not use metal money, and in all probability carried exchanges through a barter system. In return for finished goods and possibly food grains, they procured metals from the neighbouring areas by boat (they navigated the coast of the Arabian Sea) and bullock-cart. They were aware of the use of the wheel, and carts with solid wheels were in use in Harappa. It appears that the Harappans used a form of the modern *ekka* but not with the spoked wheel.

The Harappans had commercial links with Rajasthan, and also with Afghanistan and Iran. They set up a trading colony in northern Afghanistan which evidently facilitated trade with Central Asia. Their cities also had commercial links with the people of the Tigris and the Euphrates basins. Many Harappan seals have been discovered in Mesopotamia, and it appears that the Harappans imitated some cosmetics used by the urban people of Mesopotamia.

The Harappans carried on long-distance trade in lapis lazuli; lapis objects may have contributed to the social prestige of the ruling class. The Mesopotamian records from about 2350 BC onwards refer to trade relations with Meluha, which was the ancient name given to the Indus region. The Mesopotamian texts speak of two intermediate trading stations called Dilmun and Makan, which lay between Mesopotamia and Meluha. Dilmun is probably identifiable with Bahrain on the Persian Gulf. Thousands of graves await excavation in that port city.

Social Organization

Excavations indicate a hierarchy in urban habitation. Although only two localities are attributed to the city of Harappa, its structure evidences three distinct localities, and the latter is true also of Kalibangan and Dholavira. The citadel or the first locality was where the ruling class lived and the lowest tower was where the common people dwelt. The middle settlement may have been meant for bureaucrats and middle-class merchants. However, whether hierarchy in settlements corresponded to occupational divisions or socio-economic differentiation is not clear. There is no doubt that the same city was inhabited by different housing groups which were not of the same size. Social differentiation is indicated by different residential structures, with the number of rooms varying from one to twelve. The city of Harappa had two-roomed houses, probably meant for artisans and labourers.

Polity

As the Harappan culture is more or less uniform over a large area, a central authority may have contributed to this. We may identify some important elements of the state in the Indus Valley. The *Arthashastra* of Kautilya considers sovereignty, ministers, populated territory, forts, treasury, force, and friends to be the organs of the state. In the Harappan culture, the citadel may have been the seat of sovereign power, the middle town may have been the area where the bureaucrats lived or the seat of government, and the great granary at Mohenjo-daro may have been the treasury. It appears that taxes were collected in grain. Also, the entire Harappan area was a well-populated territory. Fortification was a feature of several cities. Dholavira, in particular, had forts within forts. We have no clear idea of an organized force or standing army, but a heap of sling stones and the depiction of a soldier on a potsherd at Surkotada may suggest a standing army. In any case, the state was well established in the mature Harappan phase.

In sharp contrast to Egypt and Mesopotamia, no temples have been found at any Harappan site. No religious structures of any kind have been excavated apart from the great bath, which may have been used for ablution. It would, therefore, be wrong to think that priests ruled in Harappa as they did in the cities of lower Mesopotamia. The Harappan rulers were more concerned with commerce than with conquest, and Harappa was possibly ruled by a class of merchants. However, the Harappans did not have many weapons which might mean the lack of an effective warrior class.

Religious Practices

In Harappa numerous terracotta figurines of women have been found. In one figurine, a plant is shown growing out of the embryo of a woman. The image probably represents the goddess of earth, and was intimately connected with the origin and growth of plants. The Harappans, therefore, looked upon the earth as a fertility goddess and worshipped her in the same way as the Egyptians worshipped the Nile goddess Isis. We do not, however, know whether the Harappans were a matriarchal people like the Egyptians. In Egypt, the daughter inherited the throne or property, but we do not know about the nature of inheritance in Harappan society.

Some Vedic texts indicate a reverence for the earth goddess, although she is not given any prominence. It took a long time for the worship of the supreme goddess to develop on a large scale in Hinduism. Only from the sixth century AD onwards are various mother goddesses such as Durga, Amba, Kali, and Chandi are regarded as such in the Puranas and in tantra literature. In the course of time, every village came to have its own separate goddess.

The Male Deity in the Indus Valley

The male deity is represented on a seal. This god has three-horned heads, and is represented in the sitting posture of a yogi, with one leg placed above the other. This god is surrounded by an elephant, a tiger, a rhinoceros, and below his throne there is a buffalo, and at his feet two deer. The god so depicted is identified as Pashupati Mahadeva, but the identification is doubtful because the bull is not represented here and horned gods also figure in other ancient civilizations. We also encounter the prevalence of the phallus worship, which in later times became so intimately connected with Shiva. Numerous symbols of the phallus and female sex organs made of stone have been found in Harappa, and were possibly meant for worship. The *Rig Veda* speaks of non-Aryan people who were phallus worshippers. Phallus worship thus begun in the days of Harappa was later recognized as a respectable form of worship in Hindu society.

Tree and Animal Worship

The people of the Indus region also worshipped trees. The depiction of a deity is represented on a seal amidst branches of the pipal. This tree continues to be worshipped to this day. Animals were also worshipped in Harappan times, and many of them are represented on seals. The most important of them is the one-horned animal unicorn which may be identified with the rhinoceros. Next in importance is the humped bull. Even today, when such a bull passes through the market streets, pious Hindus give way to it. Similarly, the animals surrounding 'Pashupati Mahadeva' indicate that these were worshipped. Evidently, therefore, the inhabitants of the Indus region worshipped gods in the form of trees, animals, and human beings, but the gods were not placed in temples, a practice that was common in ancient Egypt and Mesopotamia. Nor can we say anything about the religious beliefs of the Harappans without being able to read their script. Amulets have been found in large numbers. In all probability, the Harappans believed that ghosts and evil forces were capable of harming them and, therefore, they used amulets against them. The *Atharva Veda*, which is associated with the non-Aryan tradition, contains many charms and spells, and recommends amulets to ward off diseases and evil forces.

The Harappan Script

The Harappans invented the art of writing like the people of ancient Mesopotamia. Although the earliest specimen of the Harappan script was discovered in 1853 and the complete script by 1923, it has yet to be deciphered. Some scholars try to connect it with the Dravidian or the proto-Dravidian language, others with Sanskrit, and yet others with the Sumerian language, but none of these readings is satisfactory. As the script has not been deciphered, we can neither judge the Harappan contribution to literature, nor say anything about their ideas and beliefs.

There are nearly 4000 specimens of Harappan writing on stone seals and other objects. Unlike the Egyptians and Mesopotamians, the Harappans did not write long inscriptions. Most inscriptions were recorded on seals and contain only a few words. These seals may have been used by the propertied to mark and identify their private property. Altogether we have about 250 to 400 pictographs, and in the form of a picture each letter stands for some sound, idea, or object. The Harappan script is not alphabetical but largely pictographic. Attempts have been made to compare it with the contemporary scripts of Mesopotamia and Egypt, but it is the indigenous product of the Indus region and does not indicate any connection with the scripts of western Asia.

Weights and Measures

The knowledge of a script must have helped in recording private property and the maintenance of accounts. The urban people of the Indus region also needed and used weights and measures for trade and other transactions. Numerous articles used as weights have been found. They show that in weighing, largely 16 or its multiples were used: for instance, 16, 64, 160, 320, and 640. Interestingly, the tradition of 16 has continued in India up to modern times and till recently, 16 annas constituted one rupee. The Harappans also knew the art of measurement. Sticks inscribed with measure marks have been found, and one of these is made of bronze.

Harappan Pottery

The Harappans had great expertise in the use of the potter's wheel. Discovered specimens are all red and include dish-on-stand. Numerous pots have been found painted with a variety of designs. Harappan pots were generally decorated with the designs of trees and circles, and images of men also figure on some pottery fragments.

Seals and Sealings

The greatest artistic creations of the Harappan culture are seals. About 2000 seals have been found, and of these a great majority carry short inscriptions with pictures of one horned animals called unicorns, buffaloes, tigers, rhinoceroses, goats, elephants, antelopes, and crocodiles. Seals were made of steatite or faience and served as symbols of authority. They were hence used for stamping. However, there are few stamped objects, called sealings, in contrast to Egypt and Mesopotamia. Seals were also used as amulets.

Images

The Harappan artisans made beautiful images of metal. A woman dancer made of bronze is the best specimen, and she, apart from wearing a necklace, is naked. A few pieces of Harappan stone sculpture have been found. One steatite statue wears an ornamented robe passing over the left shoulder under the right arm like a shawl, and the short locks at the back of the head are held in place by a woven fillet.

Terracotta Figurines

There are many figurines made of fire-baked earthen clay, commonly called terracotta. These were either used as toys or objects of worship. They represent birds, dogs, sheep, cattle, and monkeys. Men and women also find a place in the terracotta objects, and the second outnumber the first. The seals and images were manufactured with great skill, but the terracotta pieces represent unsophisticated artistic works. The contrast between the two sets indicates the gap between the classes that utilized them, the first being used by members of the upper classes and the second by the common people.

Stone Work

We do not find much stone work in Harappa and Mohenjo-daro because stone could not be procured by the two great cities. The position was, however, different in Dholavira located in Kutch. The citadel of Dholavira built of stone is a monumental work and the most impressive among the Harappan citadels discovered so far. In Dholavira, dressed stone is used in masonry with mud bricks, which is remarkable. Stone slabs is used in three types of burials in Dholavira, and in one of these, above the grave there is a circle of stones resembling a Megalithic stone circle.

End of the Indus Culture

The mature Harappan culture, broadly speaking, existed between 2500 and 1900 BC. Throughout the period of its existence, it seems to have retained the same kind of tools, weapons, and houses. The entire lifestyle appears to have been uniform: the same town planning, the same seals, the same terracotta works, and the same long chert blades. However, the view stressing changelessness cannot be pushed too far. We do notice changes in the pottery of Mohenjo-daro over a period of time. By the nineteenth century BC, the two important cities of Harappan culture, Harappa and Mohenjo-daro, disappeared, but the Harappan culture at other sites faded out gradually and continued in its degenerate form in the outlying fringes of Gujarat, Rajasthan, Haryana, and western UP until 1500 BC.

It is difficult to account for this cultural collapse. The environmental factor may have been important. In the Harappan zone, both the Yamuna and Sutlej moved away from the Sarasvati or the Hakra around 1700 BC. This meant loss in water supply. Similarly, rainfall decreased at about that time. Some speak of dam formation in the Indus leading to a massive flooding of Mohenjo-daro. These factors may have worked adversely, but failure in human activities cannot be discounted.

It appears that crafts and commerce collapsed because of the sudden end of the long-distance land and sea trade with Mesopotamia. This trade in luxurious articles, including lapis lazuli, beads, etc., mainly passed through Elam, which was located on the eastern border of Mesopotamia and covered a substantial part of Iran. The emergence of Elam as a powerful state around 2000 BC interrupted the supply of Harappan goods to Mesopotamia and the Mesopotamian imports, including tin, to the Harappan settlements.

Beads of hard materials, especially stone, were made in the Harappan zone and sent outside. The break in their exports to Mesopotamia deprived the craftsmen of their livelihood. Similarly, the break in the supply of tin to the Valley dealt a great blow to the artisans employed in making bronze.

The exhaustion of the soil may have diminished cereal production and starved the urban people. Once the aristocracy living in the cities failed to exercise its control over crafts and cultivation, Harappan culture collapsed.

Maturity

Nearly 2800 Harappan sites have been identified. Of these, early and post-urban Harappan sites account for over half the total number. Mature Harappan settlements number 1022. Of them, 406 are located in Pakistan and 616 in India. Though mature Harappan sites are outnumbered by early and post-Harappan sites, because of their urban nature, the total area of the mature Harappan sites is larger than that of the early and post-urban sites.

The Harappan cities are indicative of well-planned growth, but their Mesopotamian counterparts show haphazard growth. Rectangular houses with brick-lined bathrooms and wells together with their stairways are found in all Harappan cities, but such town planning is not evident in the cities of western Asia. No other people in antiquity had built such an excellent drainage system except perhaps those of Crete in Knossos, nor did the people of western Asia show such skill in the use of burnt bricks as did the Harappans. The Harappans produced their own characteristic pottery and seals, and, above all, they invented their own script, which neither resembled the Egyptian nor the Mesopotamian. No contemporary culture spread over such a wide area as did the Harappan.

Post-Urban Phase

The Harappan culture seems to have flourished until 1900 BC. Subsequently, its urban phase marked by systematic town planning, extensive brickwork, the art of writing, standard weights and measures, distinction between the citadel and the lower town, use of bronze tools, and red-ware pottery painted with black designs, virtually disappeared as did its stylistic homogeneity. Some traits of post-urban Harappan culture are to be found in Pakistan, and in central and western India, in Punjab, Rajasthan, Haryana, Jammu & Kashmir, Delhi, and western UP. They broadly cover the period from 1900 to 1200 BC. The post-urban phase of Harappan culture is also known as the sub-Indus culture and was earlier considered post-Harappan, but now is better known as post-urban Harappan culture.

Post-urban Harappan cultures were primarily Chalcolithic in which tools of stone and copper were used. They did not have metal objects requiring complicated casting, although they had axes, chisels, knives, bangles, curved razors, fish-hooks, and spearheads. The Chalcolithic people in the later, post-urban phase lived in villages, subsisting on agriculture, stock raising, hunting, and fishing. Probably the dissemination of metal technology in the rural areas promoted agriculture and settlements. Some places, such as Prabhas Patan (Somnath) and Rangpur, both in Gujarat, are the direct descendants of the Harappan culture. However, in Ahar near Udaipur, only a few Harappan elements are found. Gilund, which seems to have been a regional centre of Ahar culture, even has brick structures which may be placed between 2000 and 1500 BC. Otherwise, burnt bricks have not been found anywhere else except perhaps in the late Harappan phase at

Bhagwanpura in Haryana. However, the dating of the Bhagwanpura layer to which the bricks relate is uncertain. Stray pieces occur at the OCP site of Lal Quila in Bulandshahr district in western UP. It should, however, be emphasized that few Harappan elements are to be found in the Chalcolithic culture of Malwa (*c.* 1700–1200 BC), which had its largest settlement at Navdatoli. The same is true of the numerous Jorwe sites found in the valleys of the Tapi, Godavari, and Bhima. The largest of the Jorwe settlements was Daimabad which had about 22 ha of habitation with a possible population of 4000 and may be considered proto-urban. However, a vast majority of the Jorwe settlements were villages.

Some post-urban Harappan settlements were discovered in the Swat valley in Pakistan. Here, the people practised a developed agriculture and cattle breeding together with pastoralism. They used black–grey burnished ware produced on a slow wheel. This ware resembles the pottery from the northern Iranian plateau during the third millennium BC and later. The Swat valley people also produced black-on-red painted and wheel-turned pottery with a close linkage with the Indus pottery during the early post-urban period, that is, with the post-urban culture associated with Harappa. The Swat valley may, therefore, be regarded as the northernmost outpost of late Harappan culture.

Several late or post-urban Harappan sites have been excavated in the Indian territories of Punjab, Haryana, UP, and also in Jammu. Mention may be made of Manda in Jammu, Chandigarh and Sanghol in Punjab, Daulatpur and Mitthal in Haryana, and Alamgirpur and Hulas in western UP. It seems that the Harappans took to rice when they came to Daulatpur in Haryana and Hulas in Saharanpur district of UP. *Ragi*, or finger millet, is not so far known to have been grown at any Harappan site in north India. In Alamgirpur, the late Harappans probably produced cotton, as can be inferred from the cloth impression on Harappan pottery.

The painted Harappan pottery found in the late or post-urban Harappan sites in the northern and eastern areas is replaced with less intricate designs, although there are some new pot forms. Some late Harappan pot forms are found interlocked with Painted Grey Ware remains at Bhagwanpura, but by this time the Harappan culture seems to have reached a point of complete dilution.

In the post-urban Harappan phase, no object for measuring length has been found. In Gujarat, cubical stone weights and terracotta cakes were absent in the later period. Generally, all post-urban Harappan sites lack human figurines and the characteristic painted designs. Although faience went out of fashion in Gujarat, it was freely used in north India.

Percolation of New Peoples

During the late phase of Harappan culture some exotic tools and pottery indicate the slow percolation of new peoples into the Indus basin. Some signs of insecurity and violence are evident in the last phase of Mohenjo-daro. Hoards of jewellery were buried at places, and skulls were huddled together at one place. New types of axes, daggers, knives with midribs, and flat tangs figure in the upper levels of Mohenjo-daro. They seem to betray some foreign intrusion. Traces of new peoples have been found in a cemetery related to the late phase of Harappa, where new kinds of pottery occur in the latest levels. New types of pottery also occur in some Harappan sites in Baluchistan. Baluchistan indicates that the horse and Bactrian camel existed there in 1700 BC. The new peoples may have come from Iran and south Central Asia, but they did not come in such numbers as to completely overwhelm the Harappan sites in Punjab and Sindh. Although the Rig Vedic people largely settled in the land of the Seven Rivers in which the Harappan culture once flourished, we have no archaeological evidence of any mass-scale confrontation between the late Harappans and the Indo-Aryans. Successive groups of the Vedic people may have entered the subcontinent in the post-urban Harappan phase between 1500 and 1200 BC.

Problem of Origin

Several pre-Harappan agricultural settlements sprang up in the Hakra area in the Cholistan desert in Pakistan around 4000 BC. However, agricultural settlements first arose on the eastern fringe of Baluchistan around 7000 BC in the pre-ceramic Neolithic age on the border of the Indus plains. From that time onwards, people domesticated goats, sheep, and cattle. They also produced barley and wheat. These practices of earning subsistence expanded from the fifth millennium BC when granaries were set up. In the fifth and fourth millennia BC, mud bricks began to be used. Painted pottery and female terracotta figurines also began to be made. In the northern part of Baluchistan, a site called Rahman Dheri developed as the earliest town with planned roads and houses. This site was located virtually parallel to

Harappa on the west. It is evident that the early Harappan and mature Harappan cultures developed from the Baluchistan settlements.

Sometimes the origin of Harappan culture is attributed principally to the natural environment. The current environment of the Harappan area is not favourable for crafts and cultivation, but in the third millennium BC arid and semi-desert conditions were not dominant there. In 3000–2000 BC we have evidence of both heavy rain and a substantial flow of water into the Indus and its tributary Sarasvati, virtually identical to the dried-up Hakra in Sindh. Sometimes the Indus culture is called the Sarasvati culture, but the flow of water in the Harappan Hakra was the contribution of the Yamuna and the Sutlej. These two rivers joined the Sarasvati for some centuries due to tectonic developments in the Himalayas. Therefore, the credit for helping the Harappan culture should really go to these two rivers together with the Indus and not to the Sarasvati alone. Moreover, the evidence for heavy rainfall in the Indus area cannot be ignored.

Was the Harappan Culture Vedic?

Sometimes Harappan culture is called Rig Vedic, but its principal features do not figure in the *Rig Veda*. Planned towns, crafts, commerce, and large structures built of burnt bricks mark the mature Harappan phase. The *Rig Veda* does not feature these. As will be shown later, the early Vedic people lived on cattle rearing supplemented by agriculture, and did not use bricks. The early Vedic people occupied virtually the entire Harappan zone, but also lived in Afghanistan.

The mature urban phase lasted from 2500 to 1900 BC, but the *Rig Veda* is placed around 1500 BC. Also, the Harappan and Vedic people were not aware of exactly the same plants and animals. The *Rig Veda* mentions only barley, but the Harappan knew about wheat, sesamum, and peas. The rhinoceros was known to the Harappans but unknown to the early Vedic people. The same is true of the tiger. The Vedic chiefs were horse-centred, which is why this animal is mentioned 215 times in the *Rig Veda*, but the horse was hardly known to the urban Harappans. The Harappan terracottas represent the elephant, but unlike the horse it is not important in the earliest Veda.

The Harappan writing, called the Indus script, has not been deciphered so far, but no Indo-Aryan inscriptions of Vedic times have been found in

India. We have no clear idea about the languages of the Harappans, though the Indo-Aryan language spoken by the Vedic people continues in South Asia in a variety of forms.

Problem of Continuity

Some scholars speak about the continuity of the Harappan culture, others of its change from urbanization to de-urbanization. As urbanism was the basic feature of the Harappan culture, with its collapse we cannot think of cultural continuity. Similarly, the de-urbanization of the Harappan city is not a simple transformation but meant the disappearance of towns, script, and burnt bricks for about 1500 years. These elements did not disappear in north India after the end of the Kushan towns.

It is said that the Harappan culture continued in the Gangetic plains and elsewhere in north India after its end in 1900 BC. However, no important Harappan feature appears in the Painted Grey Ware culture attributed to the first half of the first millennium BC. The PGW culture does not evidence great buildings, burnt bricks, bronze, urbanism, and writing, but it has its own characteristic pottery. Though one or two instances of burnt bricks of about 1500 BC are adduced, really fired bricks appear in north India around 300 BC in the phase of the Northern Black Polished Ware culture. Similarly, once the Harappan culture ended, writing came into currency during the NBPW phase in the form of the Brahmi script. It was, however, written from left to right whereas the Harappan script was written from right to left. Similarly, the NBP pottery cannot be related to Harappan pottery. The effective use of iron in the NBPW phase gave rise to a new socio-economic structure in the mid-Gangetic plains in the fifth century BC. However, neither iron nor coinage, which marked the NBPW phase, was characteristic of the Indus culture. Though some stray beads of the Indus culture reached the Gangetic plains, they cannot be considered an important Indus trait. Similarly, a few Harappan ceramic items and terracottas continued after 2000 BC, but these objects alone cannot represent the entirety of the mature Harappan culture. However, stray elements of the Indus culture continued in the Chalcolithic cultures of Rajasthan, Malwa, Gujarat, and upper Deccan. It appears that after the end of the urban Harappan culture in 1900 BC, there was some give and take between the Indo-Aryan and the existing cultures. The Munda and proto-Dravidian languages attributed to the Harappans continued. Through the interaction, both the

Aryan and pre-Aryan languages were enriched. We find pre-Aryan words for pottery and agriculture in Sanskrit, but the balance weighed in favour of the Indo-Aryans whose language spread in a major part of the subcontinent.

Chronology

(BC)	
7000	Earliest agricultural settlements in Baluchistan.
5th millennium	Existence of granaries, use of mud bricks.
4000	Pre-Harappan settlements in Cholistan (Pakistan).
3000–2000	Period of heavy rain and substantial flow of water into the Indus and Sarasvati.
2500–1900	Mature Harappan culture.
2000	Elam as a powerful state. The remains of a horse in Surkotada.
1900–1500	Degenerate phase of Harappan culture in Gujarat, Rajasthan, Haryana, and western UP.
1800	Use of rice in Lothal.
1900–1200	Post-urban Harappan culture.
1700	The Yamuna and Sutlej leave the Sarasvati. Existence of the horse and Bactrian camel in Baluchistan.
1500–1200	Successive groups of the Vedic people enter the Indian subcontinent.
300	Fired bricks used in north India. Writing in Brahmi script.

Chronology of Harappan Archaeology

(AD)	
1853	A. Cunningham's find of a Harappan seal.
1921	Daya Ram Sahani's excavation at Harappa.
1931	Marshall excavated Mohenjo-daro.
1938	Mackay excavated the same size.
1940	Vats excavated Harappa.
1946	Mortimer Wheeler excavated Harappa.

Post-1947 period	Harappan and associated sites excavated by Suraj Bhan, M.K. Dhavalikar, J.P. Joshi, B.B. Lal, S.R. Rao, B.K. Thapar, R.S. Bisht, and others.

11

Identity of Aryan Culture

Texts for Traits of Aryan Culture

The principal traits of Aryan culture are set out by Vedic, Iranian, and Greek literary texts and cognate terms found in the proto-Indo-European languages. The texts that help us to reconstruct the material and other aspects of Aryan culture comprise the *Rig Veda,* the *Zend-Avesta*, and Homer's *Iliad* and *Odyssey.* Specialists may differ on the criteria for dating these texts, but we may go by the generally accepted dates. The *Rig Veda* is assigned to roughly 1500 BC, although the later additions might be as late as 1000 BC. The earliest parts of the *Zend-Avesta* are roughly attributed to 1400 BC, and Homer's works are assigned to 900–800 BC. Though these texts belong to different areas, they suggest the period when copper and bronze were in use. The later portions of Homer also mention iron. Generally, the texts represent agriculture and pastoralism as the principal sources of livelihood. The people lived in temperate climate. They domesticated horses which were used for riding and for driving carts. They used spoked wheels, and fought with bows and arrows which were placed in quivers. They lived in a male-dominated society. They buried the dead body, but also practised cremation. The cults of fire and soma prevailed among the speakers of the Indo-European languages in Iran and the Indian subcontinent. However, animal sacrifice, including horse sacrifice, seems to have been practised by all the Indo-European communities.

The cultural contents of the texts date roughly to the late Neolithic and early Bronze ages. The contents seem to cover Eastern Europe and Central Asia, which are geographically linked to India, Pakistan, Afghanistan, Iran, Iraq, Anatolia, and Greece. Since ancient times various communities in a major portion of this vast territory spoke Indo-European languages.

MAP 4 Pastoral Cemetries and Other Related Sites in Central Asia. *Courtesy ASI*

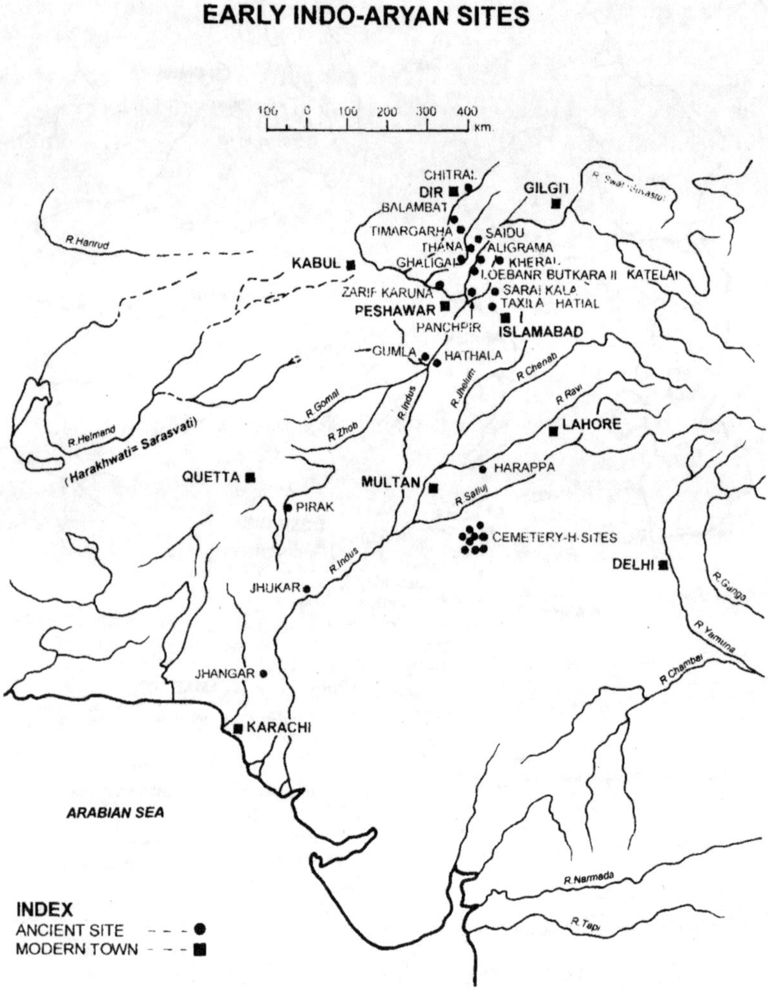

MAP 5 Early Indo-Aryan Sites. *Courtesy ASI*

The climatic conditions, birds, animals, and trees revealed by the cognate words suggest that the Aryans did not live in warmer areas. We, therefore, have to seek the speakers of the early Indo-European languages in the temperate zone covering Eastern Europe and Central Asia. We may recall that genetic signals that pass from generation to generation in human beings link together speakers of Indo-European languages. A genetic marker called M 17, which prevails in 40 per cent people of Central Asian steppes, is also found frequently in the Indo-Aryan speakers. In the Hindi-speaking area of Delhi, it is found in 35 per cent people. This suggests migration of the Indo-Aryans from Central Asia.

The Horse, its Domestication and Diffusion

The horse is regarded as an indispensable trait of the Aryan culture, for it plays a crucial role in the life of the early Indo-Europeans. The term *asva* (horse) in the *Rig Veda* and its cognates appears in Sanskrit, Avestan, Greek, Latin, and other Indo-European languages. In ancient texts, particularly Vedic and Avestan, many personal names are horse-centred. For the early Vedic period we have over fifty horse names and thirty chariot names. Similarly, the *aspa* or horse forms part of the name of several Iranian chiefs in the *Avesta*. Some Iranian tribes mentioned by Herodotus are also named after the horse. In its various forms, the term *asva* occurs 215 times in the *Rig Veda*; no other animal is mentioned so frequently. The term *go* (cow) occurs 176 times, and the term *vrsabha* (bull) 170 times. Both these terms taken together suggest the importance of cattle rearing. However, the cattle rearers were dominated by a horse-based aristocracy. The tiger and rhinoceros, characteristic of the tropical and moderately temperate climate of India, are absent in the cold conditions of Central Asia. They do not occur in the *Rig Veda*, and similar other tropical and moderately temperate zone animals such as the lion, deer, buffalo, and elephant have few references in this text in contrast to those made to the horse, cow, and bull. This difference can be attributed to the Central Asian influence on the *Rig Veda*.

The *Rig Veda* devotes two complete hymns in praise of the horse. Almost all the Vedic gods are associated with it, and this in particular applies to Indra and his companions, the Maruts. Though the Vedic people frequently pray for *praja* (children) and *pasu* (cattle), they also specifically ask for horses, sometimes as many as a thousand. In the *Avesta*, cattle wealth seems to be more significant, but the horse has its own importance. Both the horse and chariot repeatedly occur in prayers made to the Avestan Mithra who is the same as God Mitra in the *Rig Veda.* The adjective 'swift-horsed' is applied in the *Avesta* to several divinities. The text refers to the prayer to the god that the king be granted swift horses and strong sons. The horse and the horse-drawn chariot are equally important in Homer. Equerry, or the person in charge of the horses belonging to the chief, is a common term in the *Odyssey.* The Vedic, Iranian, and Greek texts, thus leave no doubt that the earliest speakers of the Indo-European languages were well acquainted with the horse.

The earliest domesticated horse is found at a considerable distance from the Indian subcontinent. It is significant that the largest number of horses appear to have been in the area between the Dnieper river in the west and the Volga river in the east. The earliest evidence of the horse is found in the south Ural region and the Black Sea area in the sixth millennium BC. In the fourth millennium BC, the horse is found in Anatolia which lay close to the Black Sea. By the third millennium BC, horses are found in large numbers in south Siberia. Evidently, the use of the horse underwent a long gestation period. Although its existence was known around 6000 BC in the area between the Black Sea and south Ural, it came into general use in Eurasia only in around 2000 BC.

The earliest inscriptional evidence of the use of the horse in western Asia is in Anatolia in the second half of the nineteenth century BC. Its effective use in western Asia is ascribed to the Kassite invasion of Babylonia in 1595 BC. When the horse first figures in Babylonia, it was called the ass from the mountain.

The War Chariot

The Indo-Europeans widely used horse-drawn chariots which are well known to the Vedic, Avestan, and Homeric texts. The chariot race prescribed in the *vajapeya* sacrifice of the later Vedic texts was also a Greek practice, and is fully described by Homer. It is held that the wheeled chariot originated in western Asia in the fourth millennium BC and reached the steppes of south Russia at about the same time. Sufficient evidence of the existence of the chariot from 3000 BC onwards appears in the excavations in south Russia. Chariots with two or three wheels of the third millennium BC have been found. The existence of horse-drawn chariots is also indicated by the names of the Mitanni rulers around 1400 BC and later. These are 'having the running chariots', 'facing the chariots', and 'having the big horses'. We also hear of the Indo-Iranian title 'horse-driver'. Dasaratha, the name of a Mitanni king, means a person possessing ten chariots. Wooden wheels are known outside India, but until 2000 BC they were generally solidly built. Clay wheels are reported in the Harappan context, though they cannot be dated earlier than 2500 BC.

Spoked Wheels

Spoked wheels appear in Hissar in Iran and in the north Caucasus around 2300 BC. A six-spoked wheeled chariot depicted on a cylindrical seal is attributed to Hissar around 1800 BC. It is said that in the nineteenth century BC, the Hittites used light-wheeled chariots to conquer Anatolia. War chariots with spoked wheels appear in the Sintashta region in the south Ural area adjoining western Kazakhistan. By 1500 BC, spoked wheels are in existence at several places in eastern Europe and western Asia.

A spoked wheel is neither identified at Harappa nor Mohenjo-daro where all the toy carts found so far show solid wheels. Banawali in Hissar district in Haryana is associated with the use of spoked wheels in the Harappan period, but this seems to be a post-Harappan phase.

The remains of horses of the second millennium BC have been found in south Central Asia, Iran, and Afghanistan. By 1500 BC the horse and the chariot are represented in Kirgizia, the Altai zone, Mongolia, the Pamir mountain ranges and, above all, in south Tajikistan.

Horse Remains in the Subcontinent

Only a few horse remains of the third millennium BC are ascribed to the Indian subcontinent, and these are of a doubtful nature. Richard Meadow, who has thoroughly studied the remains, finds no clear osteological evidence of the presence of the horse in the Indian subcontinent until 2000 BC. In his view, the Pirak complex located near the Bolan pass in the Kachi plains of Baluchistan shows the earliest true horse in South Asia around 1700 BC. The remains of horse and horse furnishings dating to 1400 BC and later appear in the burials of the Gandhara grave culture in the Swat valley situated in the North-West Frontier in Pakistan. The existence of the horse in the north-west may have helped its spread in north India. Horse bones have been found in the overlapping layers of the Painted Grey Ware and the Harappan cultures at Bhagwanpura in Haryana attributed to 1600–1000 BC. The Surkotada horse from the Kutch area may have been contemporaneous with the Pirak horse. The horse also appears in the later or the post-urban Harappan phase at Mohenjo-daro, Harappa, Lothal, and Ropar. The existence of the horse has not been reported from most recent excavations at Harappa in 1986–95. Also, although numerous bones have been found in the excavation of the Harappan site at Dholavira in Kutch, there is no indication of any bones of the horse.

The existence of the horse in the late Harappan phase at various places is consistent with its arrival in Pirak and the Swat valley from the eighteenth century BC onwards, and it becomes important in the non-Harappan/post-Harappan cultures of Pirak, Gandhara, and Painted Grey Ware sites.

Pit-dwelling

The pit-dwelling can also be associated with the Aryan culture, and may have originated in cold conditions. Around 4500 BC, the horse-users of Ukraine lived in semi-subterranean houses in addition to surface ones. With their eastward advance, pit-dwelling began in the Ural–Volga region in the fourth and third millennia BC, and in the Andronovo culture of Central Asia in the second millennium BC. Burial seems to have developed in imitation of pit-dwelling. In the Swat valley some villages show large pit-dwellings dating to around 1500 BC. These may be linked to the migrations because of which post-cremation burials are also in evidence. The practice of pit-dwelling prevailed in Burzahom near Srinagar in Kashmir and also in Haryana. This may be due to the Central Asian influence on the borders of Kashmir.

Birch

The use of birch-wood seems to be an Aryan feature along with underground houses. The birch is called *bhurja* in Sanskrit, and it has cognates in six Indo-European languages. Although this tree is found in a substantial part of Eurasia including the Ukraine, its earliest remains appear in the Andronovan settlements, where it was used to construct structures together with pine and cedar. The subterranean dwellings in particular were covered with birch. In medieval India, many manuscripts were written on the leaves of the birch tree.

Cremation

Like the use of the horse, cremation developed as an Aryan trait. Its practice is supported by the Vedic, Avestan, and Homeric texts, but does not seem to be a feature of the mature Harappan culture. The Harappans practised earth burial, and this underwent a distinct change in their later phase. This is shown by pot burial in Cemetry-H; in some cases, such burial also shows evidence of burnt bones deposited in urns.

Post-cremation burial is in evidence at several sites in the extension area of the Harappan culture in Gujarat, but it is difficult to date it in this area. Thus, the evidence at Surkotada is doubtful. In any case, even if we take a liberal view of the chronological position, the practice cannot date to earlier than 2000 BC, which marks the beginning of the post-urban phase. Its introduction may be attributed to the contact with the outside areas where the practice began much earlier. It is difficult to argue for human cremation on the basis of the burnt bones of birds and animals. Cremation is as old as the fifth millennium BC. Archaeologically, its instances are found in Holland, Germany, Eastern Europe, Iraq, and Kazakhistan in Central Asia in 5000–4000 BC. However, it is not clear when and where this practice was adopted by the horse users, but, around 1500 BC, they practised it in both Europe and Asia including the Chinese part of eastern Central Asia. In the Indian subcontinent, the earliest evidence of this practice by the horse users occurs in the Swat valley in the second half of the second millennium BC. At a distance of about 500 km from the Swat area it appears in Tajikistan around 1400 BC. Wheeler rules out the prevalence of cremation at both Harappa and Mohenjo-daro, though some late Harappans may have followed the practice under the influence of outside contacts.

The Fire Cult

The fire cult is considered to be a special trait of both the Indo-Aryans and Indo-Iranians. The fire altar or *vedi* is mentioned in the *Rig Veda*, and fire worship is very important in the *Avesta*. Some scholars consider the fire cult to be Harappan, but the veracity of the 'fire altars' found in Lothal in Gujarat and Kalibangan in Rajasthan is doubted by the excavators themselves. It is significant that the fire altars discovered in the Harappan context match neither the textual prescriptions nor the age-old traditional practices. However, as fire is so indispensable to human existence, it may have been worshipped in many regions including the Indus Valley, but whether it took the form of the Vedic altar is extremely doubtful. We may note that some structures, not exactly similar to Vedic fire altars but indicative of fire worship, dating to 4000–3500 BC have been found in Ukraine.

Animal Sacrifice

Animal sacrifice was an important Aryan ritual. However, given its almost universal practice among pastoral tribal people, it is difficult to make much of it. The earliest stock raisers did not raise cattle for the sake of milk and dairy products. A segment of the Gond tribe still believes that milk is really meant for the calf. Therefore, the early pastoralists were great meat eaters. The ritual of animal sacrifice may have been evolved because of the need for non-vegetarian food. Graves in Ukraine and south Russia dating to the fourth and third millennia BC provide numerous examples of animal sacrifice in funeral ceremonies. That is also true of south Central Asia in the second millennium BC and later. Apparently, the ritual was generally prevalent and symbolized the provision of the requirements of this world in the next world.

Horse Sacrifice

Animal sacrifice may have prevailed among many tribal peoples, but the horse sacrifice was typical of the Indo-Europeans, particularly of the Vedic people. The French Vedic scholar Louis Renou considers it to be an Indo-European ritual. Much archaeological evidence about the prevalence of horse sacrifice is found in eastern, central, western, and northern Europe, and also in the Caucasus and Central Asia. In Ukraine and south Russia, many cemeteries testify to the sacrifice of more than one horse. The practice seems to have started in the second half of the fifth millennium BC. It became widespread in later millennia and continued in Rome, medieval Ireland, and Central Asia.

Though two hymns are devoted to the horse sacrifice in the tenth book of the *Rig Veda*, the later Vedic texts transform the sacrifice into *asvamedha*.

Animals may have been sacrificed in pre-Vedic times in the subcontinent, but despite cut marks found on the bones, it cannot be said that the horses were killed for religious purposes. Archaeological evidence of horse sacrifice in Europe and Central Asia is wanting in India. Buffalo sacrifice became an important ritual in the worship of the various forms of goddess Shakti, but because of the rarity of this animal in East Europe and Central Asia, the practice did not prevail in those regions.

The Cult of Soma

The cult of soma, called *haoma* in the Avestan language, was confined to only the Iranian and Vedic peoples. The identification of the soma plant has been long debated, but now a plant called ephedra, small twigs of which have been found in vessels used for drinking rituals on the premises of the temple of Togolok-21 in Margiana in south-eastern Turkmenistan, is considered to be soma. Although this identification has been accepted by many scholars, the search for conclusive evidence is continuing.

The Svastika

Sometimes the svastika, an ancient symbol formed by a cross with equal arms, is conceived of as a mark of Aryanism. It acquired a global cachet when the Nazis adopted it as a symbol of unadulterated Aryanism. Unknown to Vedic literature, the term appears in the texts of the early Christian centuries when it had an auspicious connotation in religious art. According to Mackay, the svastika symbol originated in Elam much earlier than 2000 BC when it figured in the Harappan culture. In south Tajikistan it figured around 1200 BC. It appears that by this time it had been adopted by the Aryans, and in the early centuries of the Christian era it came to be regarded a symbol of brahmanical culture.

Language and Inscriptional Evidence

Language is the most important attribute of the Aryan culture. Linguists have reconstructed the proto-Indo-European language, which started around the seventh or the sixth millennium BC. The Indo-European language is divided into eastern and western branches, and from *c.* 4500 BC marked phonetic development took place in the eastern branch, that is, proto-Indo-Iranian. However, inscriptional evidence of the proto-Indo-Iranian or Indo-Aryan language does not date to earlier than 2200 BC. The first linguistic traces of it figure on a tablet of the dynasty of Agade in Iraq. This inscription mentions two names reconstructed as Arisena and Somasena.

Hittite inscriptions from Anatolia indicate speakers of the western branch of the Indo-European language in this area from the nineteenth to the seventeenth century BC. Similarly, Mycenaean inscriptions from Greece indicate the arrival of speakers of this branch in the fourteenth century BC. The speakers of the eastern branch are represented in the inscriptions of the Kassites and the Mittanis in Mesopotamia from the sixteenth to the fourteenth century BC, but there are no such inscriptions in India. It is, therefore, absurd to argue that speakers of the Indo-European language spread from India to Mesopotamia. Many Munda words figure in the *Rig Veda*, and evidently they entered this text in the post-Harappan phase. Had the Vedic people moved to the north-west, the Munda words would have also surfaced in that area, but they did not. Some Russian linguists consider the region south of the Caucasus to be the original home of the Indo-European language. This includes eastern Anatolia and northern Mesopotamia. Though eastern Anatolia is not far from the Black Sea area where the early horse was domesticated, neither the horse nor other characteristic traits of Indo-European culture are traceable to eastern Anatolia in the sixth–fifth millennia BC.

The finding of the Russian linguists supports an earlier hypothesis of Gordon Childe that Anatolia was the original home of the Aryans. This view has been recently reinforced by Renfrew. According to him, agriculture and the Indo-European language originated in eastern Anatolia around the seventh millennium BC. He argues that the expansion of agriculture from Anatolia led to the spread of the Indo-European language in various directions. However, much earlier, cereals were cultivated at a Mesolithic site near Jerusalem around 10,000 BC, and transition to full-fledged agriculture took place in the Palestine area around 7000 BC. However, agriculture was not confined to Palestine and Anatolia. In the sixth and seventh millennia BC, it was practised also in Iraq, Iran, and Baluchistan too. In any case, agriculture was not important in the life of the earliest speakers of the Indo-European language. This is shown by the lack of common agricultural terms used by the eastern and western groups of Indo-European language speakers from the outset. Also, if the Aryan language originated in Anatolia, why did it completely disappear from its place of origin?

Dispersal of the Indo-Aryans

We may recall the genetic signals which show the migration of the Indo-Aryans from Central Asia to India. Genetic characteristics in the blood cells of humans are known as DNA. They are hereditary and pass from generation to generation. Some special genetic signals appear in the steppe people of Central Asia from one end to the other in *c.* 8000 BC. These genetic indications are called M 17. They are found in more than 40 per cent people of Central Asia. When scientists looked for them in Delhi they discovered these in more than 35 per cent of the Hindi speakers but only in 10 per cent of the Dravidian speakers. Biologists place the Indo-Aryan migration from Central Asia after 8000 BC, but linguists and archaeologists date it *c.* 2000 BC.

We also notice a striking similarity in the use of the past tense in Russian and many Indo-Aryan languages. In Russian one uses *Ya chital* 'I read' and *Ya pishal* 'I wrote'. 'L'-ending past tense is used in Bengali, Assamese, Oriya, Maithili, Bhojpuri, and Magahi. It is also used in Marathi and sometimes in Rajasthan. In Punjabi it is rare. Linguists can better explore Russian links with Indo-Aryan languages, but the genetic evidence about the Indo-Aryan migration is decisive.

Chronology

(BC)	
10000	Cereals first cultivated at a Mesolithic site near Jerusalem.
8000	Indo-Aryan migration from Central Asia after this date.
7000	Developed agriculture in the Palestine area.
6 M	Existence of the horse in the south Ural region and the Black Sea area.
5000–4000	Cremation in Holland, Germany, eastern Europe, Iraq, and Kazakhistan in Central Asia.

4500	The horse-users of Ukraine lived in semi-subterranean houses in addition to surface houses. Introduction of the proto-Indo-Iranian language.
5 M	Horse sacrifice probably started among Indo-Europeans.
4–3 M	Pit-dwellings in the Ural–Volga region. Animal sacrifice in funeral ceremonies practised in Ukraine and south Russia.
4 M	Horse in Anatolia and wheeled chariot in western Asia and the steppes of south Russia.
3000 onwards	Sufficient evidence for the use of the chariot in excavations in south Russia.
3 M	Many horses in south Siberia. Chariots with two or three wheels in south Russia. Some horse remains ascribed to the Indian subcontinent.
2500	Clay wheels reported in the Harappan context.
2300	Spoked wheels in Hissar in Iran and in the north Caucasus.
2200	Indo-Iranian or Indo-Aryan language in an inscription of the Agade dynasty in Iraq.
2000	Wide use of the horse in Eurasia. Solidly built wooden wheels known outside India. Svastika symbol in the Harappa culture. Post-cremation burial in the late Harappan culture in Gujarat.
2 M	The horse, pit-dwellings, and post-cremation burial in the Swat valley. Pit-dwellings in the Andronovo culture of Central Asia. Horse remains in south Central Asia, Iran, and Afghanistan.
19 C	Hittites used light-wheeled chariots.
19–17 C	Western branch of Indo-European language in Anatolia in Hittite inscriptions.
1850 onwards	Earliest inscriptional evidence of the horse in Anatolia.
1800	Six-spoked wheeled chariot depicted on a Hissar seal.

1700	Pirak complex (Baluchistan) evidences the earliest true horse in South Asia.
1600–1000	Horse bones of the PGW and Harappan cultures at Bhagwanpura (Haryana) as evidenced by the overlapping layers there.
1595	Effective use of the horse during the Kassite invasion of Babylonia.
1500	Spoked wheels in eastern Europe and western Asia and representation of the horse and the chariot in Kirgizia, the Altai zone, Mongolia, the Pamir mountain ranges, and south Tajikistan.
1400	The date of the *Zend-Avesta.*
1400 and later	Existence of horse-drawn chariots indicated by the names of the Mitanni rulers.
	Remains of horses and horse furnishings in the burials of the Gandhara grave culture in the Swat valley.
	Evidence of cremation in Tajikistan.
14 C	Inscription of speakers of the western branch of the Indo-European language in Greece.
1200	Svastika in south Tajikistan.
1000	Later strata of the *Rig Veda.*
900–800	Homer's *Iliad* and *Odyssey.*

12

The Age of the *Rig Veda*

Arrival of the Indo-Aryans

The Indo-Iranians, comprising the Indo-Aryans and Iranians, moved towards India from two areas of Central Asia. The first area is archaeologically called the Andronovo culture which covered almost the whole of Central Asia during the second millennium BC. The second is archaeologically called the Bactria–Margiana Archaeological Complex (BMAC) and dated 1900–1500 BC. This cultural zone extended over south Central Asia, and included Bactria or Balkh covering Afghanistan, and Margiana covering Turkmenistan and Uzbekistan. Some ceramics from south Uzbekistan and north Afghanistan are similar to those found in the Gandhara grave culture. The Andronovo culture manifests all the important elements of Aryan life. These comprise stock breeding, widespread use of horse, spoked wheels, practice of cremation, pit-dwellings roofed with birch and other parts of wood, and the soma drink. This culture is therefore regarded as proto-Indo-Iranian. It eventually spread to both Iran and the northern part of the Indian subcontinent.

Around 1500 BC, the BMAC shows evidence of the domestic horse, chariots with spoked wheels, partial cremation, and the svastika motif. Half a dozen graveyards suggest movements of herdsmen. However, in the BMAC area, the remains of proto-urban culture of pre-Aryan times suggest that the herdsmen, who damaged it, moved from this area to the border of the Indian subcontinent. That is why the horse remains and post-cremation burials figured in the Swat valley from about 1400 BC. At about the same time, some ceramics from south Central Asia resemble those found in the Swat region.

Of the three areas covered by the BMAC, Bactria is well known in the Indian tradition. It is called Bahlika, which means an outside country coterminous with modern Balkh. Though this term is not mentioned in the *Rig Veda*, it figures in later Vedic texts. In one such text, Bahlika appears as a part of the name of a king. Bahlika also figures in classical Sanskrit texts and in inscriptions. A Gupta inscription of the fourth century refers to the conqueror of Bahlika who reached there after crossing seven mouths of the Indus. Real conquest there may not have been, but the existence of Bactria is known in the Gupta period. However, later sources considered Punjab to be Bahlika and differentiated it from Prachya or eastern India. Bactria covers a substantial part of Afghanistan, which was well known to the *Rig Veda*. Several rivers flowing in this land appear in this text. That the Aryans came to settle in Afghanistan is shown by the Aryan names of the rivers, and a part of that country is known as Araiya or Haraiya from which Herat is derived.

The earliest Aryans lived in the geographical area covered by eastern Afghanistan, the North-West Frontier Province, Punjab, and the fringes of western UP. Some rivers of Afghanistan, such as the river Kubha, and the river Indus and its five branches, are mentioned in the *Rig Veda*. The Sindhu, coterminous with the Indus, is the river par excellence of the Aryans, and it is repeatedly mentioned. Another river, the Sarasvati, is called *naditama* or the best of rivers in the *Rig Veda*. It is identified with the Ghaggar–Hakra channel in Haryana and Rajasthan, but its Rig Vedic description shows it to be the Avestan river Harakhwati or the present Helmand river in south Afghanistan from where the name Sarasvati was transferred to India. The entire region in which the Aryans first settled in the Indian subcontinent is called the Land of the Seven Rivers.

We know about the Aryans in India from the *Rig Veda*. The term *arya* occurs thirty-six times in this text, and generally denotes a cultural community that speaks the Indo-Aryan language. The *Rig Veda* is the earliest text of the Indo-European languages. It is written in Sanskrit, but also includes many Munda and Dravidian words. Probably these words percolated to the *Rig Veda* through the languages of the Harappans. It is a collection of prayers offered to Agni, Indra, Mitra, Varuna, and other gods by various families of poets or sages. It consists of ten *mandalas* or books, of which books II to VII form the earliest parts. Books I and X seem to have been the latest additions. The *Rig Veda* has many things in common with the *Avesta*, which is the oldest text in the Iranian language. The two texts use the same terms for several gods and even for social classes.

However, the earliest specimen of the Indo-European language is found in an inscription of about 2200 BC from Iraq. Later, such specimens occur in Hittite inscriptions in Anatolia (Turkey) from the nineteenth to the seventeenth centuries BC. They also figure in the Mycenaean inscriptions of Greece around 1400 BC. Aryan names appear in Kassite inscriptions of about 1600 BC from Iraq and in Mitanni inscriptions of the fourteenth century BC from Syria. However, so far no such inscriptions have been found in India.

The Aryans migrated to India in several waves. The earliest wave is represented by the Rig Vedic people, who came to the subcontinent in about 1500 BC. They came into conflict with the indigenous inhabitants called *dasas*, *dasyus*, etc. As the *dasas* are also mentioned in ancient Iranian literature, they seem to have been a branch of the early Aryans. The *Rig Veda* mentions the defeat of Sambara by a chief called Divodasa of the Bharata clan. In this case, the term *dasa* appears in the name Divodasa. In all probability, the *dasyus* in the *Rig Veda* represent the original inhabitants of India, and an Aryan chief who overpowered them was called Trasadasyu. The Aryan chief was soft towards the *dasas*, but very hostile to the *dasyus*. The term *dasyuhatya*, slaughter of the *dasyus*, is repeatedly used in the *Rig Veda*. The *dasyus* possibly worshipped the phallus and did not husband cattle for dairy products.

Tribal Conflicts

We know little about the weapons of the adversaries of the Indo-Aryan people, although we hear of many defeats inflicted by Indra on the enemies of the Aryans. In the *Rig Veda*, Indra is called Purandara which means that he destroyed dwelling units. We cannot, however, identify these units held by the pre-Aryans, some of which may have been situated in north Afghanistan. The Indo-Aryans succeeded everywhere because they had chariots drawn by horses, and introduced them for the first time into West Asia and India. The Aryan soldiers were probably also equipped with coats of mail (*varman*) and better arms.

The Indo-Aryans were engaged in two types of conflicts. First, they fought with the pre-Aryans, and secondly, they fought amongst themselves. Intra-tribal conflicts rocked the Aryan communities for a long time. According to tradition, the Aryans were divided into five tribes called *panchajana*, but there might have been other tribes too. The Aryans fought amongst themselves and sometimes enlisted the support of the non-Aryan peoples for the purpose. The Bharatas and the Tritsu were the ruling Aryan clans, and they were supported by priest Vasishtha. The country Bharatavarsha was eventually named after the tribe Bharata, which is first mentioned in the *Rig Veda.* The Bharata ruling clan was opposed by a host of ten chiefs, five of whom were heads of Aryan tribes and the remaining five of the non-Aryan people. The battle that the Bharatas fought with the host of ten chiefs is known as the Battle of Ten Kings. It was fought on the river Parushni, coterminous with the river Ravi, and it gave victory to Sudas and established the supremacy of the Bharatas. Of the defeated tribes, the most important was that of the Purus. Subsequently, the Bharatas joined hands with the Purus and formed a new ruling tribe called the Kurus. The Kurus combined with the Panchalas, and they together established their rule in the upper Gangetic basin where they played an important role in later Vedic times.

Cattle Rearing and Agriculture

We can form some idea of the material life of the Rig Vedic Aryans. They owed their success to the use of horses, chariots, and also possibly some better arms made of bronze of which we have very little archaeological evidence. In all probability, they also introduced the spoked wheel which made its debut in the Caucasus area in 2300 BC. When they settled in the western part of the subcontinent, they possibly used copper supplied by the Khetri mines in Rajasthan. The Rig Vedic people had a superior knowledge of agriculture. The ploughshare is mentioned in the earliest part of the *Rig Veda*, though some consider it to be an interpolation, and was possibly made of wood. They were acquainted with sowing, harvesting, and threshing, and knew about the different seasons. Agriculture was also well known to the pre-Aryans who lived in the area associated with the Vedic people, but was perhaps used primarily to produce fodder.

However, there are so many references to the cow and the bull in the *Rig Veda* that the Rig Vedic people can be called a predominantly pastoral people. Most of their wars were fought over cows. The terms for war in the *Rig Veda* is *gavishthi* or search for cows, and cow seems to have been the most important form of wealth. Whenever we hear of gifts made to priests, they usually consist of cows and women slaves and never of land. The Rig Vedic people may have occasionally occupied pieces of land for grazing, cultivation, and settlement, but land did not form a well-established type of private property.

The *Rig Veda* mentions such artisans as the carpenter, chariot-maker, weaver, leather worker, and potter. This indicates that they practised all these crafts. The term *ayas*, used for copper or bronze, shows that metal-working was known. We do not, however, have clear evidence of the existence of regular trade. The Aryans or the Vedic people principally used the land routes because the word *samudra* mentioned in the *Rig Veda* primarily indicates a stretch of water. Similarly, the term *pur* mentioned in that text means either a dwelling unit or a cluster of such units, not a city or a fort. Sometimes such a unit is credited with a thousand doors, but the term *sahasra* is used as an exaggeration in many places in the *Rig Veda*. Therefore, the Aryans did not live in cities, and possibly lived in some kind of fortified mud settlements which still await satisfactory identification by archaeologists. They were also familiar with caves in the mountains.

Recently a site called Bhagwanpura in Haryana and three other sites in Punjab have yielded Painted Grey Ware along with 'late Harappan' pottery. The date assigned to the Bhagwanpura finds ranges from 1600 to 1000 BC which also roughly corresponds to the period of the *Rig Veda*. The geographical area of these four sites also coincides with that of a substantial portion of the area represented by the *Rig Veda*. Although Painted Grey Ware has been found at all these sites, iron objects and cereals are missing. We may, therefore, think of a pre-iron phase of the PGW which coincided with the Rig Vedic phase. An interesting find at Bhagwanpura is a thirteen-roomed mud house whose dating has not been confirmed. This might indicate either a house for a large extended family or of a tribal chief. Cattle bones are found in substantial numbers at all these sites, and horse bones at Bhagwanpura.

Tribal Chiefdom

The administrative machinery of the Aryans in the Rig Vedic period functioned with the tribal chief, for his successful leadership in war, at the centre. He was called *rajan*. It seems that in the Rig Vedic period, the king's post had become hereditary. However, the *rajan* was a kind of chief and did not exercise unlimited power, having to reckon with the tribal organizations. We have traces of the election of the king by the tribal assembly called the *samiti.* The king was called the protector of his tribe. He protected its cattle, fought its wars, and offered prayers to the gods on its behalf.

Several tribal or kin-based assemblies such as the *sabha*, *samiti*, *vidatha*, and *gana* are mentioned in the *Rig Veda*. They exercised deliberative, military, and religious functions. Even women attended the *sabha* and *vidatha* in Rig Vedic times. The *sabha* and the *samiti* mattered a great deal in early Vedic times, so much so that the chiefs or the kings showed an eagerness to win their support.

In the day-to-day administration, the king was assisted by a few functionaries. The most important of these seems to have been the *purohita*. The two priests who played a major role in Rig Vedic times were Vasishtha and Vishvamitra. Vasishtha was a conservative and Vishvamitra a liberal. Vishvamitra composed the *gayatri* mantra to widen the Aryan world. Whoever recited the *gayatri* was admitted to the Aryan fold. Eventually, however, this mantra was made the monopoly of the three higher varnas, and priests did not permit women and shudras to recite it. The Vedic priests inspired the tribal chiefs into action and lauded their exploits in return for handsome rewards in cows and women slaves. Next in rank to the king was the *senani* or the head of the army. He used spears, axes, swords, etc. We do not learn of any officer concerned with the collection of taxes. In all probability, the people made voluntary offerings called *bali* to the *rajan.* Presents and the spoils of war were perhaps distributed in some Vedic assemblies, as is done in kin-based communities. The *Rig Veda* does not mention any officer for administration of justice. It was not, however, an ideal society but one in which there were cases of theft and burglary, and people stole cows. Spies were employed to keep an eye on such anti-social activities.

The titles of the officials do not indicate territorial administration. However, some officers appear to have been attached to territories. They enjoyed positions of authority in the pasture grounds and settled villages. The officer who enjoyed authority over a large stretch of land or pasture ground was called *vrajapati.* He led to battle the heads of the families called *kulapas*, or heads of the fighting hordes called *gramanis*. Initially the *gramani* was just the head of a small tribal kin-based fighting unit called *grama*, but when the unit settled, the *gramani* became the head of the village, and in course of time his position became the same as that of the *vrajapati.*

The king did not maintain any standing army, but in times of war he mustered a militia whose military functions were performed by various tribal groups called *vrata, gana, grama, sardha.* By and large, it was a tribal system of government in which the military element was strong. There was no civil system or territorial administration because people were in the throes of perpetual expansion and migrated from one area to another.

Tribe and Family

Kinship was the basis of the social structure, and a man was identified by the clan to which he belonged, as can be seen in the names of several Rig Vedic kings. The people's primary loyalty was to the tribe, which was called *jana.* In one of the early verses, the combined strength of the warriors of two tribes is given as twenty-one. This indicates that the total number of members in a tribe may not have exceeded 100. The term *jana* occurs at about 275 places in the *Rig Veda,* and the term *janapada* or territory is not used even once. The people were attached to the tribe as neither control over territory nor the kingdom was yet established.

Another important term which stands for tribe in the *Rig Veda* is *vis,* which is mentioned 170 times in that text. Probably the *vis* was divided into *grama*s or smaller tribal units organized to fight. When the *grama*s clashed with one another, it resulted in *samgrama* or war. The most numerous varna of the vaishyas arose out of the *vis* or the mass of the tribal people.

The term for family (*kula*) is rarely mentioned in the *Rig Veda.* It comprised not only mother, father, sons, slaves, etc., but many other people too. It seems that family in the early Vedic phase was denoted by the term *griha,* which frequently occurs in this text. In the earliest Indo-European languages, a single word is used to denote nephew, grandson, cousin, etc. This would imply that differentiation in family relationships leading to the setting up of separate households had not thus far occurred, and the family was a very large joint unit. It was obviously a patriarchal family headed by the father, as was the case in Roman society. It seems that several generations of the family lived under the same roof. As it was a patriarchal society, the birth of a son was repeatedly desired, and people prayed to the gods for brave sons to fight the wars. In the *Rig Veda* no desire is expressed for daughters, though the desire for children and cattle is a recurrent theme in the hymns.

Women could attend assemblies and offer sacrifices along with their husbands. We have an instance of five women who composed hymns, although the later texts mention twenty such women. Evidently the hymns were composed orally, and nothing written relates to that period.

The institution of marriage was established, although symbols of primitive practices survived. We hear of a proposal made by Yami, the twin-sister of Yama, to establish love relations, but the offer is resisted by Yama. We have some indications of polyandry. For instance, the Maruts are stated to have enjoyed Rodasi, and the two Asvin brothers are represented as living with Surya, the daughter of the sun god, but such instances are infrequent. Possibly they indicate matrilineal traces, and we have a few examples of sons being named after their mother, as in the case of Mamateya.

We also notice the practice of levirate and widow remarriage in the *Rig Veda*. There are no examples of child marriage, and the marriageable age in the *Rig Veda* seems to have been 16 to 17.

Social Differentiation

The *Rig Veda* displays some consciousness of the physical appearance of people in north-western India in about 1500–1000 BC. Varna was the term used for colour, and it seems that the Indo-Aryan language speakers were fair and the indigenous inhabitants dark in complexion. Colour may have provided the identifier for social orders, but its importance has been exaggerated by writers with an excessive belief in racial distinctions. The factor that contributed most to the creation of social divisions was the conquest of the indigenous inhabitants by the Indo-Aryans. The *dasa*s and the *dasyus*, who were conquered by the Aryans, were treated as slaves and shudras. The *Rig Veda* mentions the *arya* varna and *dasa* varna. The tribal chiefs and the priests acquired a larger share of the booty and naturally became wealthy at the cost of their kinsmen, thereby creating social inequalities in the tribe. Gradually the tribal society was divided into three occupational groups, warriors, priests, and the common people on the same pattern as in Iran. The fourth division called the shudras appeared towards the end of the Rig Vedic period. The term shudra is mentioned for the first time in the *Rig Veda* in its tenth book, which is the latest addition.

We repeatedly hear of slaves who were given as gifts to the priests. These were primarily women employed for domestic purposes. It is clear that in Rig Vedic times slaves were not used directly in agriculture or other productive activities.

In the age of the *Rig Veda*, differentiation based on occupations had begun, but this was very sharp. We hear of a family in which a member says: 'I am a poet, my father is a physician, and my mother is a grinder. Earning a livelihood through different means we live together ....' We hear of gifts of cattle, chariots, horses, slaves, etc. Unequal distribution of the spoils of war created social inequalities, and this aided the rise of princes and priests at the cost of the common tribal people. However, as the economy was mainly pastoral and not food producing, the scope for collecting regular tributes from the people was very limited. We do not find gifts of land, and even gifts of cereals are rare. We find domestic slaves but not wage-earners. The tribal elements in society were stronger and social divisions based on the collection of taxes or accumulation of landed property did not exist, and thus the society was still tribal and egalitarian.

Rig Vedic Gods

Every people discover their religion in their surroundings. The Aryans found it difficult to explain the coming of the rains, the appearance of the sun and the moon, and the existence of the rivers, mountains, and the like. They, therefore, personified these natural forces and looked upon them as living beings to whom they attributed human or animal attributes. We have a large number of such divinities in the *Rig Veda*, which is replete with hymns composed in their honour by the poets of sundry families. The most important divinity in the *Rig Veda* is Indra, who is called Purandara or destroyer of dwelling units. Indra played the role of a warlord, leading the Aryan soldiers to victory against the demons, and has 250 hymns devoted to him. He is considered to be the rain god and thought to be responsible for causing rainfall. The second position is held by Agni (fire god) to whom 200 hymns are devoted. Fire played a significant part in the life of primitive people because of its use in burning forests, cooking, and the like. The cult of fire occupied a central place not only in India but also in Iran. In Vedic times, Agni acted as a kind of intermediary between the gods, on the one hand, and the people, on the other. The oblations offered to Agni were supposed to be carried in the form of smoke to the sky, and thus transmitted to the gods. The third important position is occupied by Varuna who personified water. Varuna was supposed to uphold the natural order; and whatever happened in the world was thought to be the reflection of his desires. Soma was considered to be the god of plants, and an intoxicating drink is named after him. In the *Rig Veda* many hymns explain the methods of preparing this drink from plants that have not so far been satisfactorily identified. The Maruts personify the storm. Many hymns are devoted to the river Sarasvati, who was considered an important goddess. Thus we have many deities who represent the different forces of nature in one form or another but are also assigned human activities.

There are some women divinities too, such as Aditi, and Usha who represented the appearance of the dawn, but they were not prominent at the time of the *Rig Veda*. However, given the patriarchal society of the period, the male gods were far more important than the female.

The dominant mode of worshipping the gods was through the recitation of prayers and performance of sacrifices. Prayers played an important part in Rig Vedic times, both collective and individual. Originally every tribe or clan was the votary of a special god. It seems that prayers were offered to the gods in chorus by the members of an entire tribe. This also happened in the case of sacrifices: Agni and Indra were invited to partake of sacrifices made by the tribe (*jana*) as a whole. Offerings of vegetables, barley, etc., were made to gods, but in Rig Vedic times this was not accompanied by any ritual or sacrificial formulae. At this stage the magical power of the word was not considered as important as it became in later Vedic times. Why did people worship gods during the Rig Vedic period? They did not do so for their spiritual uplift or for ending the miseries of existence. They principally asked for *praja* (children), *pashu* (cattle), food, wealth, health, and the like.

Chronology

(BC)	
2300	Spoked wheel found in the Caucasus area.
2 M	The Indo-Iranian Andronovo culture covered the whole of Central Asia.
1900–1700	Specimens of Indo-European language in Hittite inscriptions in Anatolia.
1900–1500	Bactria–Margiana Archaeological Complex (BMAC) in south Central Asia.
1600	Aryan names in Kassite inscriptions from Iraq.
1600–1000	The date assigned to the PGW and late Harappan pottery from Bhagwanpura.

1500	The Aryan migration in the subcontinent represented by the *Rig Veda.* Domestic horse, chariots with spoked wheels, partial cremation, and the svastika motif in the BMAC.
1400	Specimens of the Indo-European language in the Mycenaean inscription of Greece.
1400 onwards	Horse remains and post-cremation burials in the Swat valley.
1400 onwards	Ceramics from south Central Asia similar to those of the Swat valley.
14 C	Aryan names in Mitanni inscriptions in Syria.

13

The Later Vedic Phase: Transition to State and Social Orders

Expansion in the Later Vedic Period (*c.* 1000–500 BC)

The history of the later Vedic period is based mainly on the Vedic texts which were compiled after the age of the *Rig Veda*. The collections of Vedic hymns or mantras are known as the Samhitas. The *Rig Veda Samhita* is the oldest Vedic text, on the basis of which we have described the early Vedic age. For the purpose of recitation, the prayers of the *Rig Veda* were set to tune, and this modified collection was known as the *Sama Veda*. In post-Rig Vedic times, two other collections, the *Yajur Veda Samhita* and the *Atharva Veda Samhita*, were composed. The *Yajur Veda* contains not only hymns but also rituals to accompany their recitation, the latter reflecting the social and political milieu of the time. The *Atharva Veda* contains charms and spells to ward off evils and diseases, its contents throwing light on the beliefs and practices of the non-Aryans. The Vedic Samhitas were followed by the composition of a series of texts known as the Brahmanas. These are replete with ritualistic formulae and explain the social and religious meaning of rituals. All these later Vedic texts were compiled in the upper Gangetic basin in *c.* 1000–500 BC. During the same period and in the same area, digging and exploration have brought to light nearly 700 inhabited sites. These are called Painted Grey Ware (PGW) sites because they were inhabited by people who used earthern bowls and dishes made of painted grey pottery. They also used iron weapons. With the combined evidence from the later Vedic texts and PGW iron-phase archaeology, we are able to form an idea of the life of the people in the first half of the first millennium BC in western UP and the adjoining areas of Punjab, Haryana, and Rajasthan.

The texts show that the Aryans expanded from Punjab over the whole of western UP covered by the Ganga–Yamuna doab. The Bharatas and Purus, the two major tribes, combined and thus formed the Kuru people. Initially they lived between the Sarasvati and the Drishadvati just on the fringe of the doab. Soon the Kurus occupied Delhi and the upper reaches of the doab, the area called Kurukshetra or the land of the Kurus. Gradually they coalesced with a people called the Panchalas who occupied the central part of the doab. The authority of the Kuru–Panchala people spread over Delhi, and the upper and central parts of the doab. They set up their capital at Hastinapur situated in Meerut district. The history of the Kuru tribe is important for the battle of Bharata, which is the principal theme of the great epic called the *Mahabharata*. This war is supposed to have been fought around 950 BC between the Kauravas and the Pandavas. Since both of them belonged to the Kuru clan, as a result of war virtually the whole of the Kuru clan was wiped out.

Excavations at Hastinapur, datable to the period 900 BC to 500 BC, have revealed settlements and faint beginnings of town life. They do not, however, reflect the description of Hastinapur in the *Mahabharata* because the epic was finally compiled much later in about the fourth century AD when material life had greatly advanced. In later Vedic times people hardly knew the use of burnt bricks. The mud structures that have been discovered at Hastinapur could not be imposing and lasting. From traditions we learn that Hastinapur was flooded, and the remnants of the Kuru clan moved to Kaushambi near Allahabad.

The Panchala kingdom, which covered the modern districts of Bareilley, Badaun, and Farukhabad, is famous for its philosopher kings and brahmana theologians mentioned in later Vedic texts.

Towards the end of the later Vedic period, in around 500 BC, the Vedic people spread in large numbers from the doab further east to Koshala in eastern UP and to Videha in north Bihar. Although Koshala is associated with the story of Rama, this story is not mentioned in Vedic literature. In eastern UP and north Bihar, the Vedic people had to contend against a people who used copper implements and the black-and-red earthen pots. In western UP they possibly came up against the people who used pots of ochre or red colour together with copper implements. At a few places they also came against the users of the late Harappan culture. Many Munda words occur in later Vedic texts which were compiled in the upper Gangetic basin. This would suggest that the later Vedic people also encountered the

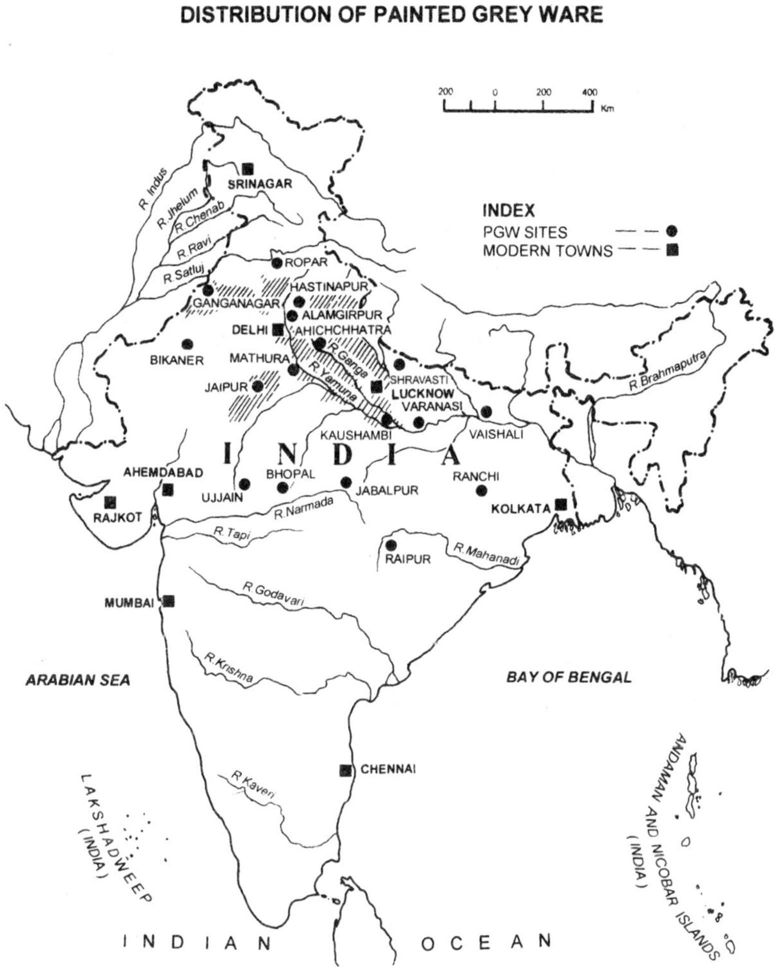

MAP 6 Distribution of Painted Grey Ware. *Courtesy ASI*

Munda speakers in this area. Whoever the opponents of the later Vedic people were, they evidently did not occupy any large and compact area, and their number in the upper Gangetic basin does not seem to have been large. The Vedic people succeeded in the second phase of their expansion because they used iron weapons and horse-drawn chariots.

Use of Iron

The story of iron is similar to that of the horse. The domesticated horse is first noticed near the Black Sea in the sixth millennium BC, but it became common only from the second millennium BC onwards. Similarly iron underwent a long gestation. Lumps of stone or iron move in outer space. When they encounter the atmosphere, they hit the ground and plummet to earth as meteorites. Such a piece was found in ancient Egypt in *c.* 3000 BC. It was identified as iron, and was called black copper from heaven in the Egyptian language.

Many copper minerals contain iron ores. It took many years to separate iron ores from these minerals and form the pure iron metal. As a pure metal, iron was first made in Mesopotamia in 5000 BC, and later in Anatolia in the third millennium BC. However, up to 1200 BC, iron was valued as a precious metal in western Asia and used as presents by rulers.

In the Indian subcontinent, iron is sometimes attributed to Lothal and to some sites in Afghanistan in Harappan times. Neither of these however represent pure iron metal nor working in iron. They are really copper objects containing iron ores. These ores have not been separated from copper and given a distinct and separate identity as a pure iron metal.

In India, pure iron at some sites in Rajasthan in the copper–stone age has been reported and also in Karnataka towards the end of that phase. Iron can thus be placed in the second half of the second millennium BC. In this phase we have no idea about its continuing use in terms of time and place.

Around 1000 BC it was used in the Gandhara area in Pakistan. Iron implements buried with dead bodies have been discovered in substantial numbers. They have also been found in Baluchistan. At about the same time, iron was used in eastern Punjab, western UP, MP, and Rajasthan. Excavations show that iron weapons, such as arrowheads and spearheads, came to be commonly used in western UP from about 800 BC onwards. With iron weapons the Vedic people may have defeated the few adversaries that they may have faced in the upper portion of the doab. The iron axe may have been used to clear the forests in the upper Gangetic basin although, because rainfall ranged between 35 cm and 65 cm, these forests may not have been very dense. Towards the end of the Vedic period knowledge of iron spread in eastern UP and Videha. The earliest iron implements discovered in this area relate to the seventh century BC, and the metal itself is called *shyama* or *krishna ayas* (black metal) in the later Vedic texts.

Agriculture

Although very few agricultural tools made of iron have been found, undoubtedly agriculture was the chief means of subsistence of the later Vedic people. Late Vedic texts speak of six, eight, twelve, and even twenty-four oxen yoked to the plough. This may be an exaggeration. Ploughing was done with a wooden ploughshare, which could function in the light soil of the upper Gangetic plains. Sufficient bullocks could not have been available because of cattle slaughter in sacrifices. Agriculture was, therefore, primitive, but there is no doubt about its wide prevalence. The *Shatapatha Brahmana* speaks at length about the ploughing rituals. According to ancient legends, Janaka, the king of Videha and Sita's father, lent his hand to the plough. In those days, even kings and princes did not hesitate to take to manual labour. Balarama, Krishna's brother, was called Haladhara or wielder of the plough. Gautama Buddha is depicted ploughing with oxen in a Bodh-Gaya sculpture. Eventually ploughing was assigned to the lower orders and prohibited for the upper varnas.

The Vedic people continued to produce barley, but during the later Vedic period rice and wheat became their chief crops. In subsequent times, wheat became the staple food of the people in Punjab and western UP. For the first time, the Vedic people became acquainted with rice in the doab, called *vrihi* in the Vedic texts, and remains of it recovered from Hastinapur relate to the eighth century BC. Rice was also grown at Atranjikhera in Etah district at around the same time. The use of rice is recommended in Vedic rituals, but that of wheat only rarely. Various kinds of lentils were also produced by the later Vedic people.

Arts and Crafts

The later Vedic period saw the rise of diverse arts and crafts. We hear of smiths and smelters, who certainly had something to do with iron working from about 1000 BC. The Vedic people were familiar with copper from the very outset. Numerous copper tools of the pre-1000 BC period found in western UP and Bihar might suggest the existence of coppersmiths in non-Vedic societies. The Vedic people may have used the copper mines of Khetri in Rajasthan, but in any event, copper was one of the first metals to be used by them. Copper objects are found in Painted Grey Ware sites. They were used principally for war and hunting, and also for ornaments.

Weaving was confined to women but practised on a wide scale. Leather work, pottery, and carpentry made great progress. The later Vedic people were acquainted with four types of pottery—black-and-red ware, black-slipped ware, Painted Grey Ware, and red-ware. The last type of pottery was the most popular, and is found almost all over western UP. However, the most distinctive pottery of the period is known as Painted Grey Ware. It consisted of bowls and dishes, that were used either for rituals or for eating or for both, probably by the emerging upper orders. Glass hoards and bangles found in the PGW layers may have been used as prestige objects by a few persons. On the whole, both Vedic texts and excavations indicate the cultivation of specialized crafts. Jewellers are also mentioned in later Vedic texts, and they possibly catered to the needs of the affluent sections of society.

Settlements

Though the term *jana* or tribal people is common in the four Vedas, *janapada* or people's settlement is not mentioned there. It first occurs in some later Vedic texts called Brahmanas dating to not earlier than 800 BC.

Agriculture and various crafts enabled the later Vedic people to lead a settled life. Excavations and explorations give us some idea about settlements in later Vedic times. Widespread Painted Grey Ware sites have been found not only in western UP and Delhi, which was the Kuru–Panchala area, but also in the adjoining parts of Punjab and Haryana, the Madra area, and in those of Rajasthan, that constituted the Matsya area. Altogether, we can count nearly 700 sites, mostly in the upper Gangetic basin, only a few sites such as Hastinapur, Atranjikhera, and Noh have been excavated. As the thickness of the material remains of habitation ranges from one to three metres, it appears that these settlements lasted from one to three centuries. By and large, these were entirely new settlements which had no immediate predecessors. People lived in mud-brick houses or in wattle-and-daub houses erected on wooden poles. Although the structures are poor, ovens and cereals (rice) recovered from the sites show that the Painted Grey Ware people, probably identifiable with the later Vedic people, were farmers who led a settled life. However, as they generally cultivated with the wooden ploughshare, the peasants were unable to produce enough to feed those engaged in other occupations, and therefore they would not contribute much to the rise of towns.

Although the term *nagara* is used in later Vedic texts only the faint beginnings of towns appear towards the end of the later Vedic period. Hastinapur and Kaushambi (near Allahabad) seem to be primitive towns dating to the end of the Vedic period, and may be called proto-urban. The Vedic texts also refer to the seas and sea voyages. Thus some form of commerce may have been stimulated by the rise of new arts and crafts.

By and large, the later Vedic phase registered a great advance in the material life of the people. The pastoral and semi-nomadic forms of living were relegated to the background and agriculture became the primary source of livelihood, and life became settled and sedentary. Equipped with diverse arts and crafts, the Vedic people now settled permanently in the upper Gangetic plains. The peasants living in the plains produced enough to maintain themselves, and were also able to spare a marginal part of their produce for the support of chiefs, princes, and priests.

Political Organization

In later Vedic times, the Rig Vedic tribal assemblies lost importance, and royal power increased at their cost. The *vidatha* completely disappeared; the *sabha* and *samiti* continued to hold their ground but their character changed. They were now controlled by chiefs and rich nobles, and women were no longer permitted to sit in the *sabha* which was now dominated by warriors and brahmanas.

The formation of larger kingdoms increased the power of the chief or king. Tribal authority tended to become territorial. The dominant tribes gave their names to territories which might be inhabited by tribes other than their own. Initially each area was named after the tribe that first settled there. First Panchala was the name of a people, and then it became the name of a region. The term *rashtra*, which indicates territory, first arose during this period. The concept of controlling people also appeared. It was indicated by the use of the term *rajya*, which meant sovereign power.

Traces of the election of the king appear in later Vedic texts. The individual considered to have the best in physical and other attributes was elected raja. A tribal who pioneered settlements, showed skill in farming, and fought bravely was elected the chief of his tribe. This may have been the case with the raja. He received voluntary presents called *bali* from his ordinary kinsmen or the common people called the *vis*. Gradually these voluntary presents assumed the form of tributes that were forcibly collected. The ruler, however, sought to perpetuate the right to receive presents and enjoy other privileges pertaining to his office by making it hereditary in his family, the post generally going to the eldest son. However, this succession was not always smooth. The *Mahabharata* tells us that Duryodhana, the younger cousin of Yudhishthira, usurped power. Battling for territory, the families of the Pandavas and Kauravas virtually destroyed themselves. The Bharata battle shows that kingship knows no kinship.

The king's influence was strengthened by rituals. He performed the *rajasuya* sacrifice, which was supposed to confer supreme power on him. He performed the *ashvamedha*, which meant unquestioned control over an area in which the royal horse ran uninterrupted. He also performed the *vajapeya* or the chariot race, in which the royal chariot drawn by a horse was made to win the race against his kinsmen. All these rituals impressed the people by demonstrating the power and prestige of the king.

During this period collection of taxes and tributes seems to have become common. These were probably deposited with an officer called *sangrihitri* who worked as the king's companion. The epics tell us that at the time of a grand sacrifice, large-scale distributions were made by the princes, and all sections of the people were sumptuously fed. In the discharge of his duties the king was assisted by the priest, the commander, the chief queen, and a few other high functionaries. At the lower level, the administration was possibly run by village assemblies, which may have been controlled by the chiefs of the dominant clans. These assemblies also tried local cases. However, even in later Vedic times the king did not have a standing army. Tribal units were mustered in times of war and, according to one ritual, for success in war, the king had to eat along with his people (*vis*) from the same plate.

Social Organization

Aryanization promoted social differentiation. In the later Vedic texts the term *arya* encapsulates brahmana, kshatriya, vaishya, and shudra. Thus it was the Vedic Aryans who introduced the varna system.

The later Vedic society came to be divided into four varnas called the brahmana, *rajanya* or kshatriya, vaishya, and shudra. The growing cult of sacrifices enormously added to the power of the brahmanas. Initially the brahmanas were only one of the sixteen classes of priests, but they gradually overshadowed the other priestly groups and emerged as the most important class. The rise of the brahmanas is a peculiar development that did not occur in Aryan societies outside India. It appears that non-Aryan elements had some role to play in the formation of the brahmana varna. They conducted rituals and sacrifices for their clients and for themselves, and also officiated at the festivals associated with agricultural operations. They prayed for the success of their patron in war, and, in return, the king pledged not to do anything to harm them. Sometimes the brahmanas came into conflict with the *rajanya*s, who represented the order of the warrior nobles, for positions of supremacy. However, whenever the two upper orders had to deal with the lower orders, they put aside their differences. From the end of the later Vedic period onwards, it began to be emphasized that the two upper orders should cooperate to rule over the rest of society.

The vaishyas constituted the common people, and they were assigned producing functions such as agriculture, cattle-breeding, and the like; some of them also worked as artisans. Towards the end of the Vedic period they began to engage in trade. The vaishyas appear to have been the only tribute payers in later Vedic times, and the brahmanas and kshatriyas are represented as living on the tributes collected from the vaishyas. The process of subjugating the mass of the tribesmen to the position of tribute payers was long and protracted. Several rituals were prescribed for making the refractory elements (*vis* or vaishya) submissive to the prince (raja) and to his close kinsmen called the *rajanya*s. This was achieved with the assistance of the priests who also fattened themselves at the cost of the people or the vaishyas. All the three higher varnas shared one common feature: they were entitled to *upanayana* or investiture with the sacred thread according to the Vedic mantras. *Upanayana* heralded the beginning of education in the Vedas. The fourth varna was deprived of the sacred thread ceremony and the recitation of the *gayatri* mantra. The *gayatri* was a Vedic mantra that could not be recited by a shudra, thereby depriving him of Vedic education. Similarly, women were also denied both the *gayatri* and *upanayana*. Thus, the imposition of disabilities on the shudras and women began towards the end of the Vedic period.

The prince, who represented the *rajanya* order, sought to assert his authority over all the three other varnas. The *Aitareya Brahmana*, a text of the later Vedic period, represents the brahmana as a seeker of livelihood and an acceptor of gifts from the prince but also removable by him. A vaishya is called tribute-paying, meant to be beaten and oppressed at will. The worst position is reserved for the shudra. He is called the servant of another, to be made to work at will by another, and to be beaten at will.

Generally, the later Vedic texts draw a line of demarcation between the three higher orders, on the one hand, and the shudras, on the other. Nevertheless, several public rituals associated with the coronation of the king in which the shudras participated, were presumably survivors of the original Aryan community. Certain sections of artisans, such as the *rathakara* or chariot maker, enjoyed a high status and were entitled to the sacred thread ceremony. Thus, in later Vedic times, varna distinctions had not advanced very far.

The family shows the increasing power of the father, who could even disinherit his son. In princely families, the right of primogeniture was getting stronger. Male ancestors came to be worshipped. Women were generally given a lower position. Although some women theologians took part in philosophical discussions and some queens participated in coronation rituals, ordinarily women were thought to be inferior and subordinate to men.

The institution of *gotra* appeared in later Vedic times. Literally, it means the cow pen or the place where cattle belonging to the entire clan are kept, but in course of time it signified descent from a common ancestor. People began to practise *gotra* exogamy. No marriage could take place between persons belonging to the same *gotra* or having the same lineage.

Ashramas or the four stages of life were not well established in Vedic times. The post-Vedic texts speak of four ashramas: that of *brahmachari* or student, *grihastha* or householder, *vanaprastha* or hermit, and *sannyasin* or ascetic who completely renounced the worldly life. Only the first three are clearly defined in the later Vedic texts; the last or the fourth stage was not well established, though ascetic life was not unknown. Even in post-Vedic times, only the stage of the householder was commonly practised by all the varnas.

Gods, Rituals, and Philosophy

In the later Vedic period, the upper doab emerged as the cradle of the Aryan culture under brahmanical influence. All the Vedic literature seems to have been compiled in this area in the land of the Kuru–Panchalas. The cult of sacrifice, central to this culture, was accompanied by rituals and formulae.

The two outstanding Rig Vedic gods, Indra and Agni, lost their former importance. On the other hand, Prajapati, the creator, came to occupy the supreme position in the later Vedic pantheon. Some of the other minor gods of the Rig Vedic period also came to the forefront. Rudra, the god of animals, became important in later Vedic times, and Vishnu came to be conceived of as the preserver and protector of the people who now led a settled life rather than a semi-nomadic one. In addition, some objects began to be worshipped as symbols of divinity; signs of idolatry appear in later Vedic times. As society became divided into social classes, such as brahmanas, *rajanyas*, vaishyas, and shudras, some social orders began to have their own deities. Pushan, who was supposed to tend to cattle, came to be regarded as the god of the shudras, although in the age of the *Rig Veda* cattle rearing was the primary Aryan occupation.

People worshipped gods for the same material reasons in this period as they did in earlier times. However, the mode of worship underwent substantial change. Prayers continued to be recited, but they ceased to be the dominant mode of placating the gods. Sacrifices became far more important, and they assumed both a public and domestic character. Public sacrifices involved the king and the entire community, which still in many cases coincided with the tribe. Private sacrifices were performed by individuals in their houses because during this period the Vedic people maintained regular households. Individuals offered oblations to Agni, and each of these took the form of a ritual or a sacrifice. Sacrifices involved the killing of animals on a large scale and, especially, the destruction of cattle wealth. The guest was known as *goghna* or one who was fed on cattle.

Sacrifices were accompanied by formulae that had to be carefully enunciated by the sacrificer. The sacrificer was known as the *yajamana*, the performer of *yajna*, and much of his success depended on the magical power of words uttered correctly during the sacrifices. Some rituals performed by the Vedic Aryans are common to the Indo-European peoples, but several of them seem to have been developed on the Indian soil.

These formulae and sacrifices were invented, adopted, and elaborated by the priests called the brahmanas who claimed a monopoly of priestly knowledge and expertise. They invented numerous rituals, some of which were adopted from the non-Aryans. The reason for the invention and elaboration of the rituals is not clear, but mercenary motives cannot be ruled out. We hear that as many as 240,000 cows were given as *dakshina* or gift to the officiating priest in the *rajasuya* sacrifice. Swami Vivekananda speaks of both orthodox and beef-eating brahmanas in Vedic times, and he recommends animal food for the Hindus in the modern context.

In addition to cows, which were usually given as sacrificial gifts, gold, cloth, and horses were also donated. Sometimes the priests claimed portions of territory as *dakshina*, but the grant of land as sacrificial fee is not established in the later Vedic period. The *Shatapatha Brahmana* states that in the *ashvamedha*, the north, south, east, and west should all be given to the priest. If this really happened then what would remain with the king? This, therefore, merely indicates the desire of the priests to grab as much property as possible. In reality, however, considerable transfer of land to priests could not have taken place. There is a reference in which land, which was being given to the priests, refused to be transferred to them.

Towards the end of the Vedic period a strong reaction arose against priestly domination, against cults and rituals, especially in the land of the Panchalas and Videha where, around 600 BC, the Upanishads were compiled. These philosophical texts criticized the rituals and laid stress on the value of right belief and knowledge. They emphasized that knowledge of the self or *atman* should be acquired and the relation of *atman* with Brahma should be properly understood. Brahma emerged as the supreme entity, comparable to the powerful kings of the period. Some of the kshatriya princes in Panchala and Videha also cultivated this form of thought and created the atmosphere for the reform of the priest-dominated religion. Their teachings promoted the cause of stability and integration. Emphasis on the changelessness, indestructibility, and immortality of the *atman* or soul served the cause of stability that was necessary to sustain the rising state power headed by the kshatriya raja. Stress on the relation of *atman* with Brahma fostered allegiance to a superior authority.

The later Vedic period saw certain important changes, such as the beginnings of territorial kingdoms, called *janapadas*, under the kshatriya rulers. Wars were fought not only for the possession of cattle but also for territory. The famous Mahabharata war, fought between the Kauravas and the Pandavas, is attributed to this period. The predominantly pastoral society of early Vedic times had become agricultural. The tribal pastoralists came to be transformed into farmers who could maintain their chief with frequent tributes. Chiefs, called *raja* or *janapadin*, grew at the expense of the tribal peasantry, and handsomely rewarded the priests who supported their patrons against the common people called the vaishyas. The shudras were still a small serving order. The tribal society broke up into a varna-divided society, but varna distinctions could not be carried too far. Despite the support of the brahmanas, the *rajanyas* or the kshatriyas could not establish a mature state system. A state cannot be set up without a regular taxation system and a standing army. The entire administrative structure, including the army, depends upon taxes, but the existing mode of agriculture did not provide scope for regular taxes and tributes.

Chronology

(BC)	
6 M	The domesticated horse in the Black Sea area.
5 M	Iron in Mesopotamia.
3 M	Iron in Anatolia. Iron in Egypt.
2nd half of the 2 M	Iron in the copper–Stone Age in Rajasthan and Karnataka.
1200	Iron used as presents by rulers in western Asia.
Pre-1000	Copper tools from western UP and Bihar.
1000	Iron use in the Gandhara area, Baluchistan, eastern Punjab, western UP, MP, and Rajasthan.
1000–500	Later Vedic texts, namely the Brahmanas compiled in the upper Gangetic basin. Nearly 700 Painted Grey Ware sites existed. People used iron weapons and cultivated rice and wheat as the principal crops.
950	The Mahabharata war.
900–500	Faint beginnings of town attributed to Hastinapur.
800	Iron commonly used in western UP.
700	Earliest iron implements in eastern UP.
600	Upanishads compiled in Panchala and Videha.
500	Spread of Vedic people to Koshala and Videha.

(AD)	
2 C	Gautama Buddha depicted ploughing with oxen.
4 C	The *Mahabharata* was finally compiled.

14

Jainism and Buddhism

Numerous religious sects arose in the mid-Gangetic plains in sixth–fifth centuries BC, and we hear of as many as sixty-two of them. Many of these sects were based on regional customs and rituals practised by different peoples living in north-east India. Of these sects, Jainism and Buddhism were the most important, and they emerged as the most potent religious reform movements.

The Causes of Origin

Post-Vedic society was clearly divided into four varnas: brahmanas, kshatriyas, vaishyas, and shudras. Each varna was assigned well-defined functions. Though varna was based on birth, the two higher varnas captured power, prestige and privileges at the cost of the lower varnas. The brahmanas, who were allotted the functions of priests and teachers, claimed the highest status in society. They demanded several privileges, including those of receiving gifts and exemption from taxation and punishment. Post-Vedic texts show many instances of such privileges enjoyed by them. The kshatriyas, who ranked second in the varna hierarchy, fought and governed, and lived on the taxes collected from the peasants. The vaishyas were engaged in agriculture, cattle rearing, and trade. They were also the principal taxpayers. However, along with the two higher varnas, they were placed in the category of *dvija* or the twice-born. A *dvija* was entitled to wear the sacred thread and study the Vedas. The shudras were meant to serve the three higher varnas, and along with women were barred from Vedic studies. They worked as domestic slaves, agricultural slaves, craftsmen, and hired labourers in post-Vedic times. They were described as cruel, greedy, and thieving in their habits, and some of them were treated as untouchables. The higher the varna, the more privileged a person was; the lower the varna of an offender, the more severe was the punishment prescribed for him.

Naturally, the varna-divided society seems to have generated tensions. We have no means of ascertaining the reactions of the vaishyas and the shudras, but the kshatriyas, who functioned as rulers, reacted strongly against the ritualistic domination of the brahmanas, and seem to have led a kind of protest movement against the importance attached to birth in the varna system. The kshatriya reaction against the domination of the brahmanas, who claimed various privileges, was one of the causes of the origin of new religions. Vardhamana Mahavira, who really founded Jainism, and Gautama Buddha, who founded Buddhism, belonged to the kshatriya clan, and both disputed the authority of the brahmanas.

However, the real cause of the rise of these new religions lay in the spread of a new agricultural economy in north-eastern India. North-east India, including the regions of eastern UP and northern and southern Bihar, has about 100 cm of rainfall. Before these areas were colonized on a large scale, they were densely forested and could not be easily cleared without the aid of iron axes. Although some people lived in these areas prior to the sixth century BC, they used implements of bone, stone, and copper, and led a precarious life on the banks of lakes and rivers and river confluences where land was opened to settlement through the process of erosion and flooding. In the mid-Gangetic plains, large-scale habitations began towards the end of the sixth century BC, when iron began to be used in this area on some scale. Given the moist nature of the soil in this area, not many iron tools of the earliest times have survived, but a fair number of axes have been found from the layers of *c.* 600–500 BC. The use of iron tools made possible clearance, agriculture, and large settlements. The agricultural economy based on the iron ploughshare required the use of bullocks, and could not flourish without animal husbandry. However, the Vedic practice of killing cattle indiscriminately in sacrifices hampered the progress of the new agriculture. The cattle wealth was gradually decimated because the cows and bullocks were being killed in the course of the numerous Vedic sacrifices, and the non-Vedic tribal people living on the southern and eastern fringes of Magadha also killed cattle for food. However, if the new agrarian economy was to stabilize, this killing had to be halted.

Around 500 BC, we see the rise of a large number of cities in north-eastern India. We may refer, for example, to Kaushambi near Allahabad, Kusinagar (in Deoria district of UP), Varanasi, Vaishali (in the newly created district of the same name in north Bihar), Chirand (in Saran district), Taradih in Bodh-Gaya, Pataliputra, Rajgir (situated at a distance of about 100 km south-east of Patna), and Champa in Bhagalpur district. Both Vardhamana Mahavira and Gautama Buddha were associated with several of these cities. In them, many artisans and traders worked who used coins for the first time. The earliest coins relate to the fifth century BC, and they were generally of the punch-marked variety. They circulated for the first time in eastern UP and Bihar. The use of coins naturally facilitated trade and commerce, which added to the importance of the vaishyas. In the brahmanical society, the vaishyas, as we have noted, ranked third, after the brahmanas and kshatriyas. Naturally they sought a religion that would improve their position. Besides the kshatriyas, the vaishyas extended generous support to both Mahavira and Gautama Buddha. The merchants, called the *setthi*s, made handsome gifts to Gautama Buddha and his disciples. There were several reasons for it. First, Jainism and Buddhism at the initial stage did not attach any importance to the existing varna system. Second, they preached the gospel of non-violence, which would put an end to wars between different kingdoms and consequently promote trade and commerce. Third, the brahmanical law-books, called the Dharmasutras, decried lending money at an interest, and condemned those who lived on interest. Therefore, the vaishyas, who lent money because of the growing trade and commerce, were held in low esteem and looked for better social status.

On the other hand, we also notice a strong reaction against various forms of private property. Old-fashioned people did not like the use and accumulation of coins made certainly of silver and copper and possibly of gold. They disliked the new dwellings and clothes, new luxurious systems of transport, and disliked war and violence. The new forms of property created social inequalities, and caused misery and suffering to the mass of ordinary people. Therefore, the common people yearned to return to a primitive lifestyle, to the ascetic ideal which dispensed with the new forms of property and the new style of life. Both Jainism and Buddhism propounded simple, puritan, ascetic living. The Buddhist and Jaina monks were asked to forego the good things of life; were not permitted to touch gold and silver. They were allowed to accept only as much from their patrons as was sufficient to keep body and soul together. They, therefore, rebelled against the material advantages stemming from the new lifestyle of the Gangetic basin. In other words, we find the same kind of reaction against changes in material life in the mid-Gangetic plain in the sixth and fifth centuries BC as occurred against the changes brought about by the Industrial Revolution of modern times. As with the coming of the Industrial Revolution, many people yearned for a return to a pre-machine age lifestyle, so in ancient times, people yearned for a return to the pre-Iron Age style of life.

Vardhamana Mahavira and Jainism

The Jainas believed that their most important religious teacher Mahavira had twenty-three predecessors who were called *tirthankaras*. If Mahavira is taken as the last or the twenty-fourth *tirthankara*, the origin of Jainism would go back to the ninth century BC. Some Jainas believe that Rishabhadeve was the first *tirthankara* or teacher of Jainism, but he is associated with Ayodhya which was settled on any scale only by 500 BC. Most *tirthankaras*, up to the fifteenth, were supposed to have been born in eastern UP and Bihar, but their historicity is extremely doubtful. No part of the mid-Gangetic plains was settled on any scale until the fifth century BC. Evidently the mythology of the *tirthankaras*, most of whom were born in the mid-Gangetic basin and attained nirvana in Bihar, seems to have been created to endow Jainism with antiquity. The earliest important teachings of Jainism are attributed to Parshvanatha, the twenty-third *tirthankara*, who hailed from Banaras, abandoned royal life, and became an ascetic. However, it was his spiritual successor Vardhamana Mahavira who was the real founder of Jainism.

It is difficult to fix the exact dates of the birth and death of the great reformers Vardhamana Mahavira and Gautama Buddha. According to one tradition, Vardhamana Mahavira was born in 540 BC in a village near Vaishali, which is coterminous with Basarh in Vaishali district of north Bihar. His father Siddhartha was the head of a famous kshatriya clan, and his mother, Trishala, was the sister of the Lichchhavi chief Chetaka, whose daughter was married to Bimbisara. Thus, Mahavira's family was connected with the royal family of Magadh, and such high connections made it easy for him to approach princes and nobles in the course of his mission.

Initially, Mahavira led the life of a householder, but in his quest for truth he abandoned the world at the age of 30 and became an ascetic. He wandered for twelve years from place to place, not staying for over a day in a village and more than five days in a town. During the course of his long journey of twelve years it is said he never changed his clothes, and abandoned them altogether at the age of 42 when he attained omniscience (*kaivalya*). Through *kaivalya* he conquered misery and happiness. Because of this conquest he is known as Mahavira or the great hero or *jina*, that is, the conqueror, and his followers are known as Jainas. He propagated his religion for thirty years, and his mission took him to Koshala, Magadha, Mithila, Champa, and elsewhere. He passed away at the age of 72 in 468 BC at a place called Pavapuri near modern Rajgir.

According to another tradition he passed away in 527 BC, but, archaeology does not support his existence in the sixth century BC. The towns and other settlements with which he was associated did not come into existence till 500 BC.

Doctrines of Jainism

Jainism taught five doctrines: (i) do not commit violence, (ii) do not tell a lie, (iii) do not steal, (iv) do not hoard, and (v) observe continence (*brahmacharya*). It is said that only the fifth doctrine was added by Mahavira: the other four were taken over by him from previous teachers. Jainism attached the utmost importance to ahimsa or non-injury to living beings. Sometimes it led to absurd results, for some Jaina kings ordered the execution of persons guilty of killing animals. Although Parshva, Mahavira's predecessor, had asked his followers to cover the upper and lower portions of their bodies, Mahavira asked them to discard their clothing altogether. This implies that Mahavira asked his followers to lead a more austere life. Because of this, in later times, Jainism split into two sects: *shvetambaras* or those who donned white garments and *digambaras* who remained naked.

Jainism recognized the existence of the gods but placed them lower than the *jina*, and did not condemn the varna system as Buddhism did. According to Mahavira, a person is born in a high or in a lower varna as a consequence of his sins committed or virtues acquired by him in his previous birth. Mahavira looks for human values even in a chandala. In his opinion, by leading pure and meritorious life, members of the lower castes can achieve liberation. Jainism principally aims at the attainment of freedom from worldly bonds. No ritual is necessary for such liberation. It can be obtained through right knowledge, right faith, and right action. These three are considered to be the three jewels or *triratna* of Jainism.

Jainism prohibited the practice of war and even agriculture for its followers because both involve the killing of living beings. Eventually the Jainas principally confined themselves to trade and mercantile activities.

Spread of Jainism

In order to spread the teachings of Jainism, Mahavira organized an order of his followers that admitted both men and women. He preached his teachings in Prakrit, the language of the common people. It is said that his followers numbered 14,000, which is not a large figure. As Jainism did not very clearly differentiate itself from the brahmanical religion, it failed to attract the masses. Despite this, Jainism gradually spread into south and west India where the brahmanical religion was weak. According to a late tradition, the spread of Jainism in Karnataka is attributed to Chandragupta Maurya (322–298 BC). The emperor became a Jaina, gave up his throne, and spent the last years of his life in Karnataka as a Jaina ascetic, but this tradition is not corroborated by any other source. The second cause of the spread of Jainism in south India is said to have been the great famine that took place in Magadha 200 years after Mahavira's death. The famine lasted for twelve years, and in order to protect themselves, many Jainas migrated to the south under the leadership of Bhadrabahu, though the rest of them stayed back in Magadha under the leadership of Sthalabahu. The emigrant Jainas spread Jainism in south India. At the end of the famine, they returned to Magadha, where they developed differences with the local Jainas. Those who returned from the south claimed that even during the famine they had strictly observed the religious rules. They alleged too that the Jaina ascetics living in Magadha had violated those rules and had become lax. In order to sort out these differences and to compile the principal teachings of Jainism, a council was convened in Pataliputra, modern Patna, but the Jainas who had returned from the south boycotted it and refused to accept its decisions. From now onwards, the southerns began to be called *digambaras* and the Magadhans *shvetambaras*. The tradition that refers to drought as the cause relates to a later period and is considered doubtful. It is, however, beyond doubt that the Jainas were divided into two sects, but epigraphic evidence of the spread of Jainism in Karnataka is not earlier than the third century AD. In subsequent centuries, especially after the fifth century, numerous Jaina monastic establishments, called *basadis* sprang up in Karnataka and were granted land by the king for their support.

Jainism spread to Kalinga in Orissa in the fourth century BC, and in the first century BC it enjoyed the patronage of the Kalinga king Kharavela who had defeated the princes of Andhra and Magadha. In the second and first centuries BC, it also seems to have reached the southern districts of Tamil Nadu. In later centuries Jainism penetrated Malwa, Gujarat, and Rajasthan, and even now these areas have a substantial number of Jainas who are principally engaged in trade and commerce. Although Jainism did not win as much state patronage as did Buddhism and did not spread very rapidly in early times, it still retains its hold in the areas where it spread. On the other hand, Buddhism virtually disappeared from the Indian subcontinent.

Contribution of Jainism

Jainism made the first serious attempt to mitigate the evils of the varna order and the ritualistic Vedic religion. The early Jainas discarded the Sanskrit language principally patronized by the brahmanas. They adopted instead Prakrit, the language of the common people to preach their doctrines. Their religious literature was written in Ardhamagadhi, and the texts were eventually compiled in the sixth century AD in Gujarat at a place called Valabhi, a geat centre of education. The adoption of Prakrit by the Jainas helped the growth of this language and its literature. Many regional languages developed out of Prakrit, particularly Shauraseni from which the Marathi language developed. The Jainas composed the earliest important works in Apabhramsha and compiled its first grammar. Jaina literature comprises epics, Puranas, novels, and drama. A large percentage of Jaina writing is still in the form of manuscripts that have yet to be published and which are to be found in the Jaina shrines of Gujarat and Rajasthan. In early medieval times, the Jainas also made substantial use of Sanskrit and wrote many texts in it. Last but not the least, they contributed to the growth of Kannada, in which they wrote extensively.

Initially, like the Buddhists, the Jainas were not image worshippers. Later they began to worship Mahavira and also the twenty-three *tirthankaras*. Beautiful and sometimes massive images in stone were sculpted for this purpose, especially in Karnataka, Gujarat, Rajasthan, and MP. Jaina art in ancient times is not as rich as its Buddhist counterpart, but Jainism contributed substantially to art and architecture in medieval times.

Gautama Buddha and Buddhism

Gautama Buddha, or Siddhartha, was a contemporary of Mahavira. According to tradition he was born in 567 BC in a Shakya kshatriya family in Lumbini in Nepal near Kapilavastu, which is identified with Piprahwa in Basti district and is close to the foothills of Nepal. Gautama's father seems to have been the elected ruler of Kapilavastu, and headed the Shakya republican clan. His mother was a princess from the Koshalan dynasty. Thus, like Mahavira, Gautama too belonged to a noble family. Born in a republic, he also inherited some egalitarian beliefs.

From early childhood Gautama showed a meditative bent of mind. He was married early, but married life did not interest him. He was moved by the misery suffered by people in the world, and sought a solution. At the age of 29, like Mahavira, he left home. He wandered from place to place for about seven years and then attained enlightenment at the age of 35 at Bodh-Gaya under a *pipal* tree. From this time onwards he began to be called the Buddha or the enlightened one.

Gautama Buddha delivered his first sermon at Sarnath in Banaras. He undertook long journeys and carried his message far and wide. He had a very strong physique, and this enabled him to walk 20 to 30 km a day. He kept wandering, preaching, and meditating continually for forty years, resting only during the annual rainy season. During this long period he encountered many staunch supporters of rival sects, including the brahmanas, but defeated them in debates. His missionary activities did not discriminate between the rich and the poor, the high and the low, and man and woman. Gautama Buddha passed away at the age of 80 in 487 BC at a place called Kusinagara, coterminous with the village called Kasia in Deoria district in eastern UP. However, as in the case of Vardhamana Mahavira, the existence of Gautama Buddha in the sixth century BC is not supported by archaeological evidence. The cities Kaushambi, Shravasti, Varanasi, Vaishali, and Rajgriha, which the Buddha visited, did not assume any urban character until the fifth century BC.

Doctrines of Buddhism

The Buddha proved to be a practical reformer who took note of the realities of the day. He did not involve himself in fruitless controversies regarding the soul (*atman*) and Brahma which raged in his time, but addressed himself to worldly problems. He said that the world was full of sorrows and that people suffered on account of desires. If desires are conquered, nirvana is attained, that is, man is free from the cycle of birth and death.

Gautama Buddha recommended an eightfold path (*ashtangika marga*) for the elimination of human misery. This path is attributed to him in a text of about the third century BC. It comprised right observation, right determination, right speech, right action, right livelihood, right effort, right awareness, and right concern. If a person follows this eightfold path, he would free himself from the machinations of priests, and would reach his destination. Gautama taught that a person should avoid an excess of both luxury and austerity, and prescribed the middle path.

The Buddha also laid down a code of conduct for his followers on the same lines as those of the Jaina teachers. The principal tenets are: (i) do not commit violence, (ii) do not covet the property of others, (iii) do not use intoxicants, (iv) do not tell a lie, and (v) do not indulge in sexual misconduct and adultery. These teachings are common to the social conduct ordained by virtually all religions.

Features of Buddhism and the Causes of its Spread

Buddhism does not recognize the existence of god and soul. This can be seen as a kind of revolution in the history of Indian religions. As early Buddhism was not enmeshed in the claptrap of philosophical discussion, it appealed to the common people, and particularly won the support of the lower orders because it attacked the varna system. People were accepted by the Buddhist order without any consideration of caste, and women too were admitted to the sangha and thus brought on a par with men. In comparison with Brahmanism, Buddhism was liberal and democratic.

Buddhism particularly appealed to the people of the non-Vedic areas where it found virgin soil for conversion. The people of Magadha responded readily to Buddhism because they were looked down upon by the orthodox brahmanas. Magadha was placed outside the pale of the holy Aryavarta, the land of the Aryas, covering modern UP. The old tradition persists, and the people of north Bihar prefer not to be cremated south of the Ganges in Magadha.

The personality of the Buddha and the method adopted by him to preach his religion helped the spread of Buddhism. He sought to fight evil by goodness and hatred by love and refused to be provoked by slander and abuse. He maintained his poise and calm under difficult circumstances and tackled his opponents with wit and presence of mind. It is said that on one occasion an ignorant person abused him. The Buddha listened on silently, and when the person had ended his abuse, the Buddha asked: 'My friend, if a person does not accept a present what will happen to it?' His adversary replied: 'It remains with the person who has offered it.' The Buddha then said: 'My friend, I do not accept your abuse.'

The use of Pali, a form of Prakrit, which began around 500 BC, contributed to the spread of Buddhism. It facilitated the spread of Buddhist doctrines amongst the common people. Gautama Buddha also organized the sangha or the religious order, whose doors were open to all irrespective of caste, creed, and sex. However, slaves, soldiers, and debtors could not be admitted. The monks were required to observe the rules and regulations of the sangha faithfully. Once they were enrolled as members of the Buddhist church, they had to take the vow of continence, poverty, and faith. There are thus three principal elements in Buddhism: Buddha, dhamma, and sangha. As a result of organized preaching under the auspices of the sangha, Buddhism made rapid strides even during Buddha's lifetime. The monarchies of Magadha, Koshala, and Kaushambi, and several republican states and their people adopted this religion.

Two hundred years after the death of the Buddha, Ashoka, the famous Maurya king, embraced Buddhism. This was an epoch-making event. Through his missionaries Ashoka spread Buddhism into Central Asia, West Asia, and Sri Lanka, and thus transformed it into a world religion. Even today Sri Lanka, Burma (Myanmar), Tibet, and parts of China and Japan profess Buddhism. Although Buddhism disappeared from the land of its birth, it continues to hold ground in the countries of South Asia, South east Asia, and East Asia.

Causes of the Decline of Buddhism

By the twelfth century Buddhism became virtually extinct in India. It had continued to exist in an altered form in Bengal and Bihar till the eleventh century, but after that Buddhism almost completely vanished from India. What caused this? We find that at the outset every religion is inspired by the spirit of reform, but eventually it succumbs to the rituals and ceremonies it originally denounces. Buddhism underwent a similar metamorphosis. It became a victim to the evils of Brahmanism against which it had initially fought. To meet the Buddhist challenge, the brahmanas reformed their religion. They stressed the need to preserve the cattle wealth and assured women and shudras of admission to heaven. Buddhism, on the other hand, changed for the worse. Gradually the Buddhist monks were cut off from the mainstream of people's lives; they gave up Pali, the language of the people, and took to Sanskrit, the language of intellectuals. From the first century onwards, they practised idol worship on a large scale and received numerous offerings from devotees. The rich offerings supplemented by generous royal grants to the Buddhist monasteries made the life of monks easy. Some of the monasteries, such as Nalanda, collected revenue from as many as 200 villages. By the seventh century, the Buddhist monasteries had come to be dominated by ease-loving people and became centres of corrupt practices which had been prohibited by Gautama Buddha. The new form of Buddhism was known as Vajrayana. The enormous wealth of the monasteries with increasing sexual activity led to further degeneration. Buddhists began looking upon women as objects of lust. The Buddha is reported to have said to his favourite disciple Ananda: 'If women were not admitted into the monasteries Buddhism would have continued for one thousand years, but because this admission has been granted it will last only five hundred years.'

The brahmana ruler Pashyamitra Shunga is said to have persecuted the Buddhists. Several instances of persecution occur in the sixth–seventh centuries. The Huna king Mihirakula, who was a worshipper of Shiva, killed hundreds of Buddhists. The Shaivite Shashanka of Gauda felled the Bodhi tree at Bodh-Gaya where the Buddha had attained enlightenment. Hsuan Tsang states that 1600 stupas and monasteries were destroyed, and thousands of monks and lay followers killed; this may not be without some truth. The Buddhist reaction can be seen in some pantheons in which Buddhist deities trample brahmanical deities. In south India both the Shaivites and Vaishnavites bitterly opposed the Jainas and Buddhists in early medieval times. Such conflicts may have weakened Buddhism.

For their riches the monasteries came to be coveted by the Turkish invaders, becoming special targets of the invaders' greed. The Turks killed a large number of Buddhist monks in Bihar, although some of the monks managed to escape to Nepal and Tibet. In any event, by the twelfth century, Buddhism had virtually disappeared from the land of its birth.

Significance and Influence of Buddhism

Despite its disappearance as an organized religion, Buddhism left its impact on Indian society and economy. The Buddhists showed a keen awareness of the problems that faced the people of north-east India from about 500 BC. The iron ploughshare-based agriculture, trade, and the use of coins enabled the traders and nobles to accumulate wealth, and we hear of people possessing eighty *kotis* of wealth. All this naturally created sharp social and economic inequalities. Buddhism therefore advised people not to accumulate wealth. According to it, poverty breeds hatred, cruelty, and violence. To eradicate these evils, the Buddha taught that farmers should be provided with grain and other facilities, traders with wealth, and the unemployed with employment. These measures were recommended to eradicate poverty in the world. Buddhism also taught that if the poor gave alms to the monks, they would be born wealthy in the next world.

The code of conduct prescribed for the monks represents a reaction against the material conditions of north-east India in the fifth–fourth centuries BC. It imposes restrictions on the food, clothing, and sexual behaviour of the monks. They could not accept gold and silver, could not resort to sale and purchase. These rules were relaxed after the death of the Buddha, but the early rules suggest a return to a kind of primitive communism, a characteristic of the tribal society in which people did not practise trade and advanced agriculture. The code of conduct prescribed for monks partially reflects a revolt against the use of money, private property and luxurious living, that was prevalent in the fifth century BC in north-east India at a time when property and money were considered luxuries.

Although Buddhism tried to mitigate the evils resulting from the new material life in the fifth century BC, it also sought to consolidate the changes in the social and economic life of the people. The rule that debtors were not permitted to be members of the sangha helped the moneylenders and richer sections of society from whose clutches the debtors could not be saved. Similarly, the rule that slaves could not join the sangha helped slave owners. Thus, the rules and teachings of Gautama Buddha took full account of the new changes in the material life of the time and strengthened them ideologically.

Although the Buddhist monks had renounced the world and repeatedly criticized the greedy brahmanas, in several ways they resembled the brahmanas. Both of them did not participate directly in production, and lived on the alms or gifts given by society. They emphasized the virtues of carrying out family obligations, protecting private property, and respecting political authority. Both supported the social order based on classes; for the monks, however, the varna was based on action and attributes but for the brahmanas it was based on birth.

Undoubtedly the objective of Buddhist teaching was to secure the salvation of the individual or nirvana. Those who found it difficult to adjust themselves to the break-up of the old egalitarian society and the rise of gross social inequalities on account of private property were provided with some way of escape, but it was confined to the monks. No escape was provided for the lay followers, who were taught to come to terms with the existing situation.

Buddhism made an important impact on society by keeping its doors open to women and shudras. As both women and shudras were placed in the same category by Brahmanism, they were neither given the sacred thread nor allowed to read the Vedas. Their conversion to Buddhism freed them from such marks of inferiority. Buddism did not deprecate manual labour. In a second-century sculpture from Bodh-Gaya, the Buddha is depicted ploughing with oxen.

With its emphasis on non-violence and the sanctity of animal life, Buddhism boosted the cattle wealth of the country. The earliest Buddhist text, *Suttanipata*, declares cattle to be givers of food, beauty, strength, and happiness (*annada, vannada, balada, sukhada*), and thus pleads for their protection. This teaching came, significantly, at a time when the non-Aryans slaughtered animals for food, and the Aryans in the name of religion. The brahmanical insistence on the sacredness of the cow and non-violence was apparently derived from Buddhist teachings.

Buddhism created and developed a new awareness in the field of intellect and culture. It taught the people not to take things for granted but to argue and judge them on merits. To a certain degree, the place of superstition was taken by logic, promoting rationalism among people. In order to preach the doctrines of the new religion, the Buddhists compiled a new type of literature, enormously enriching Pali by their writings. Early Pali literature can be divided into three categories. The first contains the sayings and teachings of the Buddha, the second deals with the rules to be observed by members of the sangha, and the third presents a philosophical exposition of the dhamma.

In the first three centuries of the Christian era, by blending Pali and Sanskrit, the Buddhists created a new language which is called Hybrid Sanskrit. The literary activities of the Buddhist monks continued even in the Middle Ages, and some famous Apabhramsa writings in east India were composed by them. The Buddhist monasteries developed as great centres of learning, and can be called residential universities. Mention may be made of Nalanda and Vikramashila in Bihar, and Valabhi in Gujarat.

Buddhism left its mark on the art of ancient India. The first human statues worshipped in India were probably those of the Buddha. Faithful devotees of the religion portrayed the various events in the life of the Buddha in stone. The panels at Bodh-Gaya in Bihar and at Sanchi and Bharhut in MP are illuminating examples of artistic activity. From the first century onwards, panel images of Gautama Buddha began to be made. The Greek and Indian sculptors worked together to create a new form of art on the north-west frontier of India known as Gandhara art. The images made in this region betray Indian as well as foreign influence. For the residence of the monks, rooms were hewn out of the rocks, and thus began the cave architecture in the Barabar hills in Gaya and also in western India around Nasik. Buddhist art flourished in the Krishna delta in the south and in Mathura in the north.

Chronology

(BC)	
Pre-600	People in north-eastern India lived alongside lakes and river banks and used stone, bone, and copper tools.
End of the 6 C	Rise in habitations in the mid-Gangetic plains.
600–500	A few iron axes in the mid-Gangetic plains.
6–5 C	Reaction against changes in material life. Numerous religious sects arose in the mid-Gangetic plains.
567	Traditional birth date of Gautama Buddha.
540	Mahavira's birth according to one tradition.
527	Traditional death of Mahavira.

500	Kaushambi, Shravasti, Varanasi, Vaishali, and Rajgriha.
487	The Buddha's death at the age of 80 years according to one tradition.
468	According to one tradition, Mahavira's death at the age of 72 years.
4 C	Jainism spread to Kalinga in Orissa.
322–298	According to a late tradition, spread of Buddhism in Karnataka attributed to Chandragupta Maurya.
3 C	Buddha's eightfold path mentioned in a text.
	Spread of Jainism in south India because of a famine in Magadh.
2–1 C	Jainism reached the southern districts of Tamil Nadu.
1 C	Jainism enjoyed the patronage of the Kalinga king Kharavela.
(AD)	
1 C onwards	Buddhists practised idol worship; panel images of Buddha began to be made.
3 C	Jainism in Karnataka according to epigraphic evidence.
6 C	The Jaina texts, written in Ardhamagadhi, finally compiled at Valabhi in Gujarat.
7 C	Buddhist monasteries, dominated by ease-loving people, became centres of practices prohibited by Gautama Buddha.
12 C	Continuing brahmanical attacks (both Shaivite and Vaishnavite), and Turkish greed for monastic wealth in Bihar Sharif destroyed Buddhism. Monks fled to Nepal and Tibet.

15

Territorial States and the Rise of Magadha

Conditions for the Rise of Large States

From the sixth century BC onwards, the increasing use of iron in eastern UP and western Bihar created conditions for the formation of large territorial states. Armed with iron weapons, the warrior class now played an important role. The new agricultural tools and implements enabled the peasants to produce far more food grains than they required for consumption. The extra produce could be collected by the princes to meet their military and administrative needs. The surplus could also be made available to the towns that had sprung up in fifth century BC. These material advantages naturally enabled the people to remain on their land, and also to expand at the cost of the neighbouring areas. The rise of large states with towns as their base of operations strengthened the territorial idea. People owed strong allegiance to the *janapada* or the territory to which they belonged rather than to their *jana* or tribe.

The *Mahajanapadas*

We may recall that a few *janapadas* arose towards the end of the Vedic-period. However, with progress in agriculture and settlement by 500 BC, they became a common feature. Around 450 BC, over forty *janapadas* covering even Afghanistan and south-eastern Central Asia are mentioned by Panini. However, the major part of southern India was excluded. The Pali texts show that the *janapadas* grew into *mahajanapadas*, that is large states or countries. These texts mention sixteen of them. Nine of them also occur in Panini not as *mahajanapadas* but as *janapadas*. In the age of the

Buddha we find sixteen large states called *mahajanapadas*. Most of these states arose in the upper and mid-Gangetic plains, including the doab area covered by the Ganges, Yamuna, and their tributaries. They were mostly situated north of the Vindhyas and extended from the north-west frontier to Bihar. Of these, Magadha, Koshala, Vatsa, and Avanti seem to have been powerful. Beginning from the east, we hear of the kingdom of Anga which covered the modern districts of Monghyr and Bhagalpur. It had its capital at Champa, which shows signs of habitation in the fifth century BC, and there is a mud fort dating to that century. Eventually the kingdom of Anga was swallowed by its powerful neighbour Magadha.

Magadha embraced the former districts of Patna, Gaya, and parts of Shahabad, and grew to be the leading state of the time. Its earlier capital was Rajgir, and later Pataliputra. Both were fortified, and show signs of habitation around the fifth century BC. North of the Ganges, in Tirhut division lay the state of the Vajjis which included eight clans. However, the most powerful dynasty was that of the Lichchhavis with their capital at Vaishali which is coterminous with the village of Basarh in Vaishali district. The Puranas push the antiquity of Vaishali to a much earlier period, but archaeologically Basarh was not settled until the sixth century BC.

Further west we find the kingdom of Kashi with its capital at Varanasi. Excavations at Rajghat show that the earliest habitations started around 500 BC, and the city was enclosed by mud embankments at about the same time. Initially Kashi appears to have been the most powerful of the states, but eventually it succumbed to the power of Koshala.

Koshala embraced the area occupied by eastern UP and had its capital at Shravasti, which is coterminous with Sahet–Mahet on the borders of Gonda and Bahraich districts of UP. Diggings indicate that Sahet–Mahet was barely settled in the sixth century BC, but we see the beginnings of a mud fort. Koshala had an important city called Ayodhya which is associated with the story in the *Ramayana*. Excavations however show that it was not settled on any scale before the fifth century BC. Koshala also included the tribal republican territory of the Shakyas of Kapilavastu. The capital of Kapilavastu is identified with Piprahwa in Basti district. Habitation at Piprahwa did not occur earlier than *c*. 500 BC. Lumbini, which is situated at a distance of 15 km from Piprahwa in Nepal, served as another capital of the Shakyas. In an Ashokan inscription, it is called the birthplace of Gautama Buddha.

In the neighbourhood of Koshala lay the republican clan of the Mallas, whose territory touched the northern border of Vajji state. One of the capitals of the Mallas was at Kushinara where Gautama Buddha passed away. Kushinara is coterminous with Kasia in Deoria district.

Further west was the kingdom of the Vatsas, along the bank of the Yamuna, with its capital at Kaushambi near Allahabad. The Vatsas were a Kuru clan who had shifted from Hastinapur and settled at Kaushambi. Kaushambi was chosen because of its location near the confluence of the Ganga and the Yamuna. In the fifth century BC, it had a mud fortification, as excavations reveal.

We also hear of the older states of the Kurus and the Panchalas which were situated in western UP, but they no longer enjoyed the political significance they had attained in the later Vedic period.

In central Malwa and the adjoining parts of MP lay the state of Avanti. It was divided into two parts, the northern part with its capital at Ujjain, and the southern part at Mahishamati. Both these towns became fairly important from the fifth century BC onwards, though eventually Ujjain surpassed Mahishamati. It developed large-scale working in iron and erected strong fortifications.

The political history of India from the sixth century BC onwards was one of struggles among these states for supremacy. Eventually the kingdom of Magadha emerged as the most powerful and founded an empire. In the north-west, Gandhara and Kamboja were important *mahajanapadas*. Kamboja is called a *janapada* in Panini and a *mahajanapada* in the Pali texts. It was located in Central Asia in the Pamir area which largely covered modern Tajikistan. In Tajikistan, the remains of a horse, chariots and spoked wheels, cremation, and svastika, which are associated with the Indo-Aryan speakers dating to between 1500 and 1000 BC, have been found. Around 500 BC, both Sanskrit and Pali were spoken in Kamboja, which was connected with Pataliputra by the *uttarapatha*.

The Rise and Growth of the Magadhan Empire

Magadha came into prominence under the leadership of Bimbisara of the Haryanka dynasty and a contemporary of the Buddha. He began the policy of conquest and aggression which ended with the Kalinga war of Ashoka. Bimbisara acquired Anga and placed it under the viceroyalty of his son

Ajatashatru at Champa. He also strengthened his position by marriage alliances. He had three wives. Bimbisara's first wife was the daughter of the king of Koshala and the sister of Prasenajit, the son and successor of the Koshalan king. The Koshalan bride brought Bimbisara as dowry a Kashi village yielding a revenue of 100,000 which suggests that revenues were collected in terms of coins. The marriage bought off the hostility of Koshala and gave Bimbisara a free hand in dealing with the other states. His second wife, Chellana, was a Lichchhavi princess from Vaishali who gave birth to Ajatashatru, and his third wife was the daughter of the chief of the Madra clan of Punjab. Marriage relations with the different princely families lent enormous diplomatic prestige and paved the way for the expansion of Magadha westward and northward.

Magadha's most serious rival was Avanti with its capital at Ujjain. Its king, Chanda Pradyota Mahasena, fought Bimbisara, but eventually the two thought it wise to make up. Later, when Pradyota was afflicted by jaundice, at the Avanti king's request, Bimbisara sent the royal physician Jivaka to Ujjain. Bimbisara is also said to have received an embassy and a letter from the ruler of Gandhara with which Pradyota had fought unsuccessfully. Therefore, through his conquests and diplomacy, Bimbisara made Magadha the dominant state in the sixth century BC. His kingdom is said to have consisted of 80,000 villages, a number which sounds conventional.

The earliest capital of Magadha was at Rajgir, which was called Girivraja at that time. It was surrounded by five hills, the openings in which were closed by stone walls on all sides, which made it impregnable.

According to the Buddhist chronicles, Bimbisara ruled for fifty-two years, roughly from 544 to 492 BC. He was succeeded by his son Ajatashatru (492–60 BC). Ajatashatru killed his father and seized the throne for himself. His reign saw the high watermark of the Bimbisara dynasty. He fought two wars and made preparations for the third. Throughout his reign he pursued an aggressive policy of expansion. This provoked a combination of Kashi and Koshala against him. There began a prolonged conflict between Magadha and Koshala. Eventually Ajatashatru got the best of the war, and the Koshalan king was compelled to purchase peace by giving his daughter in marriage to Ajatashatru and leaving him in sole possession of Kashi.

Ajatashatru was no respecter of relations. Although his mother was a Lichchhavi princess, this did not prevent him from making war against Vaishali. The excuse was that the Lichchhavis were the allies of Koshala. He sowed dissension within the ranks of the Lichchhavis and eventually ended their independence by invading their territory and by defeating them in battle. This took him full sixteen years. He was eventually successful in doing so because of a war engine like a catapult which was used to hurl stones. He also possessed a chariot to which a mace was attached, and this facilitated mass killings. The Magadhan empire was thus enlarged with the addition of Kashi and Vaishali.

Ajatashatru faced a stronger rival in the ruler of Avanti. Avanti had defeated the Vatsas of Kaushambi and now threatened an invasion of Magadha. To meet this threat Ajatashatru began the fortification of Rajgir, the remains of the walls of which can still be seen. However, the invasion did not materialize during his lifetime.

Ajatashatru was succeeded by Udayin (460–44 BC). His reign is important because he is said to have built a fort at the confluence of the Ganges and Son at Patna. This was done because Patna lay at the centre of the Magadhan kingdom, which now extended from the Himalayas in the north to the hills of Chhotanagpur in the south. Patna's position, as will be seen later, was crucially strategic.

Udayin was succeeded by the dynasty of Shishunagas, who temporarily moved the capital to Vaishali. Their greatest achievement was the destruction of the power of Avanti with its capital at Ujjain. This brought to an end the 100-year old rivalry between Magadha and Avanti. From now onwards Avanti became a part of the Magadhan empire and continued to be so till the end of Maurya rule.

The Shishunagas were succeeded by the Nandas, who proved to be the most powerful rulers of Magadha. So great was their power that Alexander, who invaded Punjab at that time, dared not move towards the east. The Nandas extended the Magadhan power by conquering Kalinga from where they brought an image of *jina* as a victory trophy. All this took place during the reign of Mahapadma Nanda. This ruler claimed to be *ekarat,* the sole sovereign who had destroyed all the other ruling princes. It seems that he captured not only Kalinga but also Koshala which had probably rebelled against him.

The Nandas were fabulously rich and enormously powerful. It is said that they maintained 200,000 infantry, 60,000 cavalry, and 3000 to 6000 war elephants. Such a huge army could be maintained only through an effective taxation system. Obviously these considerations prevented Alexander from advancing against the Nandas.

The later Nandas proved to be weak and unpopular. Their rule in Magadha was supplanted by that of the Maurya dynasty under which the Magadhan empire reached the apex of glory.

Causes of Magadha's Success

The march of the Magadhan empire during the two centuries preceding the rise of the Mauryas is like the march of the Iranian empire during the same period. The formation of the largest state in India during this period was the work of several enterprising and ambitious rulers such as Bimbisara, Ajatashatru, and Mahapadma Nanda. They employed all the means in their power, fair and foul, to enlarge their kingdoms and to strengthen their states. This, however, was not the only reason for the expansion of Magadha.

There were some other important ones. Magadha enjoyed an advantageous geographical position in the age of iron, because the richest iron deposits were situated not far away from Rajgir, the earliest capital of Magadha. The ready availability of the rich iron ores in the neighbourhood enabled the Magadhan princes to equip themselves with effective weapons which were not easily available to their rivals. Iron mines are also located in eastern MP, and were not far from the kingdom of the Avanti with their capital at Ujjain. Around 500 BC, iron was certainly forged and smelted in Ujjain, and probably the smiths manufactured weapons of good quality. On account of this Avanti proved to be Magadha's most serious competitor for supremacy in north India, and Magadha took about a hundred years to subjugate Ujjain.

Magadha enjoyed certain other advantages. The two capitals of Magadha, the first at Rajgir and the second at Pataliputra, were situated at very strategic points. Rajgir was surrounded by a group of five hills, and so it was impregnable in those days when there was no easy means of storming citadels such as cannons. In the fifth century BC, the Magadhan princes shifted their capital from Rajgir to Pataliputra, which occupied a pivotal position commanding communications on all sides. Pataliputra was situated at the confluence of the Ganges, the Gandak, and the Son, and a fourth river called the Ghaghra joined the Ganges not far from Pataliputra. In pre-industrial days, when communications were difficult, the army could move north, west, south, and east by following the courses of the rivers. Also, the position of Patna itself was rendered invulnerable because it was virtually surrounded by rivers. While the Ganges and the Son girdled it on the north and west, the Poonpun girdled it on the south and east. Pataliputra was therefore a true water fort (*jaladurga*).

Magadha lay at the centre of the mid-Gangetic plains, the Ganges providing a means of both transport and agricultural facilities. As most of the *mahajanapadas* were located in the Gangetic plains, they could be reached by navigating the rivers. There was also an abundance of timber as can be seen in the palisades of the sixth century BC found south of Patna. Megasthenes speaks of the wooden walls and houses in Pataliputra. Thus boats could be easily manufactured and they played an important part in promoting the advance of Magadha towards the east and the west. Similarly, environmental factors conducive to agriculture helped Magadha. The alluvium, once cleared of jungles, proved immensely fertile. Given the heavy rainfall, the area could be made productive even without irrigation. The countryside produced varieties of paddy, which are mentioned in the early Buddhist texts. This area was far more productive than the areas to the west of Allahabad. This naturally enabled the peasants to produce a considerable surplus, which could be mopped up by the rulers in the form of taxes.

The princes of Magadha also benefited from the rise of towns and use of metal money. A Pali text speaks of twenty towns in the age of the Buddha. Most of them were located in the mid-Gangetic plains. They contributed to trade and commerce in north-east India. This enabled the princes to levy tolls on the sale of commodities and accumulate wealth to pay and maintain their army.

Magadha enjoyed a special advantage in military organization. Although the Indian states were well acquainted with the use of horses and chariots, it was Magadha which first used elephants on a large scale in its wars against its neighbours. The eastern part of the country could supply elephants to the princes of Magadha, and we learn from Greek sources that the Nandas maintained 6000 elephants. Elephants could be used to storm fortresses and to march across marshy and other areas lacking roads and other means of transport.

Finally, we may refer to the unorthodox character of Magadhan society. It was inhabited by the Kiratas and Magadhas, who were held in low esteem by the orthodox brahmanas. It however underwent a happy ethnic admixture with the coming of the Vedic people. As it had been recently Vedicized, it demonstrated a greater enthusiasm for expansion than the kingdoms that had been brought under the Vedic influence earlier. For all these reasons,

Magadha succeeded in defeating the other kingdoms and in founding the first empire in India.

Chronology

(BC)	
6 C	Basarh (Vaishali) was not settled.
6 C onwards	Struggles among large states (*mahajanapadas*).
544–492	Bimbisara ruled Magadha.
500	Habitation at Piprahwa, capital of Kapilavastu, not earlier than this date.
5 C	Champa evidences habitation and a mud fort.
	Kaushambi also had a mud fortification. Surplus food grains available to towns on the basis of iron tool agriculture.
492–60	Ajatashatru's rule in Magadha.
460–44	Udayin's reign in Magadha. The fort on the confluence of the Ganges and the Son built by him.

16

Iranian and Macedonian Invasions

Iranian Invasion

In north-east India, smaller principalities and republics gradually merged with the Magadhan empire. North-west India, however, presented a different picture in the sixth century BC. Several small principalities, such as those of the Kambojas, Gandharas, and Madras fought one another. This area did not have any powerful kingdom like that of Magadha to weld the warring communities into one organized kingdom. As the area was fertile and rich in natural resources, it attracted the attention of its neighbours. In addition, it could be easily penetrated through the passes in the Hindu Kush.

The Achaemenian rulers of Iran, who expanded their empire at the same time as the Magadhan princes, took advantage of the political disunity on the north-west frontier. The Iranian ruler Darius penetrated north-west India in 516 BC and annexed the Punjab, west of the Indus, and Sindh. This area was converted into the twentieth province or satrapy of Iran, which had a total number of twenty-eight satrapies. The Indian satrapy included Sindh, the north-west frontier, and the part of Punjab that lay to the west of the Indus. It was the most fertile and populous part of the empire. It paid a tribute of 360 talents of gold, which accounted for one-third of the total revenue Iran received from its Asian provinces. The Indian subjects were also enrolled in the Iranian army. Xerxes, Darius's successor, employed Indians in the long war against the Greeks. It appears that India continued to be a part of the Iranian empire till its invasion by Alexander.

Results of the Contact

The Indo-Iranian contact lasted for about 200 years. It gave an impetus to Indo-Iranian trade and commerce. The cultural results were more significant.

Iranian scribes brought into India a form of writing that came to be known as the Kharoshthi script. It was written from right to left like the Arabic. Some Ashokan inscriptions in north-west India were written in the third century BC in this script, which continued to be used in India till the third century AD. Iranian coins are also found in the north-west frontier region which points to the exchange of goods with Iran. It is, however, wrong to think that the punch-marked coins came into use in India as a result of contact with Iran. However, Iranian influence on Maurya sculpture is clearly perceptible. The monuments of Ashoka's time, especially the bell-shaped capitals, owed something to the Iranian models. Iranian influence may also be traced in the preamble to Ashoka's edicts as well as in certain terms used in them. For instance, for the Iranian term *dipi,* the Ashokan scribe used the term *lipi.* Also it appears that through the Iranians, the Greeks learnt about the great wealth of India, which whetted their greed and led to Alexander's invasion of India.

Alexander's Invasion

In the fourth century BC, the Greeks and the Iranians fought for the supremacy of the world. Under the leadership of Alexander of Macedonia, the Greeks eventually destroyed the Iranian empire. Alexander conquered not only Asia Minor and Iraq but also Iran. From Iran he marched to India, obviously attracted by its great wealth. Herodotus, who is called the father of history, and other Greek writers had painted India as a fabulous land, which tempted Alexander to invade it. Alexander also had a strong passion for geographical inquiry and natural history. He had heard that the Caspian Sea continued on the eastern side of India. He was also inspired by the mythical exploits of past conquerors whom he wanted to emulate and surpass.

The political condition of north-west India suited his plans. The area was parcelled out into many independent monarchies and tribal republics, which were strongly wedded to the soil and had a fierce dedication to the principality in which they lived. Alexander found it easy to conquer these principalities one by one. Among the rulers of these territories, two were well known: Ambhi, the prince of Taxila, and Porus whose kingdom lay between the Jhelum and the Chenab. Together they might have effectively resisted Alexander's advance, but they could not put up a joint front; and the Khyber pass remained unguarded.

Following the conquest of Iran, Alexander moved on to Kabul, from where he marched to India through the Khyber pass in 326 BC. It took him five months to reach the Indus. Ambhi, the ruler of Taxila, readily submitted to the invader, augmenting Alexander's army and replenishing his treasure. When he reached the Jhelum, Alexander encountered the first and the strongest resistance from Porus. Although Alexander defeated Porus, he was impressed by the bravery and courage of the Indian prince. He therefore restored his kingdom to him and made him his ally. He then advanced as far as the Beas river. He wanted to move still further eastward, but his army refused to accompany him. The Greek soldiers had grown war-weary, and diseased. The hot climate of India and ten years of continuous campaigning had made them terribly homesick. They had also had a taste of Indian fighting qualities on the banks of the Indus, which made them desist from advancing further. As the Greek historian Arrian tells us: 'In the art of war the Indians were far superior to the other nations inhabiting the area at that time.' In particular, the Greek soldiers were told of a formidable power on the Ganges. This was obviously the kingdom of Magadha ruled by the Nandas who maintained an army far outnumbering Alexander's. So, despite the repeated appeals by Alexander for their advance, the Greek soldiers refused to budge. Alexander lamented: 'I am trying to rouse the hearts that are disloyal and crushed with craven fears.' The king who had never known defeat at the hands of his enemies had to accept defeat from his own men. He was forced to retreat, and his dream of an eastern empire remained unfulfilled. On his return march Alexander vanquished many small republics until he reached the end of the Indian frontier. He remained in India for nineteen months (326–5 BC) of continual battle, leaving him barely any time to organize his conquests. Still, he made some arrangements. Most of the conquered states were restored to their rulers who submitted to his authority. His own territorial possessions were however divided into three parts and placed under three Greek governors. He also founded a number of cities to maintain his power in this area.

Effects of Alexander's Invasion

Alexander's invasion provided the first occasion when ancient Europe came into close contact with ancient South Asia. Alexander's Indian campaign was a triumphant success. He added to his empire an Indian province which was much larger than that conquered by Iran. However, the Greek possessions in India were soon lost to the Maurya rulers.

The most important outcome of this invasion was the establishment of direct contact between India and Greece in various fields. Alexander's campaign opened up four distinct routes by land and sea, paving the way for Greek merchants and craftsmen, and increasing the existing facilities for trade.

Although we hear of some Greeks living on the north-west even prior to Alexander's invasion, the invasion multiplied Greek settlements in this area. The most important of these were the city of Alexandria in the Kabul region, Boukephala on the Jhelum, and Alexandria in Sindh. Although the entire area was conquered by the Mauryas, the Greeks continued to live under both Chandragupta Maurya and Ashoka.

Alexander was deeply interested in the geography of the mysterious ocean which he saw for the first time at the mouth of the Indus. He therefore dispatched his new fleet under his friend Nearchus to explore the coast and search for harbours from the mouth of the Indus to that of the Euphrates. As a result Alexander's historians left valuable geographical accounts and also clearly dated records of Alexander's campaign, which enable us to definitively establish Indian chronology for subsequent events. Alexander's historians also provide us with important information about the social and economic conditions of the time. They tell us about the sati system, the sale of girls in marketplaces by poor parents, and the fine breed of oxen in north-west India. Alexander sent from there 200,000 oxen to Macedonia for use in Greece. The art of carpentry was the most flourishing craft in India, and carpenters built chariots, boats, and ships.

By destroying the power of petty states in north-west India, Alexander's invasion paved the way for the expansion of the Maurya empire in that area. According to tradition, Chandragupta Maurya, who founded the Maurya empire, had seen something of the working of Alexander's military machine and had acquired some knowledge that helped him to destroy the power of the Nandas.

Chronology

(BC)

6 C	In north-east India, the independent principalities and republics merged with the Magadha empire.

516	The Iranian ruler Darius annexed Punjab and Sindh.
4 C	The Greeks conquered the Iranian empire.
326	Alexander invaded India.
326–5	Alexander remained in India for nineteen months.
3 C–AD 3 C	Kharoshthi script brought by Iranian scribes to India.

17

State Structure and the Varna System in the Age of the Buddha

Second Urbanization

A picture of material life in north India, especially in eastern UP and Bihar, can be drawn on the basis of the Pali texts and the Sanskrit Sutra literature in combination with archaeological material. Archaeologically, the fifth century BC marks the beginning of the Northern Black Polished Ware (NBPW) phase in the Gangetic plains, and this was a very glossy, shining type of pottery. This pottery was made of very fine material and apparently served as tableware for the rich. In association with this pottery are found iron implements, especially those meant for crafts and agriculture. This phase also saw the beginning of metal money. The use of burnt bricks and ring wells began in the middle of the NBPW phase, that is, in the third century BC.

Studies of the doab sites show that Chalcolithic settlements started in the black-and-red ware phase in pre-PGW times, and increased substantially in the PGW phase. A survey of Kanpur district shows that the settled area in the PGW phase was thrice the area in the black-and-red ware phase. Also, this settled area expanded over two and a half times during the NBPW phase. As settlements expanded, the population kept increasing. Thus, the NBPW phase, starting around 500 BC, saw a considerable increase in both settlements and population.

The NBPW phase marked the beginning of the second urbanization in India. The Harappan towns disappeared in 1900 BC. Following that, for about 1500 years, no towns were established in India. However, from about 1200 BC we notice settlements in the doab and the neighbouring areas. We find two types of settlements in the lower doab in 1000–600 BC, based on

MAP 7 Distribution of Northern Black Polished Ware. *Courtesy ASI*

size and location. In the same area and on the same basis, four types of settlements are located some parts. This settlement hierarchy is regarded as the most important indicator of urbanization. Large settlements may enjoy some advantages over the smaller ones, but without crafts, coins, trade, and agricultural surplus even a large settlement cannot grow into a town. Towns arose in the mid-Gangetic basin in the fifth century BC, and thus a second urbanization began in India. Many towns mentioned in the Pali and Sanskrit texts, such as Kaushambi, Shravasti, Shringaverapur, Ayodhya, Kapilavastu, Varanasi, Vaishali, Rajgir, Pataliputra, and Champa have been excavated, and in each case signs of habitation and mud structures relating to the early NBPW phase or to the middle period of it have been found. Wooden palisades have been found in Patna, and these possibly relate to pre-Maurya times. Relating to the seventh–sixth centuries BC, these are the earliest wooden enclosures in the mid-Gangetic plains. The houses were mostly made of mud brick, and wood, which naturally disintegrated in the moist climate of the mid-Gangetic basin. Although seven-storeyed palaces are mentioned in the Pali texts, these have not been discovered anywhere. The structures that have so far been excavated are generally unimpressive, though together with the other material remains they indicate a great increase in population in comparison to the PGW settlements.

Many towns were seats of government, but whatever be the causes of their origin, they eventually became markets and came to be inhabited by artisans and merchants. The city of Champa near Bhagalpur is called Vaniyagama in a Prakrit text, and means a settlement of merchants. Some places were centres of artisans: Saddalaputta at Vaishali had 500 potters' shops. Both artisans and merchants were organized into guilds under their respective headmen.

We hear of eighteen guilds of artisans but only the guilds of smiths, carpenters, leather workers, and painters are specified. Both artisans and merchants lived in fixed localities in towns. We hear of *vessa*s or merchants' streets in Varanasi, and of the street of ivory workers. Thus, specialization in crafts developed on the strength of the guild system as well as localization. Generally crafts were hereditary, and the son learned his family trade from the father.

The products of crafts were transported by merchants over long distances. We repeatedly hear of 500 cartloads of goods. These contained fine textiles, ivory objects, pots, and the like. All the important cities of the period were situated on river banks and trade routes, and connected with one another. Shravasti was linked with both Kaushambi and Varanasi. The latter was considered to be a great centre of trade in the age of the Buddha. The route from Shravasti passed eastward and southward through Kapilavastu and Kushinara (Kasia) and linked to Vaishali. Traders crossed the Ganges near Patna and travelled to Rajgir, and also via this river to Champa. If we are to believe the Jataka tales, the traders of Koshala and Magadha went via Mathura as far north as Taxila. Similarly, from Mathura they travelled southward and westward to Ujjain and the Gujarat coast.

Trade was facilitated by the use of money. The coin or metal money bearing the stamp of an authority was invented in the seventh century BC in Lydia in Asia Minor. How it was first introduced in India is not clear. The terms *nishka* and *satamana* in the Vedic texts are taken to be names of coins, but they seem to have been prestige objects made of metal. It appears that in Vedic times, exchange was conducted through barter, and the mutual gift system served as a mode of exchange in pre-Buddhist times. Sometimes cattle served the purpose of currency. Coins made of metal appear first in the age of Gautama Buddha. The earliest were made largely of silver, though a few copper coins also existed. They are called punch-marked because pieces of silver and copper were punched with certain marks, such as a hill, tree, fish, bull, elephant, and crescent. In Maurya and later times cast coins and die-struck coins of different metals were also used. The earliest hoards of coins have been found in eastern UP and Magadha, although some early coins have also been found in Taxila. The Pali texts indicate plentiful use of money and show that coins were used to pay wages and buy goods. The use of money had become so universal that even the price of a dead mouse was estimated in it.

By 300 BC we notice full-fledged urbanization that led to a great increase in population. It is estimated that 270,000 people lived in Pataliputra, 60,000 in Mathura, 48,000 in Vidisha or modern Besnagar and Vaishali, 40,000 in Kaushambi and old Rajgir, and 38,000 in Ujjain. Such sizable populations cannot be suggested for earlier times.

Urbanization strengthened the state, increased trade, and promoted reading and writing. After the end of the Harappan culture, writing probably began a couple of centuries before Ashoka. The earliest records have been destroyed, probably because they were written on wood and similar perishable material. Writing led to the compilation not only of laws and rituals but also facilitated bookkeeping, which was so essential to trade, tax-collection, and the maintenance of a large professional army. The period produced texts dealing with sophisticated measurement (Sulvasutras), which presuppose writing and which may have helped in the demarcation of fields and houses.

Rural Economy

Although rural settlements of the NBPW phase have not been excavated, sherds of this ware have been found at over 400 sites in the plains of Bihar and those of eastern and central UP. However, the NBPW also extended over MP and Maharashtra. We cannot think of the beginning of crafts, commerce, and urbanization in the mid-Gangetic basin without a strong rural base. Princes, priests, artisans, traders, administrators, military personnel, and numerous other functionaries could not live in towns unless taxes, tributes, and tithes were available in sufficient measure to support them. Non-agriculturists living in towns had to be fed by agriculturists living in villages. In return, artisans and traders living in towns made tools, cloth, and the like available to the rural folk. We hear of a village trader depositing 500 ploughs with a town merchant, and these were evidently iron ploughshares. From the NBPW phase in Kaushambi, iron tools consisting of axes, adzes, knives, razors, nails, sickles, etc., have been discovered. A substantial number of them relate to the layers of about the fifth–fourth centuries BC, and were probably meant for the use of the peasants who bought them with cash or kind.

Numerous villages are mentioned in the Pali texts, and towns seem to have been situated amidst clusters of villages. It seems that the nucleated rural settlement in which all the people settled at one place with their agricultural lands mostly outside the settlement were first established in the mid-Gangetic plains during the age of Gautama Buddha. The Pali texts speak of three types of villages. The first category included the typical village inhabited by various castes and communities, and these villages seem to have been the largest in number and each village headed by a village headman called *bhojaka*. The second included suburban villages that were in the nature of craft villages; for instance, a carpenters' village or chariot-makers' village was situated in the vicinity of Varanasi. Obviously such villages served as markets for the other villages and linked the towns with the countryside. The third category consisted of border villages situated at the outer limits of the countryside which merged with the surrounding forests. People living in these villages were principally fowlers and hunters who largely lived on food gathering.

The village lands were divided into cultivable plots which were allotted to each family. Every family cultivated its plots in conjunction with its members supplemented by agricultural labourers. Fields were fenced and irrigation channels dug collectively by the peasant families under the supervision of the village headman.

The peasants had to pay one-sixth of their produce as tax. Taxes were collected directly by royal agents, and generally no intermediate landlords existed between the peasants, on the one hand, and the state, on the other. Some villages were however granted to brahmanas and big merchants. We also hear of large plots of land worked with the help of slaves and agricultural labourers. Rich peasants were called *gahapatis* (Pali term), who were of almost the same status as a section of the vaishyas.

Rice was the staple cereal produced in eastern UP and Bihar during this period. Various types of paddy and paddy fields are described in the Pali texts. Although rice was used in India in the second and third millennia BC, like iron, it became far more effective in the NBPW phase. The use of the term *shali* for transplantation is found in the Pali, Prakrit, and Sanskrit texts of the period, and it appears that large-scale paddy transplantation began in the age of the Buddha. Until *c.* 500 BC, paddy seeds were sown and grown exclusively in watery areas. Subsequently however the paddy seedlings were removed from their original fields and planted elsewhere on a good scale. This method revolutionized rice production. Paddy transplantation or wet paddy production added enormously to the yield. In addition, the peasants also produced barley, pulses, millets, cotton, and sugarcane. Agriculture made great strides through the use of the iron ploughshare, and, with the immense fertility of the alluvial soil in the area between Allahabad and Rajmahal, production more than doubled. The surplus grain comprising rice and other cereals formed the basis of the very existence of those not directly engaged in agricultural production.

Technology became central to the progress of the rural and urban economy. Iron played a crucial role in opening the rainfed, forested, hard-soil areas of the mid-Gangetic basin to clearance, cultivation, and settlement. The production of low carbon steel began from about 600 BC. The smiths knew how to harden iron tools, and some tools from Rajghat (Varanasi) show that they were made out of the iron ores obtained from Singhbhum and Mayurbhanj. It thus appears that people became acquainted with the richest iron mines in India which ensured the supply of tools for crafts and agriculture.

The picture of the economy that emerges from a study of the mid-Gangetic material remains and the Pali texts is very different from the rural economy of later Vedic times in western UP, and also differs from the economy of the Chalcolithic communities in Bihar and UP. For the first time an advanced food-producing economy spread over the alluvial soil of the mid-Gangetic plains and led to the beginning of an urban economy in this area. It was an economy that provided subsistence not only to direct producers but also to many others who were neither farmers nor artisans. This made the collection of taxes and the maintenance of armies possible on a long term basis, and created conditions in which large territorial states could be formed and sustained.

Administrative System

Although we hear of many states in this period, only Koshala and Magadha emerged as powerful. Both of them became mature states ruled by the hereditary monarchs belonging to the kshatriya varna. The Jatakas or tales relating to the previous births of the Buddha tell us that oppressive kings and their chief priests were expelled by the people and new kings installed. However, instances of expulsion were as rare as those of election. The king enjoyed the highest official status and special protection of his person and property. He yielded ground only to great religious leaders of the stature of the Buddha. The king was primarily a warlord who led his kingdom from victory to victory. This is well illustrated by the careers of Bimbisara and Ajatashatru.

The kings ruled with the aid of officials, both high and low. Higher officials were called *mahamatras*, and performed a variety of functions such as those of minister (*mantrin*), commander (*senanayaka)*, judge, chief accountant, and head of the royal harem. Probably a class of officers *ayukta*s also performed similar functions in some states.

Ministers played an important part in administration. Varsakara of Magadha and Dirghacharayana of Koshala proved to be effective and influential ministers. The first succeeded in sowing seeds of dissension in the ranks of the Lichchhavis of Vaishali, enabling Ajatashatru to conquer the republic. The second assisted the king of Koshala. It seems that high officers and ministers were largely recruited from the brahmana priestly class. They do not in general seem to have belonged to the clan of the king. This substantially undermined the kin-based polity of Vedic times.

In both Koshala and Magadha, despite the use of the punch-marked coins made of silver, some influential brahmanas and *setthis* were paid by the grant of the revenue of a cluster of villages. In doing so, the king did not have to obtain the consent of the clan, as was the case in later Vedic times, but the beneficiaries were granted only the revenue and not any administrative authority.

The rural administration was in the hands of the village headmen. Initially the headmen functioned as leaders of the tribal regiments, and were therefore called *gramini* which means the leader of the *grama* or a tribal military unit. As life became sedentary and plough cultivation well-established, tribal contingents settled down to agriculture. The *gramini* was therefore transformed into a village headman in pre-Maurya times. The village headmen were known by a variety of titles such as *gramabhojaka*, *gramini* or *gramika*. The title *gramini* prevails in Sri Lanka to this day. Eighty-six thousand *gramikas* are said to have been summoned by Bimbisara. The number may be conventional, but it shows that the village headmen enjoyed considerable importance and had direct links with the kings. The village headmen assessed and collected taxes from the villagers and also maintained law and order in their locality. Sometimes oppressive headmen were taken to task by the villagers.

Army and Taxation

The real increase in state power is indicated by the formation of a large professional army. At the time of Alexander's invasion, the Nanda ruler of Magadha maintained 20,000 cavalrymen, 200,000 infantry, 2000 four-horse chariots, and about 6000 elephants. The horse-chariots were losing their importance not only in north-east India but also in the north-west, where they had been introduced by the Vedic people. Very few elephants were maintained by the rulers of the states in north-west India, though some of them maintained as many horses as did the Magadhan king. The possession of numerous elephants gave an edge to the Magadhan princes.

The large, long-service army had to be fed by the state exchequer. We are told that the Nandas possessed enormous wealth which must have enabled them to maintain the army, but we have no idea of the special measures they adopted to raise taxes, though the fiscal system was well-established. Warriors and priests, that is, the kshatriyas and the brahmanas, were exempted from payment of taxes, and the burden fell on the peasants who were mainly vaishyas or *grihapatis*. *Bali*, a voluntary payment made by the tribesmen to their chiefs in Vedic times, became a compulsory payment to be made by the peasants in the age of the Buddha, and officers called *balisadhakas* were appointed to collect it. It appears that one-sixth of the produce was collected as tax by the king from the peasant. Taxes were assessed and collected by the royal agents with the help of village headmen. The advent of writing may have helped in the assessment and collection of taxes. The discovery of many hoards of punch-marked coins suggests that payment was made in both cash and kind. In north-eastern India, payment was made in paddy. In addition to these taxes, the peasants were subjected to forced labour for royal work. The Jatakas state that sometimes peasants left the country of the king in order to escape the oppressive burden of taxes.

Artisans and traders too had to pay taxes. Artisans were made to work for a day in a month for the king, and the traders had to pay customs on the sale of their commodities. The tolls were collected by officers known as *shaulkika* or *shulkadhyaksha*.

The territorial kings discarded the *sabha* and *samiti*. Popular tribal assemblies had virtually disappeared in post-Vedic times. They dwindled and disappeared as tribes disintegrated into varnas and lost their identity. Their place was taken by varna and caste groups, and therefore caste laws and customs were given due weight by the writers of the law-books. However, these regulations were largely confined to social matters. Popular assemblies were able to succeed only in small kingdoms where members of the tribe could easily be summoned, as may have been the case in the Vedic period. With the emergence of the large states of Koshala and Magadha, it was not possible to hold large assemblies attended by people belonging to the different social classes and different parts of the empire, and the very difficulty of communications made regular meetings impossible. Also, being tribal, the old assembly was unable to find a place for the many non-Vedic tribes which lived in the new kingdoms. The changed circumstances, therefore, were not congenial for the continuance of the old assemblies. They were replaced by a small body called *parishad* consisting exclusively of the brahmanas. Even during this period, assemblies existed, but this was not the case in the monarchies. They flourished in the smaller republican states of the Shakyas, Lichchhavis, and the like.

The Republican Experiment

The republican system of government existed either in the Indus basin or in the foothills of the Himalayas in eastern UP and Bihar. The republics in the Indus basin may have been the remnants of the Vedic tribes, although some monarchies may have been followed by republics. In some instances in UP and Bihar, people were possibly inspired by the old ideals of tribal equality which did not give much prominence to the single raja.

Both Panini and the Pali text, speak of the non-monarchical states. According to Panini, the *janapada* or the territorial state was generally headed by *ekaraja* or one king. He specifies nineteen one-king *janapadas*, but he also speaks of the *samgha* or multi-ruler *janapadas* which were republics.

In the republics, real power lay in the hands of tribal oligarchies. In the republics of Shakyas and Lichchhavis, the ruling class belonged to the same clan and the same varna. Although in the case of the Lichchhavis of Vaishali, 7707 rajas sat in the assembly held in the motehall, the brahmanas were not mentioned in this context. In post-Maurya times in the republics of the Malavas and the Kshudrakas, the kshatriyas and the brahmanas were given citizenship, but slaves and hired labourers were excluded from it. In a state situated on the Beas river in the Punjab, membership was restricted to those who could supply the state with at least one elephant, and it was characteristic of the oligarchy of the Indus basin.

The administrative machinery of the Shakyas and Lichchhavis was simple. It consisted of *raja*, *uparaja* (vice-king), *senapati* (commander), and *bhandagarika* (treasurer). We hear of as many as seven courts in hierarchical order trying the same case in succession in the Lichchhavi republic, but this seems to be too good to be true!

In any event, certain states in the age of the Buddha were not ruled by hereditary kings but by persons who were responsible to the assemblies. Thus, although the people living in the old republics may not have shared political power equally, the republican tradition in India is as old as the age of the Buddha.

The republics differed from the monarchies in several ways. In the monarchies the king claimed to be the sole recipient of revenue from the peasant, but in the republics, this claim was advanced by every tribal oligarch who was known as raja. Each one of the 7707 Lichchhavi rajas maintained his own storehouse and apparatus of administration. Again, every monarchy maintained its regular standing army and did not permit any group or groups of people to carry arms within its boundaries. However, in a tribal oligarchy, each raja was free to maintain his own little army under his *senapati*, enabling each of them to compete with the other. The brahmanas exercised great influence in a monarchy, but they had no place in the early republics, nor did they recognize these states in their law-books. Finally, the principal difference between a monarchy and a republic was the same as that between one-man rule and many-men rule. The republic functioned under the leadership of oligarchic assemblies but the monarchy under the leadership of an individual.

The republican tradition became feeble from the Maurya period. Even in pre-Maurya times, monarchies were far stronger and more common. Naturally, ancient thinkers looked upon kingship as the commonest and most important form of government. To them, the state, government, and kingship meant the same thing. As the state was well established in the age of the Buddha, thinkers began to speculate about its possible origins. The *Digha Nikaya,* one of the oldest Buddhist texts in Pali, points out that in the earliest stage human beings lived happily. Gradually they began to own private property and set up house with their wives, and this led to quarrels over property and women. In order to put an end to such quarrels, they elected a chief who would maintain law and order and protect the people. In return for protection, the people promised to give the chief a part of the paddy. The chief came to be called king, and that is how kingship or the state originated.

Social Orders and Legislation

The Indian legal and judicial system originated in this period. Formerly people were governed by the tribal law, which did not recognize any class distinction. However, by now the tribal community had been clearly divided into four orders: brahmanas, kshatriyas, vaishyas, and shudras. The Dharmasutras therefore set out the duties of each of the four varnas, and the civil and criminal law came to be based on the varna division. The higher the varna, the purer it was, and the higher the level of moral conduct expected of the upper varna by civil and criminal law. All forms of disabilities were imposed on the shudras. They were deprived of religious and legal rights and relegated to the lowest position in society; the *upanayana* or sacred thread could not be conferred on them. Crimes committed by them against the brahmanas and others were severely punished, but those committed against the shudras were lightly treated. The lawgivers spread the fiction that the shudras were born from the feet of the creator. Therefore, members of the higher varnas, especially the brahmanas, shunned the company of the shudra, avoided the food touched by him, and refused to enter into marriage relations with him. A shudra could not be appointed to high posts, and more importantly he was specifically asked to serve the twice-born as slave, artisan, and agricultural labourer.

Jainism and Buddhism themselves did not materially change the shudra's position. Although he could be admitted to the new religious orders, his general position continued to be low. It is said that Gautama Buddha visited the assemblies of the brahmanas, kshatriyas, and *gahapatis* or householders, but assemblies of the shudras are not mentioned in this context. The Pali texts mention ten despicable crafts and castes including the chandalas. They are called *hina* which means poor, inferior, and despicable. In contrast the kshatriyas and brahmanas are called the *uttama* or best castes.

The civil and criminal law set out in the Dharmashastras was administered by royal agents, who inflicted rough and ready punishments such as scourging, beheading, and tearing out of the tongue. In many instances, punishments for criminal offences were governed by the idea of revenge, that is, a tooth for a tooth and an eye for an eye.

Although the brahmanical law-books took into account the social status of the different varnas in framing their laws, they did not ignore the customs of the non-Vedic tribal groups which were gradually absorbed into the brahmanical social order. Some of these indigenous tribals were given fictitious social origins and allowed to be governed by their own customs.

Conclusion

Gautama Buddha stayed in several mid-Gangetic cities during the rainy seasons. Archaeologically these cities are not dateable to earlier than the fifth century BC. Therefore, the age of the Buddha roughly covers the fifth century BC. This period is important because ancient Indian polity, economy, and society really took shape in its course. Agriculture based on the use of iron tools and paddy transplantation gave rise to an advanced food-producing economy, particularly in eastern UP and Bihar. This created conditions for the rise of towns, based on trade, industry, and the use of metal money. Also, higher levels of cereal production made it possible to collect taxes from the peasants. Therefore, on the basis of regular taxes and tributes, large states could be founded. In order to continue this polity, the varna order was devised, and the functions of each varna were clearly demarcated. According to the law-books, rulers and fighters were called kshatriyas, priests and teachers were called brahmanas, peasants and taxpayers were called vaishyas, and those who served all the higher orders as labourers were called shudras. The Buddhists too recognized the varna system though they did not base it on birth. They, however, gave the kshatriya the highest place in the system.

Chronology

(BC)	
1900	Harappan towns disappeared.
1200 onwards	Settlements in the doab.
1000–600	Hierarchy of settlement in the lower doab, based on size and location.
7–6 C	Earliest wooden enclosures in Patna.
5 C	First towns in the middle Gangetic basin, first coins.

18

The Maurya Age

Chandragupta Maurya

The Maurya dynasty was founded by Chandragupta Maurya, who seems to have belonged to an ordinary family. According to the brahmanical tradition, he was born of Mura, a shudra woman in the court of the Nandas. However, an earlier Buddhist tradition speaks of the Mauryas as the ruling clan of the little republic of Pipphalivana in the region of Gorakhpur near the Nepalese terai. In all likelihood, Chandragupta was a member of this clan. He took advantage of the Nandas in the last days of their rule. With the help of Chanakya, who is known as Kautilya, he overthrew the Nandas and established the rule of the Maurya dynasty. The machinations of Chanakya against Chandragupta's enemies are described in detail in the *Mudrarakshasa*, a play written by Vishakhadatta in the ninth century. In modern times, several plays have been based on it.

Justin, a Greek writer, says that Chandragupta overran the whole of India with an army of 600,000. This may or may not be true, but Chandragupta liberated north-western India from the thraldom of Seleucus, who ruled over the area west of the Indus. In the war with the Greek viceroy, Chandragupta seems to have emerged victorious. Eventually peace was concluded between the two, and in return for 500 elephants, Seleucus gave him not only his daughter but also eastern Afghanistan, Baluchistan, and the area west of the Indus. Chandragupta thus built up a vast empire which included not only Bihar and substantial parts of Orissa and Bengal but also western and north-western India, and the Deccan. Aside from Kerala, Tamil Nadu, and parts of north-eastern India, the Mauryas ruled over virtually the entire subcontinent. In the north-west, they held sway over certain areas that did not even form part of the British empire. The Mauryas also conquered the republics or *samghas* which Kautilya considered obstacles to the growth of the empire.

Imperial Organization

The Mauryas organized a very elaborate system of administration. We know about this from the account of Megasthenes and the *Arthashastra* of Kautilya. Megasthenes was a Greek ambassador sent by Seleucus to the court of Chandragupta Maurya. He lived in the Maurya capital of Pataliputra and wrote an account not only of the administration of the city of Pataliputra but also of the Maurya empire as a whole. Megasthenes's account does not survive in full, but quotations from it occur in the works of several subsequent Greek writers. These fragments have been collected and published in the form of a book entitled *Indika,* which throws valuable light on the administration, society, and economy of Maurya times.

Megasthenes's account can be supplemented by the *Arthashastra* of Kautilya. Although the *Arthashastra* was finally compiled a few centuries after Maurya rule, some of its books contain material that provides authentic information about the Maurya administration and economy. These two sources enable us to draw a picture of the administrative system of Chandragupta Maurya.

Chandragupta Maurya was evidently an autocrat who concentrated all power in his hands. If we are to believe a statement in the *Arthashastra,* the king had set a high ideal. He stated that in the happiness of his subjects lay his happiness and in their troubles lay his troubles. We do not however know how far the king acted up to these ideals. According to Megasthenes, the king was assisted by a council whose members were noted for wisdom. There is nothing to show that their advice was binding on him, though the high officers were chosen from among the councillors.

The empire was divided into a number of provinces, and each of these was placed under a prince who was a scion of the royal dynasty. The provinces were divided into still smaller units, and arrangements were made for both rural and urban administration. Excavations show that a large number of towns relate to Maurya times. Pataliputra, Kaushambi, Ujjain, and Taxila were the most important cities. Megasthenes states that numerous cities existed in India, but he considered Pataliputra to be the most important. He calls it Palibothra. This Greek term means a city with gates. According to him, Pataliputra was bounded by a deep ditch and a wooden wall crowned with 570 towers, and had 64 gates. The ditch, timber palisades, and also wooden houses have been found in excavations. According to Megasthenes, Pataliputra was 9.33 miles long and 1.75 miles broad. This size tallies with that of Patna even today, because Patna is all length with little breadth. Given this conformity, it is possible to trust Megasthenes's other statements.

The Greek ambassador also refers to the administration of Pataliputra, the capital of the Mauryas. The city was administered by six committees, each of which consisted of five members. These committees were entrusted with sanitation, care of foreigners, registration of birth and death, regulation of weights and measures, and similar other functions. Various types of weights belonging to Maurya times have been found in several places in Bihar.

According to Kautilya, the central government maintained about two dozen departments of state, which controlled social and economic activities at least in the areas that were in proximity to the capital. The most striking feature of Chandragupta's administration was its maintenance of a huge army. A Roman writer called Pliny states that Chandragupta maintained 600,000 foot soldiers, 30,000 cavalrymen, and 9000 elephants. Another source tells us that the Mauryas maintained 8000 chariots. In addition to these, it appears that the Mauryas also maintained a navy. The administration of the armed forces, according to Megasthenes, was carried on by a board of thirty officers divided into six committees, each committee consisting of five members. It seems that each of the six wings of the armed forces, the army, the cavalry, the elephants, the chariots, the navy, and the transport, was assigned to the care of a separate committee. The Mauryas' military strength was almost three times that of the Nandas, and this was apparently because of a much larger empire and thus far greater resources.

How did Chandragupta Maurya manage to meet the expenses of such a huge army? If we rely on the *Arthashastra* of Kautilya, it would appear that the state controlled almost all the economic activities in the realm. The state brought new land under cultivation with the aid of cultivators and shudra labourers. The virgin land that was opened to cultivation yielded handsome income to the state in the form of revenue collected from the newly settled peasants. It appears that taxes collected from the peasants varied from one-fourth to one-sixth of the produce. Those who were provided with irrigation facilities by the state had to pay for it. In addition, in times of emergency, peasants were compelled to raise more crops. Tolls were also levied on commodities brought to town for sale, and they were collected at the gate. Moreover, the state enjoyed a monopoly in mining, sale of liquor, manufacture of arms, etc. This naturally brought vast resources to the royal exchequer. Chandragupta thus established a well-organized administrative system and gave it a sound financial base.

Ashoka (273–32 BC)

Chandragupta Maurya was succeeded by Bindusara, whose reign is important for its continuing links with the Greek princes. His son, Ashoka, is the greatest of the Maurya rulers. According to Buddhist tradition, he was so cruel in his early life that he killed his ninety-nine brothers to win the throne. However, as this statement is based on a legend, it may be mythical. Ashoka's biography, written by Buddhist authors, is so full of fiction that it cannot be taken seriously.

Ashokan Inscriptions

The history of Ashoka is reconstructed on the basis of his inscriptions, thirty-nine, in number, that are classified into Major Rock Edicts, Minor Rock Edicts, Separate Rock Edicts, Major Pillar Edicts, and Minor Pillar Edicts. The name Ashoka occurs in copies of Minor Rock Edict I found at three places in Karnataka and at one in MP. Thus, altogether, the name Ashoka occurs four times. It is significant that Ashoka's name does not occur in any of his inscriptions from north or north-west India. The inscriptions which do not carry his name mention only *devanampiya piyadasi*, dear to the gods, and leave out the name Ashoka. The title *devanampiya* or 'dear to gods' adopted by Ashoka was not unique but also adopted by his ancestors. However, *piyadasi* or 'good looking' seems to have been his unique title. Ashokan inscriptions have been found in India, Nepal, Pakistan, and Afghanistan. Altogether, they appear at forty-seven places, and the total number of versions is 182 including two edicts which are considered spurious. It is significant that Ashokan inscriptions which were generally located on ancient highways, have been found at six places in Afghanistan. Composed in Prakrit, they were written in Brahmi script in the greater part of the subcontinent. However, in the north-western part of the subcontinent they appeared in Aramaic language and Kharoshthi script, and in Afghanistan they were written in both Aramaic and Greek scripts and languages. He was the first Indian king to speak directly to the people through his inscriptions which carry royal orders. The inscriptions throw light on Ashoka's career, his external and domestic polices, and the extent of his empire.

Impact of the Kalinga War

The ideology of Buddhism guided Ashoka's state policy at home and abroad. After his accession to the throne, Ashoka fought only one major war called the Kalinga war. According to him, 100,000 people were killed in the course of it, several lakhs died, and 150,000 were taken prisoners. These numbers are exaggerated, because the number 'a hundred thousand' is used as a cliché in Ashokan inscriptions. At any rate, it appears that the king was deeply moved by the massacre in this war. The war caused great suffering to the brahmana priests and Buddhist monks, and this in turn brought upon Ashoka much grief and remorse. He therefore abandoned the policy of physical occupation in favour of one of cultural conquest. In other words, *bherighosha* was replaced with *dhammaghosha.* We quote below the words of Ashoka from his Thirteenth Major Rock Edict:

> When he had been consecrated eight years the Beloved of the Gods, the King Piyadasi, conquered Kalinga. A hundred and fifty thousand people were deported, a hundred thousand were killed and many times that number perished. Afterwards, now that Kalinga was annexed, the Beloved of the Gods very earnestly practised *dhamma,* desired *dhamma*, and taught *dhamma.* On conquering Kalinga the Beloved of the Gods felt remorse, for when an independent country is conquered the slaughter, death and deportation of the people is extremely grievous to the Beloved of the Gods and weighs heavily on his mind. What is even more deplorable to the Beloved of the Gods, is that those who dwell there, whether brahmanas, *shramanas*, or those of other sects, or householders who show obedience to their teachers and behave well and devotedly towards their friends, acquaintances, colleagues, relatives, slaves, and servants, all suffer violence, murder and separation from their loved ones .... Today if a hundredth or a thousandth part of those people who were killed or died or were deported when Kalinga was annexed were to suffer similarly, it would weigh heavily on the mind of the Beloved of the Gods .... The Beloved of the Gods considers victory by *dhamma* to be the foremost victory ....

Ashoka now appealed ideologically to the tribal people and the frontier kingdoms. The subjects of the independent states in Kalinga were asked to obey the king as their father and to repose confidence in him. The officials appointed by Ashoka were instructed to propagate this idea among all sections of his subjects. The tribal peoples were similarly asked to follow the principles of *dhamma* (dharma). He no longer treated foreign dominions as legitimate areas for military conquest. He took steps for the welfare of men and animals in foreign lands, which was a new thing considering the conditions in those times. He sent ambassadors of peace to the Greek kingdoms in West Asia and Greece. All this is based on Ashoka's inscriptions. If we rely on the Buddhist tradition, it would appear that he sent missionaries for the propagation of Buddhism to Sri Lanka and Central Asia, and there is inscriptional evidence to support Ashoka's initiatives to propagate Buddhism in Sri Lanka. As an enlightened ruler, Ashoka tried to enlarge his sphere of influence through propaganda.

It would be wrong to think that the Kalinga war caused Ashoka to become an extreme pacifist. He did not pursue the policy of peace for the sake of peace under all circumstances, but adopted the practical policy of consolidating his empire. He retained Kalinga after its conquest and incorporated it into his empire. There is also nothing to show that he disbanded the huge army maintained from the time of Chandragupta Maurya. Although he repeatedly asked the tribal people to follow the policy of dharma, he threatened adverse consequences if they violated the established rules of social order and righteousness (dharma). Within the empire he appointed a class of officers known as the *rajukas*, who were vested with the authority not only to reward people but also to punish them when necessary. Ashoka's policy to consolidate the empire in this way bore fruit. The Kandahar inscription speaks of the success of his policy with the hunters and fishermen, who gave up killing animals and possibly took to a settled agricultural life.

Internal Policy and Buddhism

Ashoka was converted to Buddhism as a result of the Kalinga war. According to tradition, he became a monk, made huge gifts to the Buddhists, and undertook pilgrimages to the Buddhist shrines. His visits to Buddhist shrines is also suggested by the dhamma *yatras* mentioned in his inscriptions.

According to tradition, Ashoka held the third Buddhist council (*sangiti*) and missionaries were sent not only to south India but also to Sri Lanka, Myanmar (Burma), and other countries to convert the people there. Brahmi inscriptions of the second and first centuries BC have been found in Sri Lanka.

Ashoka set a very high ideal for himself, and this was the ideal of paternal kingship. He repeatedly asked his officials to tell his subjects that the king looked upon them as his children. As agents of the king, the officials were also asked to take care of the people. Ashoka appointed *dhammamahamatras* to propagate dharma among various social groups, including women, and appointed *rajukas* for the administration of justice in his empire.

Ashoka disapproved of rituals, especially those observed by women. He forbade killing certain birds and animals, prohibited the slaughter of animals in the royal kitchen, and forbade the slaughter of animals in sacrifices. He banned gay social functions in which people indulged in an excess of revelry.

Ashoka's dharma was not however a narrow dharma and cannot be regarded as a sectarian faith. His Kandahar Greek inscription preaches amity between the sects. Ashoka's inscriptions are called *dhammalipi*, which cover not only religion and morality but also embrace social and administrative matters. They can be compared to the Dharmashastras or law-books written in Sanskrit under brahmanical influence. Though the *dhammalipis* were written in Prakrit under Buddhist influence, they try to regulate the social order like the Dharmashastras. The Ashokan edicts can be also compared to the *shasanas* or royal edicts issued in Sanskrit by the brahmanized kings. The broad objective was to preserve the social order. He ordained that people should obey their parents, pay respect to the brahmanas and Buddhist monks, and show mercy to slaves and servants. Above all, the *dhammalipi* asks the people to show firm devotion (*dridha bhakti*) or loyalty to king. These instructions are found in both the Buddhist and brahmanical faiths.

Ashoka taught people to live and let live. He emphasized compassion towards animals and proper behaviour towards relatives. His teachings were meant to strengthen the institution of family and the existing social classes. He held that if the people behaved well they would go to heaven, but never said that they would attain nirvana, which was the goal of Buddhist teachings. Ashoka's teachings were thus intended to maintain the existing social order on the basis of tolerance. He does not seem to have preached any sectarian faith.

Ashoka's Place in History

It is said that Ashoka's pacific policy destroyed the Maurya empire, but this is not true. On the contrary, Ashoka has a number of achievements to his credit. He was certainly a great missionary ruler in the history of the ancient world. He enthusiastically worked with great devotion for his mission and achieved a great deal at home and abroad.

Ashoka brought about the political unification of the country. He bound it further by one dharma, one language, and virtually one script called Brahmi which was used in most of his inscriptions. In unifying the country he respected such non-Indian scripts as Kharoshthi, Aramaic, and Greek. His inscriptions appear not only in different types of the Indian languages like Prakrit, but also in Greek and particularly in Aramaic which was a Semitic language of ancient Syria. His multi-script and multi-lingual inscriptions enabled him to contact literate people. Ashoka followed a tolerant religious policy, not attempting to foist his Buddhist faith on his subjects; on the contrary, he made gifts to non-Buddhist and even anti-Buddhist sects.

Ashoka was fired with a zeal for missionary activity. He deputed officials in the far-flung parts of the empire. He helped administration and promoted cultural interaction between the developed Gangetic basin and distant backward provinces. The material culture, characteristic of the heart of the empire, spread to Kalinga, the lower Deccan, and northern Bengal.

Above all, Ashoka is important in history for his policy of peace, non-aggression, and cultural conquest. He had no model in early Indian history for the pursuit of such a policy; nor was there any comparable example elsewhere except in Egypt where Akhnaton had pursued a pacific policy in the fourteenth century BC. But Ashoka was not aware of his Egyptian predecessor. Although Kautilya advised the king to be always intent on physical conquest, Ashoka followed quite the reverse policy. He asked his successors to give up the policy of conquest and aggression, followed by the Magadhan princes till the Kalinga war, and counselled them to adopt a policy of peace sorely needed after a period of aggressive wars lasting for two centuries. He consistently adhered to his policy, for though he possessed sufficient resources and maintained a huge army, he did not wage any war after the conquest of Kalinga. In this sense, Ashoka was certainly far ahead of his day and generation.

However, Ashoka's policy did not have any lasting impact on his viceroys and vassals, who declared themselves independent in their respective areas after the king retired in 232 BC. Similarly, the policy did not succeed in converting his neighbours, who swooped on the north-western frontier of his empire within thirty years of Ashoka's giving up power in 232 BC.

Chronology

(BC)

14 C	The Egyptian king Akhnaton pursued a pacific policy.
273–32	Ashoka's reign.
232	Ashoka gives up power.
2–1 C	Brahmi inscriptions found in Sri Lanka.

19

The Significance of Maurya Rule

State Control

The brahmanical law-books repeatedly stressed that the king should be guided by the laws laid down in the Dharmashastras and by the customs prevalent in India. Kautilya advises the king to promulgate dharma when the social order based on the varnas and ashramas (stages in life) collapses. He calls the king *dharmapravartaka* or promulgator of the social order. That the royal orders were superior to other orders was asserted by Ashoka in his inscriptions. Ashoka promulgated dharma and appointed officials to inculcate and enforce its essentials throughout India.

An assertion of royal absolutism was a natural culmination of the policy of military conquest adopted by the princes of Magadha. Anga, Vaishali, Kashi, Koshala, Avanti, Kalinga, etc., one by one were annexed to the Magadhan empire. Military control over these areas eventually turned into a coercive control over the lives of the people. Magadha had the requisite power of the sword to enforce its overall authority. In order to control various spheres of life the state had to maintain a vast bureaucracy. In no other period of ancient history do we hear of as many officers as in Maurya times.

The administrative mechanism was backed by an elaborate system of espionage. Various types of spies collected intelligence about foreign enemies and kept an eye on numerous officers. They also promoted superstitious practices to collect money from credulous people. Important functionaries were called *tirthas*. It appears that most functionaries were paid in cash, the highest among whom, the minister (*mantrin*), high priest (*purohita*), commander-in-chief (*senapati*) and crown prince (*yuvaraja*), were paid generously. They received as much as 48,000 *panas* (*pana* was a silver coin equal to three-fourths of a *tola*). In sharp contrast to them, the lowest officers were given 60 *panas* in consolidated pay although some employees were paid as little as 10 or 20 *panas*. Thus there was great disparity in the salaries of employees.

Economic Regulations

If we rely on the *Arthashastra* of Kautilya, it would appear that the state appointed twenty-seven superintendents (*adhyakshas*), principally to regulate its economic activities. They controlled and regulated agriculture, trade and commerce, weights and measures, crafts such as weaving and spinning, mining, and the like. The state also provided irrigation facilities and regulated water supply for the benefit of agriculturists. Megasthenes informs us that in the Maurya empire the officials measured the land as in Egypt and inspected the channels through which water was distributed into smaller channels.

According to the *Arthashastra* of Kautilya, a striking social development of the Maurya period was the employment of slaves in agricultural operations. Megasthenes states that he did not notice any slaves in India, but there is little doubt that there had been domestic slaves from Vedic times onwards. It seems that during the Maurya period slaves were engaged in agricultural work on a large scale. The state maintained farms on which numerous slaves and hired labourers were employed. About 150,000 war-captives brought by Ashoka from Kalinga to Pataliputra may have been engaged in agriculture, but the number of 1,50,000 seems to be exaggerated. However, ancient Indian society was not a slave society. The tasks that slaves performed in Greece and Rome were undertaken by the shudras in India. The shudras were regarded as the collective property of the three higher varnas. They were compelled to serve them as slaves, artisans, agricultural labourers, and domestic servants.

Several reasons suggest that royal control was exercised over a very large area, at least in the core of the empire. This was because of the strategic position of Pataliputra, from where royal agents could sail up and down the Ganges, Son, Punpun, and Gandak rivers. Besides this, the royal road ran from Pataliputra to Nepal through Vaishali and Champaran. We also hear of a road at the foothills of the Himalayas which passed from Vaishali through Champaran to Kapilavastu, Kalsi (in Dehra Dun district), Hazra, and eventually to Peshawar. Megasthenes speaks of a road connecting north-western India with Patna. Roads also linked Patna with Sasaram, and from there they ran to Mirzapur and central India. The capital was also connected with Kalinga via a route through eastern MP, and Kalinga in turn was linked with Andhra and Karnataka. All this facilitated transport in which horses may have played an important part. The Ashokan inscriptions appear on important highways. The stone pillars were made in Chunar near Varanasi from where they were transported to north and south India. Maurya control over the settled parts of the country may have matched that of the Mughals and perhaps of the East India Company. Medieval transport improved as a consequence of more settlements on the highways and the use of stirruped horses. In the late eighteenth century, when the dominions of the Company extended up to Allahabad, tax collections were transported by boat from eastern UP to Calcutta, and the transport system was much improved when steam navigation began on the Ganges around 1830.

In the distant areas the Maurya imperial authority may not have been effective. Pataliputra was the chief centre of royal power, but Tosali, Suvarnagiri, Ujjain, and Taxila were seats of provincial power. Each of them was governed by a governor called *kumara* or prince, and thus every governor hailed from the royal family. The princely governor of Tosali administrated Kalinga and also parts of Andhra, and that of Suvarnagiri ruled the Deccan area. Similarly, the princely governor of Ujjain ruled the Avanti area while that of Taxila the frontier area. The princely governors may have functioned as autonomous rulers, and although some governors oppressed their subjects, Ashoka's authority was never seriously questioned.

The Maurya rulers did not have to deal with a large population. All told, their army did not exceed 650,000 men. If 10 per cent of the population was recruited, the total population in the Gangetic plains may not have been over six and a half million.

Ashokan inscriptions show that royal writ ran throughout the country except the extreme east and south. Nineteen Ashokan inscriptions have been found in AP and Karnataka, but rigid state control may not have proved effective much beyond the mid-Gangetic zone owing to difficulty in means of communications.

The Maurya period constitutes a landmark in the system of taxation in ancient India. Kautilya names many taxes which were collected from peasants, artisans, and traders. This required a strong and efficient machinery for assessment, collection, and storage. The Mauryas attached greater importance to assessment than to storage and deposit. The *samaharta* was the highest officer in charge of assessment and collection, and the *sannidhata* was the chief custodian of the state treasury and storehouse. The assessor-cum-collector was far more important than the chief treasurer. The damage inflicted on the state by the first was thought to be more serious than any inflicted by the second. In fact, an elaborate machinery for assessment was first set up during the Maurya period. The list of taxes mentioned in the *Arthashastra* is impressive, and, if these were really collected, very little would have been left to the people to live on.

The epigraphic evidence we have for the existence of rural storehouses shows that taxes were also collected in kind. These granaries were probably also meant to help local people in times of famine, drought, etc.

It seems that the punch-marked silver coins, which carry the symbols of the peacock and crescented hill, formed the imperial currency of the Mauryas. They have been discovered in large numbers. Copper coins were also punch-marked. Besides punch-marked silver and copper coins, cast copper coins and die-struck coins were also issued. Without doubt, all these different types of coins helped the collection of taxes and payment of officers in cash. Also, because of its uniformity, the currency must have facilitated market exchange in a wider area.

The term empire is used for the territories conquered by the Magadhan kings, but this pre-industrial empire was different from the colonial empire of the industrial period. The pre-industrial empire was essentially territorial, based on taxes and tributes. The pre-industrial rulers collected taxes from a limited area under their direct control but also received tributes from distant rulers who acknowledged the suzerainty of the emperor. In the colonial empires of the industrial age, the rulers obtained raw material from their dominions for the manufacture of various goods which were sold to the dominions. Thus cotton was almost unknown to Europe, and Indian textiles were sold in Britain. However, with the establishment of their rule, the British imported huge quantities of cotton from India, and sold cotton cloth to India in addition to woollen fabrics. In this context the pre-British empires were quite different.

Art and Architecture

The Mauryas made a remarkable contribution to art and architecture, and introduced stone masonry on a wide scale. Megasthenes states that the Maurya palace at Pataliputra was as splendid as that in the capital of Iran.

Fragments of stone pillars and stumps, indicating the existence of an 84-pillared hall, have been discovered at Kumrahar on the outskirts of modern Patna. Although these remains do not recall the magnificence mentioned by Megasthenes, they certainly attest to the high technical skill achieved by Maurya artisans in polishing the stone pillars, which are as shining as the Northern Black Polished Ware. It was a very difficult task to transport the huge blocks of stone from the quarries and to polish and embellish them when they were erected. The whole process suggests a great feat of engineering. Each pillar is made of a single piece of buff-coloured sandstone. Only their capitals, which are beautiful pieces of sculpture in the form of lions or bulls, are joined to the pillars on the top. The erection of the polished pillars throughout India shows the spread of the technical knowledge involved in the art of polishing them. It also shows that transport had spread far and wide. The Maurya artisans also started the practice of hewing out caves from rocks for monks to live in. The earliest examples are the Barabar caves at a distance of 30 km from Gaya. Later, this form of cave architecture spread to western and southern India.

In the central phase of the Northern Black Polished Ware around 300 BC, the central Gangetic plains became the centre of terracotta art. In Maurya times terracottas were produced on a large scale. They generally represented animals and women. The women included mother goddesses, and animals included elephants. These terracottas were however modelled by hand. The stone statue of Yakshini in the form of a beautiful woman found in Didarganj (Patna) is noted for its Maurya polish.

Spread of Material Culture and the State System

The Mauryas created for the first time a well-organized state machinery which operated at the heart of the empire. Their conquest also opened the doors for trade and missionary activity. It appears that the contacts established by administrators, traders, and Jaina and Buddhist monks led to the spread of the material culture of the Gangetic basin to areas situated on the periphery of the empire. The new material culture in the Gangetic basin was based on an intensive use of iron, the prevalence of writing, punch-marked coins, an abundance of beautiful pottery called Northern Black Polished Ware, the introduction of burnt bricks and ring wells, and above all, on the existence of towns in north-eastern India. A Greek writer called Arrian states that it is not possible to record with accuracy the number of cities on account of their multiplicity. Thus, the Maurya period witnessed a rapid development of material culture in the Gangetic plains. Given the access to the rich iron ores of south Bihar, people used more and more of this metal. This period evidences socketed axes, hoes, spades, sickles, and ploughshares. Besides these iron implements, the spoked wheel also began to be used. Although arms and weapons were the monopoly of the Maurya state, the use of the other iron tools was not restricted to any class. Their use and manufacture must have spread from the Gangetic basin to distant parts of the empire. In the end of the Maurya period burnt bricks were used for the first time in north-eastern India. Maurya constructions made of burnt bricks have been found in Bihar and UP. Houses were made of bricks, and also timber which was available in abundance because of the dense vegetation in ancient times. Megasthenes speaks of the wooden structure at the Maurya capital Pataliputra. Excavations show that logs of wood were also used as an important line of defence against flood and invasion. The use of burnt bricks spread in the outlying provinces of the empire. Because of the moist climate and heavy rainfall, it was not possible to have large, lasting structures made of mud or mud-brick, as was the case in the dry zones. Therefore, diffusion of the use of burnt-brick proved to be a great boon, eventually leading to the growth of towns in the different parts of the empire. Similarly, ring wells, which were first constructed under the Mauryas in the Gangetic plains spread beyond the heart of the empire. As ring wells supplied water to people for domestic use, it was no longer imperative to found settlements on the banks of rivers. Ring wells also served as soak pits in congested settlements.

The principal elements of the mid-Gangetic material culture seem to have been transferred with modifications to northern Bengal, Kalinga, Andhra, and Karnataka, but, of course, the local cultures of these regions also developed independently. In Bangladesh, the Mahasthana inscription in Bogra district is in Maurya Brahmi. NBPW has been found at Bangarh in Dinajpur district and sherds of it at Chandraketugarh in the 24 Parganas in West Bengal. Gangetic associations can be attributed to settlements at Sisupalgarh in Orissa. The settlement of Sisupalgarh is ascribed to Maurya times in the third century BC, and it contains NBPW, iron implements, and punch-marked coins. As Sisupalgarh is situated near Dhauli and Jaugada, where Ashokan inscriptions have been found on the ancient highway passing along the eastern coast of India, the material culture may have reached this area as a result of contact with Magadha. This contact may have started in the fourth century BC when the Nandas are said to have conquered Kalinga, but it deepened after the conquest of Kalinga in the third century BC. Possibly as a measure of pacification after the Kalinga war, Ashoka promoted some settlements in Orissa which had been incorporated into his empire.

Although we find iron weapons and implements at several places in Andhra and Karnataka in the Maurya period, the advance of iron technology in that area was the contribution of the megalith builders noted for various kinds of large stone burials including those of a round form. However, some of these places have Ashokan inscriptions as well as sherds of the NBPW of the third century BC. For example, Ashokan inscriptions have been found at Amaravati and three other sites in Andhra and at nine places in Karnataka. It therefore appears that, from the eastern coast, ingredients of the material culture percolated through Maurya contacts into the lower Deccan plateau.

The art of making steel may have spread through Maurya contacts across some other parts of India. Steel objects relating to about 200 BC or an earlier date have been found in the mid-Gangetic plains. The spread of steel may have led to jungle clearance and the use of better methods of cultivation in Kalinga, and could have created the conditions for the rise of the Cheti kingdom in that region. Although the Satavahanas rose to power in the Deccan in the first century BC, yet in some ways their state was a projection of the Maurya. As will be shown later, they also issued inscriptions in Prakrit, and adopted some of the administrative measures of the Mauryas.

It seems that stimulus to state formation in peninsular India came from the Mauryas not only in the case of the Chetis and the Satavahanas but also that of the Cheras (Keralaputras), the Cholas, and the Pandyas. According to Ashokan inscriptions, all the three last-mentioned people came together with the Satyaputras, and the people of Tamraparni or Sri Lanka lived on the borders of the Maurya empire, and were, therefore, familiar with the Maurya state. The Pandyas were known to Megasthenes who visited the Maurya capital. Ashoka called himself 'dear to the gods', a title which was translated into Tamil and adopted by the chiefs mentioned in the Sangam texts.

The existence of inscriptions, occasional NBPW sherds, and punch-marked coins in parts of Bangladesh, Orissa, Andhra, and Karnataka from about the third century BC shows that during the Maurya period attempts were made to spread elements of the mid-Gangetic basin culture in distant areas. The process seems to be in accord with the instructions of Kautilya.

Kautilya advised that new settlements should be founded with the help of cultivators, who were apparently vaishyas, and with that of shudra labourers who should be drafted from overpopulated areas. In order to bring the virgin soil under cultivation, the new peasants were allowed a remission in tax and supplied with cattle, seeds, and money. The state did this in the expectation that it would recover what it had given. Such settlements were necessary in those areas where people were not acquainted with the use of the iron ploughshare, and this policy led to the opening of large areas to cultivation and settlement.

How far the Maurya towns facilitated the diffusion of the material culture of the Gangetic plains into the tribal belt of central India, extending from Jharkhand in the east to the Vindhyas in the west, cannot be said. It is however quite clear that Ashoka maintained intimate contacts with the tribal people, who were exhorted to observe dharma. Their contact with the *dhammamahamatras* appointed by Ashoka must have enabled them to imbibe rudiments of the higher culture prevalent in the Gangetic basin. In this sense, Ashoka launched a deliberate and systematic policy of acculturation. He states that as a result of the diffusion of dhamma, men would mingle with gods. This implies that tribal and other people would take to the habits of a settled, taxpaying, peasant society and develop a respect for paternal power, royal authority, and for the monks, priests, and officers who helped in enforcing his authority. His policy succeeded. Ashoka claims that hunters and fishermen had given up killing and practised dhamma, which implies that they had taken to a settled agricultural life.

Causes of the Fall of the Maurya Empire

The Magadhan empire, which had been reared by successive wars culminating in the conquest of Kalinga, began to disintegrate after the exit of Ashoka in 232 BC. Several causes seem to have brought about the decline and fall of the Maurya empire.

Brahmanical Reaction

The brahmanical reaction began as a result of Ashoka's policy. There is no doubt that Ashoka adopted a tolerant policy and asked the people to respect even the brahmanas, but he issued his edicts in Prakrit and not in Sanskrit. He prohibited the killing of birds and animals, and derided superfluous rituals performed by women. The anti-sacrifice attitude of Buddhism adopted by Ashoka adversely affected the incomes of brahmanas. Further, Ashoka appointed *rajukas* to govern the countryside and introduce *vyavaharasamata* and *dandasamata*. This meant the same civil and criminal law for all varnas. But the Dharmashastra compiled by the brahmanas prescribed varna discrimination. Naturally this policy infuriated the brahmanas.

Some new kingdoms that arose on the ruins of the Maurya empire were ruled by the brahmanas. The Shungas and the Kanvas, who ruled in MP and further east on the remnants of the Maurya empire, were brahmanas. Similarly, the Satavahanas, who founded kingdom in the western Deccan and Andhra, claimed to be brahmanas. These brahmana dynasties performed Vedic sacrifices that were discarded by Ashoka.

Financial Crisis

The enormous expenditure on the army and payment to the bureaucracy created a financial crisis for the Maurya empire. As far as we know, in ancient times the Mauryas maintained the largest army and the largest regiment of officers. Despite the range of taxes imposed on the people, it was difficult to maintain this huge superstructure. It seems that Ashoka made large donations to the Buddhist monks which left the royal treasury empty. Towards the end, in order to meet expenses, they were obliged to melt gold images.

Oppressive Rule

Oppressive rule in the provinces was an important cause of the break-up of the empire. In the reign of Bindusara, the citizens of Taxila bitterly complained against the misrule of wicked bureaucrats (*dushtamatyas*). Their grievance was redressed by the appointment of Ashoka, but when Ashoka became emperor, a similar complaint was made by the same city. The Kalinga edicts show that Ashoka was much concerned about oppression in the provinces and, therefore, asked the *mahamatras* not to tyrannize the townsmen without due cause. For this purpose he introduced rotation of officers in Tosali (in Kalinga), Ujjain and Taxila. He himself spent 256 nights on a pilgrimage which may have helped administrative supervision. All this however failed to stop oppression in the outlying provinces, and after his retirement Taxila took the earliest opportunity to throw off the imperial yoke.

New Knowledge in the Outlying Areas

We may recall that Magadha owed its expansion to certain basic material advantages. Once the knowledge of the use of these elements of culture spread to central India, the Deccan, and Kalinga as a result of the expansion of the Magadhan empire, the Gangetic basin, which formed the heart of the empire, lost its special advantage. The regular use of iron tools and weapons in the peripheral provinces coincided with the decline and fall of the Maurya empire. On the basis of the material culture acquired from Magadha, new kingdoms could be founded and developed. This explains the rise of the Shungas and Kanvas in central India, of the Chetis in Kalinga, and of the Satavahanas in the Deccan.

Neglect of the North-West Frontier and the Great Wall of China

Since Ashoka was primarily preoccupied with missionary activities at home and abroad, he was unable to pay attention to safeguarding the passes through the north-western frontier. This had become necessary in view of the movement of tribes in Central Asia in the third century BC. The Scythians were in a state of constant flux. A nomadic people principally reliant on the use of the horse, they posed a serious danger to the settled empires in China and India. The Chinese ruler Shih Huang Ti (247–10 BC) constructed the Great Wall of China in about 220 BC to shield his empire against the attacks of the Scythians, but Ashoka took no such measures. Naturally, when the Scythians made a push towards India, they forced the Parthians, the Shakas, and the Greeks to move towards this subcontinent. The Greeks had set up a kingdom in north Afghanistan which was known as Bactria, and they were the first to invade India in 206 BC. This was followed by a series of invasions that continued till the beginning of the Christian era.

The Maurya empire was finally destroyed by Pushyamitra Shunga in 185 BC. Although a brahmana, he was a general of the last Maurya ruler called Brihadratha. He is said to have killed Brihadratha in public and forcibly usurped the throne of Pataliputra. The Shungas ruled in Pataliputra and central India. They performed several Vedic sacrifices to mark the revival of the brahmanical way of life, and are said to have persecuted the Buddhists. They were succeeded by the Kanvas who were also brahmanas.

Chronology

(BC)	
4 C	The elements of the mid-Gangetic material culture started to spread to northern Bengal, Kalinga, Andhra, and Karnataka. The Nandas of Magadha are said to have conquered Kalinga.
3 C	Conquest of Kalinga by Ashoka. Rise of Sisupalgarh settlement.
232	The Magadhan empire began to disintegrate.
247–10	Date of Shih Huang Ti, the ruler of China.
220	The Great Wall of China was constructed by the Chinese ruler Shih Huang Ti to shield his empire against attacks.
206	The Greeks invaded India.
200	Steel objects of around this time found in the mid-Gangetic plains.
185	The Maurya empire finally destroyed by Pushyamitra Shunga.

20

Central Asian Contact and Mutual Impact

I Political Aspects

The period that began in about 200 BC did not witness a large empire like that of the Mauryas, but it is notable for intimate and widespread contacts between Central Asia and India. In the eastern and central parts of India and in the Deccan, the Mauryas were succeeded by several native rulers such as the Shungas, the Kanvas, and the Satavahanas. In north-western India they were succeeded by a number of ruling dynasties from Central Asia. Of them, the Kushans became the most famous.

The Indo-Greeks

A series of invasions began in about 200 BC. The first to cross the Hindu Kush were the Greeks, who ruled Bactria, or Bahlika, situated south of the Oxus river in the area covered by north Afghanistan. The invaders came one after another, but some of them ruled simultaneously. One important cause of the invasions was the weakness of the Seleucid empire that had been established in Bactria and the adjoining areas of Iran called Parthia. On account of growing pressure from the Scythian tribes, the later Greek rulers were unable to sustain power in this area. With the construction of the Chinese wall, the Scythians were pushed back from the Chinese border. They therefore turned their attention towards the neighbouring Greeks and Parthians. Pushed by the Scythian tribes, the Bactrian Greeks were forced to invade India. The successors of Ashoka were too weak to stem the tide of foreign invasions that began during this period.

The first to invade India were the Greeks, who are called the Indo-Greeks or Indo-Bactrians. In the beginning of the second century BC, the Indo-Greeks occupied a large part of north-western India, a much larger area than that conquered by Alexander. It is said that they pushed forward as far as Ayodhya and Pataliputra. However, the Greeks failed to establish united rule in India. Two Greek dynasties simultaneously ruled north-western India on parallel lines. The most famous Indo-Greek ruler was Menander (165–45 BC), also known as Milinda. He had his capital at Sakala (modern Sialkot) in the Punjab; and invaded the Ganga–Yamuna doab. He had a great many cities in his dominions including Sakala and Mathura. He is known for the variety and wide spread of coins in his dominions. He was converted to Buddhism by Nagasena, who is also known as Nagarjuna. Menander asked Nagasena many questions relating to Buddhism. These questions and Nagasena's answers were recorded in the form of a book known as *Milinda Panho* or the *Questions of Milinda.*

Indo-Greek rule is important in the history of India because of the large number of coins that the Greeks issued. The Indo-Greeks were the first rulers in India to issue coins that can be definitively attributed to particular kings. This is not possible in the case of the early punch-marked coins, which cannot be assigned with certainty to any particular dynasty. The Indo-Greeks were also the first to issue gold coins in India, and these increased in number under the Kushans. Greek rule introduced features of Hellenistic art in the north-west frontier of India, but this was not purely Greek but the outcome of Greek contact with non-Greek conquered peoples after Alexander's death. The best example of this was Gandhara art.

The Shakas

The Greeks were followed by the Shakas. The Shakas or the Scythians destroyed Greek power in both Bactria and India, and controlled a much larger part of India than had the Greeks. There were five branches of the Shakas with their seats of power in different parts of India and Afghanistan. One branch of the Shakas settled in Afghanistan; the second in the Punjab with Taxila as their capital; the third in Mathura where they ruled for about two centuries; the fourth branch established its hold over western India, where the Shakas continued to rule until the fourth century; the fifth branch established its power in the upper Deccan.

The Shakas did not face any effective resistance from the rulers and peoples of India. In about 57–58 BC we hear of the king of Ujjain who effectively fought against the Shakas and succeeded in driving them out during his reign. He called himself Vikramaditya, and an era called Vikrama Samvat is reckoned from his victory over the Shakas in 57 BC. From this time onwards, Vikramaditya became a coveted title. Whoever achieved anything great adopted this title just as the Roman emperors adopted the title Caesar to demonstrate their great power. As a result of this practice, we have as many as fourteen Vikramadityas in Indian history, Chandragupta II of the Gupta dynasty being the most famous of them. The title continued to be fashionable with the Indian kings till the twelfth century, and it was especially prevalent in the western part of India and the western Deccan.

Although the Shakas established their rule in different parts of the country, only those who ruled in western India held power for any considerable length of time, for about four centuries or so. They benefited from the sea-borne trade in Gujarat and issued numerous silver coins. The most famous Shaka ruler in India was Rudradaman I (AD 130–50). He ruled not only over Sindh, but also over a substantial part of Gujarat, Konkan, the Narmada valley, Malwa, and Kathiawar. He is famous in history because of the repairs he undertook to improve the Sudarshana lake in the semi-arid zone of Kathiawar which had been in use for irrigation for a long time and dated back to the Mauryas.

Rudradaman was a great lover of Sanskrit. Although he had Central Asian ancestors, he issued the first-ever long inscription in chaste Sanskrit. All the earlier longer inscriptions that we have in India were composed in Prakrit which had been made the state language by Ashoka.

The Parthians

Shaka domination in north-western India was followed by that of the Parthians, and in many ancient Indian Sanskrit texts, the two people are mentioned together as Shaka–Pahlavas. In fact, both of them ruled over India in parallel for some time. Originally the Parthians or the Pahlavas lived in Iran from where they moved to India. In comparison to the Greeks and the Shakas, they occupied only a small portion of north-western India in the first century AD. The most famous Parthian king was Gondophernes during whose reign St Thomas is said to have come to India to propagate

Christianity. In course of time, the Parthians, like the Shakas before them, became an integral part of Indian polity and society.

The Kushans

The Parthians were followed by the Kushans, who are also called Yuechis or Tocharians. The Tocharians were considered to be the same as the Scythians. The Kushans were one of the five clans into which the Yuechi tribe was divided. A nomadic people from the steppes of north Central Asia living in the neighbourhood of China, the Kushans first occupied Bactria or north Afghanistan where they displaced the Shakas. Gradually they moved to the Kabul valley and seized Gandhara by crossing the Hindu Kush, replacing the rule of the Greeks and Parthians in these areas. They eventually established their authority over the lower Indus basin and the greater part of the Gangetic basin.

Their empire extended from the Oxus to the Ganges, from Khorasan in Central Asia to Pataliputra in Bihar. A substantial part of Central Asia now included in the Commonwealth of Independent States (in the former USSR), a portion of Iran, a portion of Afghanistan, almost the whole of Pakistan, and almost the whole of northern India were brought under one rule by the Kushans. Because of this, the Kushan empire in India is sometimes called a Central Asian empire. In any case, the empire created a unique opportunity for the interaction of peoples and cultures, and the process gave rise to a new type of culture which embraced nine modern countries.

There were two successive dynasties of Kushans. The first was founded by a house of chiefs who were called Kadphises and who ruled for twenty-eight years from about AD 50 under two kings. The first was Kadphises I, who issued coins south of the Hindu Kush, minting copper coins in imitation of Roman coins. The second king was Kadphises II, who issued a large number of gold money and spread his kingdom east of the Indus.

The house of Kadphises was succeeded by that of Kanishka. Its kings extended Kushan power over upper India and the lower Indus basin. The early Kushan kings issued numerous gold coins with a higher degree of metallic purity than is found in the Gupta gold coins. Although the gold coins of the Kushans are found mainly west of the Indus, their inscriptions are distributed not only in north-western India and Sindh but also in Mathura, Shravasti, Kaushambi, and Varanasi. Hence, besides the Ganga–Yamuna doab they had established their authority in the greater part of the middle Gangetic basin. Kushan coins, inscriptions, constructions, and pieces of sculpture found in Mathura show that it was their second capital in India, the first being Purushapura or Peshawar, where Kanishka erected a monastery and a huge stupa or relic tower which excited the wonder of foreign travellers.

Kanishka was the most famous Kushan ruler. Although outside the borders of India, he seems to have suffered defeat at the hands of the Chinese, he is known to history for two reasons. First, he started an era in AD 78, which is now known as the Shaka era and is used by the Government of India. Secondly, Kanishka extended his wholehearted patronage to Buddhism. He held a Buddhist council in Kashmir, where the doctrines of the Mahayana form of Buddhism were finalized. Kanishka was also a great patron of art and architecture. Kanishka's successors continued to rule in north-western India till about AD 230, and some of them bore a typical Indian name such as Vasudeva.

The Kushan empire in Afghanistan and in the area west of the Indus was supplanted in the mid-third century by the Sassanian power which originated in Iran. However, Kushan principalities continued to exist in India for about a century. The Kushan authority seems to have lingered in the Kabul valley, Kapisa, Bactria, Khorezm, and Sogdiana (coterminous with Bokhara and Samarkand in Central Asia) in the third–fourth centuries. Many Kushan coins, inscriptions, and terracottas have been found in these areas. This is especially so at a place called Toprak-Kala in Khorezm, situated south of the Aral Sea on the Oxus, where a huge Kushan palace of the third–fourth centuries has been unearthed. It housed an administrative archive containing inscriptions and documents written in Aramaic script and the Khorezmian language.

The Indo-Sassanians

However, by the middle of the third century, the Sassanians had occupied the lower Indus region. Initially they called this region Hindu, not in the sense of religion but in the sense of the Indus people. A Sassanian inscription of AD 262 uses the term Hindustan for this region. Thus the term Hindustan used for India in Mughal and modern times was first used in the third century AD. The Sassanians, also called the Indo-Sassanians, ruled in India for less than a century but they contributed to the Indian economy by issuing a large number of coins.

II Cultural Consequences

Structures and Pottery

The Shaka–Kushan phase saw a distinct advance in building activities. Excavations have revealed several layers of construction, sometimes over half a dozen, at various sites in north India. In them we find the use of burnt bricks for flooring and tiles for both flooring and roofing. However, the use of tiles may not have been adopted from outside. The period also saw the construction of brick-walls. The characteristic pottery is red ware, both plain and polished, with medium to fine fabric. The distinctive pots are sprinklers and spouted channels. They remind us of red pottery with thin fabric found in the same period in Kushan layers in Central Asia. Red pottery techniques were widely known in Central Asia and are to be found even in regions such as Farghana which lay on the peripheries of the Kushan cultural zone.

Better Cavalry

The Shakas and Kushans added new ingredients to Indian culture and enriched it immensely. They settled in India for good and completely identified themselves with its culture. As they did not have their own script, written language, or any organized religion, they adopted these components of culture from India and became an integral part of Indian society to which they contributed considerably. They introduced better cavalry and the use of the riding horse on a large scale.

They popularized the use of reins and saddles, which appear in the Buddhist sculpture of the second and third centuries AD. The Shakas and the Kushans were excellent horsemen. Their passion for horsemanship is shown by numerous equestrian terracotta figures of Kushan times discovered from Begram in Afghanistan. Some of these foreign horsemen were heavily armoured and fought with spears and lances. Presumably they also used some form of toe stirrup made of rope which facilitated their movements. The Shakas and Kushans introduced the turban, tunic, trousers, and heavy long coat. Even now Afghans and Punjabis wear turbans, and the *sherwani* is a successor of the long coat. The Central Asians also brought in cap, helmet, and boots which were used by warriors. Given these advantages, they made a clean sweep of their opponents in Iran, Afghanistan, Pakistan, and India. Later, when this military technology spread in India, the dependent princes turned them to good use against their former conquerors.

Trade and Agriculture

The coming of the Central Asian people established intimate contacts between Central Asia and India. India received a great fund of gold from the Altai mountains in Central Asia. Gold may also have been received by it through trade with the Roman empire. The Kushans controlled the Silk Route, which started from China and passed through their empire in Central Asia and Afghanistan to Iran, and western Asia which formed part of the Roman empire in the eastern Mediterranean zone. This route was a source of substantial income for the Kushans, and they built a large prosperous empire on the strength of the tolls levied from traders. It is significant that the Kushans were the first rulers in India to issue gold coins on a wide scale.

The Kushans also promoted agriculture. The earliest archaeological traces of large-scale irrigation in Pakistan, Afghanistan, and western Central Asia date to the Kushan period.

Polity

The Central Asian conquerors imposed their rule on numerous petty native princes. This led to the development of a feudatory organization. The Kushans adopted the pompous title of 'king of kings', which indicates that they collected tributes from numerous small princes.

The Shakas and Kushans strengthened the idea of the divine origin of kingship. Ashoka called himself 'dear to the gods', but the Kushan kings called themselves sons of god. This title was adopted by the Kushans from the Chinese, who called their king the son of heaven. It was naturally used in India to legitimize the royal authority. The brahmanical lawmaker Manu asks people to respect the king even if he is a child because he is a great god ruling in the form of a human being.

The Kushans strengthened the satrap system of government adopted by the Shakas. The empire was divided into numerous satrapies, and each placed under the rule of a satrap. Some curious practices such as hereditary dual rule, that is, two kings ruling in the same kingdom simultaneously, were begun, with instances of father and son ruling jointly at the same time. It thus appears that there was less of centralization under these rulers.

The Greeks also introduced the practice of military governorship, the governors called *strategos*. Military governors were necessary to maintain the power of the new rulers over the conquered people.

New Elements in Indian Society

The Greeks, the Shakas, the Parthians, and the Kushans eventually lost their identity in India, in the course of time becoming completely Indianized. As most of them came as conquerors they were absorbed in Indian society as a warrior class, that is, as kshatriyas. Their placement in the brahmanical society was explained in a curious way. The lawmaker Manu stated that the Shakas and the Parthians were kshatriyas who had deviated from their duties and fallen in status. In other words, they came to be considered second class kshatriyas. In no other period of ancient Indian history were foreigners assimilated into Indian society on such a large scale as they were in post-Maurya times.

Religious Developments

Some rulers and others from Central Asia adopted Vaishnavism, which means the worship of Vishnu, the god of protection and preservation. The Greek ambassador called Heliodorus set up a pillar in honour of Vasudeva at Besnagar near Vidisa (headquarters of Vidisa district) in MP around the middle of the second century BC.

A few other rulers adopted Buddhism. The famous Greek ruler Menander became a Buddhist. The questions and the answers that he exchanged with the Buddhist teacher Nagasena, also called Nagarjuna, is a good source for the intellectual history of the post-Maurya period. The Kushan rulers worshipped both Shiva and the Buddha, and the images of these two gods appeared on the Kushan coins. Seveal Kushan rulers were worshippers of Vishnu, as was certainly the case with the Kushan ruler Vasudeva, whose very name is a synonym for Krishna, an incarnation of Vishnu.

The Origin of Mahayana Buddhism

Indian religions underwent changes in post-Maurya times partly due to a great leap in trade and artisanal activity and partly due to the large influx of people from Central Asia. Buddhism was especially affected. The monks and nuns could not afford to lose the cash donations from the growing body of traders and artisans concentrated in towns. Large numbers of coins are found in the monastic areas of Nagarjunakonda in AP. Also, the Buddhists welcomed foreigners who were non-vegetarians. All this meant laxity in the day-to-day living of the nuns and monks who led an austere life. They now accepted gold and silver, took to non-vegetarian food, and wore elaborate robes. Discipline became so lax that some renunciates even deserted the religious order or the samgha and resumed the householder's life. This new form of Buddhism came to be called Mahayana or the Great Vehicle. In the old puritan Buddhism, certain things associated with the Buddha were worshipped as his symbols. These were replaced with his images at the time when the Christian era began. Image worship started with Buddhism but was followed on a large scale in Brahmanism. With the rise of Mahayana the old puritan school of Buddhism came to be known as the Hinayana or the Lesser Vehicle.

Fortunately for the Mahayana school, Kanishka became its great patron. He convened in Kashmir a council, whose members composed 300,000 words, thoroughly elucidating the three *pitaka*s or collections of Buddhist literature. Kanishka got these commentaries engraved on sheets of red copper, enclosed them in a stone receptacle, and raised a stupa over it. If this tradition is correct, the discovery of the stupa with its copper inscriptions could shed new light on Buddhist texts and teachings. Kanishka set up many other stupas to perpetuate the memory of the Buddha.

Gandhara and Mathura Schools of Art

The foreign princes became enthusiastic patrons of Indian art and literature, and displayed the zeal characteristic of new converts. The Kushan empire brought together masons and other artisans trained in different schools and countries. This gave rise to several schools of art: Central Asian, Gandhara, and Mathura. Pieces of sculpture from Central Asia show a synthesis of both local and Indian elements influenced by Buddhism.

Indian craftsmen came into contact with the Central Asians, Greeks, and Romans, especially in the north-western frontier of India in Gandhara. This gave rise to a new form of art in which images of the Buddha were made in the Graeco-Roman style, and his hair fashioned in the Graeco-Roman style.

The influence of Gandhara art also spread to Mathura, which was primarily a centre of indigenous art. Mathura produced beautiful images of the Buddha, but it is also famous for the headless erect statue of Kanishka whose name is inscribed at its lower end. It also produced several stone images of Vardhamana Mahavira. Its pre-Gupta sculpture and inscriptions ignore Krishna, although Mathura is considered his birthplace and the scene of his early life. The Mathura school of art flourished in the early centuries of the Christian era, and its products made of red sandstone are found even outside Mathura. Currently the Mathura Museum possesses the largest collection of the pieces of Kushan sculpture in India.

During the same period, beautiful works of art were created at several places south of the Vindhyas. Wonderful Buddhist caves were constructed out of rock in Maharashtra. In AP, Nagarjunakonda and Amaravati became great centres of Buddhist art, and stories associated with the Buddha were portrayed on numerous panels. The earliest panels dealing with Buddhism are to be found at Bodh-Gaya, Sanchi, and Bharhut, and relate to the second century BC. However, further development in sculpture occurred in the early centuries of the Christian era.

Language, Literature, and Learning

The Kushans were conscious of the fact that the people used various scripts and languages in their dominions, and therefore issued their coins and inscriptions in the Greek, Kharoshthi, and Brahmi scripts. Similarly, they used Greek, Prakrit, and Sanskrit-influenced Prakrit, and towards the end of their rule pure Sanskrit. The rulers thus officially recognized three scripts and four languages, and Kushana coins and inscriptions suggest the commingling and coexistence of different scripts and languages. The Kushan method of communicating with the people also indicates literacy in their times. More importantly, although the Mauryas and Satavahanas patronized Prakrit, some Central Asian princes patronized and cultivated Sanskrit literature. The earliest specimen of the *kavya* style is found in the Junagadh inscription of Rudradaman in Kathiawar in about AD 150. From then onwards, inscriptions began to be composed in chaste Sanskrit, although the use of Prakrit in composing inscriptions continued till the fourth century and even later.

It appears that some of the great creative writers such as Ashvaghosha enjoyed the patronage of the Kushans. Ashvaghosha wrote the *Buddhcharita*, which is a biography of the Buddha, and also composed *Saundarananda*, a fine example of Sanskrit *kavya*.

The development of Mahayana Buddhism led to the composition of numerous *avadanas* (life history and teachings). Most of these texts were composed in what is now known as Buddhist Hybrid Sanskrit with the sole objective of communicating the teachings of Mahayana Buddhism to the people. Examples of important books of this genre were *Mahavastu* and *Divyavadana*.

It is suggested that Indian theatre owed much to Greek influence. Both outdoor and indoor theatres appear in the caves of Ramgarh hill, 160 miles south of Banaras, and there is also a rest house for an actress. The plan of the theatre is supposed to be of Greek origin. Some scholars doubt this type of Greek influence, but there is little doubt that the curtain entered Indian theatre under Greek influence. As it was borrowed from the Greeks, it came to be known as *yavanika*, a word derived from the term *yavana*, a Sanskritized form of Ionian, a branch of the Greeks known to the ancient Indians. Initially, the term *yavana* referred to the Greeks, but subsequently it began to be used for all foreigners.

However, India's contribution to the development of theatre is undeniable. Around 150 BC, Patanjali mentions the presentation of such scenes as the binding of Bali or the killing of Kansa. More importantly, Bharata's *Natyasastra* was an important work on rhetoric and dramaturgy, and marked the entry of full-fledged theatre into India.

The best example of secular literature is the *Kamasutra* of Vatsyayana. Attributed to the third century AD, it is the earliest work on erotics dealing with sex and lovemaking. It gives us a picture of the life of a city-bred person or *nagaraka* who lived in a period of thriving urbanism.

Science and Technology

In post-Maurya times Indian astronomy and astrology profited from contact with the Greeks. Many Greek terms concerning the movement of planets appear in Sanskrit texts. Indian astrology was influenced by Greek ideas, and from the Greek term *horoscope* was derived the term *horashastra* that denotes astrology in Sanskrit. The Greek coins, which were properly shaped and stamped, were a great improvement on punch-marked coins. The Greek term *drachma* came to be known as *drama.* In return, the Greek rulers used the Brahmi script and represented some Indian motifs on their coins. Dogs, cattle, spices, and ivory pieces were exported by the Greeks, but whether they learnt any craft from India is not clear.

However, the Indians did not owe anything striking to the Greeks in medicine, botany, and chemistry. These three subjects were dealt with by Charaka and Sushruta. The *Charakasamhita* contains names of numerous plants and herbs from which drugs were prepared. The processes described for pounding and mixing the plants give us an insight into the developed knowledge of chemistry in ancient India. For the cure of ailments the ancient Indian physician relied chiefly on plants, for which the Sanskrit word is *oshadhi,* and as a result medicine itself came to be known as *aushadhi.*

In the field of technology too, the Indians seem to have benefited from the contact with the Central Asians. Kanishka is represented as wearing trousers and long boots. The introduction of the stirrup is also attributed to the Kushans. Possibly the practice of making leather shoes began in India during their period. In any event, the Kushan copper coins in India were imitations of Roman coins. Similarly, gold coins in India were struck by the Kushans in imitation of the Roman gold coins. We hear of two embassies being exchanged between the Indian kings and their Roman counterparts. Embassies were sent from India to the court of the Roman emperor Augustus in AD 27–8 and also to the Roman emperor Trajan in AD 110–20. Thus, the contacts of Rome with ancient India may have introduced new practices in technology. Working in glass during this period was especially influenced by foreign ideas and practices. In no other period in ancient India did glass-making progress as much as it did during this period.

Chronology

(BC)

200	Intimate and widespread contacts with Central Asia began.
2 C	The earliest Buddhist panels in Bodh-Gaya, Sanchi, and Bharhut. The Indo-Greeks occupied a part of the north-west, a much larger region than that occupied by Alexander. The Greek ambassador, Haliodorus, set up a pillar in honour of Vasudeva near Vidisa.

165–145	Date of Menander or Milinda.
58–57	The tradition that Vikramaditya, the king of Ujjain, defeated the Shakas and an era called Vikrama Samvat started from this time.
(AD)	
27–8	Indian missions sent to the court of the Roman emperor Augustus.
50	Kadphises group of Kushan rulers ruled from this date.
78	The Shaka era started by Kanishka.
110–20	Embassies sent from India to the Roman emperor Trajan.
130–50	The reign of the Shaka ruler Rudradaman I.
150	The earliest specimen of the *kavya* style in the Junagarh inscription of Rudradaman.
2–3 C	The Shakas and Kushans introduced the rope stirrup.
230	The end of Kushan rule in north-western India.
250	The Kushan empire in Afghanistan and west of the Indus supplanted by the Sassanian power of Iran.
Early centuries	The Mathura school of art flourished.
3 C	The *Kamasutra* of Vatsyayana.
262	A Sassanian inscription of this date mentions the term Hindustan, used later in Mughal and modern India.
3–4 C	Kushan coins, inscriptions, and terracottas of this period have been found in a substantial part of Central Asia, especially the excavation of a huge Kushan palace of this date at Toprak-Kala in Khorezm on the Oxus.
4 C	Prakrit inscriptions continued till this time. The branch of Shakas who occupied western India continued to rule there until this time.
12 C	The title Vikramaditya favoured by the kings till this time.

21

The Satavahana Phase

Political History

The most important of the native successors of the Mauryas in the north were the Shungas followed by the Kanvas. In the Deccan and in central India, the Satavahanas succeeded the Mauryas, although after a gap of about 100 years. The Satavahanas are considered to be the same as the Andhras mentioned in the Puranas. The Puranas speak only of Andhra rule and not of Satavahana rule, and the name Andhra does not figure in Satavahana inscriptions. Pre-Satavahana settlements are indicated by the finds of red ware, black-and-red ware, and russet-coated painted ware at many sites in the Deccan. Most of these are associated with the iron using megalith builders who were stimulated to new activity by contacts with the material culture from the north. The use of the iron ploughshare, paddy transplantation, the growth of urbanism, writing, etc., created conditions for state formation under the Satavahanas. According to some Puranas, the Andhras ruled altogether for 300 years although this period is assigned to the rule of the Satavahana dynasty. The earliest inscriptions of the Satavahanas relate to the first century BC, when they defeated the Kanvas and established power in parts of central India. The early Satavahana kings ruled not in Andhra but in north Maharashtra where their earliest coins and inscriptions have been found, establishing power in the upper Godavari valley, which currently produces rich and diverse crops in Maharashtra.

Gradually the Satavahanas extended their power over Karnataka and Andhra. Their greatest competitors were the Shakas, who had established power in the upper Deccan and western India. At one stage the Satavahanas were dispossessed of their dominions by the Shakas in Maharashtra and western India. The fortunes of the family were restored by Gautamiputra

Satakarni (AD 106–30) who called himself the only brahmana. He defeated the Shakas and destroyed many kshatriya rulers. He claimed to have ended the Kshaharata lineage to which his adversary Nahapana belonged. This claim is true because over 8000 silver coins of Nahapana, found near Nasik, bear the marks of having been re-struck by the Satavahana king. He also occupied Malwa and Kathiawar which were controlled by the Shakas. It seems that the empire of Gautamiputra Satakarni extended from Malwa in the north to Karnataka in the south, and he possibly also exercised general authority over Andhra.

The successors of Gautamiputra ruled till AD 220. The coins and inscriptions of his immediate successor Vashishthiputra Pulumayi (AD 130–54) have been found in Andhra, and show that by the middle of the second century this area had become a part of the Satavahana kingdom. He set up his capital at Paithan or Pratishthan on the Godavari in Aurangabad district. The Shakas resumed their conflict with the Satavahanas for the possession of the Konkan coast and Malwa. Rudradaman I (AD 130–50), the Shaka ruler of Saurashtra (Kathiawar), defeated the Satavahanas twice, but did not destroy them because of shared matrimonial relations. Yajna Sri Satakarni (AD 165–94) was the last great king of the Satavahana dynasty, and recovered north Konkan and Malwa from the Shaka rulers. He was a patron of trade and navigation, and his coins appear not only in Andhra but also in Maharashtra, MP, and Gujarat. His enthusiasm for navigation and overseas trade is demonstrated by the representation of a ship on his coins.

The successors of Yajna Sri Satakarni were unable to retain the Satavahana kingdom which was destroyed by AD 220.

Aspects of Material Culture

The material culture of the Deccan under the Satavahanas was a fusion of local elements and northern ingredients. The megalith builders of the Deccan were fairly well acquainted with the use of iron and agriculture. Although prior to *c.* 200 BC we find some iron hoes, the number of such tools increased substantially in the first two or three centuries of the Christian era. We do not notice much change in the form of hoes from the megalithic to the Satavahana phase, except that the hoes in the latter were fully and properly socketed. Besides socketed hoes, sickles, spades, ploughshares, axes, adzes, razors, etc., relate to the Satavahana layers of the excavated sites. Tanged and socketed arrowheads as well as daggers have also been discovered.

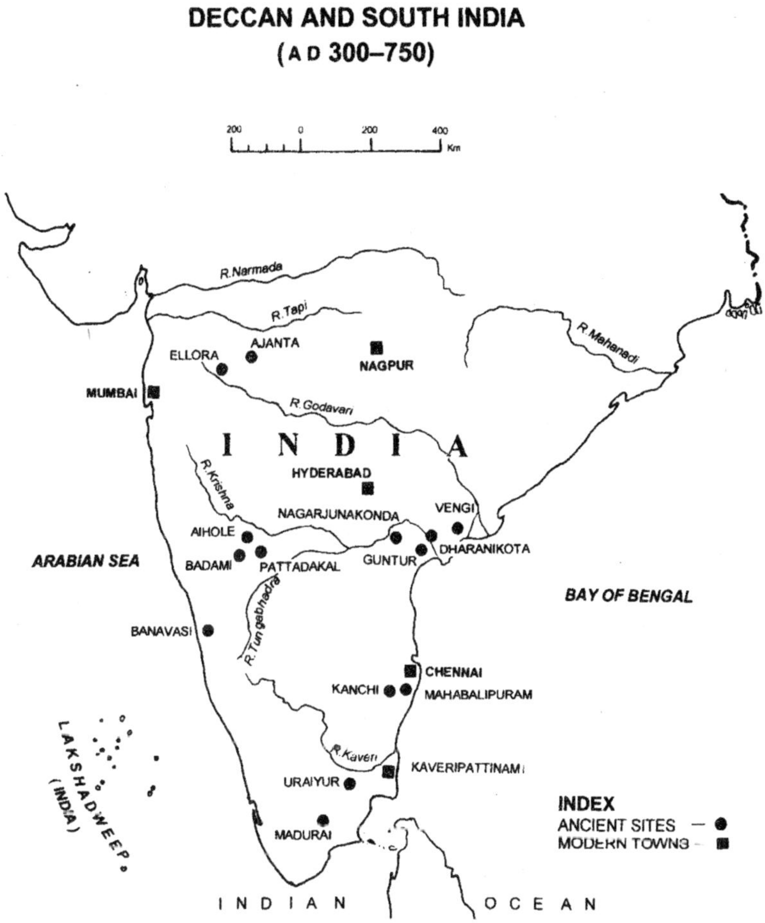

Map 8 Deccan and South India. *Courtesy ASI*

At a site in Karimnagar district, even a blacksmith's shop is found. The Satavahanas may have exploited the iron ores of Karimnagar and Warangal, for these districts show signs of iron working that dates to the megalithic phase in the first millennium BC. Evidence of ancient gold workings has been found in the Kolar fields in the pre-Christian centuries and later. The Satavahanas may have used gold as bullion, for they did not issue gold coins as did the Kushans. By and large they issued coins of lead which is found in the Deccan. They also issued potin, copper, and bronze money. The Ikshvakus, who succeeded the Satavahanas in the early third century AD in eastern Deccan, also issued coins. Both the Satavahanas and Ikshvakus seem to have exploited the mineral resources of the Deccan.

The people of the Deccan were aware of the art of paddy transplantation, and in the first two centuries of the Christian era, the area between the Krishna and the Godavari, especially at the mouths of the two rivers, formed a great rice bowl. The people of the Deccan also produced cotton. In foreign accounts, Andhra is considered to be famous for its cotton products. Thus, a substantial part of the Deccan developed a very advanced rural economy. According to Pliny, the Andhra kingdom maintained an army of 100,000 infantry, 2000 cavalry and 1000 elephants. This presupposes a large rural population, and apparently the peasants produced enough to support this military strength.

Through contacts with the north, the people of the Deccan learnt the use of coins, burnt bricks, ring wells, the art of writing, and the like. These components of material life became quite important in the Deccan. In Peddabankur (200 BC–AD 200) in Karimnagar district, we find regular use of fire-baked bricks, and that of flat, perforated roof tiles. Although roof tiles were found in Kushan constructions, they were more widely used in the Deccan and western India under the Satavahanas. All this must have contributed to the longevity of constructions. It is remarkable that as many as twenty-two brick wells belonging to the second century have been discovered at Peddabankur. These naturally facilitated dense habitation. The site also shows covered underground drains to channel waste water into soakage pits. Towns developed in Maharashtra by the first century BC when we find several crafts, but in eastern Deccan they developed a century later. Pliny informs us that the Andhra country in eastern Deccan included thirty walled towns, besides numerous villages. Several towns of the second and third centuries in this area are known from inscriptions and excavations. Increasing trade is indicated by numerous Roman and Satavahana coins which appeared about a century later in eastern Deccan in the Godavari–Krishna area.

Social Organization

The Satavahanas originally seem to have been a Deccan tribe. They however were so brahmanized that they claimed to be brahmanas. Their most famous king, Gautamiputra Satakarni, described himself as a brahmana and claimed to have established the fourfold varna system which had fallen into disorder. He boasted that he had put an end to the intermixture between the people of different social orders. Such confusion was probably caused by the Shaka infiltration and by the superficial brahmanization of the tribes living in the Deccan. The absorption of the Shakas in brahmanical society as kshatriyas was facilitated by intermarriage between the Shakas and the Satavahanas. Similarly, the indigenous tribal people were increasingly acculturated by the Buddhist monks who were induced by land grants to settle in western Deccan. It is suggested that traders too supported the Buddhist monks, for the earliest caves seem to have been located on the trade routes. The Satavahanas were also the first rulers to make land grants to brahmanas, although we find more instances of such grants being made to Buddhist monks.

According to the Dharmashastras, it was the function of the kshatriyas to rule, but the Satavahana rulers called themselves brahmanas. Gautamiputra boasted that he was the true brahmana. As the Andhras are identified with the early Satavahanas, they were probably a local tribe that was brahmanized. The orthodox brahmanas of the north viewed the Andhras as a mixed caste which would appear to indicate that the Andhras were a tribal people brought within the fold of brahmanical society as a mixed caste.

Increasing craft and commerce during this period brought many merchants and artisans to the fore. Merchants took pride in naming themselves after the towns to which they belonged, and both artisans and merchants made generous donations to the Buddhist cause and set up small memorial tablets. Among the artisans, the *gandhika*s or perfumers are repeatedly mentioned as donors. At a later stage, the term *gandhika* became so general as to connote all kinds of shopkeepers. The modern title Gandhi is derived from this ancient term.

The most interesting detail about the Satavahanas relates to their family structure. In the Aryan society of north India, the father enjoyed greater importance than the mother, and the north Indian princes generally belonged to a patriarchal society. The Satavahanas however show traces of a matrilineal social structure. It was customary for their king to be named after his mother. Such names as Gautamiputra and Vashishthiputra indicate that in their society the mother enjoyed a great deal of importance. Sometimes an inscription is issued both under the authority of the king and his mother. At present in peninsular India, the son's name includes a part of the father's name, and there is no place in it for the mother's, indicative of patriarchal influence. Queens made important religious gifts in their own right, and some of them acted as regents. However, the Satavahana ruling family was basically patriarchal because succession to the throne passed to the male member.

Pattern of Administration

The Satavahana rulers strove for the royal ideal set forth in the Dharmashastras. The king was represented as the upholder of dharma, and to him were assigned new divine attributes. The Satavahana king is represented as possessing the qualities of mythical heroes such as Rama, Bhima, Keshava, and Arjuna, and is compared in prowesss and lustre to these legendary figures and to supernatural forces. This was evidently meant to attribute divinity to the Satavahana king.

The Satavahanas retained some administrative structures of Ashokan times. Their district was called *ahara*, as it was known in the time of Ashoka, and their officials were known as *amatyas* and *mahamatras*, as was the case in Maurya times. However, their administrative divisions were also called *rashtra*, and their high officials were styled *maharashtrikas*.

We notice certain military and feudal traits in the administration of the Satavahanas. It is significant that the *senapati* was appointed provincial governor. As the tribal people in the Deccan were not thoroughly brahmanized and reconciled to the new rule, it was necessary to keep them under strong military control. The administration in the rural areas was placed in the hands of a *gaulmika*, the head of a military regiment consisting of nine chariots, nine elephants, twenty-five horses, and forty-five foot-soldiers. The head of this regiment was posted in the countryside to maintain peace and order.

The military character of Satavahana rule is also evident from the common use of such terms as *kataka* and *skandhavara* in their inscriptions. These were military camps and settlements which served as administrative centres when the king was there. Thus, coercion played a key role in the Satavahana administration.

The Satavahanas started the practice of granting tax-free villages to brahmanas and Buddhist monks. The cultivated fields and villages granted to them were declared free from intrusion by royal policemen, soldiers, and other royal officers. These areas therefore became small independent islands within the Satavahana kingdom. Possibly the Buddhist monks also preached peace and spelt out rules of good conduct to the people among whom they lived, and taught them to respect political authority and social order. The brahmanas, of course, helped enforce the rules of the varna system which promoted social stability.

The Satavahana kingdom had three grades of feudatories. The highest grade was formed by the king who was called raja and had the right to strike coins. The second grade was formed by the *mahabhoja*, and the third grade by the *senapati*. It seems that these feudatories and landed beneficiaries enjoyed some authority in their respective localities.

Religion

The Satavahana rulers were brahmanas, and they represented the march of triumphant Brahmanism. From the very outset, kings and queens performed such Vedic sacrifices as *ashvamedha*, and *vajapeya* paying liberal sacrificial fees to the brahmanas. They also worshipped a large number of Vaishnava gods such as Krishna and Vasudeva.

However, the Satavahana rulers promoted Buddhism by granting land to the monks. In their kingdom, the Mahayana form of Buddhism commanded a considerable following, especially amongst the artisan class. Nagarjunakonda and Amaravati in AP became important seats of Buddhist culture under the Satavahanas, and more so under their successors, the Ikshvakus. Similarly, Buddhism flourished in the Nasik and Junar areas in western Deccan in Maharashtra, where it seems to have been supported by traders.

Architecture

In the Satavahana phase, many *chaityas* (sacred shrines) and monasteries were cut out of solid rock in north-western Deccan or Maharashtra with great skill and patience. In fact, the process had started about a century earlier in about 200 BC. The two common religious constructions were the Buddhist temple which was called *chaitya* and monastery which was called *vihara*. The *chaitya* was a large hall with a number of columns, and the *vihara* consisted of a central hall entered by a doorway from a verandah in front. The most famous *chaitya* is that of Karle in western Deccan. About 40 m long, 15 m wide, and 15 m high, it is a most impressive specimen of massive rock architecture.

The *viharas* or monasteries were excavated near the *chaityas* for the residence of monks during the rainy season. At Nasik there are three *viharas*. Since they carry the inscriptions of Nahapana and Gautamiputra, they belong to first–second centuries AD.

Rock-cut architecture is also found in Andhra in the Krishna–Godavari region, but the region is really famous for independent Buddhist structures, mostly in the form of stupas. The most famous of them are those of Amaravati and Nagarjunakonda. The stupa was a large round structure erected over some relic of the Buddha. The Amaravati stupa was begun in around 200 BC but was completely reconstructed in the second half of the second century AD. Its dome measured 53 m across the base, and it seems to have been 33 m in height. The Amaravati stupa is full of sculptures that depict various scenes from the life of the Buddha.

Nagarjunakonda prospered most in the second–third centuries under the patronage of the Ikshvakus, the successors of the Satavahanas. It possesses both Buddhist monuments and the earliest brahmanical brick temples. Nearly two dozen monasteries can be counted here. Together with its stupas and *mahachaityas* Nagarjunakonda appears to have been the richest area in terms of structures in the early centuries of the Christian era.

Language

The official language of the Satavahanas was Prakrit. All their inscriptions were composed in this language and written in the Brahmi script, as was the case in Ashokan times. Some Satavahana kings may have composed Prakrit books. One Prakrit text called *Gathasattasai*, or the *Gathasaptasati*, is attributed to a Satavahana king called Hala. It consisted of 700 verses, all written in Prakrit, but it seems to have been finally re-touched much later, possibly after the sixth century.

Chronology

(BC)	
1 M	Karimnagar and Warangal districts (Deccan) show indications of iron working in the megalithic phase.
200	*Chaityas* and monasteries began to be built in north-western Deccan. The Amaravati stupa began to be built.
200–AD 200	Regular use of fire-baked bricks and flat perforated roof tiles in Karimnagar district.
Pre-Christian centuries and later	Gold workings in Kolar fields.
1 C	The earliest Satavahana inscriptions. Development of towns in Maharashtra.
(AD)	
1–2 C	*Viharas* at Nasik with inscriptions of Nahapana and Gautamiputra Satakarni. Paddy transplantation in the Deccan.
106–30	Date of Gautamiputra Satakarni.
130–50	Date of Rudradaman I.
130–54	Date of Vashishthiputra Pulumayi.
165–94	Date of Yajna Sri Satakarni, the last great king of the Satavahana dynasty.
2 C	Twenty-two brick wells in Peddabankur in Karimnagar district. Reconstruction of Amaravati stupa.
2–3 C	Coins are known from inscriptions and excavations. Nagarjunakonda prospered most under the Ikshvakus, the successors of the Satavahanas.
220	End of the Satavahana kingdom.
3 C	Increasing trade is indicated by numerous Roman and Satavahana coins in the Deccan.
Post-6 C	Prakrit *Gathasattasai*, or *Gathasaptasati*, finalized.

22

The Dawn of History in the Deep South

The Megalithic Background

After the prehistoric period, several elements mark the beginning of the historical period. These are: settlements of large-scale rural communities which carry on plough agriculture with the aid of the iron ploughshare, formation of the state system, rise of social classes, introduction of writing, introduction of metal coinage, and the beginnings of written literature. All these phenomena did not come into being at the tip of the peninsula with the Kaveri delta as the nuclear zone until about the second century BC. Up to the second century BC, the upland portions of the peninsula were inhabited by people who are called megalith builders. They are known not from their actual settlements which are rare, but from their funerary structures. The graves are called megaliths because they were encircled by large pieces of stone. They contain not only the skeletons of the people who were buried but also pottery and iron objects. We have a list of 104 excavated megalithic and black-and-red ware sites of the early Iron Age or early historic period. Though some of them are found in Maharashtra, MP, and UP, most of them are located in south India. The megalithic people used various types of pottery, including red ware, but black-and-red ware seems to have been popular with them. It was so widespread and important that initially black-and-red ware was called megalithic ware by archaeologists. Obviously the practice of burying goods in the graves with the dead bodies was based on the belief that the dead would need all these in the next world. These goods give us an idea of their sources of livelihood. We find arrowheads, spearheads, and also hoes and sickles, all made of iron. Tridents, which later came to be associated with Shiva, have also been found in the megaliths. However, in comparison to the number of agricultural tools that were buried, those meant for fighting and hunting are larger in number. This would indicate that the megalithic people did not practise an advanced type of agriculture.

The megaliths are found in all the upland areas of the peninsula, but their concentration seems to be in eastern Andhra and in Tamil Nadu. The beginnings of the megalithic culture can be traced to *c*. 1000 BC, though in many instances, the megalithic phase lasted from about the fifth to the first century BC, and in a few places, this phase persisted even as late as the early centuries of the Christian era.

The Cholas, Pandyas, and Keralaputras (Cheras) mentioned in Ashokan inscriptions were probably in the late megalithic phase of material culture. The megalithic people in the southern districts of Tamil Nadu had certain noteworthy characteristics. They buried the skeletons of the dead in urns made of red pottery in pits. In many instances, these urns were not surrounded by stone circles, and there were not many grave goods. The practice of urn burial was different from that of cist burial or pit burial surrounded by stone circles, that prevailed in the Krishna–Godavari valley. However, despite the use of iron, the megalithic people preferred the slopes of hills for settlement and funerary structures. Although the megalithic people produced paddy and *ragi,* apparently the area of cultivable land used by them was very limited, and they generally did not settle on the plains or lowlands due to their thick forest cover.

State Formation and the Development of Civilization

By the second century BC, the megalithic people had moved from the uplands into fertile river basins and reclaimed marshy deltaic areas. Under the stimulus of contact with the elements of material culture brought from the north to the extreme end of the peninsula by traders, conquerors, and Jaina, Buddhist, and some brahmana missionaries, they began practising wet paddy cultivation, founded numerous villages and towns, and developed social classes. Cultural and economic contacts between the north and the deep south, known as Tamizhakam, became extremely important from the fourth century BC onwards. The route to the south, called Dakshinapatha, was valued by the northerners because the south supplied gold, pearls, and various precious stones. The Pandya state was known to Megasthenes who lived in

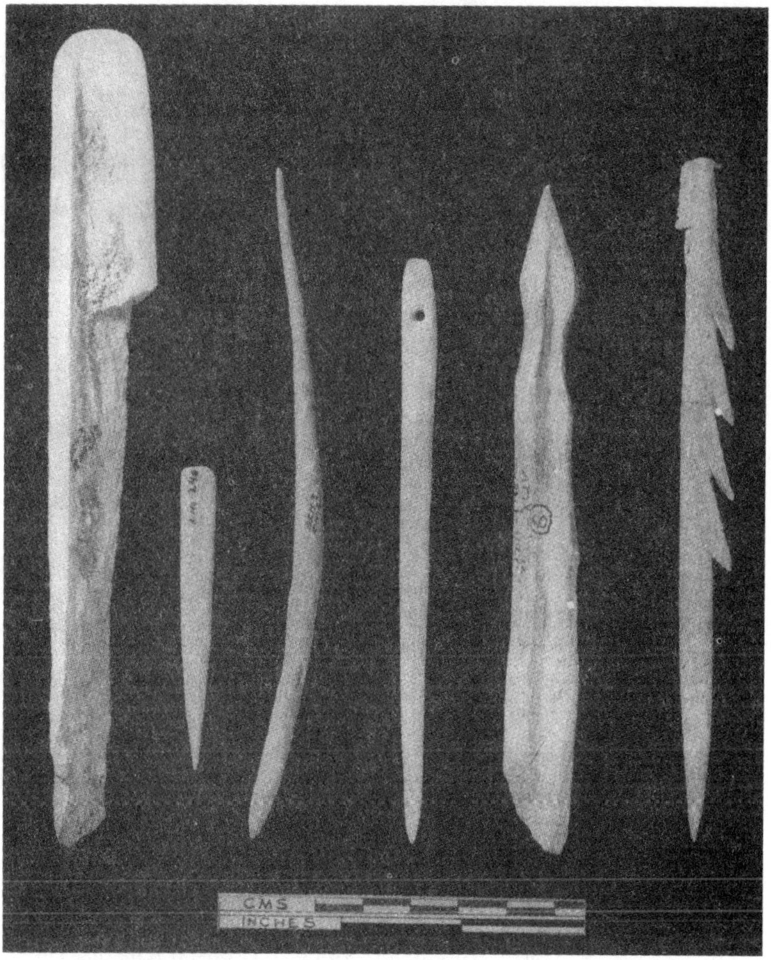

PLATE 1 Neolithic Bone Tools, Burzahom. *Courtesy Archaeological Survey of India (ASI)*

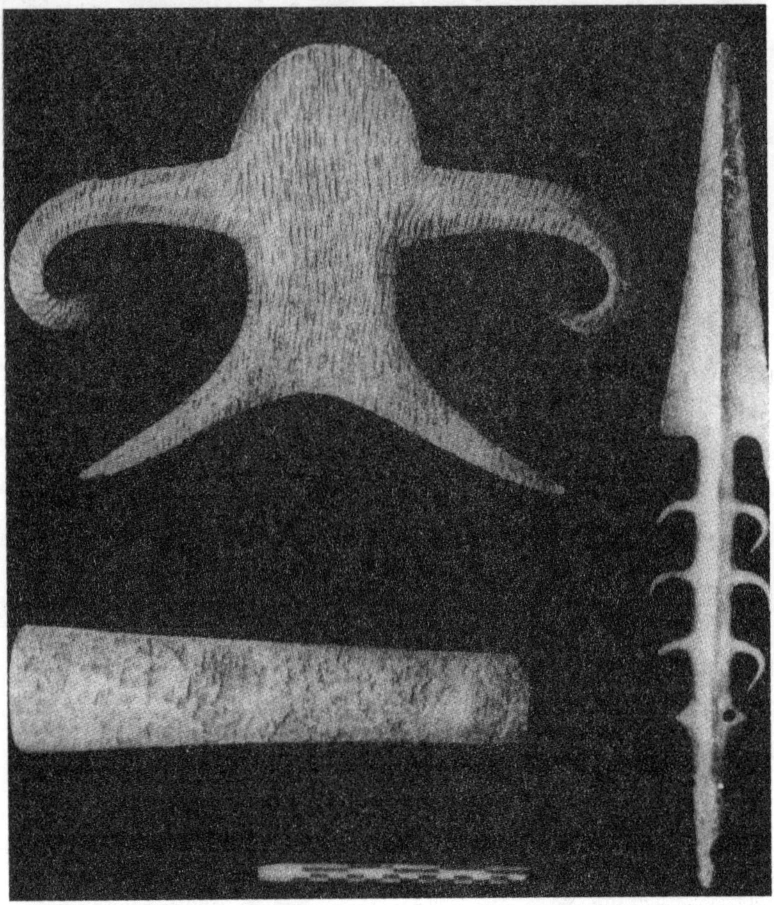

PLATE 2 Copper Hoards, Anthropomorph Figure, Bharat Kala Bhawan, Banaras. *Courtesy ASI*

PLATE 3 Mother Goddess, Terracotta, Mohenjo-daro. *Courtesy ASI*

PLATE 4 Bull Seal, Mohenjo-daro. *Courtesy ASI*

Plate 5 North Gate, Dholavira. *Courtesy ASI*

PLATE 6 Apsara, Ajanta. *Courtesy ASI*

PLATE 7 Sanchi, 200 BC–AD 200. *Courtesy ASI*

PLATE 8 Vidisha, 200 BC–AD 200. *Courtesy ASI*

PLATE 9 Buddha, Mathura, 200 BC–AD 200. *Courtesy ASI*

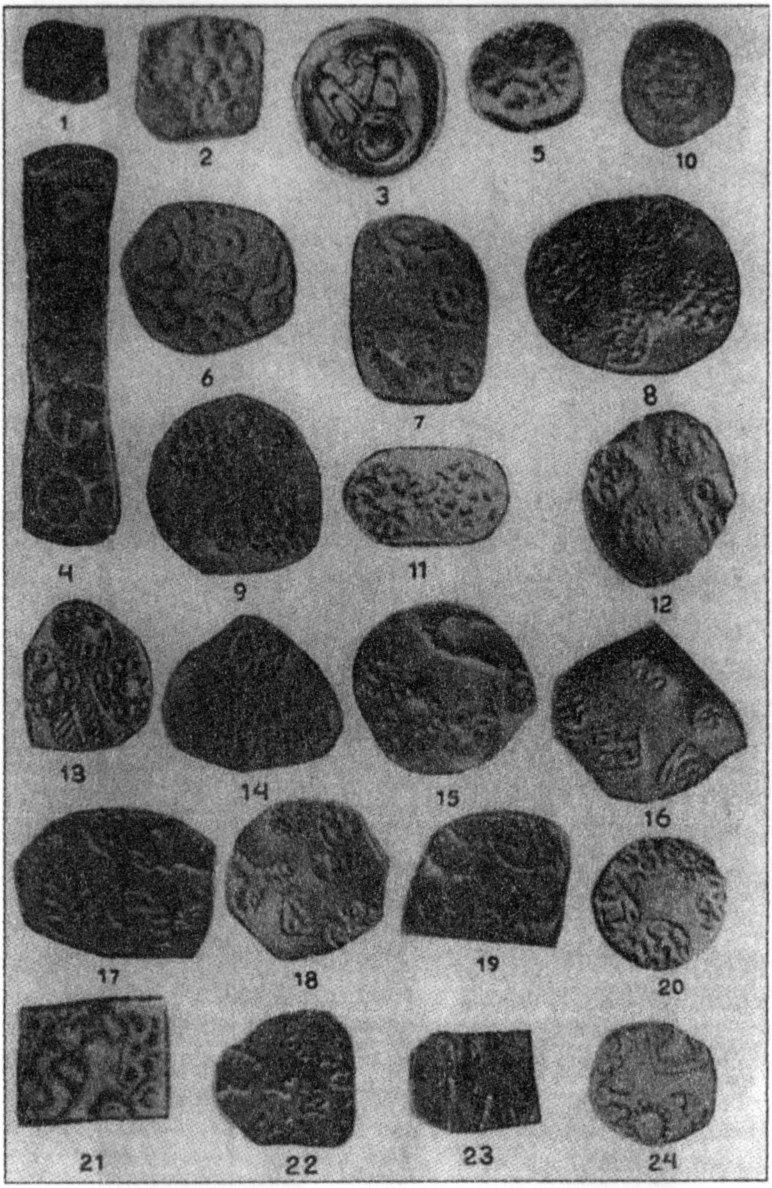

PLATE 10 Punch-marked Coins, Age of Buddha. *Courtesy ASI*

PLATE 11 Scene from *Mrichchakatika*, Mathura, Kushan, Second Century AD. *Courtesy ASI*

PLATE 12 Stupa Site III, Nalanda, Gupta Period. *Courtesy ASI*

PLATE 13 Gupta Coins. *Courtesy ASI*

PLATE 14 Rathas, Mahabalipuram, Gupta Period. *Courtesy ASI*

PLATE 15 Nara-Narayana, Deogarh, Gupta Period. *Courtesy ASI*

Pataliputra. The earlier Sangam texts are familiar with the rivers Ganges and Son, and also with Pataliputra, the capital of the Magadhan empire. The Ashokan inscriptions mention the Cholas, Pandyas, Keralaputras, and Satyaputras living on the borders of the empire; of these only the Satyaputras are not clearly identified. Tamraparnis, or the people of Sri Lanka, are also mentioned. Ashoka's title 'dear to the gods' was adopted by a Tamil chief. All this was the result of the missionary and acculturating activities of the Jainas, Buddhists, Ajivikas, and brahmanas, as well as the traders who accompanied their train. It is significant that Ashokan inscriptions were set up on important highways. In the earliest stage much of the influence of Gangetic culture over the south was felt through the activities of the heterodox sects that are mentioned in the earliest Tamil Brahmi inscriptions. The brahmanical influence also percolated in a large measure to Tamizhakam, but this really happened after the fourth century AD. Eventually many elements of Tamil culture spread to the north, and in the brahmanical texts, the Kaveri came to be regarded as one of the holy rivers of India.

These southern kingdoms would not have developed without the spread of iron technology which promoted forest clearance and plough cultivation. The distribution of the punch-marked coins of the *janapada* and of the imperial Magadhan type are indicative of the development of north–south trade.

Flourishing trade with the Roman empire contributed to the formation of three states, respectively under the Cholas, Cheras, and Pandyas. From the first century AD onwards, the rulers of these peoples derived benefit from the export and import activity that was carried on between the coastal parts of south India, on the one hand, and the eastern dominions of the Roman empire, especially Egypt, on the other.

Three Early Kingdoms

The southern end of the Indian peninsula situated south of the Krishna river was divided into three kingdoms: Chola, Pandya, and Chera or Kerala. The Pandyas are first mentioned by Megasthenes, who says that their kingdom was celebrated for pearls. He also speaks of it being ruled by a woman, which suggests some matriarchal influence in Pandya society.

The Pandya territory occupied the southernmost and the south-eastern portion of the Indian peninsula, and it roughly included the modern districts of Tirunelveli, Ramnad, and Madurai in Tamil Nadu with its capital at

Madurai. The literature compiled in the Tamil academies in the early centuries of the Christian era and called the Sangam literature refers to the Pandya rulers, but it does not provide any coherent account. One or two Pandya conquerors are mentioned. However, this literature shows clearly that the state was wealthy and prosperous. The Pandya kings profited from trade with the Roman empire and sent ambassadors to the Roman emperor Augustus. The brahmanas enjoyed considerable influence, and the Pandya king performed Vedic sacrifices in the early centuries of the Christian era.

The Chola kingdom, which came to be called Cholamandalam (Coromandel), in early medieval times, was situated to the north-east of the territory of the Pandyas, between the Pennar and the Velar rivers. We have some idea of the political history of the Cholas from the Sangam texts. Their chief centre of political power lay at Uraiyur, a place famous for cotton trade. It seems that in the mid-second century BC, a Chola king named Elara conquered Sri Lanka and ruled over it for nearly fifty years. A clearer history of the Cholas begins in the second century AD with their famous king Karikala. He founded Puhar and constructed 160 km of embankment along the Kaveri river. This was built with the labour of 12,000 slaves who were brought as captives from Sri Lanka. Puhar is coterminous with Kaveripattanam, the Chola capital. It was a great centre of trade and commerce, and excavations show that it had a large dock. One of the principal sources of the wealth of the Cholas was trade in cotton cloth. They maintained an efficient navy.

Under Karikala's successors Chola power rapidly declined. Their capital, Kaveripattanam, was overwhelmed and destroyed. Their two neighbouring powers, the Cheras and the Pandyas, expanded at the cost of Cholas. What remained of the Chola power was almost wiped out by the attacks of the Pallavas from the north. From the fourth to the ninth century, the Cholas played only a marginal part in south Indian history.

The Chera or the Kerala country was situated to the west and north of the land of the Pandyas. It included the narrow strip of land between the sea and the mountains, and covered portions of both Kerala and Tamil Nadu. In the early centuries of the Christian era, the Chera state was as important as the states of the Cholas and Pandyas, and owed its position to trade with the Romans. The Romans set up two regiments at Muziris, coterminous with Cranganore in the Chera state, to protect their interests. It is said that they also built there a temple of Augustus.

The history of the Cheras is a continuing battle with the Cholas and Pandyas. Although the Cheras killed the father of the Chola king Karikala, the Chera king also lost his life. Later, the two kingdoms temporarily became friends and concluded a matrimonial alliance. The Chera king next allied himself with the Pandya rulers against the Cholas, but the Cholas defeated the allies, and it is said that as the Chera king was wounded in the back, he felt shamed and committed suicide.

According to the Chera poets, their greatest king was Senguttuvan, the Red or Good Chera. He routed his rivals and established his cousin securely on the throne. It is said that he invaded the north and crossed the Ganges. All this however seems an exaggeration. After the second century, Chera power declined, and we know nothing of its history until the eighth century.

The principal interest of the political history of these three kingdoms lies in the continuing wars they fought with one another and also with Sri Lanka. Although these states were weakened by the wars, they greatly profited from their natural resources and foreign trade. They grew spices, especially pepper, which was in great demand in the Western world. Their elephants supplied ivory, which was highly valued in the West. The sea yielded pearls and their mines produced precious stones, and both these were exported to the West in substantial quantities. In addition, they produced muslin and silk. We hear of cotton cloth as thin as the slough of a snake. The early Tamil poems also mention the weaving of complex patterns on silk. Uraiyur was noted for its cotton trade. In ancient times, the Tamils traded with the Greek or Hellenistic kingdom of Egypt and Arabia, on the one hand, and with the Malay archipelago and China, on the other. As a result of trade, the words in Greek for rice, ginger, cinnamon, and several other articles were derived from Tamil. When Egypt became a Roman province and the monsoon was discovered at about the beginning of first century AD, this trade received great impetus. Thus, for the first two and a half centuries, the southern kingdoms conducted a lucrative trade with the Romans. With the decline of this trade, these kingdoms began to decay.

The Purse and the Sword

Trade, local and long distance, constituted a very important source of royal revenue. We know how the customs officers functioned in Puhar. Transit duties were also collected from merchants who moved from place to place with their goods. For the safety of merchants and prevention of smuggling, soldiers maintained constant vigil along the road.

The spoils of war further added to the royal income. However, the real foundation of war and polity lay in the regular income from agriculture. The share of the agricultural produce claimed and collected by the king is not specified. The tip of the peninsula and the adjacent regions were extremely fertile. The land produced paddy, *ragi*, and sugarcane. It was said of the Kaveri delta that the space in which an elephant could lie down produced enough to feed seven persons. In addition, the Tamil region produced grains, fruit, pepper, and turmeric. It seems that the king had a share in all this produce.

Apparently, out of the taxes collected from the peasantry, the state maintained a rudimentary army. It consisted of chariots drawn by oxen, elephants, cavalry, and infantry. Elephants played an important role in war. Horses were imported into the Pandyan kingdom by sea. The nobles and princes or the captains of the army rode elephants, and the commanders used chariots. The footmen and horsemen wore leather sandles to protect their feet.

Rise of Social Classes

Income from trade, war booty, and agricultural produce enabled the king to maintain groups of professional warriors and also to pay the bards and priests who were largely brahmanas. The brahmanas first appear in the Tamil land in the Sangam age. An ideal king was one who never hurt the brahmanas. Many brahmanas functioned as poets, and in this role they were generously rewarded by the king. Karikala is said to have given one poet 1,600,000 gold pieces, but this seems to be an exaggeration. Besides gold, the poets or bards also received cash, land, chariots, horses, and even elephants. The Tamil brahmanas partook of meat and wine. The kshatriyas and vaishyas appear as regular varnas in the Sangam texts. The warrior class was an important element in the polity and society. The captains of the army were invested with the title of *enadi* at a formal ceremony. However, we have no clear idea about the vaishyas. Civil and military offices were held under both the Cholas and Pandyas by *vellalas* or rich peasants. The ruling class was called *arasar,* and its members had marriage relations with the *vellalas*, who formed the fourth caste. They held the bulk of the land

and thus constituted the cultivating class, divided into the rich and the poor. The rich did not plough the land themselves but employed labourers to undertake this. Agricultural operations were generally the task of members of the lowest class (*kadaisiyar*), whose status appears to have differed little from that of slave.

Some artisans were not differentiated from agricultural labourers. The *pariyars* were agricultural labourers who also worked with animal skins and used them as mats. Several outcastes and forest tribes suffered from extreme poverty and lived from hand to mouth. We notice sharp social inequalities in the Sangam age. The rich lived in houses of brick and mortar, and the poor in huts and humbler dwellings. In the cities rich merchants lived in the upper storey of their houses. It is not however clear whether rites and religion were used to maintain social inequalities. We notice the emergence of the brahmanas and the ruling caste, but the acute caste distinctions of later times did not exist in the early Sangam age.

Beginnings of Brahmanism

The state and society that were formed in the Tamil state in the early centuries of the Christian era developed under the impact of Brahmanism. However, brahmanical influence was confined to a small part of the Tamil territory and only to the upper levels of the Tamil society in that area. The kings performed Vedic sacrifices; the brahmanas, who were the followers of the Vedas, conducted disputations. However, the chief local god worshipped by the people of the hilly region was Murugan, who came to be called Subramaniya in early medieval times. The worship of Vishnu is also mentioned, although it may have been a later practice. The megalithic practice of providing for the dead continued, paddy being offered to the dead. Cremation was introduced, but inhumation followed in the megalithic phase was not abandoned.

Tamil Language and Sangam Literature

All that has been stated above about the life of the Tamils in the beginning of the historical period is based on the Sangam literature. As shown earlier, the Sangam was a college or assembly of Tamil poets held probably under the patronage of the chiefs or kings. We, however, neither know the number of Sangams nor the period for which they were held. It is stated in a Tamil commentary of the middle of the eighth century that three Sangams lasted for 9990 years and were attended by 8598 poets, and had 197 Pandya kings as patrons. All this is wild exaggeration. All that can be said is that a Sangam was held under royal patronage in Madurai.

The available Sangam literature, which was produced by these assemblies, was compiled in *c.* AD 300–600. However, parts of this literature look back to at least the second century AD. The Sangam literature can roughly be divided into two groups, narrative and didactic. The narrative texts are called *Melkannakku* or Eighteen Major Works. They comprise eighteen major works consisting of eight anthologies and ten idylls. The didactic works are called *Kilkanakku* or Eighteen Minor Works.

Social Evolution from Sangam Texts

Both these types of texts suggest several stages of social evolution. The narrative texts are considered works of heroic poetry in which heroes are glorified and perpetual wars and cattle raids are frequently mentioned. They show that the early Tamil people were primarily pastoral. Traces of early megalithic life appear in the Sangam texts. The earliest megalithic people seem to be primarily pastoralists, hunters, and fishermen, though they also produced rice. Hoes and sickles occur at many sites in peninsular India but not ploughshares. Other iron objects include wedges, flat celts, arrowheads, long swords and lances, spikes and spearheads, horse-bits, and the like. These tools were meant primarily for war and hunting. This has some parallels in the Sangam texts which speak of perpetual war and cattle raids. The texts suggest that war booty was an important source of livelihood. They also state that when a hero dies he is reduced to a piece of stone. This reminds us of the circles of stone that were raised over the graves of the megalithic people. This may have led to the later practice of raising hero stones called *virarkal* in honour of the heroes who had died fighting for kine and other things. It is likely that the earliest phase of social evolution reflected in the Sangam works relates to the early megalithic stage.

The narrative Sangam texts give some idea of the state formation in which the army consisted of groups of warriors, and the taxation system and judiciary arose in a rudimentary form. The texts also tell us about trade, merchants, craftsmen, and farmers. They speak of several towns such as Kanchi, Korkai, Madurai, Puhar, and Uraiyur. Of them, Puhar or Kaveripattanam was the most important. The Sangam references to towns and economic activities are corroborated by Greek and Roman accounts, and by the excavation of the Sangam sites.

Many of the Sangam texts, including the didactic ones, were written by the brahmana scholars of Prakrit or Sanskrit. The didactic texts cover the early centuries of the Christian era and prescribe a code of conduct not only for the king and his court but also for the various social groups and occupations. These categories could have been possible only after the fourth century when brahmanas rose in number under the Pallavas. The texts also refer to grants of villages, and also to the descent of kings from the solar and lunar dynasties.

Besides the Sangam texts, we have a text called *Tolkkappiyam*, which deals with grammar and poetics. Another important Tamil text deals with philosophy and wise maxims, and is called *Tirukkural.* In addition, we have the twin Tamil epics *Silappadikaram* and *Manimekalai*. The two were composed around the sixth century. The first is considered to be the brightest gem of early Tamil literature. It deals with a love story in which a dignitary called Kovalan prefers a courtesan called Madhavi of Kaveripattanam to his wedded wife Kannagi from a noble family. The author apparently seems to be a Jaina and tries to locate the scenes of the story in all the kingdoms of the Tamil state. The other epic, *Manimekalai*, was written by a grain merchant of Madurai. It deals with the adventures of the daughter born of the union of Kovalan and Madhavi. However, this epic is of greater religious than literary interest. It is claimed in the prologues to the two epics that the authors were friends and contemporaries of the Chera king Senguttuvan, who ruled in the second century AD. Though the epics cannot be dated so early, they throw light on the social and economic life of the Tamils up to about the sixth century.

The art of writing was doubtless known to the Tamils before the beginning of the Christian era. Twelve findspots of Ashokan inscriptions in Brahmi script appear in the south, three in Andhra, and nine in Karnataka. Over seventy-five short inscriptions in the Brahmi script dating to about two centuries later have been found in natural caves, mainly in the Madurai region. They provide the specimens of the earliest form of Tamil mixed with Prakrit words. They relate to the second–first centuries BC when the Jaina and Buddhist missionaries came to this area. Inscribed potsherds have been found at several places during recent excavations, These inscriptions provide examples of the Tamil language at the beginning of the Christian era. It is because of the practice of writing that considerable Sangam literature was produced in the early centuries of the Christian era, although it was finally compiled by AD 600.

Chronology

(BC)	
1000	The beginnings of the megalithic culture.
5–1 C	Wide megalithic presence.
4 C	Cultural and economic contact between the north and the deep south known as Tamizhakam.
2 C	The megalithic people moved from the uplands into the fertile river basins. A Chola king conquered Sri Lanka in the middle of this century.
2–1 C	Seventy-five short inscriptions in the Brahmi script, found in the Madurai caves, provide the earliest form of Tamil mixed with Prakrit words.
(AD)	
1 C	Discovery of the monsoon. Tamil language in potsherd inscriptions.
Early centuries	The megalithic phase persisted at some places. The south Indian rulers benefited from trade between the coastal parts of south India and the eastern dominions of the Roman empire, especially Egypt.
2 C	The Chera power declined after this date. Composition of parts of the Sangam literature.
300–600	Final composition of the Sangam literature.
4 C	After this time, brahmana Prakrit–Sanskrit scholars composed many Sangam texts. Brahmanical influence ended in Tamizhakam after this time.
6 C	The marginal role of the Cholas from this time. Composition of the two Tamil epics, *Silappadikaram* and *Manimekalai*, at about this time.
9 C	The Cholas re-emerge as an important power.

23

Crafts, Commerce, and Urban Growth (200 BC–AD 250)

Crafts and Craftsmen

Although a substantial number of non-producing people concentrated in the cities, the age of the Shakas, Kushans, Satavahanas (200 BC–AD 250) and the first Tamil states was the most flourishing period in the history of crafts and commerce in ancient India. Arts and crafts in particular witnessed remarkable growth. We do not hear of so many kinds of artisans in the earlier texts as are mentioned in the writings of the period. The *Digha Nikaya,* which relates to pre-Maurya times, mentions nearly two dozen occupations, but the *Mahavastu*, which relates to this period, catalogues thirty-six kinds of workers living in the town of Rajgir, and the list is not exhaustive. The *Milinda Panho* or the *Questions of Milinda* enumerates as many as seventy-five occupations, sixty of which are connected with various crafts. A Tamil text known in English as *The Garland of Madurai* supplements the information supplied by the two Buddhist texts on crafts and craftsmen. This text does not distinguish between craftsmen and shopkeepers. According to it, many artisans work in their shops, including painters, weavers, clothiers, florists, goldsmiths, and coppersmiths. Such artisan–shopkeepers were found in both urban and rural areas, but in the literary texts, craftsmen are mostly associated with towns. Some excavations indicate that they also inhabited villages. In a village settlement in Karimnagar in Telangana, carpenters, blacksmiths, goldsmiths, potters, and the like, lived in separate quarters, and agricultural and other labourers lived at one end.

Eight crafts were associated with the working of gold, silver, lead, tin, copper, brass, iron, and precious stones or jewels. Various types of crafts associated with brass, zinc, antimony, and red arsenic are also mentioned.

This indicates great advance and specialization in mining and metallurgy. Technological knowledge about iron work had made great progress, and iron artefacts have been discovered in large numbers in Kushan and Satavahana layers at sundry excavated sites. The Telangana region of Andhra seems to have been the richest in this respect, and in addition to weapons, balance rods, socketed axes and hoes, sickles, ploughshares, razors, and ladles have been discovered in the Karimnagar and Nalgonda districts of this region. Indian iron and steel, including cutlery, were exported to the Abyssinian ports, and they enjoyed great prestige in western Asia.

The techniques of cloth-making, silk-weaving, and the manufacture of arms and luxury articles also developed. Mathura was a great centre for the manufacture of a special type of cloth which was called *shataka*. Dyeing was a thriving craft in some south Indian towns. A brick-built dyeing vat has been unearthed at Uraiyur, a suburb of Tiruchirapalli town in Tamil Nadu, and similar dyeing vats were excavated at Arikamedu. These structures relate to the first–third centuries when the handloom textile industry in these towns flourished. The manufacture of oil increased because of the use of the oil wheel. The inscriptions of the period mention weavers, goldsmiths, dyers, workers in metal and ivory, jewellers, sculptors, fishermen, smiths, and perfumers as constructors of caves, and also as donors of pillars, tablets, cisterns, etc., to the Buddhist monks. This suggests that their crafts were flourishing.

Of the handicrafts meant for manufacturing luxury articles, ivory work, glass manufacture, and bead-cutting may be mentioned; the shell industry was thriving. Many products of crafts have been found as a result of digging in the Kushan complexes. Indian ivories have been found in Afghanistan and Rome. They are likened to ivory objects found in excavations at Satavahana sites in the Deccan. Roman glass objects are found in Taxila and in Afghanistan, but it was around the beginning of the Christian era that the knowledge of glass-blowing reached India and attained its peak. Similarly, large numbers of beads of semiprecious stones have been found in post-Maurya layers, which show numerous beads and bangles made of shell. Coin-minting was an important craft, and the period is noted for numerous types of coins made of gold, silver, copper, bronze, lead, glass, and potin. The craftsmen also made fake Roman coins. Various coin moulds relating to the period have been found in both north India and in the Deccan. A coin mould from a Satavahana level shows that it could turnout half a dozen coins at a time. The Greeks, Sakas, Satavahanas, and Kushans

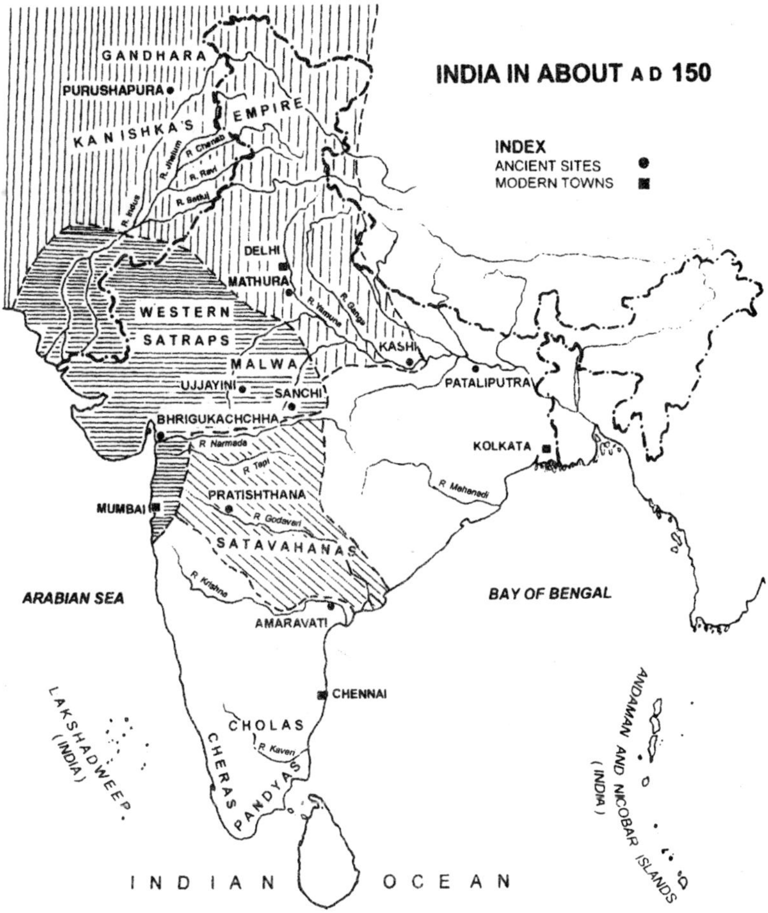

MAP 9 India in about AD 150. *Courtesy ASI*

all contributed to the spread of coins. However, if we go by the coin collections in museums, it appears that the Satavahanas issued the largest number. Even those dynasties which ruled for short periods issued a large number of coins. This is the case with the Indo-Sassanians whose coins are found in half a dozen museums including the British Museum.

Coin moulding and other urban handicrafts were supplemented by the manufacture of beautiful pieces of terracotta, which abound at several places. They have been found at almost all the Kushan and Satavahana sites, but Yelleshwaram in Nalgonda district deserves special mention. There the largest number of terracottas and the moulds in which they were manufactured have been excavated. Terracottas and their moulds are also found at Kondapur, located about 65 km from Hyderabad. Terracottas were used largely by the upper classes in towns. It is significant that with the decline of towns in the Gupta, and especially in the post-Gupta period, such terracottas virtually went out of fashion.

Artisans were organized into guilds which were called *shrenis*. In the second century AD in Maharashtra, lay devotees of Buddhism deposited money with the guilds of potters, oilmen, and weavers to provide the monks with robes and other necessities. During the same century, money was deposited by a chief with the guild of flour-makers at Mathura so that its monthly income could daily feed a hundred brahmanas. On the basis of different texts we can say that artisans of this period were organized into at least two dozen guilds. Most artisans known from inscriptions were confined to the Mathura region and to western Deccan which lay on the trade routes leading to the ports on the western coast.

Types of Merchants

The Garland of Madurai calls the streets broad rivers of people who buy and sell in the market place. The importance of shopkeepers is indicated by the repetition of the term *apana* in the description of the city of Sakala. Its shops appear as filled with various types of cloth made in Kashi, Kotumbara, and elsewhere. Many artisans and merchants were organized into guilds called *sreni* and *ayatana*, but how these organizations functioned is indicated neither in the *Mahavastu* nor in the *Milinda-Panho*. Both merchants and craftsmen were divided into high, low, and middle ranks.

The Buddhist texts mention the *sresthi*, who was the chief merchant of the *nigama*, and the *sarthavaha*, the caravan leader who was the head of the corporation of merchants (*vanijgramo*). It also speaks of nearly half a dozen petty merchants called *vanija*. They dealt in fruits, roots, cooked food, sugar, bark cloth, sheaves of corn or grass, and bamboo. We also hear of many shopkeepers in a Tamil text. They sold sweet cakes, scented powder, fetal quids, and flower garlands. These merchants thus met the varied needs of the urban folk including food, clothing, and housing. To them we can add perfumers or all-purpose merchants called *gandhika*. Various types of oilmen, some of them dealing in perfumed oils, are covered by the term. The term *vyavahari,* that is, one who transacts business, is also used, but the term *vyapari* or trader seems to be missing. The term *agrivanija* seems to be obscure, but these merchants may have been the predecessors of the *agrawalas* if we allow for some linguistic change. Whatever may be the meaning of this term, there were certainly wholesale merchants who conducted both internal and external trade.

Trade Routes and Centres

The most important economic development of the period was the thriving trade between India and the eastern Roman empire. Initially, a substantial amount of this trade was conducted overland, but the movement of the Shakas, Parthians, and Kushans disrupted overland trade. Although the Parthians of Iran imported iron and steel from India, they presented great obstacles to India's trade with the lands further west of Iran. However, since the first century AD trade was conducted mainly by sea. It seems that around the beginning of the Christian era, the monsoon was understood, and this enabled sailors to sail in much less time directly from the eastern coast of the Arabian Sea to the western coast, and easily call at the various ports along the route such as Broach and Sopara situated on the western coast of India, and Arikamedu and Tamralipti situated on the eastern coast. Of all these ports, Broach seems to have been the most important and prosperous. To it were brought not only commodities produced in the Satavahana kingdom but also the goods produced in the Shaka and Kushan kingdoms. The Shakas and the Kushans used two routes from the north-western frontier to the western sea coast. Both these routes converged at Taxila, and were connected with the Silk Route passing through Central Asia. The first route directly ran from the north to the south, linking Taxila with the lower Indus basin from where it passed on to Broach. The second route, called the *uttarapatha*, was in more frequent use. From Taxila it passed through modern Punjab up to the eastern bank of the Yamuna. Following the course of the Yamuna, it went southward to Mathura, from Mathura passing on to Ujjain in Malwa, and again from Ujjain to Broach on the western coast. Ujjain was the meeting point of another route which started from Kaushambi near Allahabad.

Goods in Foreign Trade

Although the volume of trade between India and Rome seems to have been large, it was not conducted in articles of daily use for the common people. There was a brisk commerce in luxury goods, which are sometimes called articles of aristocratic necessities. The Romans first started trade with the southernmost part of India, as their earliest coins are found in the Tamil kingdoms which lay outside the Satavahana dominions. The Romans mainly imported spices for which south India was famous, and also muslin, pearls, jewels, and precious stones from central and south India. Iron goods, especially cutlery, formed an important item of export to the Roman empire. Pearls, ivory, precious stones, and animals were considered luxuries, but plants and plant products served the basic religious, funerary, culinary, and medicinal needs of the people. Kitchenware may have been included in the items of import, and cutlery may have been important for the higher class of people.

In addition to the goods directly supplied by India, certain articles were brought to India from China and Central Asia and then passed on to the eastern part of the Roman empire. Silk was directly sent from China to the Roman empire via the Silk Route passing through north Afghanistan and Iran. However, the establishment of the Parthian rule in Iran and the neighbouring areas created difficulties. Therefore, silk had to be diverted to the western Indian ports through the north-western part of the subcontinent. Sometimes it also found its way from China to the east coast of India, and from there went to the West. Thus there was considerable transit trade in silk between India and the Roman empire.

In return for the articles exported by India to the Roman empire, the Romans exported to India wine, wine-amphorae, and various other types of pottery which were discovered in excavations at Tamluk in West Bengal, Arikamedu near Pondicherry, and at several other sites in south India. Sometimes Roman goods travelled as far as Guwahati. Lead, which was used for making coins by the Satavahanas, seems to have been imported from Rome in the form of coiled strips. The Roman goods do not appear in any substantial quantities in north India, but there is no doubt that under the Kushans, the north-western part of the subcontinent in the second century traded with the eastern part of the Roman empire. This was facilitated by the conquest of Mesopotamia, which was made a Roman province in AD 115. The Roman emperor Trajan not only conquered Muscat but also explored the Persian Gulf. As a result of trade and conquest, the Roman goods reached Afghanistan and north-western India. At Begram, 72 km north of Kabul, large glass jars made in Italy, Egypt, and Syria have been found. Also found there were bowls, bronze stands, steel yards, and weights of Western origin, small Graeco-Roman bronze statues, jugs, and other vessels made of alabaster. Taxila, which is coterminous with the modern Sirkap in the North-West Frontier Province of Pakistan, has yielded fine examples of the Graeco-Roman sculpture in bronze. Silver ornaments, some bronze pots, one jar, and coins of the Roman emperor Tiberius were also found. However, Arretine pottery, which is regularly found in south India, appears neither in central or western India nor in Afghanistan. Evidently these places did not receive popular western articles, which have been found mostly south of the Vindhyas in the Satavahana kingdom and further south. Thus the kingdoms of both the Satavahanas and the Kushans profited from trade with the Roman empire, although the largest profit seems to have accrued to the Satavahanas.

The most significant Roman export to India was the large number of coins, invariably made of gold and silver, though some Roman copper coins are also found. About 150 finds of Roman coins appear in the subcontinent as a whole, and most of them from the south of the Vindhyas. The total number of Roman gold and silver coins that have been found in India does not exceed 6000, but it is difficult to say that only this number of coins came from Rome. The number seems to have been much larger. This justifies the complaint of the Roman writer Pliny, who wrote his account called *Natural History* in Latin in AD 77. He believed that Rome was being drained of gold on account of its trade with India. This may be an exaggeration, but as early as AD 22, we hear of complaints against excessive expenditure on the purchase of pepper from the East. As Westerners were very fond of Indian pepper, it is called *yavanapriya* in Sanskrit. There was also a strong reaction against the use of Indian-made steel cutlery for which the Roman nobles paid very high prices. The concept of the balance of trade may not have then been known, but numerous finds of Roman coins and pottery in the peninsula leave no doubt that India was a gainer in its trade with the Roman empire. The loss of Roman money was so deeply felt that eventually steps had to be taken in Rome to ban its trade with India in pepper and steel goods.

It appears that the major role in the Indo-Roman trade and shipping was played by the Romans. Although Roman traders lived in south India, there is little evidence of Indian residents in the Roman empire. Some potsherds with graffiti in Tamil suggest that some Tamil merchants lived in Egypt in Roman times.

Money Economy

How did the Indians use the silver and gold currency which came to India from Rome? The Roman gold coins were naturally valued for their intrinsic worth, but they may also have circulated in major transactions. In the north, the Indo-Greek rulers issued a few gold coins, but the Kushans issued gold coins in considerable numbers. It is wrong to think that all Kushan gold coins were minted out of Roman gold. As early as the fifth century BC, India had paid a tribute of 320 talents of gold to the Iranian empire. This gold may have been extracted from the gold mines in Sindh. The Kushans probably obtained gold from Central Asia, and may also have procured it either from Karnataka or from the gold mines of Dhalbhum in Jharkhand which later came under their sway. On account of the contact with Rome, the Kushans issued the dinar type of gold coins which became abundant under the Gupta rule. Gold coins may not however have been used in day-to-day transactions, which were carried on in coins of lead, potin, or copper. Both lead and copper deposits are found in Andhra, and gold deposits in Karnataka. The Andhras issued a large number of lead or potin coins in the Deccan. Although the Satavahanas did not issue gold coins, the museums show that they seem to have issued the largest number of coins. Some punch-marked and early Sangam age coins have been found at the tip of the peninsula. The Kushans issued the largest number of copper coins in northern and north-western India. The Indo-Sassanians, the successors of the Kushans in lower Sindh, also issued many coins. Copper and bronze coins were used in large quantities by the rulers of some indigenous dynasties such as the Nagas who ruled in central India, the Yaudheyas who ruled in eastern Rajasthan together with the adjacent areas of Haryana, Punjab, and UP, and by the Mitras who ruled in Kaushambi, Mathura, Avanti, and

Ahichchhatra (Bareilly district in UP). The period roughly between 200 BC and AD 300 evidences the largest number of coins, and these were issued not only by Indian and Central Asian rulers and but also by many cities and tribes. In ancient times, this phase has the highest number of dies and moulds for the manufacture of coins. Perhaps in no other period had the money economy penetrated so deeply into the lives of the common people of the towns and their suburbs as this. This development fits in well with the growth of arts and crafts and India's thriving trade with the Roman empire.

Urban Growth

The growing crafts and commerce, and the increasing use of money, promoted the prosperity of numerous towns during this period. Important towns in north India, such as Vaishali, Pataliputra, Varanasi, Kaushambi, Shravasti, Hastinapur, Mathura, and Indraprastha (Purana Qila in New Delhi), are all mentioned in literary texts, and some of them are also described by the Chinese pilgrims. Most of them flourished during the Kushan period in the first and second centuries. Excavations have revealed superior constructions of the Kushan age. Several sites in Bihar such as Chirand, Panr, Sonpur, and Buxar, and others in eastern UP such as Khairadih and Mason saw prosperous Kushan phases. Similarly, in UP, towns such as Sohgaura, Bhita, Kaushambi, Shringaverapur, and Atranjikhera were prosperous. Rangmahal in Rajasthan, and many other sites in the western areas throve in Kushan times. The excavations at Sonkh in Mathura reveal as many as seven levels of the Kushan phase, and only one of the Gupta phase. Current excavation shows Sachnan Kot, 50 km from Lucknow, to be the largest Kushan town in Northern India. It covers 9 sq. km and contains many brick-houses and copper coins. Again, sites in Jalandhar, Ludhiana, and Ropar, all located in Punjab, and several Haryana sites reveal the quality of Kushan constructions.

In many instances, the Gupta period structures were poorly built and made of used Kushan bricks. On the whole, the material remains from the Kushan phase indicate urbanization at its peak. This also applies to towns in the Shaka kingdom of Malwa and western India. The most important town was Ujjain as the nodal point of two routes, one from Kaushambi and the other from Mathura. It was however also important because of its export of agate and carnelian stones. Excavations show that agate, jasper, and carnelian were worked on a large scale for the manufacture of beads after

200 BC. This was possible because the raw material could be obtained in abundance from the trap bedrock in the bed of the Sipra river in Ujjain.

Towns throve in the Satavahana kingdom during the same period as they did under the Shakas and Kushans. Tagar (Ter), Paithan, Dhanyakataka, Amaravati, Nagarjunakonda, Broach, Sopara, Arikamedu, and Kaveripattanam were prosperous towns in western and south India, during the Satavahana period. Several Satavahana settlements, some of which may be coterminous with the thirty walled towns of the Andhras mentioned by Pliny, have been excavated in Telangana. They had originated much earlier than the towns in coastal Andhra although not much later than those in western Maharashtra. The decline of towns in Maharashtra, Andhra, and Tamil Nadu generally started in the mid-third century or later.

Towns prospered in the Kushan and Satavahana empires because they conducted thriving trade with the Roman empire. India then traded with the eastern part of the Roman empire as well as with Central Asia. Towns in Punjab and western UP throve because the centre of Kushan power lay in north-western India. Most Kushan towns in India lay exactly on the north-western or *uttarapatha* route passing from Mathura to Taxila. The Kushan empire ensured security along the routes, and its demise in the third century dealt a great blow to these towns. The same thing happened in the Deccan. The end of the Satavahana power together with the ban on trade with India imposed by the Roman empire in the third century impoverished the urban artisans and merchants. Archaeological excavations in the Deccan clearly suggest a decline in urban settlements after the Satavahana phase.

Chronology

(BC)	
5 C	India paid Iran a tribute of 320 talents of gold probably extracted from the gold mines in Sindh.
200	Ujjain exported beads, agate, and carnelian stones after this time. Stone was obtained from the bed-rock in the Sipra river.
200 BC–AD 250	The age of the Shakas, Kushans, Satavahanas, and the first Tamil states had flourishing crafts and commerce. Thriving trade between India and the eastern Roman empire.
200 BC–AD 300	The largest number of coins.

1 C	The movement of the Shakas, Parthians, and Kushans from this time disrupted overland trade.
(AD)	
1 C	Trade conducted principally by sea, and, because of the monsoon, sailing took less time. The knowledge of glass-blowing reached India.
22	Complaints against costly purchase of pepper from the East by the Romans.
77	The date of Pliny's *Natural History* in Latin.
1–2 C	Prosperity of towns in north India during the Kushan period.
1–3 C	Dyeing vats in Arikmedu and Tiruchirapalli.
115	Mesopotamia was conquered by the Romans and made a Roman province.
2 C	In Maharashtra, Buddhist devotees deposited money with the various guilds of artisans for the provision of robes and other necessities for the monks. Trade between the north-western part of the subcontinent and the eastern part of the Roman empire under the Kushans.
3 C	Impact of the end of the Kushan empire on towns on the north-western or *uttarapatha* route from Mathura to Taxila. Impact of the end of the Satavahana power on towns and Indo-Roman trade.

24

Rise and Growth of the Gupta Empire

Background

After the break-up of the Maurya empire, the Satavahanas and Kushans emerged as the two large powers. The Satavahanas acted as a stabilizing factor in the Deccan and the south to which they provided political unity and economic prosperity on the strength of their trade with the Roman empire. The Kushans performed the same role in the north. Both these empires came to an end in the mid-third century.

On the ruins of the Kushan empire arose a new empire that established its sway over a substantial part of the former dominions of the Kushans. This was the empire of the Guptas, who may have been of vaishya origin. Different titles are recommended for the different varnas by the Dharmashastras. The title *sharman* or auspicious is recommended for the brahmana, *varman* or armour for the kshatriya, *gupta* or hidden (also protected) for the vaishya, and *dasa* or servile for the shudra. Although the Gupta empire was not as large as the Maurya empire, it kept north India politically united for over a century from AD 335 to 455. The original kingdom of the Guptas comprised UP and Bihar at the end of the third century. UP appears to have been a more important province for the Guptas than Bihar, because early Gupta coins and inscriptions are largely found in that state. If we exclude some feudatories and private individuals whose inscriptions are largely found in MP, UP stands out as the most important area in relation to finds of Gupta antiquities. UP therefore seems to have been the place from where the Guptas operated and fanned out in different directions. Probably with their centre of power at Prayag, they spread into the neighbouring regions.

The Guptas were possibly feudatories of the Kushans in UP, and seem to have succeeded them without any considerable time-lag. At many places in UP and Bihar, Kushan antiquities are immediately followed by Gupta antiquities. It is likely that the Guptas learnt the use of the saddle, reins, buttoned coats, trousers, and boots from the Kushans. All these gave them mobility and made them excellent horsemen. In the Kushan scheme of things, horse-chariots and elephants had ceased to be important, horsemen playing the central role. This also seems to have been the case with the Guptas on whose coins horsemen are represented. Although some Gupta kings are described as excellent and unrivalled chariot warriors, their basic strength lay in the use of horses.

The Guptas enjoyed certain material advantages. The centre of their operations lay in the fertile land of Madhyadesh covering Bihar and UP. They were able to exploit the iron ores of central India and south Bihar. Also, they took advantage of their proximity to the areas in north India that conducted the silk trade with the eastern Roman empire, also known as the Byzantine empire. Given these favourable factors, the Guptas established their rule over Anuganga (along the Ganges in the mid-Gangetic basin), Prayag (modern Allahabad), Saketa (modern Ayodhya), and Magadha. In the course of time, this kingdom became an all-India empire. The Kushan power in north India came to an end around AD 230, and then a substantial part of central India fell under the rule of the Murundas, who were possibly kinsmen of the Kushans. The Murundas continued to rule till AD 250. Twenty-five years later, in about AD 275, the Gupta dynasty came to power.

Chandragupta I (AD 319–34)

The first important king of the Gupta dynasty was Chandragupta I. He married a Lichchhavi princess, in all probability from Nepal, which strengthened his position. The Guptas were probably vaishyas, and hence marriage into a kshatriya family lent them prestige. Chandragupta I seems to have been a ruler of considerable importance because he started the Gupta era in AD 319–20, which marked the date of his accession. Later many inscriptions of the Gupta era came to be dated in this era.

MAP 10 The Gupta Empire at the Close of the Fourth Century.
Courtesy ASI

Samudragupta (AD 335–80)

The Gupta kingdom was enlarged enormously by Chandragupta's son and successor Samudragupta (AD 335–80). He was the opposite of Ashoka. Ashoka believed in a policy of peace and non-aggression, but Samudragupta delighted in violence and conquest. His court poet Harishena wrote a glowing account of the military exploits of his patron, and, in a long inscription, the poet enumerate the peoples and countries that were conquered by Samudragupta. The inscription is engraved at Allahabad on the same pillar that carries the inscriptions of the peace-loving Ashoka.

The places and the countries conquered by Samudragupta can be divided into five groups. Group one includes the princes of the Ganga–Yamuna doab who were defeated and whose kingdoms were incorporated into the Gupta empire. Group two includes the rulers of the eastern Himalayan states and of some frontier states such as Nepal, Assam, and Bengal, which were made to feel the weight of Samudragupta's arms. It also covers some republics of Punjab. The republics, which flickered on the ruins of the Maurya empire, were finally crushed by Samudragupta. Group three includes the forest kingdoms situated in the Vindhya region and known as Atavika *rajyas* which Samudragupta brought under his control. Group four includes twelve rulers of the eastern Deccan and south India who were conquered and liberated. Samudragupta's arms reached as far as Kanchi in Tamil Nadu, where the Pallavas were compelled to recognize his suzerainty. Group five includes the names of the Shakas and Kushans, some of them ruling in Afghanistan. It is said that Samudragupta swept them out of power and received the submission of the rulers of distant lands. The prestige and influence of Samudragupta spread even outside India. According to a Chinese source, Meghavarman, the ruler of Sri Lanka, sent a missionary to Samudragupta for permission to build a Buddhist temple at Gaya. This was granted, and the temple was developed into a huge monastic establishment. If we are to believe the eulogistic inscription at Allahabad, it would appear that Samudragupta never knew defeat, and because of his bravery and generalship he is called the Napoleon of India. There is no doubt that Samudragupta forcibly unified the greater part of India under him, and his power was felt in a much larger area than that of his predecessors.

Chandragupta II (AD 380–412)

The reign of Chandragupta II saw the high watermark of the Gupta empire. He extended the limits of the empire by marriage alliance and conquest. Chandragupta married his daughter Prabhavati to a Vakataka prince of the brahmana caste and ruled in central India. The prince died, and was succeeded by his young son. Prabhavati thus became the virtual ruler. As testified to by some of her land charters, which betray the influence of the eastern Gupta writing, she promoted the interests of her father Chandragupta. Thus Chandragupta exercised indirect control over the Vakataka kingdom in central India, and this afforded him great advantage. With his great influence in this area, Chandragupta II conquered Mathura from the Kushans. More importantly, he occupied western Malwa and Gujarat, which had for about four centuries been under the rule of the Shaka Kshatrapas. The conquest gave Chandragupta control over the western sea coast, famous for trade and commerce. This contributed to the prosperity of Malwa, and its chief city Ujjain. Ujjain seems to have been made the second capital by Chandragupta II.

The exploits of a king called Chandra are glorified in an iron pillar inscription fixed near Qutb Minar in Delhi. If Chandra corresponds to Chandragupta II, it would appear that he established Gupta authority in north-western India and in a substantial part of Bengal. However, the epigraphic eulogy seems to be exaggerated.

Chandragupta II adopted the title of Vikramaditya, which had been first used by an Ujjain ruler in 58–57 BC as a mark of victory over the Shaka Kshatrapas of western India. This Ujjain ruler is traditionally called Shakari or the enemy of the Shakas. The Vikrama *samvat* or era was started in 58–57 BC by Shakari. However, Chandragupta II proved to be a greater Shakari and Vikramaditya. The court of Chandragupta II at Ujjain was adorned by numerous scholars including Kalidasa and Amarasimha.

It was during Chandragupta's reign that the Chinese pilgrim Fa-hsien (AD 399–414) visited India and wrote an elaborate account of the life of its people.

Fall of the Empire

The successors of Chandragupta II had to face an invasion by the Hunas from Central Asia in the second half of AD fifth century. Although initially the Gupta king Skandagupta took effective measures to stem the march of the Hunas into India, his successors proved to be weak and were unable to cope with the Huna invaders who excelled in horsemanship and possibly used stirrups made of metal. They could move quickly, and being excellent archers they seem to have achieved considerable success not only in Iran but also in India.

By AD 485, the Hunas occupied eastern Malwa and a substantial portion of central India where their inscriptions have been found. The intermediate regions, such as Punjab and Rajasthan, also passed into their hands. This must have drastically reduced the extent of the Gupta empire at the beginning of the sixth century. Although the Huna power was soon overthrown by Yashodharman of Malwa who belonged to the Aulikara feudatory family, the Malwa prince successfully challenged the authority of the Guptas and set up in AD 532 a pillar of victory commemorating his conquest of almost the whole of northern India. Yashodharman's rule was short-lived, but it dealt a severe blow to the Gupta empire.

The Gupta empire was further undermined by the rise of the feudatories. The governors appointed by the Gupta kings in north Bengal and their feudatories in Samatata or south-east Bengal tended to declare themselves independent. The later Guptas of Magadha established their power in Bihar. Alongside them, the Maukharis rose to power in Bihar and UP, and had their capital at Kanauj. It seems that by AD 550, Bihar and UP had passed out of Gupta hands. By the beginning of the sixth century we find independent princes issuing land grants in their own right in northern MP, though they used the Gupta era in dating their charters. The rulers of Valabhi established their authority in Gujarat and western Malwa. After the reign of Skandagupta, that is, AD 467, hardly any Gupta coin or inscription has been found in western Malwa and Saurashtra. The loss of western India, which seems to have been complete by the end of the fifth century, must have deprived the Guptas of the rich revenues from trade and commerce and crippled them economically. In north India, the princes of Thanesar established their power in Haryana and then gradually moved on to Kanauj.

The Gupta state may have found it difficult to maintain a large professional army because of the growing practice of giving land grants for religious and other purposes, which was bound to reduce revenues. Their income may have been also lost by the decline of foreign trade. The migration of a guild of silk-weavers from Gujarat to Malwa in AD 473 and their adoption of non-productive professions show that there was no great demand for the cloth produced by them. The advantages from Gujarat trade gradually disappeared. After the middle of the fifth century, the Gupta kings made desperate attempts to maintain their gold currency by reducing the content of pure gold in it, but this proved to be of no avail. Although the rule of the imperial Guptas lingered till the sixth century, the imperial glory had vanished a century earlier.

Chronology

(AD)	
3 C	The original kingdom of the Guptas comprised UP and Bihar at the end of this century.
230	End of the Kushan power in north India. The Murundas ruled till AD 250.
275	The dynasty of the Guptas gained power.
319–20	The Gupta era started by the first Gupta emperor Chandragupta I.
319–34	Chandragupta I.
335–80	Samudragupta, the son and successor of Chandragupta I.
380–412	Chandragupta II.
399–414	Visit of Chinese pilgrim Fa-hsien.
5 C	The Huna invasion in the second half of this century.
467	End of Skandagupta's reign.
473	Migration of a guild of silk weavers from Gujarat to Malwa.
485	The Hunas occupied eastern Malwa and a part of central India.
532	Yashodharman, the Malwa prince, challenged the Guptas and set up a victory pillar claiming his conquest of northern India.
550	The Guptas lost Bihar and UP.

25

Life in the Gupta Age

System of Administration

In contrast to the Maurya rulers, the Gupta kings adopted pompous titles such as *parameshvara*, *maharajadhiraja*, and *paramabhattaraka* which signify that they ruled over many lesser kings in their empire. Kingship was hereditary, but royal power was limited by the want of a firm adherence to primogeniture. The throne did not always go to the eldest son, creating uncertainties of which the chiefs and high officials took advantage. The Guptas made munificent gifts to the brahmanas, who expressed their gratitude by comparing the king to different gods. He was looked upon as Vishnu, the protector and preserver. The goddess Lakshmi is invariably represented on Gupta coins as Vishnu's wife.

The numerical strength of the Gupta army is not known. Evidently the king maintained a standing army, which was supplemented by the forces occasionally supplied by his feudatories. Horse chariots receded into the background, and cavalry came to the fore. Horse archery became an important element in military tactics.

During the Gupta period land taxes increased in number, and those on trade and commerce decreased. Probably the king collected taxes varying from one-fourth to one-sixth of the produce. In addition, whenever the royal army passed through the countryside, the local people had to feed it. The peasants had also to supply animals, food grains, furniture, etc., for the maintenance of royal officers on duty in rural areas. In central and western India, the villagers were also subjected to forced labour called *vishti* by the royal army and officials.

The judicial system was far more developed under the Guptas than in earlier times. Several law-books were compiled during this period, and for the first time civil and criminal laws were clearly demarcated. Theft and adultery fell under criminal law, disputes regarding various types of property under civil law. Elaborate laws were laid down about inheritance. As in earlier times, many laws continued to be based on varna differentiation. It was the duty of the king to uphold the law, and try cases with the help of brahmana priests. The guilds of artisans, merchants, and others were governed by their own laws. Seals from Vaishali and from Bhita near Allahabad indicate that these guilds flourished during Gupta times.

The Gupta bureaucracy was not as elaborate as that of the Mauryas. The most important officers in the Gupta empire were the *kumaramatyas*. They were appointed by the king in the home provinces and possibly paid in cash. As the Guptas were possibly vaishyas, recruitment was not confined to the upper varnas only, but several offices were combined in the hands of the same person, and posts became hereditary. This naturally weakened royal control.

The Guptas organized a system of provincial and local administration. The empire was divided into divisions called *bhukti*s, and each *bhukti* was placed under the charge of an *uparika*. The *bhukti*s were divided into districts (*vishayas*), which were placed under the charge of a *vishayapati*. In eastern India, the *vishaya*s were divided into *vithi*s, which again were subdivided into villages.

The village headman gained in importance in Gupta times, managing village affairs with the assistance of elders. With the administration of a village or a small town, leading local elements were associated. No land transactions could be effected without their consent.

In the urban administration, organized professional bodies were given a considerable say. The sealings from Vaishali show that artisans, merchants, and the head of the guild served on the same corporate body, and in this capacity they obviously conducted the affairs of the town. The administrative board of the district of Kotivarsha in north Bengal (Bangladesh) included the chief merchant, the chief trader, and the chief artisan. Their consent to land transactions was considered necessary. Artisans and bankers were organized into their own separate guilds. We hear of numerous guilds of artisans, traders, etc., at Bhita and Vaishali. At Mandasor in Malwa and at Indore, silk weavers maintained their own guilds. In the district of Bulandshahar in western UP, the oil-pressers were organized into guilds. It seems that these guilds, especially those of merchants, enjoyed certain immunities. In any event, they looked after the affairs of their own members and punished those who violated the laws and customs of the guild.

The system of administration described above applied only to north Bengal, Bihar, UP, and some adjoining areas of MP, which were ruled directly by the officers appointed by the Gupta kings. The major part of the empire was held by feudatory chiefs, many of whom had been subjugated by Samudragupta. The vassals who lived on the edge of the empire had three obligations to fulfil. As subordinate princes, they offered homage to the sovereign by personal attendance at his court, paid tribute to him, and presented to him daughters in marriage. It seems that in return they obtained charters to rule their areas, and these, marked with the royal Garuda seal, seem to have been issued to the vassals. The Guptas thus controlled several tributary princes in MP and elsewhere.

The second important feudal development that surfaced under the Guptas was the grant of fiscal and administrative concessions to priests and administrators. Started in the Deccan by the Satavahanas, the practice became a regular affair in Gupta times, particularly in MP. Religious functionaries were granted land, free of tax, for posterity, and they were authorized to collect from the peasants all the taxes that once went directly to the emperor. The villages granted to the beneficiaries could not be entered by royal agents, retainers, and others, and the beneficiaries were also empowered to punish criminals.

Whether state officials were paid by grants of land in Gupta times is not clear. The abundance of gold coins would suggest that higher officials continued to be paid in cash, but some of them may have been remunerated by land grants.

As much of the imperial administration was managed by feudatories and beneficiaries, the Gupta rulers did not require as many officials as did the Mauryas, and also because, in contrast to the Maurya state, the Gupta state did not regulate economic activities on any substantial scale. The participation of leading artisans, merchants, elders, and others in the rural and urban administration also lessened the need to maintain a large retinue of officers. The Guptas neither needed nor had the elaborate administrative machinery of Maurya times, and in some ways their political system appears to have been feudal.

Trends in Trade and the Agrarian Economy

We get some idea of the economic life of the people of Gupta times from Fa-hsien, who visited different parts of the Gupta empire. The Chinese traveller informs us that Magadha was full of cities and its rich people believed in and supported it with charitable offerings.

In ancient India, the Guptas issued the largest number of gold coins, which were called *dinaras* in their inscriptions. Regular in size and weight, they appear in many types and sub-types. They vividly portray Gupta kings, indicating the latter's love for war and art. Although in gold content the Gupta coins are not as pure as the Kushan ones, they not only served to pay the officers in the army and administration but also to meet the needs of the sale and purchase of land. After the conquest of Gujarat, the Guptas issued a large number of silver coins mainly for local exchange, in which silver occupied an important position under the Western Kshatrapas. In contrast to those of the Kushans, the Gupta copper coins are very few in number. This would suggest that the use of money did not touch the common people as much as it did under the Kushans.

In comparison to the earlier period we notice a decline in long-distance trade. Till AD 550 India carried on some trade with the eastern Roman or Byzantine empire, to which it exported silk. Around AD 550, the people of the eastern Roman empire learnt from the Chinese the art of growing silk, which adversely affected India's export trade. Even before the mid-sixth century, the demand for Indian silk abroad had slackened. In the mid-fifth century, a guild of silk weavers left their original home in western India in the state of Lata in Gujarat and migrated to Mandasor in Malwa where they abandoned their original occupation and adopted other professions.

The striking development of the Gupta period, especially in eastern and central MP, was the emergence of priestly landlords at the cost of local peasants. Land grants made to the priests certainly brought many virgin areas under cultivation, but these beneficiaries were imposed from above on local tribal peasants who were reduced to a lower status. In central and western India, the peasants were also subjected to forced labour. However, a substantial amount of virgin soil was brought under cultivation, and better knowledge applied to agriculture in the tribal areas of central India by the brahmana beneficiaries.

Social Developments

Large-scale land grants to the brahmanas suggest that the brahmana supremacy increased in Gupta times. The Guptas, who probably were originally vaishyas, came to be looked upon as kshatriyas by the brahmanas. The brahmanas presented the Gupta kings as possessing god-like attributes. All this helped to legitimize the position of the Gupta princes, who became great supporters of the brahmanical order. The brahmanas accumulated wealth on account of the numerous land grants made to them and therefore claimed many privileges, which are listed in the *Narada Smriti*, the law-book of Narada, a work of about the fifth century.

The castes proliferated into numerous sub-castes as a result of two factors. A large number of foreigners had been assimilated into Indian society, and each group of foreigners was considered a kind of caste. As the foreigners largely came as conquerors they were given the status of kshatriya in society. The Hunas, who came to India towards the close of the fifth century, eventually came to be recognized as one of the thirty-six clans of the Rajputs. Even now some Rajputs bear the title Hun. The other reason for the increase in the number of castes was the absorption of many tribal people into brahmanical society through the process of land grants. The tribal chiefs were assigned a respectable origin, but most of their ordinary kinsmen were assigned a low origin, and every tribe became a kind of caste in its new incarnation. This process continued in some ways up to the present.

The position of shudras improved during this period. They were now permitted to listen to recitations of the *Ramayana*, the *Mahabharata*, and the Puranas. The epics and the Puranas represented the kshatriya tradition, whose myths and legends won loyalty to the social order. The shudras could also worship a new god called Krishna and were also permitted to perform certain domestic rites which naturally meant fees for the priests. This can all be linked to some improvement in the economic status of the shudras. From the seventh century onwards, they were mainly represented as agriculturists; in the earlier period, they generally figured as servants, slaves, and agricultural labourers working for the three higher varnas.

However, during this period, the number of untouchables increased, especially the chandalas. The chandalas entered the society as early as the fifth century BC. By the fifth century AD, their number had become so enormous and their disabilities so glaring that these attracted the attention of the Chinese pilgrim Fa-hsien. He informs us that the chandalas live outside the village and deal in meat and flesh. Whenever they enter the town, they strike a piece of wood to announce their arrival so that others may avoid them. In the Gupta period, like the shudras, women were also allowed to listen to the *Ramayana*, the *Mahabharata*, and the Puranas, and were advised to worship Krishna. However, women of the higher orders did not have access to independent sources of livelihood in pre-Gupta and Gupta times. The fact that women of the two lower varnas were free to earn their livelihood, which gave them considerable freedom, but this was denied to women of the upper varnas. It was argued that the vaishya and shudra women take to agricultural operations and domestic services and are therefore outside the control of their husbands. In contrast, by Gupta times, members of the higher orders came to acquire more and more land which made them more polygamous and more property-minded. In a patriarchal set-up, they began to treat women as items of property, to such a degree that a woman was expected to follow her husband to the next world. The first example of the immolation of a widow after the death of her husband occurred during the Gupta period in AD 510. However, some post-Gupta law-books held that a woman could remarry if her husband was dead, destroyed, impotent, had become a renouncer, or had been excommunicated.

The principal reason for the subordination of women of the upper varnas was their complete dependence on men for their livelihood, and lack of proprietary rights. However, the oldest Smritis or law-books state that gifts of jewellery, ornaments, garments, and similar other presents made to the bride on the occasion of her marriage were considered her property. Gupta and post-Gupta law-books substantially enlarged the scope of these gifts. According to them, presents received by the bride not only from her parents' side but also from her parents-in-law at marriage and on other occasions formed the *stridhana*. Katyayana, a lawmaker of the sixth century, held that a woman could sell and mortgage her immovable property along with her *stridhana*. This clearly implies that women received shares in landed property according to this lawmaker, but generally a daughter was not allowed to inherit landed property in the patriarchal communities of India.

Niyoga, according to which a younger brother or kinsman could marry the wife of the elder brother after the latter's death, was practised by the brahmanas and kshatriyas in Vedic times, but was not allowed to them by the law-books of Gupta and earlier times. Similarly, widow remarriage was not allowed to members of the higher orders, but the shudras could practise both *niyoga* or levirate and widow remarriage.

The State of Buddhism

Buddhism ceased to receive royal patronage during the Gupta period. Fa-hsien gives the impression that this religion was flourishing, but in reality it was not as important during the Gupta period as it had been in the days of Ashoka and Kanishka. However, some stupas and *viharas* were constructed, and Nalanda became a centre of Buddhist education.

The Origin and Growth of Bhagavatism

Bhagavatism originated in post-Maurya times and centred around the worship of Vishnu or Bhagavata. Vishnu was a minor god in Vedic times. He represented the sun and also the fertility cult. By the second century BC he was merged with a god called Narayana, and came to be known as Narayana–Vishnu. Originally Narayana was a non-Vedic tribal god called *bhagavata*, and his worshippers were called *bhagavatas*. This god was conceived as a divine counterpart of the tribal chief. Just as a tribal chief received presents from his kinsmen and distributed shares among them, Narayana also was supposed to bestow shares or good fortune (*bhaga*) on his *bhakta* or worshippers. In return the worshippers or *bhaktas* offered their loving devotion or bhakti to him. The worshippers of Vishnu and those of Narayana were brought under a single umbrella by merging Vishnu with Narayana. The former was a Vedic god and the latter emerged subsequently with non-Vedic associations, but the two cultures, the two types of peoples, and the two gods mingled and merged.

Besides, Vishnu came to be identified with a legendary hero of the Vrishni tribe living in western India who was known as Krishna–Vasudeva. The great epic *Mahabharata* was recast to show that Krishna and Vishnu were one. Thus, by 200 BC the three streams of gods and their worshippers merged into one and resulted in the creation of Bhagavatism or Vaishnavism.

Bhagavatism was marked by bhakti and ahimsa. Bhakti meant the offer of loving devotion. It was a kind of loyalty offered by a tribal to his chief or by a subject to his king. Ahimsa, or the doctrine of non-killing of animals, suited the agricultural society and was in keeping with the old cult of life-giving fertility associated with Vishnu. People worshipped the image of Vishnu, and offered it rice, sesamum, etc. Out of their aversion to killing animals, some of them took to an entirely vegetarian diet.

The new religion was sufficiently liberal to attract foreigners. It also appealed to artisans and merchants who became important under the Satavahanas and Kushans. Krishna taught in the *Bhagavadgita* that even women, vaishyas, and shudras who were born of sin could seek refuge in him. This religious text dealt with the Vaishnava teachings, as did the *Vishnu Purana*, and also to an extent the *Vishnu Smriti*.

Bhagavatism or Vaishnavism overshadowed Mahayana Buddhism by Gupta times. It preached the doctrine of incarnation, or avatar. History was presented as a cycle of the ten incarnations of Vishnu. It was believed that whenever the social order faced a crisis, Vishnu appeared in human form to save it. Each incarnation of Vishnu was considered necessary for the salvation of dharma which coincided with the varna divided society and the institution of the patriarchal family protected by the state.

By the sixth century Vishnu became a member of the trinity of gods along with Shiva and Brahma, but was a dominant god in his own right. After the sixth century, several texts were written to popularize the virtues of worshipping him, but the most important was the *Bhagavata Purana.* The story in that text was recited by priests for several days. In medieval times *bhagavataghara*s or places meant for Vishnu worship and recitation of the legends associated with him began to be established in eastern India. Several religious recitations, including the *Vishnusahasranama*, were composed for the benefit of Vishnu worshippers.

A few Gupta kings were worshippers of Shiva, the god of destruction, but he came to the fore at a later stage, and does not seem to have been as important as Vishnu in the early phase of the Gupta rule.

Idol worship in the temples became a common feature of Hinduism from the Gupta period onwards and many festivals also began to be celebrated. Agricultural festivals observed by different classes of people were lent a religious garb and colour, and turned into useful sources of income for the priests.

The Gupta kings followed a policy of tolerance towards different religious sects. We find no example of the persecution of the followers of Buddhism and Jainism. This was also due to the change in the character of Buddhism which had come to acquire many features of Brahmanism or Hinduism.

Art

The Gupta period is called the Golden Age of ancient India. This may not be true in the economic field because several towns in north India declined during this period. However, the Guptas possessed a large quantity of gold, whatever its source, and they issued the largest number of gold coins. Princes and the rich could divert a part of their income to support those who were engaged in art and literature. Both Samudragupta and Chandragupta II were patrons of art and literature. Samudragupta is represented on his coins playing the lute (vina), and Chandragupta II is credited with maintaining in his court nine luminaries.

In ancient India, art was largely inspired by religion. Survivals of non-religious art from ancient India are few. Buddhism gave great impetus to art in Maurya and post-Maurya times and led to the creation of massive stone pillars, the hewing of beautiful caves, and the raising of high stupas or relic towers. The stupas appeared as dome-like structures on round bases, principally of stone. Innumerable images of the Buddha were sculptured.

During the Gupta period a life-size copper image of the Buddha of more than 6 feet was made. It was discovered at Sultanganj near Bhagalpur, and is now displayed in Birmingham. During the Gupta period beautiful images of the Buddha were fashioned at Sarnath and Mathura, but the finest specimens of Buddhist art in Gupta times are the Ajanta paintings. Although these paintings covered the period from the first century BC to the seventh century AD, most of them relate to Gupta times. They depict various events in the life of Gautama Buddha and the previous Buddhas whose birth stories are related in the Jatakas. These paintings are lifelike and natural, and the brilliance of their colours has not faded even after fourteen centuries. However, there is nothing to show that the Guptas were the patrons of the Ajanta paintings.

As the Guptas supported Brahmanism, images of Vishnu, Shiva, and some other Hindu gods were fashioned for the first time during their period. At many places, the entire pantheon is portrayed with the chief god at the centre surrounded by his retainers and subordinates. The leading god is represented as large in size, with his retainers and subordinate gods drawn on a smaller scale. This reflects clear social hierarchy and discrimination.

The Gupta period was poor in terms of architecture. All that we find are a few temples made of brick in UP and a stone temple. The brick temples of Bhitargaon in Kanpur, Bhitari in Ghazipur, and Deogarh in Jhansi may be mentioned. The Buddhist university at Nalanda was set up in the fifth century, and its earliest structure, made of brick, relates to this period.

Literature

The Gupta period is remarkable for the production of secular literature, which consisted of a fair degree of ornate court poetry. Bhasa was an important poet in the early phase of the Gupta period and wrote thirteen plays. He wrote in Sanskrit, but his dramas also contain a substantial amount of Prakrit. He was the author of a drama called *Dradiracharudatta*, which was later refashioned as *Mrichchhakatika* or the *Little Clay Cart* by Shudraka. The play deals with the love affair of a poor brahmana trader with a beautiful courtesan, and is considered one of the best works of ancient drama. In his plays Bhasa uses the term *yavanika* for the curtain, which suggests Greek contact. However, what has made the Gupta period particularly famous is the work of Kalidasa who lived in the second half of the fourth and the first half of the fifth century. He was the greatest poet of classical Sanskrit literature and wrote *Abhijnanashakuntalam* which is very highly regarded in world literature. It relates the love story of King Dushyanta and Shakuntala, whose son Bharata appears as a famous ruler. *Shakuntalam* was one of the earliest Indian works to be translated into European languages, the other work being the *Bhagavadgita*. The plays produced in India during the Gupta period have two common features. First, they are all comedies; no tragedies are found. Secondly, characters of the higher and lower classes do not speak the same language; women and shudras featuring in these plays use Prakrit whereas the higher classes use Sanskrit. We may recall that Ashoka and the Satavahanas used Prakrit as the state language.

This period also shows an increase in the production of religious literature. Most works of the period had a strong religious bias. The two great epics, namely the *Ramayana* and the *Mahabharata,* were almost completed by the fourth century AD. Although the epics and Puranas seem to have been compiled by the brahmanas, they represent the kshatriya tradition. They are replete with myths, legends, and exaggerations. They may reflect social developments but are not dependable for political history. The *Ramayana* relates the story of Rama, who was banished by his father Dasharatha from the kingdom of Ayodhya for fourteen years on account of the machinations of his stepmother Kaikeyi. He faithfully carried out his father's orders and went to live in a forest, from where his wife Sita was abducted by Ravana, the king of Lanka. Eventually Rama with the help of Sugriva succeeded in rescuing Sita. The story has two important moral strands. First, it idealizes the institution of family in which a son must obey his father, the younger brother must obey his elder brother, and the wife must be faithful to her husband under all circumstances. Second, Ravana symbolizes the force of evil, and Rama the force of righteousness. In the end, righteousness triumphs over the forces of evil, and a good order over a bad order. The story of Rama had a much wider social and religious appeal than the main narrative of the *Mahabharata*. There are many versions of the *Ramayana* in all the important Indian languages and also in those of Southeast Asia.

The *Mahabharata* is essentially the story of conflict between two groups of cousins, the Kauravas and the Pandavas. It shows that kingship knows no kinship. Although the Pandavas were entitled to their share in the kingdom ruled by Dhritarashtra, the Kauravas refused to give them even a single inch of territory. This led to a prolonged fratricidal war between the Pandavas, patronized by Krishna, and the Kauravas fighting on their own. Eventually the Kauravas were worsted in the battle, and the Pandavas emerged victorious. This story too symbolizes the victory of righteousness over the forces of evil. The *Bhagavadgita* forms an important part of the *Mahabharata*. It teaches that a person must carry out the duties assigned to him by his caste and rank under all circumstances without any desire for reward.

The Puranas follow the lines of the epics, and the earlier ones were finally compiled in Gupta times. They are full of myths, legends, sermons, etc., which were meant for the education and edification of the common people. The period also saw the compilation of various Smritis or the law-books in which social and religious norms were written in verse. The phase of writing commentaries on the Smritis begins after the Gupta period.

The Gupta period also saw the development of Sanskrit grammar based on the work of Panini and Patanjali. This period is particularly memorable for the compilation of *Amarakosha* by Amarasimha, who was a luminary in the court of Chandragupta II. This lexicon is learnt by heart by students learning Sanskrit in the traditional way. Overall, the Gupta period was a bright phase in the history of classical literature and one that developed an ornate style that was different from the old simple Sanskrit. From this period onwards we find a greater emphasis on verse than on prose, and also a few commentaries. Sanskrit was undoubtedly the court language of the Guptas, and although the period produced much brahmanical religious literature, it also gave birth to some of the earliest pieces of secular literature.

Science and Technology

In mathematics, the period saw, in the fifth century, a work called *Aryabhatiya* written by Aryabhata who belonged to Pataliputra. It appears that this mathematician was well versed in various kinds of calculations. Aryabhata displays an awareness of both the zero system and the decimal system. A Gupta inscription of AD 448 from Allahabad district suggests that the decimal system was known in India at the beginning of the fifth century. In the field of astronomy, a book called *Romaka Sidhanta* was compiled, its title indicating that it was influenced by Greek and Roman ideas.

The Gupta craftsmen distinguished themselves by their work in iron and bronze. Bronze images of the Buddha began to be produced on a considerable scale because of the knowledge the smiths had of advanced metal technology. With regard to iron objects, the best example is the iron pillar found at Mehrauli in Delhi. Manufactured in the fourth century AD, the pillar has not gathered any rust over the subsequent fifteen centuries which is a great tribute to the technological skill of the craftsmen, although the arid conditions in Delhi may also have contributed to its preservation. It was impossible to produce such a pillar in any iron foundry in the West until about a century ago. It is a pity that the later Indian craftsmen could not develop this knowledge further.

Chronology

(BC)	
5 C	The chandalas appeared in Indian society.
200	Emergence of Bhagavatism or the Krishna cult.
2 C	Krishna merged with Narayana and came to be known as Narayana–Vishnu.
(AD)	
1–5 C	Period of the Ajanta paintings.
4 C	The iron pillar was set-up at Mehrauli in Delhi.

5 C	The date of the *Narada Smriti* and Aryabhata's *Aryabhatiya*. Awareness of the zero and decimal systems. Fa-hsien states that the chandalas lived outside the village and dealt in meat and flesh.
448	A Gupta inscription of 448 from Allahabad district suggests the knowledge of the decimal system.
510	The first inscriptional evidence of sati.
550	Around this year, the people of the eastern Roman empire learnt from the Chinese the art of growing silk which adversely affected the Indian trade.

26

Spread of Civilization in Eastern India

Signs of Civilization

A region is considered to be civilized if its people know writing, set up a system for collecting taxes, and maintaining order, form social classes and produce specialists for performing priestly, administrative, and production functions. Above all, a civilized society is able to produce enough to sustain not only the actual producers comprising artisans and peasants but also consumers who are not engaged in production. A combination of these elements makes for civilization. They were apparent in a recognizable form very late in a large part of eastern India. Virtually no written records have been found in the greater portions of eastern MP and the adjoining areas of Orissa, West Bengal, Bangladesh, and Assam that relate to a period prior to the mid-fourth century AD.

The period from the fourth to the seventh century is remarkable for the diffusion of an advanced rural economy, formation of state systems, and delineation of social classes in eastern MP, Orissa, eastern Bengal, south-east Bengal, and Assam. This is indicated by the distribution of a substantial number of Sanskrit inscriptions in these areas in Gupta times. Many inscriptions are dated in the Gupta era and appear in the form of land grants made by feudatory princes and others for religious purposes to brahmanas, Vaishnavite temples, and Buddhist monasteries. These beneficiaries played an important role in spreading and strengthening the elements of an advanced culture. The process can be understood by attempting a survey by region.

Orissa, and Eastern and Southern MP

Kalinga, or coastal Orissa south of the Mahanadi, rose to importance under Ashoka, though a strong state had been founded in that area in the first century BC. Its ruler, Kharavela had advanced as far as Magadha. In the first and second centuries AD, the ports of Orissa conducted a brisk trade in pearls, ivory, and muslin. Excavations at Shishupalgarh, the site of Kalinganagari, of Kharavela's capital at a distance of 60 km from Bhubaneswar, yielded several Roman objects indicating trade contacts with the Roman empire. However, the greater part of Orissa, particularly north Orissa, neither experienced state formation nor much commercial activity. In the fourth century Kosala and Mahakantara figured in the list of the regions conquered by Samudragupta, and covered parts of northern and western Orissa. From the second half of the fourth century to the sixth century, several states were formed in Orissa, and at least five of them can be clearly identified. The most important of those was the state of the Matharas, also known as Pitribhaktas, who at the peak of their power dominated the area between the Mahanadi and the Krishna. Their contemporaries and neighbours were the Vasishthas, the Nalas, and the Manas. The Vasishthas ruled on the borders of Andhra in south Kalinga, the Nalas in the forest area of Mahakantara, and the Manas in the coastal area in the north beyond the Mahanadi. Each state developed its system of taxation, administration, and military organization. The Nalas, and probably the Manas, also evolved their system of coinage. Each kingdom favoured the brahmanas with land grants and even invited them from outside, and most kings performed Vedic sacrifices not only for spiritual merit but also for power, prestige, and legitimacy.

During this period elements of advanced culture were not confined to the coastal belt known as Kalinga, but were also apparent in the other parts of Orissa. The find of Nala gold coins in the tribal Bastar area in MP is significant. It presupposes an economic system in which gold money was used in large transactions, and served as a medium of payment to high functionaries. Similarly, the Manas seem to have issued copper coins, which implies the use of metal money even by artisans and peasants. The various states added to their income by forming new fiscal units in rural areas. The Matharas created a district called Mahendrabhoga in the area of the Mahendra mountains, and also ruled over a district called Dantayavagubhoga, which apparently supplied ivory and rice-gruel to its administrators though it had been created in a backward area. The Matharas made endowments called *agraharas*, which consisted of land and income from villages and were meant to support the religious and educational activities of the brahmanas. Some *agraharas* had to pay taxes although elsewhere in the country they were tax-free. The induction of the brahmanas through land grants in tribal, forest, and red soil areas brought new lands under cultivation and introduced better methods of agriculture, based on a better understanding of weather conditions. Formerly the year was divided into three units, each of four months, and time was reckoned on the basis of three seasons. Under the Matharas, in the mid-fifth century, people began the practise of dividing the year into twelve lunar months. This implied a sound idea of weather conditions which was useful for agricultural operations.

In coastal Orissa, writing had certainly been known since the third century BC, and inscriptions up to the mid-fourth century AD were written in Prakrit, but from about AD 350 onwards Sanskrit began to be used. What is more significant, charters in this language appear outside the coastal belt beyond the Mahanadi in the north. Thus, the art of writing and the use of the Sanskrit language spread over a substantial part of Orissa, and some of the finest Sanskrit verses have been found in the epigraphs of the period. Sanskrit served as the vehicle not only of brahmanical religion and culture but also of property laws and social regulations in the new area. Verses from the Puranas and Dharmashastras are quoted in Sanskrit charters, and kings claim to be the preservers of the varna system. The affiliation of the people to the culture of the Gangetic basin is emphasized. A dip in the Ganges at Prayag at the confluence of the Ganges and the Yamuna was considered holy, and victorious kings visited it.

Bengal

As regards Bengal, parts of north Bengal, now in Bogra district, provide evidence of the prevalence of writing during Ashoka's reign. An inscription indicates several settlements maintaining a storehouse filled with coins and food grains for the upkeep of Buddhist monks. Clearly, the local peasants could spare a part of their produce to pay taxes and make gifts. Also, people of this area knew Prakrit and professed Buddhism. Similarly, an inscription found in the coastal district of Noakhali in south-east Bengal indicates that the people of the area knew Prakrit and the Brahmi script in the second century BC. However, for the greater part of Bengal we do not hear anything until up to the fourth century AD. In about the middle of the fourth century, a king with the title 'maharaja' ruled in Pokharna on the Damodara in Bankura district. He knew Sanskrit and was a devotee of Vishnu, for whose worship he possibly granted a village.

The area situated between the Ganges and the Brahmaputra now covering Bangladesh emerged as a settled and fairly Sanskrit-educated region in the fifth and sixth centuries. The Gupta governors, who seem to have become independent after about AD 550, occupied north Bengal; some part of it may also have been seized by the rulers of Kamarupa. Local vassal princes called *samanta* maharajas had created their own administrative apparatus and built their military organization consisting of horses, elephants, foot soldiers, and boats to fight the local peasantry. By AD 600 the area came to be known as Gauda and functioned as an independent state ruled by Shashanka, Harsha's adversary.

For a century from AD 432–3 we notice a series of land sale documents recorded on copperplates in Pundravardhanabhukti, which covered almost the whole of north Bengal, now mostly in Bangladesh. Most of the land transactions indicate that land was purchased with gold coins called *dinara*. However, once land was given for religious purposes, the donees did not have to pay any tax. The land transactions show the involvement of leading scribes, merchants, artisans, landed classes, and the like in local administration, which was manned by governors appointed by the Gupta emperors. The land sale documents not only indicate the existence of different social groups and local functionaries but also shed valuable light on the expansion of agriculture. Generally, land purchased for religious endowments is described as fallow, uncultivated and, therefore, untaxed. Without doubt, the effect of the grants was to bring such plots of land within the purview of cultivation and settlement.

The deltaic portion of Bengal formed by the Brahmaputra and called Samatata, which was made to acknowledge the authority of Samudragupta in the fourth century, covered south-east Bengal. A part of this territory may have been populated and important enough to attract the attention of the Gupta conqueror. However, possibly it was not ruled by brahmanized princes, and consequently it neither used Sanskrit nor adopted the varna system as was the case in north Bengal. From about AD 525 onwards, the area developed a fairly organized state covering Samatata and a portion of Vanga which lay on the western boundary of Samatata. It is called the kingdom of Samatata or Vanga whose rulers, including Sama Haradeva, issued a substantial number of gold coins in the second half of the sixth century.

In addition to this state, in the seventh century, there existed the state of the Khadgas, literally swordsmen, in the Dhaka area. There was also the kingdom of a brahmana feudatory called Lokanatha and that of the Ratas, both in the Comilla area. All these princes of south-east and central Bengal issued land grants in the sixth and seventh centuries. Like the Orissa kings, they too created *agraharas*. The land charters show the cultivation of Sanskrit, in which some sophisticated metres were used in the second half of the seventh century. At the same time, they attest to the expansion of cultivation and rural settlements. A fiscal and administrative unit called *Dandabhukti* was formed in the border areas between Bengal and Orissa. *Danda* means punishment, and *bhukti* enjoyment. The unit was apparently to pacify and suppress the tribal inhabitants of that region and may have promoted Sanskrit and other elements of culture in the tribal areas. This was also true of Vardhamanabhukti (Burdwan) of which we hear in the sixth century. In south-east Bengal in the Faridpur area, five plots of land granted to a Buddhist monastery were declared waste and water-logged and they paid no tax to the state. Similarly, 200 brahmanas were given a large area in Comilla district within a forest region full of deer, boars, buffaloes, tigers, serpents, and the like. All such instances are sufficient proof of the progress of colonization and civilization in new areas.

The two centuries from about the middle of the fifth appear to have been very momentous in the history of Bengal. They saw the progress of Brahmanism and the coming of Buddhism. The statues of the Buddha are virtually non-existent in early centuries, after which they are found in Bodh-Gaya, Sanchi, Mathura, and Gandhara. In the fifth century, however, statues were set up at several places in Bengal. In early medieval times, monasteries were established not only in Bihar but also in north Bengal. The fifth to seventh centuries also saw the formation of about half a dozen states, some large and others small; some independent and others feudatory. However, each had its victory or military camp where it maintained its infantry, cavalry, elephants, and boats. Each had its fiscal and administrative districts with its machinery for tax collection and maintenance of order. Each practised expansion through war and through land grants to Buddhists and brahmanas. The number of endowments had increased to such a degree that eventually an officer called *agraharika* had to be appointed to look after them. Land gifts led to rural expansion and created new rights in land. Generally, land was owned by individual families, but its sale and purchase were subject to the overall control of the local communities dominated by leading artisans, merchants, landowners, and scribes, who assisted the local agents of the king. However, ordinary cultivators were also consulted about the sale of land in the village. It seems that originally land could not be alienated without the consent of the tribe or the community. Therefore, even when individuals owned their land and made gifts for religious purposes, the community exercised its say in the matter. Probably, at an earlier stage, the community donated land to the priests for religious services and paid taxes to the princes for military and political services. Later the king received from the community a substantial part of the land and arrogated to himself much more, which enabled him to make land grants. The king was entitled to taxes and also enjoyed rights over waste and fallow land. The administrative functionaries of each state knew Sanskrit, the official language. They were also familiar with the teachings of the Puranas and the Dharmashastras. The period is therefore very significant because it witnessed the development of civilization in this area.

Assam

Kamarupa, coterminous with the Brahmaputra basin running from east to west, shot into prominence in the seventh century. Excavations, however, show settlements in Ambari near Guwahati from the fourth century of the Christian era. In the same century Samudragupta received tributes from Davaka and Kamarupa. Davaka possibly accounted for a portion of Nowgong district, and Kamarupa covered the Brahmaputra basin. The rulers who submitted to Samudragupta may have been chiefs living on the tributes collected from the tribal peasantry.

The Ambari excavations near Guwahati show that settlements were fairly developed in the sixth and seventh centuries, and this is supported by inscriptions. By the beginning of the sixth century, the use of Sanskrit and the art of writing are clearly in evidence. The Kamarupa kings adopted the title *varman,* which obtained not only in northern, central, and western India but also in Bengal, Orissa, Andhra, Karnataka, and Tamil Nadu. This title, which means armour and symbolizes a warrior, was given to the kshatriyas by Manu. The kshatriyas strengthened their position through land grants to the brahmanas. In the seventh century Bhaskaravarman emerged as the head of a state which controlled a substantial part of the Brahmaputra basin and some areas beyond it. Buddhism also acquired a foothold, and the Chinese traveller Hsuan Tsang (Hieun Tsang) visited this state.

The Formative Phase

Although different parts of eastern India acquired prominence at different times, the formative phase ranged from the fourth to the seventh century. During this period, writing, Sanskrit learning, Vedic rituals, brahmanical social classes, and state systems spread and developed in eastern MP, north Orissa, West Bengal, parts of Bangladesh, and Assam. Cultural contacts with the Gupta empire stimulated the spread of civilization in the eastern zone. North Bengal and north-west Orissa came under Gupta rule; in other areas of these regions, the Gupta influence can be inferred from the use of the Gupta era dates in inscriptions. In Bengal new states were formed by feudatories, who maintained a substantial number of elephants, horses, boats, etc., in their military camps. They obviously collected regular taxes from the rural communities to maintain these professional armies. For the first time, the fifth and sixth centuries clearly show large-scale writing, use of Sanskrit, formation of a varna society, and the growth of Buddhism and Brahmanism in the form of Shaivism and Vaishnavism in this area. Though, the remnants of communal authority over land continued, there is evidence of private property in land, and the use of gold coins with which it could be purchased. All this presupposes an advanced food producing economy. It was apparently based on iron ploughshare agriculture, wet paddy cultivation, and knowledge of a variety of crafts. Kalidasa refers to the transplantation of paddy seedling in Vanga; but we do not know whether the practice was indigenous or came from Magadha. North Bengal produced high quality sugarcane. All this made for sufficient agricultural production to sustain both people and government, and fostered widespread rural settlements in such areas as were either sparsely inhabited or unoccupied. A connected narrative of the princes and dynasties and their feudatories, all revolving around a central power cannot be written, but there is no doubt about cultural evolution and the development of civilization in the outlying provinces in the eastern zone.

The decline and fall of the Gupta empire therefore coincided with considerable progress in the outlying regions. Many obscure areas, which were possibly ruled by tribal chiefs and were thinly settled, came into limelight. This applied to the red soil areas of West Bengal, north Orissa, and the adjoining areas of MP, which formed part of Jharkhand and were difficult to cultivate and settle. It applied even more to the jungle areas with alluvial soil and heavy rainfall in Bangladesh and to the Brahmaputra basin.

Chronology

(BC)	
3 C	Writing known in Orissa.
2 C	In south-east Bengal people knew Prakrit and the Brahmi script.
1 C	In Kalinga, south of the Mahanadi, a strong state was founded by Kharavela who advanced up to Magadha.
(AD)	
1–2 C	Orissa conducted a brisk trade in pearls, ivory, and muslin.
4 C	Settlements in Ambari near Guwahati. Samatata, the deltaic portion of Bengal, acknowledged the authority of Samudragupta who conquered Kosala and Mahakantara. No written records exist for the study of the life of the people in eastern MP and the adjoining areas of Orissa, West Bengal, Bangladesh, and Assam till the middle of this century though Prakrit inscriptions figure in coastal Orissa.
350	Around this date, a maharaja ruled in Pokharna on the Damodara in Bankura district. He knew Sanskrit. From this time onwards, Sanskrit began to be used.
4–6 C	Several states formed in Orissa, and five of them can be identified.
4–7 C	Diffusion of an advanced rural economy, state formation, and delineation of social classes in eastern MP, Orissa, Bengal, and Assam. A formative phase in writing, Sanskrit learning, Vedic rituals, etc.
432–3	Land sale documents recorded on copperplates in Pundravardhanabhukti.
5 C	From about the middle of this century, half a dozen states were formed. People began the practice of dividing the year into twelve lunar months.

5–6 C	Use of Sanskrit, formation of a varna society, and progress of Buddhism and Brahmanism. The area between the Ganges and the Brahmaputra (Bangladesh) emerged as a settled and fairly Sanskrit-educated area.
525	A fairly organized state in Samatata and a part of Vanga on the western boundary of Samatata.
6 C	In the second half of this century, the rulers of Samatata issued a substantial number of gold coins. A fiscal and administrative unit, called Vardhamanabhukti (Burdwan), was created to pacify and suppress the tribal inhabitants of that region.
550	The Gupta governors, probably independent after this date, occupied north Bengal.
600	The area covered by Bangladesh came to be known as Gauda, and became an independent state ruled by Shashanka.
7 C	Kamarupa, coterminous with the Brahmaputra basin from east to west, rose to prominence.
	Bhaskaravarman emerged as the head of a state that controlled the Brahmaputra basin and some other areas. The Chinese pilgrim Hsuan Tsang visited Bhaskarvarman's state. The state of Khadgas was formed in the Dhaka area. The kingdom of a brahmana feudatory called Lokanatha and that of the Ratas were formed in the Comilla area. These princes created *agraharas*. Land charters evidence the cultivation of Sanskrit with some sophisticated metres.

27

Harsha and His Times

Harsha's Kingdom

The Guptas, with their seat of power in UP and Bihar, ruled over north and western India for about 160 years until the mid-sixth century. Then north India again split up into several kingdoms. The white Hunas established their supremacy over Kashmir, Punjab, and western India from about AD 500 onwards. North and western India passed under the control of about half a dozen feudatories who parcelled out the Gupta empire among themselves. Gradually one of these dynasties ruling at Thanesar in Haryana extended its authority over all the other feudatories. The ruler who brought this about was Harshavardhana (AD 606–47). As a result of the excavation of 'Harsha ka Tila' in Thanesar, some brick buildings have been discovered, but they cannot be taken to be parts of a palace.

Harsha made Kanauj his seat of power, and from there he extended his authority in all directions. By the seventh century Pataliputra fell on bad days and Kanauj came to the fore. How did this happen? Pataliputra owed its power and importance to trade and commerce, and the widespread use of money. Tolls could be collected from the traders who came to the city from the east, west, north, and south across four rivers.

However, once trade declined, money became scarce, and officers and soldiers were paid through land grants, the city lost its importance. Power shifted to military camps (*skandhavaras*), and places of strategic importance which dominated long stretches of land. To this class belonged Kanauj. Situated in Farrukhabad district of UP, it shot into political prominence from the second half of the sixth century onwards. Its emergence as a centre of political power from the reign of Harsha onwards typifies the coming of the feudal age in north India just as Pataliputra largely represents the pre-feudal order. Fortification of places in the plains was far more difficult, but Kanauj was situated on an elevated area which was easily fortifiable. Located right at the centre of the doab, it was well-fortified in the seventh century. Therefore, to exercise control over the eastern and western wings of the doab, soldiers could be moved by both land and water routes.

The early history of Harsha's reign is reconstructed from a study by Banabhatta, who was his court poet and who wrote a book called *Harshacharita*. This can be supplemented by the account of the Chinese pilgrim Hsuan Tsang, who visited India in the seventh century and stayed in the country for about fifteen years. Harsha's inscriptions speak of various types of taxes and officials.

Harsha is called the last great Hindu emperor of India, but he was neither a staunch Hindu nor the ruler of the whole country. His authority was limited to north India excluding Kashmir. Rajasthan, Punjab, UP, Bihar, and Orissa were under his direct control, but his sphere of influence spread over a much wider area. It appears that the peripheral states acknowledged his sovereignty. In eastern India he faced opposition from the Shaivite king Shashanka of Gauda, who felled the Bodhi tree at Bodh-Gaya. However, Shashanka's death in AD 619 put an end to this hostility. Harsha's southward march was stopped at the Narmada river by the Chalukya king Pulakeshin, who ruled over a great part of modern Karnataka and Maharashtra with his capital at Badami in the modern Bijapur district of Karnataka. Apart from this, Harsha did not face any serious opposition and succeeded in giving a measure of political unity to a large part of India.

Administration

Harshavardhana's reign is an example of transition from ancient to medieval times. Harsha governed his empire on the same lines as did the Guptas, but his administration had become feudal and decentralized. It is stated that Harsha had 100,000 horses and 60,000 elephants. This appears astonishing because the Mauryas, who ruled over virtually the entire country except the deep south, maintained only 30,000 cavalry and 9000 elephants. Harsha could have had a larger army only if he was in a position to mobilize the support of all his feudatories in the time of war. Evidently every feudatory contributed his quota of foot soldiers and horses, and thus enormously added to the imperial army. The vast numbers of the imperial army suggests a great increase in population.

Land grants continued to be made to priests for special services rendered to the state. More importantly, Harsha is credited with the grant of land to the officers by issuing charters. These grants allowed the same concessions to priests as were allowed by the earlier grants. The Chinese pilgrim Hsuan Tsang informs us that Harsha's revenues were divided into four parts. One part was earmarked for the expenditure of the king, a second for scholars, a third for the endowment of officials and public servants, and a fourth for religious purposes. He also tells us that ministers and high officers of the state were endowed with land. The feudal practice of rewarding and paying officers with grants of land seems to have begun under Harsha. This explains why we do not have very many coins issued by this king.

In Harsha's empire, law and order was not well maintained. Hsuan Tsang, about whose welfare, special care may have been taken by the government, was robbed of his belongings, although he reports that according to the laws of the land, severe punishments were inflicted for crime. Robbery was considered to be a second treason for which the right hand of the robber was amputated. It however appears that, under the influence of Buddhism, the severity of punishment was mitigated and criminals were imprisoned for life.

The reign of Harsha is historically important because of the visit of the Chinese pilgrim Hsuan Tsang, who left China in AD 629 and travelled all the way to India. After a long stay in India, he returned to China in AD 645. He had come to study at the Buddhist university of Nalanda situated in the district of the same name in Bihar and to collect Buddhist texts from India. The pilgrim spent many years in Harsha's court and travelled widely in India. Under his influence Harsha became a great supporter of Buddhism and made generous endowments to it. The pilgrim vividly describes Harsha's court and life in those days, and this account is richer and more reliable than that of Fa-hsien, shedding light on the social and economic life as well as the religious sects of the period.

The Chinese account shows that Pataliputra was in a state of decline, as was Vaishali. On the other hand, Prayag and Kanauj in the doab had become important. The brahmanas and kshatriyas are reported to have led a simple life, but the nobles and priests led a luxurious life. This indicates differentiation in the ranks of each of the two higher varnas. The majority in each of them may have taken to agriculture. Hsuan Tsang calls the shudras agriculturists, which is significant. The earlier texts represent them as serving the three higher varnas. The Chinese pilgrim notes the living conditions of the untouchables such as scavengers, and executioners. The untouchables lived outside the villages, and ate garlic and onion, and when they entered the town, they announced their entry by shouting loudly so that people might keep away from them.

Buddhism and Nalanda

The Buddhists were divided into eighteen sects when the Chinese pilgrim was in India. The old centres of Buddhism had fallen on bad days. The most famous centre was Nalanda, which maintained a great Buddhist university meant for Buddhist monks. It is said to have had as many as 10,000 students, all monks. They were taught Buddhist philosophy of the Mahayana school. Although all the mounds of Nalanda have not been dug, excavations have exposed a very impressive complex of buildings. These were raised and renovated over a period of 700 years from the fifth century onwards. The buildings exposed by excavations do not have the capacity to accommodate 10,000 monks. In AD 670, another Chinese pilgrim, I-tsing, visited Nalanda, and he mentions that only 3000 monks lived there. This is reasonable because, even if the remaining mounds are excavated, the buildings cannot have been sufficiently spacious to have accommodated 10,000 monks. According to Hsuan Tsang, the monastery at Nalanda was supported from the revenues of 100 villages. I-tsing raises this number to 200. Nalanda thus had a huge monastic establishment during the reign of Harshavardhana.

Harsha followed a tolerant religious policy. A Shaiva in his early years, he gradually became a great patron of Buddhism. As a devout Buddhist he convened a grand assembly at Kanauj to widely publicize the doctrines of Mahayana. The assembly was attended not only by Hsuan Tsang and the Kamarupa ruler Bhaskaravarman, but also by the kings of twenty states and by several thousand priests belonging to different sects. Two thatched halls were built to accommodate 1000 persons each. However, the most important construction was a huge tower in the middle of which a golden statue of the Buddha, as tall as the king himself, was placed. Harsha worshipped the image and gave a public dinner. The discussion in the conference was initiated by Hsuan Tsang who dilated on the virtues of Mahayana Buddhism and challenged the audience to refute his arguments. However, nobody came forward for five days, and then his theological rivals conspired to take the pilgrim's life. Hearing of this plot, Harsha threatened to behead anybody causing Hsuan Tsang the slightest harm. Suddenly the great tower caught fire and there was an attempt to assassinate Harsha. Harsha then arrested 500 brahmanas. He banished most of them, and also executed a few. This would indicate that Harsha was not as tolerant as he is painted. After Kanauj, he held at Prayag a great assembly which was attended by all the tributary princes, ministers, nobles, etc. On this occasion, an image of the Buddha was worshipped, and discourses were given by Hsuan Tsang. At the end of it, Harsha made huge donations, and according to a tradition, he gave away everything except his personal clothing. Hsuan Tsang speaks of Harsha in glowing terms. The king was kind, courteous, and helpful to him, and the pilgrim was able to visit the various parts of the empire.

Banabhatta gives us a flattering account of the early years of his patron in his book *Harshacharita* in an ornate style which became a model for later writers. Harsha is remembered not only for his patronage and learning but also for the authorship of three plays: *Priyadarshika*, *Ratnavali*, and *Nagananda*. Bana attributes great poetical skill to him, and some later authors consider him to have been a literary monarch. However, Harsha's authorship of the three dramas is doubted by several medieval scholars. It is held that they were composed by a person called Dhavaka in the name of Harsha for some consideration. Harsha may have composed some pieces, but the proverb goes that royal authors are only half authors. In both ancient and medieval India, various achievements, including high literary attainments, were ascribed to a king in order to boost his image. The practice of praising the patron initiated by Harishena in the time of Samudragupta became common and well established under Harsha. Evidently, the object in such cases was not only to win the favour of the king but also to validate and exalt his position in the eyes of his rivals and subjects.

Chronology

(AD)

5 C	Foundation of the Buddhist structural complex at Nalanda. Establishment of white Huna supremacy over Kashmir, Punjab, and western India.
6 C	The Guptas ruled over north and western India for about 160 years until the middle of the century.
606–47	The reign of Harshavardhana.
629	Hsuan Tsang left China for India.

645	Hsuan Tsang's return to China.
670	The Chinese pilgrim I-tsing visited Nalanda.
7 C	*Harshacharita* by Banabhatta and Hsuan Tsang's account.

28

Brahmanization, Rural Expansion, and Peasant Protest in the Peninsula

The New Phase

The period *c.* AD 300–750 marks the second historical phase in the regions south of the Vindhyas. It continued some of the processes that had begun in the first historical phase (*c.* 200 BC–AD 300) of the peninsula. It however shows some new features that were not regarded as significant in earlier times. The first phase shows the ascendancy of the Satavahanas over the Deccan, and that of the Tamil kingdoms over the southern districts of Tamil Nadu. In that period, northern Tamil Nadu, southern Karnataka, a part of southern Maharashtra, and the land between the Godavari and the Mahanadi broadly owed allegiance to the seats of political authority established outside their areas. They themselves did not have their own states. Now in these areas and also in Vidarbha, between AD 300 and 600 there arose about two dozen states which are known to us from their land charters. Eventually, by the beginning of the seventh century, the Pallavas of Kanchi, the Chalukyas of Badami, and the Pandyas of Madurai emerged as the rulers of the three major states. The first historical phase is marked by numerous crafts, internal and external trade, widespread use of coins, and a large number of towns. Trade, towns, and coinage seem to have been in a state of decline in the second phase, but in that phase numerous land grants free of taxes were made to the temples and brahmanas. The grants suggest that many new areas were brought under cultivation and settlement. This period therefore saw a far greater expansion of agrarian economy.

We also notice the march of triumphant Brahmanism. In the first phase we encounter extensive Buddhist monuments in both Andhra and Maharashtra. Cave inscriptions probably indicate the influence of Jainism and also of Buddhism in the southern districts of Tamil Nadu. Now however Jainism was confined to Karnataka, and the peninsula as a whole shows numerous instances of the performance of Vedic sacrifices by the kings. This phase also marked the beginning of the construction of stone temples for Shiva and Vishnu in Tamil Nadu under the Pallavas, and in Karnataka under the Chalukyas of Badami. By the beginning of the second phase, south India had ceased to be the land of megaliths, and towards its end began the process that made it a land of temples.

Culturally, the Dravidian element seems to have dominated the scene in the first phase, but during the second phase Aryanization and brahmanization came to the fore. This happened because of land grants made by the rulers who were either brahmanas or firm supporters of them. As managers of temple lands, the brahmanas guided cultural and religious activities. They spread Sanskrit, which became the official language. The Ashokan inscriptions found in Andhra and Karnataka show that the people knew Prakrit in the third century BC. Also, epigraphs between the second century BC and the third century AD were largely written in Prakrit. The Brahmi inscriptions that have been found in Tamil Nadu also contain Prakrit words, but from about AD 400 onwards Sanskrit became the official language in the peninsula and most charters were composed in it.

States of the Deccan and South India

In northern Maharashtra and Vidarbha (Berar), the Sātavahanas were succeeded by the Vakatakas, a local power. The Vakatakas, who were brahmanas themselves, are known from a large number of copperplate land grants issued by them. They were great champions of the brahmanical religion and performed numerous Vedic sacrifices. Their political history is more linked to north India than to south India. We may recall how Chandragupta II married his daughter Prabhavati Gupta into the Vakataka royal family and with its support conquered Malwa and Gujarat from the Shaka Kshatrapas in the last quarter of the fourth century AD. Culturally however the Vakataka kingdom served as a channel for the transmission of brahmanical ideas and social institutions to the south.

The Vakataka power was followed by that of the Chalukyas of Badami who played an important role in the history of the Deccan and south India for about two centuries until AD 757, when they were overthrown by their feudatories, the Rashtrakutas. The Chalukyas claimed their descent from Brahma or Manu or the Moon. They boasted that their ancestors ruled at Ayodhya, but all this was done to acquire legitimacy and respectability. In actuality they seem to have been a local Kanarese people who were accommodated in the ruling varna with brahmanical blessings.

The Chalukyas set up their kingdom towards the beginning of the sixth century in the western Deccan. They established their capital at Vatapi, modern Badami, in the district of Bijapur, which forms a part of Karnataka. They later branched off into several independent ruling houses, but the main branch continued to rule at Vatapi for two centuries. During this period, no other power in the Deccan was as important as the Chalukyas of Badami until we come to Vijayanagar in later medieval times.

On the ruins of the Satavahana power in the eastern part of the peninsula, there arose the Ikshvakus in the Krishna–Guntur region. They seem to have been a local tribe who adopted the exalted name of the Ikshvakus in order to demonstrate the antiquity of their lineage, and also claimed to be brahmanas. They have left behind many monuments at Nagarjunakonda and Dharanikota. They began the practise of land grants in the Krishna–Guntur region, where several of their copperplate inscriptions have been discovered.

The Ikshvakus were supplanted by the Pallavas. The term *pallava* means creeper, and is a Sanskrit version of the Tamil word *tondai*, which also carries the same meaning. The Pallavas were possibly a local tribe who established their authority in the Tondainadu or the land of creepers. It however took them some time to become completely civilized and acceptable because in Tamil, the word *pallava* is also a synonym of robber. The authority of the Pallavas extended over both southern Andhra and northern Tamil Nadu. They set up their capital at Kanchi, identical with modern Kanchipuram, which under them became a town of temples and Vedic learning.

The early Pallavas came into conflict with the Kadambas, who had established their control over northern Karnataka and Konkan in the fourth century. They claimed to be brahmanas, and generously rewarded their fellow caste men.

The Kadamba kingdom was founded by Mayurasharman. It is said that he came to receive education at Kanchi but was unceremoniously driven out. Smarting under this insult, the Kadamba chief set up his camp in a forest, and defeated the Pallavas, possibly with the help of the forest tribes.

Eventually, the Pallavas avenged the defeat but recognized the Kadamba authority by formally investing Mayurasharman with the royal insignia. Mayurasharman is said to have performed eighteen *ashvamedhas* or horse sacrifices and granted numerous villages to brahmanas. The Kadambas established their capital at Vaijayanti or Banavasi in north Kanara district of Karnataka.

The Gangas were another important contemporary dynasty of the Pallavas. They established their kingdom in southern Karnataka around the fourth century. The kingdom was situated between that of the Pallavas in the east and of the Kadambas in the west. They are called the Western Gangas or Gangas of Mysore in order to differentiate them from the Eastern Gangas who ruled in Kalinga from the fifth century onwards. For most of their reign, the Western Gangas were feudatories of the Pallavas. Their earliest capital was located at Kolar which, given its gold mines, may have helped the rise of this dynasty.

The Western Gangas made land grants mostly to the Jainas; the Kadambas also made grants to the Jainas, though they favoured the brahmanas more. The Pallavas for their part granted numerous villages free of taxes largely to the brahmanas. We have as many as sixteen land charters of the early Pallavas. A few, which seem to be earlier, are written on stone in Prakrit, but most of them were recorded on copperplates in Sanskrit. The villages granted to the brahmanas were exempted from payment of all taxes and forced labour to the state. This implied that these were collected from the cultivators by the brahmanas for their personal use and profit. As many as eighteen types of immunities were granted to the brahmanas in a Pallava grant of the fourth century. They were empowered to enjoy the fruits of the land so granted and exempted from payment of land tax, from supply of forced labour, from supply of provisions to royal officers living in the town, and free from the interference of royal agents and constabulary.

The Pallavas, the Kadambas, the Chalukyas of Badami, and their other contemporaries were great champions of Vedic sacrifices. They performed *ashvamedha* and *vajapeya* sacrifices, which legitimatized their position, enhanced their prestige, and enormously increased the income of the priestly class. The brahmanas therefore emerged as an important class at the expense of the peasantry, from whom they collected their dues directly. They also received as gifts a substantial proportion of the taxes collected by the king from his subjects.

The Kalabhra Revolt

Although the period between AD 300 and 750 was extremely important for state formation and agrarian expansion in the peninsula, very little is known about what happened at the tip of the peninsula after the eclipse of the Cholas, the Cheras, and the Pandyas. The only important event is a revolt led by the Kalabhras in the sixth century. The Kalabhras seem to have been a tribal people who captured power, particularly at the cost of the Cholas, and ruled for seventy-five years. Their rule also affected the Pallavas as well as their neighbouring contemporaries. The Kalabhras are called evil rulers, who overthrew innumerable kings and established their hold on the Tamil land. The Kalabhra revolt was a powerful peasant protest directed against the landed brahmanas. The repeated teaching that those who attack land grants are condemned to hell for sixty thousand years failed to change their minds. They put an end to the *brahmadeya* rights granted to the brahmanas in numerous villages. It appears that the Kalabhras were of Buddhist persuasion as they patronized Buddhist monasteries. The Kalabhras' revolt was so widespread that it could be quelled only through the joint efforts of the Pandyas, the Pallavas, and the Chalukyas of Badami. By the last quarter of the sixth century, according to a tradition, the Kalabhras had imprisoned the Chola, the Pandya, and the Chera kings, which underlines how formidable their revolt was. The confederacy of the kings formed against the Kalabhras, who had revoked the land grants made to the brahmanas, shows that the revolt was directed against the existing social and political order in south India.

It, therefore, appears that some land grants had been made between AD 300 and 500 to the brahmanas by the kings of the deep south. The Sangam texts tell us that villages were granted to the warriors by the chief for their acts of bravery. Land grants seem to have stimulated agrarian expansion under the Pallavas in south Andhra and north Tamil Nadu from the end of the third century onwards, but they seem to have adversely affected the peasants.

Conflict between the Pallavas and the Chalukyas

The principal interest in the political history of peninsular India from the sixth to the eighth century centres around the long struggle for supremacy between the Pallavas of Kanchi and the Chalukyas of Badami. The Pandyas, who were in control of Madurai and Tirunelveli districts of Tamil Nadu, joined this conflict as a poor third. Although both the Pallavas and the Chalukyas championed Brahmanism, performed Vedic sacrifices, and made grants to the brahmanas, the two quarrelled with each other over plunder, prestige, and territorial resources. Both tried to establish supremacy over the land lying between the Krishna and the Tungabhadra. This doab was again the bone of contention in late medieval times between the Vijayanagar and the Bahmani kingdoms. Time and again, the Pallava princes tried to cross the Tungabhadra, which formed the natural historic boundary between many a kingdom of the Deccan and the deep south. The struggle continued over a long period with varying fortunes.

The first important event in this long conflict took place during the reign of Pulakeshin II (AD 609–42), the most famous Chalukya king. He is known to us from the eulogy written on him by the court poet Ravikirti in the Aihole inscription. This inscription is an example of the poetic excellence achieved in Sanskrit, and despite its exaggeration is a valuable source for the life of Pulakeshin. He subjugated the Kadamba capital at Banavasi and compelled the Gangas of Mysore to acknowledge his suzerainty. He also defeated Harsha's army on the Narmada and checked his advance towards the Deccan. In his conflict with the Pallavas, he almost reached the Pallava capital, but the Pallavas purchased peace by ceding their northern provinces to Pulakeshin II. Around AD 610 Pulakeshin II also conquered the entire area between the Krishna and the Godavari, which came to be known as the province of Vengi. Here, a branch of the main dynasty was set up and is known as the eastern Chalukyas of Vengi. However, Pulakeshin's second invasion of Pallava territory ended in failure. The Pallava king Narasimhavarman (AD 630–68) occupied the Chalukya capital at Vatapi in about AD 642, when Pulakesin II was probably killed in a battle against the Pallavas. Narasimhavarman assumed the title of Vatapikonda or the conqueror of Vatapi. He is also said to have defeated the Cholas, the Cheras, the Pandyas, and the Kalabhras.

Towards the end of the seventh century, there was a lull in this conflict, which was again resumed in the first half of the eighth century. The Chalukya king Vikramaditya II (AD 733–45) is said to have overrun Kanchi three times. In AD 740 he completely routed the Pallavas. His victory ended the Pallava supremacy in the far south although the ruling house continued for over a century thereafter. However, the Chalukyas were unable for long to enjoy the fruits of their victory over the Pallavas because their own hegemony was brought to an end in AD 757 by the Rashtrakutas.

Temples

Besides the performance of Vedic sacrifices, the worship of Brahma, Vishnu, and Shiva, especially of the last two, was becoming popular. From the seventh century onwards, the Alvar saints, who were great devotees of Vishnu, popularized the worship of this god. The Nayanars rendered a similar service to the cult of Shiva. From the seventh century onwards, the cult of bhakti began to dominate the religious life of south Indians, and the Alvars and Nayanars played a great part in propagating it.

The Pallava kings constructed a number of stone temples in the seventh and eighth centuries for housing these gods. The most famous of them are the seven *ratha* temples at Mahabalipuram, at a distance of 65 km from Chennai. These were built in the seventh century by Narasimhavarman, who founded the port city of Mahabalipuram or Mamallapuram. This city is also famous for the Shore Temple, which was a structural construction erected independently and not hewn out of rock. In addition, the Pallavas constructed several such structural temples at their capital Kanchi. A very good example was the Kailashanath temple built in the eighth century. The Chalukyas of Badami erected numerous temples at Aihole, which has as many as seventy, from about AD 610. The work was continued in the adjacent towns of Badami and Pattadakal. Pattadakal has ten temples built in the seventh and eighth centuries, the most celebrated of which are the Papanatha temple (*c.* AD 680) and the Virupaksha temple (*c.* AD 740). The first of these, although 30 m long, has a low and stunted tower in the northern style; the second was constructed in purely southern style. The latter is about 40 m in length and has a very high square and storeyed tower (*shikhara*). The temple walls are adorned with beautiful pieces of sculpture, representing scenes from the *Ramayana*.

We have no clear idea of how these early temples were maintained. After the eighth century, land grants to temples became a common practice in south India, and usually they were recorded on the walls of the temples. Most temples were managed by the brahmanas. By early medieval times, such temples came to own three-fifths of the arable land, and became centres of religious rituals and caste-based ideology in south India. However, the earlier temples seem to have been constructed and maintained out of the taxes directly collected by the king from the common people. Some temples in Karnataka under the Chalukyas were erected by Jaina traders. The common people worshipped their village gods by offering them paddy and toddy, but those who could afford it might have made rich offerings to acquire status and satisfy their religious cravings.

Demands on the Peasantry

To conduct wars, to cultivate art and literature, to promote religion, and to maintain the administrative staff, enormous resources were needed. These were apparently provided by the peasantry. The nature of burdens imposed on the agrarian communities was more or less the same in the Vakataka and the Pallava kingdoms although the former was in Vidarbha and Maharashtra, and the latter in southern Andhra and northern Tamil Nadu. In addition to land tax, which was a part of the produce, the king could demand donations of cereals and gold, and could bore certain trees such as the palmyra to obtain salt and substances derived from plants such as sugar and liquor. Of course, all the natural resources beneath the earth in the villages belonged to him. In addition, he demanded flowers and milk, wood and grass, and could compel the villagers to carry loads free of charge. The king was also entitled to forced labour or *vishti*.

When royal officials visited the villages either to collect taxes or to punish criminals, and also when the army was on the march, the rural communities had to fulfil several obligations. They had to supply bullocks for carts and provide beds, charcoal, ovens, cooking pots, and attendants.

This whole list of imposts indicates that the state made heavy demands on the labour and produce of the peasantry. Most of these are covered by the eighteen types of immunities granted to the brahmanas from the fourth century AD onwards. Later, more and more demands were made on the peasantry.

Land Grants and Rural Expansion

These numerous demands made by the king on the agrarian population presuppose a capacity to pay on the part of the peasantry. Collection could not have been possible without an increase in agricultural production. In this period we witness the formation of new states in the trans-Vindhyan regions. Each state had a number of feudatory chiefdoms, which were small states within a large state. Each of them, large or small, paramount or feudatory, needed its own administrative machinery, and a substantial number of priestly and other functionaries. Every state, therefore, required resources that could be obtained from its rural base. Therefore, the states could not multiply without the proliferation of rural communities or an increase in the agricultural production of the existing villages. It seems that in tribal areas, the brahmanas were granted land, and the tribal peasantry learnt the value of preserving cattle and better methods of cultivation from them. The peasants also learnt from the brahmanas the new calendar that helped agriculture. Certain areas suffered from a dearth of labour power. In order to sustain the economy of such areas, it was also found necessary to make over some sharecroppers and weavers to the brahmanas, as is known from an early Pallava grant. Therefore, the large number of grants made to the brahmanas played an important role in spreading new methods of cultivation and increasing the size of the rural communities.

This period saw three types of villages in south India: *ur*, *sabha*, and *nagaram*. The *ur* was the usual type of village inhabited by peasant castes, who perhaps held their land in common; it was the responsibility of the village headman to collect and pay taxes on their behalf. These villages were mainly found in southern Tamil Nadu. The *sabha* type of village consisted of *brahmadeya* villages or those granted to the brahmanas, and of *agrahara* villages. The brahmana owners enjoyed individual rights in the land but carried on their activities collectively. The *nagaram* type of village consisted of a village settled and dominated by combinations of traders and merchants. This possibly happened because trade declined and merchants moved to villages. In the Chalukya areas, rural affairs were managed by village elders called *mahajana*. On the whole, the period *c*. AD 300–750 provides good evidence of agricultural expansion, rural organization, and more productive use of land.

Social Structure and Brahmanization

We can present a rough outline of the social structure that developed in this period. Society was dominated by princes and priests. The princes claimed the status of brahmanas or kshatriyas, though many of them were local clan chiefs promoted to the second varna through benefactions made to the priests. The priests invented respectable family trees for these chiefs and traced their descent from age-old solar and lunar dynasties. This process enabled the new rulers to acquire acceptability in the eyes of the people. The priests were mainly brahmanas, though the Jaina and Buddhist monks may also be placed in this category. In this phase, priests through land grants gained in influence and authority. Many south Indian rulers claimed to be brahmanas, which shows that the kshatriyas were not as important in the south as in the north. The same seems to have been the case with the vaishyas. Though the varna system was introduced in south India, in practice its operation was different from that in Aryavarta or the main part of north India.

However, like the north, below the princes and priests came the peasantry, which was divided into numerous peasant castes. Possibly most of them were called shudras in the brahmanical system. If the peasant and artisan castes failed to produce and render services and payments, it was considered a departure from the established dharma or norm. Such a situation was described as the age of Kali. It was the duty of the king to put an end to such a state of affairs and restore peace and order which worked in favour of chiefs and priests. The title *dharma-maharaja* was, therefore, adopted by the Vakataka, Pallava, Kadamba, and Western Ganga kings. The real founder of the Pallava power, Simhavarman, is credited with coming to the rescue of dharma when it was beset with the evils typical of the Kaliyuga. This apparently refers to his suppression of the Kalabhra, peasants who upset the existing social order.

Chronology

200 BC–AD 300	The ascendancy of the Satavahanas over the Deccan and that of the Tamil kingdoms over southern Tamil Nadu. Non-Ashokan epigraphs in Andhra and Karnataka in Prakrit.
(AD)	
300–500	Land grants to the brahmanas by the kings of the deep south.
300–600	About two dozen states in the peninsula, including Vidarbha.
300–750	Rural expansion and better use of land south of the Vindhyas. More state formation in the peninsula.
4 C	Eighteen types of immunities for the brahmanas in peninsular India. The rise of Western Ganga rule in southern Karnataka. Chandragupta II captured

	Malwa and Gujarat from the Shaka Kshatrapas. The Kadamba controlled northern Karnataka and Konkan. From now Sanskrit became the official language in the peninsula.
5 C	The Eastern Gangas ruled Kalinga from this century onwards.
6 C	The Kalabhra revolt. The Chalukyas set up their kingdom in the western Deccan.
6–8 C	Struggle between the Pallavas of Kanchi and the Chalukyas of Badami.
7 C	Emergence of the Pallavas of Kanchi, the Chalukyas of Badami, and the Pandyas of Madurai as major states. The reign of the Chalukya king Pulakeshin II according to the Aihole inscription.
610	Erection of temples.
630–68	The reign of the Pallava king Narasimhavarman.
680	The Papanatha temple of Pattadakal.
733–45	The reign of the Chalukya king Vikramaditya II.
740	The Virupaksha temple of Pattadakal.
757	Pallava hegemony brought to an end.
775	The end of the role of the Chalukyas of Badami in the Deccan.

29

Developments in Philosophy

Goals of Life

Once the state and the varna-divided social order had been firmly established, the ancient thinkers advocated that a person should strive for the attainment of four goals. These were regulation of the social order or dharma, economic resources or *artha*, physical pleasures or *kama*, and salvation or *moksha*. Each of these objectives was expounded in writing. Matters relating to economy were treated in the *Arthashastra*, the well-known book written by Kautilya. Laws governing the state and society became the subject of the *Dharmashastra*, and physical pleasures were discussed in the *Kamasutra*. All these three branches of knowledge were primarily concerned with the material world and its problems. They occasionally touched marginally on the question of salvation. Salvation or *moksha* became the central subject of the texts on *darshana* or philosophy. It meant deliverance from the cycle of birth and death, which was first recommended by Gautama Buddha but later emphasized by some brahmanical philosophers.

By the beginning of the Christian era, six schools of philosophy developed. These were known as Samkhya, Yoga, Nyaya, Vaisheshika, Mimamsa, and Vedanta.

Samkhya

Samkhya, literally 'count', seems to have originated first. According to the early Samkhya philosophy, the presence of divine agency is not essential to the creation of the world. The world owes its creation and evolution more to Nature or *prakriti* than to God. This was a rational and scientific view. Around the fourth century AD, in addition to *prakriti*, *purusha* or spirit was introduced as an element in the Samkhya system, and the creation of the world was attributed to both. According to the new view, Nature and the spiritual element together create the world. Thus, at the outset the Samkhya school of philosophy was materialistic, but later it tended to become spiritualistic. Initially, according to this school, a person can attain salvation through the acquisition of real knowledge, and his misery can be ended for ever. This knowledge can be acquired through perception (*pratyaksha*), inference (*anumana*), and hearing (*shabda*). Such a method is characteristic of a scientific system of inquiry.

Yoga

According to the Yoga school, a person can attain salvation through meditation and physical application. Practice of control over pleasure, the senses, and bodily organs is central to this system. In order to obtain salvation, physical exercises in various postures called *asana*s are prescribed, and a breathing exercise called *pranayama* is recommended. It is thought that through these methods, the mind gets diverted from worldly matters and achieves concentration. These exercises are important because they not only presuppose some development of the knowledge of physiology and anatomy in ancient times, but they also indicate a tendency to run away from worldly difficulties.

Nyaya

Nyaya, or the school of analysis, was developed as a system of logic. According to it, salvation can be attained through the acquisition of knowledge. What is more important, the veracity of a proposition or statement can be tested through inference, hearing, and analogy. An example of how they used logic is given below:

1. There is fire in the mountain
2. because it emits smoke;
3. whatever emits smoke contains fire such as the hearth.

The stress laid on the use of logic influenced Indian scholars who took to systematic thinking and reasoning.

Vaisheshika

The Vaisheshika school gives importance to the discussion of material elements or *dravya*. They draw a line between particularities and their aggregate. Earth, water, fire, air, and ether (sky), when combined, give rise to new objects. The Vaisheshika school propounded the atom theory believing that all material objects are made up of atoms. The Vaisheshika thus marked the beginning of physics in India, but the scientific view was diluted by a belief in god and spiritualism, and this school put its faith in both heaven and salvation.

Mimamsa

Mimamsa literally means the art of reasoning and interpretation. However, reasoning was used to provide justifications for various Vedic rituals, and the attainment of salvation was made dependent on their performance. According to the Mimamsa school, the Vedas contain the eternal truth. The principal object of this philosophy was to acquire heaven and salvation. A person will enjoy the bliss of heaven so long as his accumulated acts of virtue last. When his accumulated virtues are exhausted, he will return to earth, but if he attains salvation he will be completely free from the cycle of birth and death in the world.

In order to attain salvation, the Mimamsa school strongly recommended the performance of Vedic sacrifices, which needed the services of priests and legitimized the social distance between the various varnas. Through the propagation of the Mimamsa philosophy, the brahmanas sought to maintain their ritual authority and preserve the social hierarchy based on Brahmanism.

Vedanta

Vedanta means the end of the Veda. The *Brahmasutra* of Badarayana compiled in the second century BC formed its basic text. Later, two famous commentaries were written on it, one by Shankara in the ninth century and the other by Ramanuja in the twelfth. Shankara considers *brahma* to be without any attributes, but Ramanuja's *brahma* had attributes. Shankara considered knowledge or *jnana* to be the chief means of salvation, but Ramanuja's road to salvation lay in practising devotion/loving faith.

Vedanta philosophy is traced to the earlier Upanishads. According to it, *brahma* is the reality and everything else is unreal (*maya*). The self (soul) or atma coincides with *brahma*. Therefore, if a person acquires the knowledge of the self (atma), he acquires the knowledge of *brahma*, and thus attains salvation. Both *brahma* and atma are eternal and indestructible. Such a view promotes the idea of stability and unchangeability. What is true spiritually could also be true of the social and material situation in which a person is placed.

The theory of karma came to be linked to Vedanta philosophy. It means that in his present birth, a person has to bear the consequences of his actions performed in his previous birth. Belief in rebirth or *punarjanma* becomes an important element not only in the Vedanta system but also in several other systems of Hindu philosophy. It implies that people suffer not because of social or worldly causes but because of causes which they neither know nor which they can control.

Charvaka and the Materialistic View of Life

By and large, the six systems of philosophical teaching promoted the idealistic view of life. All of them became paths of attaining salvation. The Samkhya and Vaisheshika systems advanced the materialistic view of life. Kapila, the earliest exponent of the Samkhya, teaches that a man's life is shaped by the forces of nature and not by any divine agency. Materialistic ideas also figure in the doctrines of the Ajivikas, a heterodox sect in the time of the Buddha. Charvaka, however, was the main expounder of the materialistic philosophy which came to be known as the Lokayata, which means the ideas derived from the common people. It underlined the importance of intimate contact with the world (*loka*), and showed a lack of belief in the other world. Many teachings are attributed to Charvaka. He was opposed to the quest for spiritual salvation. He denied the existence of any divine or supernatural agency. He accepted the existence/reality of only those things that could be experienced by human senses and organs. This implied a clear lack of faith in the existence of *brahma* and god. According to Charvaka, the brahmanas manufactured rituals in order to acquire gifts (*dakshina*). To discredit Charvaka, his opponents highlight only one of his teachings. According to it, a person should enjoy himself as long as he lives; he should borrow to eat well (that is, take ghee). However, Charvaka's real contribution lies in his materialistic outlook. He denies the operation of divine and supernatural agencies and makes man the centre of all activities.

The schools of philosophy with emphasis on materialism developed in the period of an expanding economy and society between 500 BC and AD 300. The struggle against the difficulties presented by nature in founding settlements and leading day-to-day life in the Gangetic plains and elsewhere led to the origin and growth of iron-based agricultural technology, the use of metal money, and the thriving of trade and handicrafts. The new environment gave rise to a scientific and materialistic outlook which was principally reflected in Charvaka's philosophy and also figured in that of several traditional schools.

By the fifth century AD, materialistic philosophy was overshadowed by the exponents of idealistic philosophy who constantly criticized it and recommended the performance of rituals and cultivation of spiritualism as a path to salvation; they attributed worldly phenomena to supernatural forces. This view hindered the progress of scientific inquiry and rational thinking. Even the enlightened found it difficult to question the privileges of the priests and warriors. Steeped in the idealistic and salvation schools of philosophy, the people could resign themselves to the inequities of the varna-based social system and the strong authority of the state represented by the king.

Chronology

500 BC–AD 300	Development of materialist philosophy.
2 C	Compilation of the *Brahmasutra* of Badarayana.
(AD)	
4 C AD	In addition to *prakriti, purusha* or spirit introduced as an element in the Samkhya system, and the creation of the world attributed to both.
5 C	Materialistic philosophy overshadowed by the idealistic philosophy.
9 C	Shankara wrote a famous commentary on the *Brahmasutra*.
12 C	Ramanuja's commentary on the *Brahmasutra*.

30

Cultural Interaction with Asian Countries

India's Relations with the Outside World

Medieval lawgivers and commentators ordained that a person should not cross the seas. This would imply that India shunned all relations with the outside world, but this is not so, for India has maintained contacts with its Asian neighbours since Harappan times. Indian traders went to the cities of Mesopotamia, where their seals dating to the second half of the third millennium BC have been found. From the beginning of the Christian era onwards, India maintained commercial contacts with China, Southeast Asia, West Asia, Central Asia, and the Roman empire. We may recall how the Indian land routes were connected with the Chinese Silk Route, and also India's commercial intercourse with the eastern part of the Roman empire. India also sent its missionaries, conquerors, and traders to the neighbouring countries where they founded settlements.

Buddhism in Sri Lanka, Myanmar, China, and Central Asia

The propagation of Buddhism promoted India's contacts with Sri Lanka, Myanmar, China, and Central Asia. Buddhist missionaries were sent to Sri Lanka in the reign of Ashoka in the third century BC. Short inscriptions in Brahmi script relating to the second and first centuries BC have been found in Sri Lanka. In the course of time, Buddhism came to acquire a permanent stronghold in Sri Lanka. In the early centuries of the Christian era, Buddhism spread from India to Burma (modern Myanmar). The Burmese developed the Theravada form of Buddhism, and erected many temples and statues in honour of the Buddha. What is more significant, the Burmese and Sri Lankan Buddhists produced a rich corpus of Buddhist literature not to be found in India. All the Pali texts were compiled and commented upon in Sri Lanka. Although Buddhism disappeared from India, it continued to command a large following in Myanmar and Sri Lanka, and this remains the case to this day.

Beginning with the reign of Kanishka, a large number of Indian missionaries went to China, Central Asia, and Afghanistan to preach their religion. China emerged as a great centre of Buddhism. The Chinese records mention 162 visits made by the Chinese monks during the fifth to the eighth centuries. But the visit of only one Indian scholar called Bodhidharma to China is recorded in this period. All these visits were concerned with Buddhist texts and translations. Thus despite linguistic differences we notice an amazing contact between India and China in the Buddhist context. From China, Buddhism spread to Korea and Japan, and it was in search of Buddhist texts and doctrines that several Chinese pilgrims, such as Fa-hsien and Hsuan Tsang, came to India. Eventually this contact proved fruitful to both the countries. A Buddhist colony arose at Tun Huang, which was the starting point of the companies of merchants crossing the desert. The Indians learnt the art of growing silk from China, and the Chinese learnt from India the art of Buddhist painting.

The two other great centres of Buddhism in ancient times were Afghanistan and Central Asia. In Afghanistan, many statues of the Buddha and Buddhist monasteries have been discovered. Begram and Bamiyan situated in the north of this country are famous for such relics. Begram is famous for ivory work, which is similar to Indian workmanship in Kushan times. Bamiyan had the distinction of boasting of the tallest Buddha statue sculptured out of rock in the early centuries of the Christian era; unfortunately this was recently destroyed by aggressive, fundamentalist Afghan Muslims. Bamiyan has thousands of natural and artificial caves in which the monks lived. Buddhism continued to hold its ground in Afghanistan until the seventh century when it was supplanted by Islam.

A similar process took place in Central Asia. Excavations have revealed Buddhist monasteries, stupas, and inscriptions and manuscripts written in Indian languages at several places in Central Asia. As a result of the extension of Kushan rule, Prakrit written in Kharoshthi script spread to Central Asia, where we find many Prakrit inscriptions and manuscripts relating to the

fourth century AD. Written language was used for official and day-to-day correspondence as well as for the preservation and propagation of Buddhism. In Central Asia, Buddhism continued to be a dominant religious force.

Christianity and West Asian Relations

Though trade with the Roman and Byzantine empires declined, religious relations continued. Buddhism connected India with Central and East Asia, but Christianity linked it with West Asia. In the sixth century, the Alexandrian scholar Kosmos speaks of a thriving Christian community in both India and Sri Lanka. A bishop appointed from Persia served the Christians in Kalyan near modern Mumbai. Thus, the Christians lived in western India along with Jain, Buddhist, and Hindu communities.

Indian Culture in Southeast Asia

Indian culture also spread to Southeast Asia, but not through the medium of Buddhism. Except in the case of Burma it was mostly diffused through the brahmanical cults. The name Suvarnabhumi was given to Pegu and Moulmein in Burma, and merchants from Broach, Banaras, and Bhagalpur traded with Burma. Considerable Buddhist remains of Gupta times have been found in Burma. From the first century AD onwards India established close trading relations with Java in Indonesia, which was called Suvarnadvipa or the island of gold by the ancient Indians. The earliest Indian settlements in Java were established in AD 56. In the second century of the Christian era, several small Indian principalities were set up. When the Chinese pilgrim Fa-hsien visited Java in the fifth century, he found the brahmanical religion prevalent there. In the early centuries of the Christian era, the Pallavas founded their colonies in Sumatra. Eventually these flowered into the kingdom of Sri Vijaya, which continued to be an important power and a centre of Indian culture from the fifth to the tenth century. The Indian settlements in Java and Sumatra became channels for the radiation of Indian culture. The process of founding settlements continued subsequently.

In Indo-China, which is at present divided into Vietnam, Cambodia, and Laos, the Indians set up two powerful kingdoms in Kamboja and Champa. The powerful kingdom of Kamboja, coterminous with modern Cambodia, was founded in the sixth century. Its rulers were devotees of

Shiva, and developed Kamboja into a centre of Sanskrit learning, and numerous inscriptions were composed.

In the neighbourhood of Kamboja at Champa, embracing southern Vietnam and the fringes of northern Vietnam, it seems that the traders set up colonies. The king of Champa was also a Shaiva, and the official language of Champa was Sanskrit. This country was considered to be a great centre of education in the Vedas and Dharmashastras.

Indian settlements in the Indian Ocean continued to flourish until the thirteenth century, and during this period, their inhabitants intermingled with the local peoples. Continuing commingling gave rise to a new type of art, language, and literature. We find in these countries several art objects that show evidence of a happy blending of both Indian and indigenous elements. It is astonishing that the greatest Buddhist temple is to be found not in India but in Borobudur in Java. Considered to be the largest Buddhist temple in the world, it was constructed in the eighth century, and 436 images of the Buddha engraved on it illustrate his life.

The temple of Ankor Vat in Cambodia is larger than that of Borobudur. Although this temple dates to medieval times, it can be compared to the best artistic achievements of the Egyptians and Greeks. The stories of the *Ramayana* and *Mahabharata* are narrated in relief on the walls of the temple. The story of the *Ramayana* is so popular in Indonesia that many folk plays based on it are performed. The language of Indonesia, Bahasa Indonesia, contains numerous Sanskrit words.

Cultural Give and Take

With regard to sculpture, the head of the Buddha from Thailand, the head from Kamboja, and the magnificent bronze images from Java are regarded as the best examples of the fusion of Indian art with the local art traditions of Southeast Asia. Similarly, beautiful examples of painting, comparable to those of Ajanta are found not only in Sri Lanka but also in the Tun Huang caves on the Chinese border.

It would be wrong to think that religion alone contributed to the spread of Indian culture. Missionaries were backed by traders and conquerors. Trade evidently played a vital part in establishing India's relations with Central Asia and Southeast Asia. The very names Suvarnabhumi and Suvarnadvipa, given to territories in Southeast Asia, suggest Indians' search for gold. Trade led not only to the exchange of goods but also to that of elements of culture. It would be inaccurate to hold that Indians alone contributed to the culture of their neighbours; it was a two-way traffic. The Indians acquired the craft of minting gold coins from the Greeks and Romans, they learnt the art of growing silk from China, that of growing betel leaves from Indonesia, and adopted several other products from the neighbouring countries. Similarly, the method of growing cotton spread from India to China and Central Asia. However, the Indian contribution seems to have been significant in art, religion, script, and language. Nevertheless, no culture which developed in the neighbouring countries was a replica of the Indian culture. Just as India retained and developed its own identity in spite of foreign influences, similarly, each country in Southeast Asia developed its own characteristic culture by synthesizing Indian elements with indigenous elements.

Chronology

(BC)	
3 M	Indian traders went to the cities of Mesopotamia, where their seals have been found.
3 C	The Buddhist missionaries sent to Sri Lanka in the reign of Ashoka. India began commercial contacts with China, Southeast Asia, West Asia, Central Asia, and the Roman empire.
(AD)	
56	The earliest Indian settlement in Java.
Early Christian centuries	Buddhism spread from India to Burma (modern Myanmar). Indian Buddhist missionaries in China, Central Asia, and Afghanistan in Kanishka's time and later. The tallest Buddha statue sculpted out of rock at Bamiyan. The Pallavas founded colonies in Sumatra.
4 C	Many Prakrit inscriptions and manuscripts found in Central Asia.
5 C	Fa-hsien visited Java.
5–11 C	Sri Vijay as an important power and a centre of Indian culture.

6 C	The kingdom of Kamboja, coterminous with modern Cambodia, founded.
7 C	Buddhism in Afghanistan supplanted by Islam.
8 C	Construction of the largest Buddhist temple in the world, the Borobudur temple, in Indonesia.

31

From Ancient to Medieval

Social Crisis and Agrarian Changes

The central factor that eventually transformed ancient Indian society into a medieval society was the practice of land grants. How did this practice begin on a large scale? The charters state that the givers, mainly kings, wanted to acquire religious merit, and the receivers, mainly monks and priests, needed the means to perform religious rites. However, the practice really came into being because of a serious crisis that affected the ancient social order. The varna society was based on the producing activities of the peasants who were called vaishyas, and of the labourers who were called shudras. The taxes collected by the royal officers from the vaishyas enabled the kings to pay salaries to their officials and soldiers, reward their priests, and purchase luxury and other articles from merchants and rich artisans. However, in the third–fourth centuries AD, a deep social crisis, described as Kaliyuga in the Puranas, afflicted this system. Contemporary Puranic texts complain of a situation in which the varnas or social classes had discarded the functions assigned to them. The lower orders attempted to arrogate to themselves the status and functions of the higher orders. In other words, they refused to pay taxes and provide free labour. This led to *varnasamkara* or intermixture of social classes. Varna barriers were attacked because the producing masses were oppressed with heavy taxes and impositions, and were denied protection by the kings. This state of affairs is known as Kaliyuga in the Puranic passages of the third–fourth centuries.

Several measures were adopted to overcome the crisis. The almost contemporary law-book of Manu advises that the vaishyas and shudras should not be allowed to deviate from their duties, and this may have led to coercive measures. However, a more important step to meet the situation was to grant land to priests and officials in lieu of salaries and remuneration. Such a practice had the advantage of throwing the burden of collecting taxes and maintaining law and order in the donated areas on the beneficiaries who could deal with recalcitrant peasants on the spot. The practice could also bring new lands under cultivation. Moreover, by implanting brahmanas in the conquered tribal areas, the tribal people could be taught the brahmanical way of life, and the need to obey the king and pay taxes to him.

Rise of Landlords

Land grants became frequent from the fifth century AD. According to this, the brahmanas were granted villages free from taxes which were collected by the king from the villages. In addition, the beneficiaries were given the right to govern the people living in the donated villages. Government officials and royal retainers were not permitted to enter the gifted villages. Up to the fifth century, the ruler generally retained the right to punish the thieves, but in later times, the beneficiaries were authorized to punish all criminal offenders. Thus, the brahmanas not only collected taxes from the peasants and artisans but also maintained law and order in the villages granted to them. Villages were made over to the brahmanas in perpetuity. Thus, the power of the king was heavily undermined from the end of the Gupta period onwards. In the Maurya period, taxes were assessed and collected by the agents of the king, and law and order were maintained by them. In the initial stage, land grants attest to the increasing power of the king. In Vedic times, the king was considered the owner of cattle or *gopati*, but in Gupta times and later, he was regarded as *bhupati* or owner of land. However, eventually land grants undermined the authority of the king, and the pockets that were free from royal control multiplied.

Royal control was further eroded through the payment of government officials by land grants. In the Maurya period, the officers of the state, from the highest to the lowest, were generally paid in cash. The practice continued under the Kushans, who issued a large number of copper and gold coins, and it lingered on under the Guptas whose gold coins were evidently meant for payment of the army and high functionaries. However, from the sixth century onwards, the position seems to have changed. The law-books of that century recommended that services should be rewarded in land. Accordingly, from the reign of Harshavardhana, public officials were paid in land revenues and one-fourth of the royal revenue was earmarked for the endowment of great public servants. The governors, ministers, magistrates, and officers were given portions of land for their personal upkeep. All this created vested interests at the cost of royal authority. Thus, by the seventh century, there is a distinct evolution of the landlordism and a devolution of the central state authority.

New Agrarian Economy

We notice an important change in the agrarian economy. Landed beneficiaries could neither cultivate land nor collect revenues on their own. The actual cultivation was entrusted to peasants or sharecroppers who were attached to the land but did not legally own it. The Chinese pilgrim I-tsing states that most Indian monasteries got their lands cultivated by servants and others. Hsuan Tsang describes the shudras as agriculturists, which suggests that they no longer cultivated land just as slaves and agricultural labourers, but possibly occupied it temporarily. This evidently happened in the old settled areas in north India.

When villages were granted in the tribal areas, the agriculturists were placed under the control of religious beneficiaries, especially the brahmanas, because the brahmanas began to be granted land on a large scale from the fifth–sixth centuries onwards. From the sixth century onwards, sharecroppers and peasants were particularly asked to remain on the land granted to the beneficiaries in the backward and mountainous areas such as Orissa and Deccan. From there, the practice spread to the Ganges basin. In north India too, artisans and peasants were asked not to leave the villages granted to the beneficiaries, thus preventing them from moving from one village to another, greatly undermining mass mobility.

Decline of Trade and Towns

From the sixth century onwards, a sharp decline began. Trade with the main part of the Roman empire ended in the third century, and the silk trade with Iran and the Byzantium stopped in the mid-sixth century. India carried on some commerce with China and Southeast Asia, but its benefits were reaped by the Arabs who acted as middlemen. In the feudal set-up, horse trade became more important because of military needs. In the sixth century, horses from Persia were imported, and traders did not have to pay custom duties. Before the rise of Islam, the Arabs had virtually monopolized India's export trade. The decline of trade for well over 300 years after the sixth century is strikingly demonstrated by the virtual absence of gold coins in India. The paucity of metallic money after the sixth century is true not only of north India but also of south India.

The decline of trade led to the decay of towns. Towns flourished in west and north India under the Satavahanas and Kushans and a few cities continued to thrive in Gupta times. However, the post-Gupta period witnessed the ruin of many old commercial cities in north India. Excavations show that several towns in Haryana and East Punjab, Purana Qila (Delhi), Mathura, Hastinapur (Meerut district), Shravasti (UP), Kaushambi (near Allahabad), Rajghat (Varanasi) Chirand (Saran district), Vaishali, and Pataliputra began to decline in the Gupta period, and largely disappeared in post-Gupta times. The Chinese pilgrim Hsuan Tsang visited several towns considered sacred on account of their association with the Buddha but found them virtually deserted or dilapidated. On account of the restricted market for Indian exports, artisans and merchants living in these towns flocked to the countryside and took to cultivation. In the late fifth century, a group of silk weavers from the western coast migrated to Mandasor in Malwa, gave up silk weaving, and adopted other professions. On account of the decay of trade and towns, the villages had to meet their needs of oil, salt, spices, cloth, etc., on their own. This gave rise to smaller units of production, each unit meeting its own needs.

Most merchants could have become cultivators, but some were appointed managers of land administration. Like temples and brahmanas, some merchants were also granted land by the king in Gupta and post-Gupta times. In such cases, they directly looked after their land grants, but indirectly they looked after grants of lands of which they had been appointed trustees or managers, that is, land endowed on temples and monasteries. The role of the merchants as landlords was linked to the decline of trade and towns.

Changes in the Varna System

From the sixth century onwards, some changes occurred in social organization. In the Gangetic plains in north India, the vaishyas were regarded as free peasants, but land grants created landlords between the peasants, on the one hand, and the king, on the other, so the vaishyas were reduced to the level of the shudras. This modified the old brahmanical order, which spread from north India into Bengal and south India as a result of land grants to the brahmanas, brought from the north from the fifth–sixth centuries onwards. In the outlying areas there were largely two orders, brahmanas and shudras.

Frequent seizures of power and land grants gave rise to several categories of landed people. When a person acquired land and power, he naturally sought a high position in society. He might belong to a lower varna, but he was favoured with generous land grants by his master. This created difficulties because, though economically well off, socially and ritually he was low. According to the Dharmashastras, social positions had hitherto been largely regulated by the varna system. The people were divided into four varnas, the brahmanas being the highest and the shudras the lowest. The economic rights of a person were also determined by the varna to which he belonged. So some changes had to be made in the written texts to recognize the position of the new landed classes. An astrologer of the sixth century, Varahamihira, prescribed houses in sizes that varied according to the varna, as was the ancient practice, but he also fixed the size according to the grades of various classes of ruling chiefs. Thus, formerly all things in society were graded according to the varnas, but now they were also determined by a person's possession of land.

Though some law-books allowed *niyoga* (levirate) or widow remarriage, these concessions were confined to the women of the lower orders. From the very outset, women were denied property rights, and immovable property could not be inherited by them.

From the seventh century onwards, numerous castes were created. A Purana of the eighth century states that thousands of mixed castes were produced by the connection of vaishya women with men of lower castes. This implies that the shudras and untouchables were divided into countless sub-castes, as were the brahmanas and Rajputs who constituted an important element in Indian polity and society around the seventh century. The number of castes increased given the nature of the economy in which people could not move from one place to another. Although people living in different areas followed the same occupation, they became divided into sub-castes in relation to the territory to which they belonged. In addition, many tribal people were admitted into brahmanical society on the basis of land grants given to the brahmanas in the aboriginal tracts. Most of these people were enrolled as shudras and mixed castes. Every tribe or kin group was now given the status of a separate caste in brahmanical society.

Rise of Regional Identities

Around the sixth–seventh centuries, there began the formation of cultural units which later came to be known as Karnataka, Maharashtra, Orissa, Rajasthan, Tamil Nadu, etc. The identity of the various cultural groups is recognized by both foreign and Indian sources. The Chinese traveller Hsuan Tsang mentions several nationalities. The Jaina texts of the late eighth century notice the existence of eighteen major peoples or nationalities and describe the physical features of sixteen. They reproduce samples of their language and say something about their character. Vishakhadatta, an author of about the ninth century, speaks of different regions inhabited by peoples different in customs, clothing, and language.

Since the seventh century, a remarkable development takes place in the linguistic history of India, the birth of Apabhramsha, the final stage of the middle Indo-Aryan. This language is placed roughly halfway between Prakrit that preceded it and modern Indo-Aryan languages that succeeded it. It roughly covers the period from AD 600 to 1000. Extensive Jaina literature was written in this language towards the end of this period. Glimpses of modern languages are traceable in both Jaina and Buddhist writings in Apabhramsha. Buddhist writings from eastern India show faint glimmerings of Bengali, Assamese, Maithili, Oriya, and Hindi. Similarly, the Jaina works of the same period reveal the beginnings of Gujarati and Rajasthani.

In the south, Tamil was the oldest language, but Kannada began to grow at about this time. Telugu and Malayalam developed much later. It seems that each region came to develop its own language because of its isolation from the other. When the Gupta empire broke up, several independent principalities rose, and this naturally hindered countrywide contacts and communication. The decline of trade meant lack of communication between the people of the various regions, and this promoted the growth of regional languages.

Regional scripts became more prominent in AD seventh century and later. From Maurya to Gupta times, although the script changed to some degree, more or less the same script continued to be used throughout the greater part of India. Thus, a person who has mastered the script of the

Gupta age can read inscriptions of that period from different parts of the country, but from the seventh century onwards, every region had its own script, and therefore it is not possible to read post-Gupta inscriptions from different parts without mastering the regional scripts.

Trends in Literature

In the history of literature, the sixth and seventh centuries are equally important. Sanskrit continued to be used by the ruling class from the second century AD. In line with the pomp, vanity, and splendour of the feudal lords, the style of Sanskrit prose and poetry became ornate. Writing became replete with metaphors, imagery, adjectives, and adverbs that made it difficult for the reader to comprehend its essential meaning. Bana's prose is a typical example. In poetry, many metres were invented and elaborated to meet the requirements of the new ornate, verbose, high-flown style. In line with the dominance of landed magnates over the social hierarchy, artificial prose and poetry became fashionable with the elitist authors, who widened the chasm between the landlords and the peasants. Kosambi considers the combination of sex and religion to be a distinctive feature of feudal literature. A leisured landed class sought the support of the Sanskrit writers who wrote on sex and tantrism. Sexual union came to be seen as union with the supreme divine being. According to the Vajrayani tantrikas, supreme knowledge, which amounted to supreme bliss, could be realized through the sexual union of the male and female. Spiritualism was thus inverted to justify eroticism in art and literature.

The medieval period produced a large corpus of commentaries on ancient texts in Sanskrit, Pali, and Prakrit, and these were written between the fifth and eighteenth centuries. They discussed not only the Dharmasutras and Smrtis but also Panini's grammar, the Grhyasutras, Srautasutras, Sulvasutras, and medical and philosophical texts. Commentaries on the Pali texts are called *atthakatha,* and those on Prakrit texts *curni, bhasya,* and *niryukti.* This literature greatly strengthened the authoritarian trend in intellectual life, seeking to preserve the state- and varna-based patriarchal society, and to adapt it to new situations. Several law-books were also composed between AD 600 and 900. In order to make themselves acceptable, some of the lawgivers called themselves Vrddha Manu or Brhat Parasara. In any event, the commentaries helped to perpetuate the essentials of social inequality and adapt the law and rituals to the new inequalities that had arisen from the unequal distribution of land and power. Commentaries and digests continued till the eighteenth century. They emphasized continuity, and the dominant trend in medieval times was that of a closed mind linked to a closed economy that killed creativity.

The Divine Hierarchy

In sculpture and the construction of temples, every region began evolving its own style from the seventh–eighth centuries onwards. South India, in particular, tended to become the land of stone temples. Stone and bronze were the two principal media for the representation of deities, and bronze statues began to be manufactured on an impressive scale. Although they figured in substantial numbers in the Himalayan territories, they predominated in south India. In the south, they were used in brahmanical temples, and in eastern India in Buddhist temples and monasteries. Although the same gods and goddesses were worshipped throughout India, people of every region portrayed them in their own way.

We notice increasing divine hierarchy in post-Gupta times. The various divinities began to be arranged according to grade in the pantheons. Just as society was divided into unequal classes based on ritual, landed property, military power, and the like, so too were the deities divided into unequal ranks. Vishnu, Shiva, and Durga figured as supreme deities, presiding over many other gods and goddesses, who were placed in lower positions as retainers and attendants. The supreme deity in the pantheon was depicted in the largest size, and the subordinate deities in comparatively smaller sizes. The pantheons suggest that the deities worshipped by the various tribes and lower orders were forcibly absorbed into the divine hierarchy. We find the practice of worshipping Brahma, Ganapati, Vishnu, Shakti, and Shiva, called the *panchadeva* or five divinities. The chief god Shiva or some other deity was installed in the main temple, around which four subsidiary shrines were erected to house the other four deities. Such temples were known as *panchayatana.* The Vedic gods Indra, Varuna, and Yama were reduced to the position of *lokapala*s or security guards. The early medieval pantheons give us a good idea of the divine hierarchy based on worldly hierarchy. In many of them, the supreme mother goddess was represented in a dominating posture in relation to several other deities. We find such pantheons not only in Shaivism, Shaktism, and Vaishnavism but also in Jainism and Buddhism where gods were depicted and placed according to their position in the hierarchy.

The monastic organization of the Jainas, Shaivites, Vaishnavites, and others was also divided into about five ranks. The highest rank was occupied by the *acharya*, whose coronation took place in the same manner as that of a prince, with the *upadhyaya* and *upasaka* occupying lower positions.

The Bhakti Cult

From the seventh century onwards, the Bhakti cult spread throughout India, and especially in the south. Bhakti meant that people made all kinds of offerings to the god in return for which they received the *prasada* or the favour of the god. This implied the total surrender of the devotees to their god. This practice is comparable to the complete dependence of the tenants on the landowners. Just as the tenants offered and provided various services to the lord and then received land and protection as a kind of favour from him, a similar relation came to be established between the individual and his god. As elements of feudalism persisted in the country for a very long time, Bhakti became deeply embedded in the Indian ethos.

Tantrism

The most remarkable development in India in the religious field from about the sixth century onwards was the spread of tantrism. Like the Bhakti cult, tantrism can also be seen in the context of socio-economic changes. In the fifth–seventh centuries, many brahmanas received land in Nepal, Assam, Bengal, Orissa, central India, and the Deccan, and it is at about this time that tantric texts, shrines, and practices came into being. Tantrism admitted both women and shudras into its ranks, and laid great stress on the use of magic rituals. Some of the rituals may have been in use in earlier times, but they were systematized and recorded in the tantric texts from about the sixth century onwards. They were intended to satisfy the material desires of the devotees for physical possessions and to cure diseases and injuries suffered by them. Tantrism obviously arose as a consequence of the large-scale admission of the aboriginal peoples in brahmanical society. The brahmanas adopted many of the tribal rituals, charms, and symbols, which were now officially compiled, sponsored, and fostered by them. In the course of time, these were distorted by the priests to serve the interests of their rich patrons. Tantrism permeated Jainism, Buddhism, Shaivism, and Vaishnavism. From the seventh century onwards, it continued to hold ground throughout the medieval age. Many medieval manuscripts found in different parts of India deal with tantrism and astrology, and the two are completely intermixed.

Summary

On the whole, the sixth and seventh centuries evidence some striking developments in polity, society, economy, language, literature, script, and religion. During this period, the dominant features of ancient Indian life were making way for those of medieval life. Taken together, these changes herald the transition to a different type of society and economy dominated by the landlords who now stood between the state and the peasants. They ran the administration that had hitherto been manned largely by officers appointed by the state. This development was similar to what happened in Europe where landlords acquired effective authority from the sixth century onwards, following the fall of the Roman empire. Both the Roman and Gupta empires were attacked by the Hunas, but the consequences were dissimilar. So strong was the pressure of the Hunas and other tribes on the Roman empire that independent peasants were compelled for self-preservation and protection, to surrender their freedom to the lords. The Huna invasions of India did not lead to such a result.

Unlike Roman society, ancient Indian society did not employ slaves in production on any scale. In India, the principal burden of production and taxation fell on the peasants, artisans, merchants, and agricultural labourers, who were placed in the categories of vaishyas and shudras. We find signs of revolt against this system which made it difficult for the state officials to collect taxes directly from the producers. Therefore, land began to be granted on a large scale to remunerate various functionaries. The earliest grants were made to the brahmanas and temples just as they were made in Europe to the Church.

Both India and Europe show a clear trend of decline in artisanal and commercial activity after the sixth century. In the fifth–sixth centuries, towns as a whole decayed in both India and the Roman empire. Both India and Europe witnessed agrarian expansion which gave rise to many rural settlements. In India, this was promoted by the practice of land grants. The emergence of landlords as a powerful class became a conspicuous feature of the social, economic, and political landscape after the end of the ancient period in both Europe and India. Whether they held land for religious or other purposes, the landlords played the key role in shaping the course of society, religion, art and architecture, and literature in India from the seventh century onwards.

Chronology

(AD)	
2 C	Sanskrit continued to be used by the ruling class.
3 C	End of trade with the western part of the Roman empire.
3–4 C	The Kaliyuga social crisis.
5 C	Land grants frequent. The ruler retained the right to punish thieves up to this century, but later passed it on to the beneficiaries of land grants. A group of silk weavers from the western coast migrated to Mandasor in Malwa and adopted other professions.
5–18 C	The period of commentaries in Sanskrit, Pali, and Prakrit.
5–6 C	Land grants created landlords, and vaishya peasants were virtually reduced to the status of shudras.
5 C	Towns generally decayed in both India and the Roman empire.
6 C	The law-books recommended land grants for services. The silk trade with Iran and the Byzantium ended. Varahamihira prescribed both varna- and property-based house sizes. Origin and spread of tantrism, open to both women and shudras. Ornate Sanskrit prose and poetry. Regional units began which later came to be known as Karnataka, Maharashtra, Orissa, Rajasthan, Tamil Nadu, etc.
600–900	The decline of trade for 300 years suggested by the virtual absence of gold coins.

7 C	The key role of the landlords in shaping society, religion, art and architecture, and literature in India from this century. Paucity of metallic money in both north and south India. Proliferation of castes. Rajputs became an important element in Indian polity and society. Buddhist writings from eastern India provide glimpses of the beginnings of Bengali, Assamese, Maithili, Oriya, and Hindi. Jaina Prakrit works provide glimpses of the beginnings of Gujarati and Rajasthani. Kannada began to grow. Telugu and Malayalam developed much later. Lack of communications promoted regional languages. From this century, every region began to have its own script and the Bhakti cult spread throughout the country.
7–8 C	In sculpture and the construction of temples, every region came to evolve its own style from this time.
8 C	Jaina texts refer to the existence of eighteen major peoples or nationalities.
9 C	Vishakhadatta speaks of different regions inhabited by peoples with various religions, languages, and apparel.

32

Sequence of Social Changes

Introduction

There are no written texts for the study of society in pre-Vedic times. Archaeology tells us that people lived in small groups in the hilly areas in the Palaeolithic age. Their principal source of subsistence was the game they hunted, and the wild fruits and roots they collected. Man learnt to produce food and live in houses towards the end of the Stone Age and the beginning of the use of the metal. The Neolithic and Chalcolithic communities lived on the uplands in the proximity of hills and rivers. Gradually peasant villages were established in the Indus basin area, and eventually they blossomed into the urban society of Harappa, with large and small houses. However, once the Harappan civilization disappeared, urbanism did not reappear in Indian subcontinent for about 1500 years.

Tribal and Pastoral Phase

For the history of society from the time of the *Rig Veda* onwards, we can use written texts. They tell us that the Rig Vedic society, despite its mastery of agriculture, was primarily pastoral. People were semi-nomadic, and their principal possessions were cattle and horses. The terms for cow, bull, and horse frequently figure in the *Rig Veda*. Cattle were considered to be synonymous with wealth, and a wealthy person was called *gomat*. Wars were fought over cattle and, therefore, the raja, whose principal responsibility was to protect the cows was called *gopa* or *gopati*. The cow was so central to the subsistence of the family that the daughter was called *duhitr*, that is, one who milks. So intimate was the acquaintance of the Vedic people with kine that when they encountered the buffalo in India they called it *govala* or cow-haired. In contrast to references to cows and bulls, those to agriculture are fewer and occur in the late hymns of the *Rig Veda*. Cattle-rearing was thus the principal source of livelihood.

In such a society, people were barely able to produce anything over and above their barest subsistence. Tribesmen could afford only occasional presents for their chiefs. The principal income of a chief or a prince came from the spoils of war. He captured booty from enemy tribes and extracted tributes from them and from his own tribal compatriots. The tribute received by him was called *bali*. It appears that tribal kinsmen reposed trust in the tribal chief and gave him voluntary presents. In return, the chief led them from victory to victory and stood by them in difficult times. The respect and irregular gifts received by the prince from his tribesmen may have become customary in Vedic times. However, defeated hostile tribes were forced to pay tributes. Periodic sacrifices provided an important occasion for the distribution of these gifts and tributes. The lion's share went to the priests in lieu of the prayers they offered to the gods on behalf of their patrons. In one passage in the *Rig Veda*, the god invoked is asked to bestow wealth only on priests, princes, and sacrificers. This suggests an attempt at unequal distribution. Princes and priests sought to increase their share at the cost of the common people, although people voluntarily gave a large share to their chiefs and princes out of deference and because of their military qualities and the services they provided. Ordinary members of the tribe received a share known as *amsa* or *bhaga*, which was distributed in folk gatherings assemblies attended by the rajas and their clansmen.

Although artisans, peasants, priests, and warriors figure even in the earlier portions of the *Rig Veda*, society as a whole was tribal, pastoral, semi-nomadic, and egalitarian. The spoils of war and cattle constituted the principal forms of property. Cattle and women slaves were generally offered as gifts. Gifts of cereals are hardly mentioned because these were not produced on any sizeable scale. Therefore, apart from the booty captured in wars, there was no other substantial source for the maintenance of princes and priests. It was possible to have high ranks but not high social classes. Princes and priests employed women slaves for domestic service, but their number were probably not large. The Rig Vedic society did not have a serving order which was, later formed by the shudras.

Agriculture and the Origin of the Upper Orders

When the Vedic people moved from Afghanistan and Punjab to western UP, they largely became agriculturists. Archaeology shows that in later Vedic times, there was continuing settlement for two or three centuries. This gave rise to territorial chiefdoms. From tributes obtained from peasants and others, the princes could perform sacrifices and reward their priests. The later Vedic peasant paid the nobles and warriors who in turn made donations to the priests; and in addition also paid sacrificial fees to the priests. The peasant supplied food to the smiths, chariot-makers, and carpenters, who largely served the emerging class of warriors. However, the later Vedic peasant was unable to contribute to the rise of trade and towns; and this feature was conspicuous in the age of the Buddha. The later Vedic society used iron on a limited scale, but the use of metal money was unknown.

The Vedic communities had established neither a taxation system nor a professional army. Tax collectors, apart from the kinsmen of the prince, did not exist. Payment made to the king was not very different from the sacrificial offering made to the gods. The tribal militia of the pastoral society was replaced by the peasant militia of agricultural society. The *vis* or the tribal peasantry formed the *sena* or the army. The peasantry in later Vedic times was called *bala* (force). The army to protect the *ashvamedha* horse comprised both the kshatriyas and the *vis*. Armed with bows, quivers, and shields, the former acted as military captains and leaders; armed with staves, the latter constituted the rank and file. In order to achieve victory, the chief or noble was required to eat from the same vessels as the *vis*. The priests stressed through rituals the subjection of the peasantry or vaishyas to the warrior nobles, but even then the process of transforming the tribesmen into taxpaying peasants was very indistinct. The use of the wooden ploughshare and indiscriminate killing of cattle in sacrifices made it impossible for the peasants to produce much over and above their subsistence needs, and this in turn prevented them from paying regular taxes. On the other hand, princes were not completely alienated from the peasants. In consonance with tribal practices, the rajas were expected to extend agriculture and even to put their hands to the plough, and therefore the gap between the vaishya and the *rajanya* was not very wide. Although the nobles and warriors ruled over their peasant kinsmen, they had to depend upon a peasant militia to fight against enemies and could not grant land without the consent of the tribal peasantry. All this placed the nobles and warriors in a difficult position and prevented sharp distinctions between the rulers and the ruled.

The Varna System of Production and Government

Three processes coincided with one another in post-Vedic times. These were Aryanization, ironization, and urbanization. Aryanization meant the spread of the Indo-Aryan languages such as Sanskrit, Prakrit, and Pali. It also meant the dominance of the upper orders and the subjugation of women. In the later Vedic texts, the term *arya* denoted the first three varnas, excluding the shudras and *dasa*s. Even in the Buddhist context, the *arya* was considered a noble. In post-Vedic times, Aryanization meant the adaptation of the non-Aryan tribals to the brahmanical culture. Ironization meant the spread of tools and weapons made of low carbon steel. It revolutionized agriculture and crafts and multiplied settlements. This process also increased the military powers of the rulers who extended the boundaries of their states and supported the varna system. Urbanization, or the growth of towns, helped the traders and artisans and also led to an increase in the income of the state treasury.

The use of iron tools for crafts and cultivation created conditions for the transformation of the comparatively egalitarian Vedic society into a caste-divided social order around the fifth century BC. In the earlier period, people were not very familiar with iron tools whose number was limited. Now however the situation changed. Once the forested areas of the Gangetic plains were cleared with the aid of fire and the iron axe, one of the most fertile parts of the world was opened to settlement. From 500 BC onwards, numerous rural and urban settlements were established. Large territorial states resulted in the formation of the Magadhan empire. All this was possible because, using the iron ploughshare, sickles, and other tools, peasants produced a good deal more than was needed for their bare subsistence. Peasants needed the support of artisans, who not only provided them with tools, clothing, and the like but also supplied weapons and luxury goods to the princes and priests. The new agricultural production techniques in post-Vedic times attained a much higher level than those in the Vedic age.

The new techniques and the use of force enabled some people to own large stretches of land which needed a substantial number of slaves and hired labourers to till it. In Vedic times, people cultivated their fields with the assistance of family members only; there is no word for wage-earner in Vedic literature. However, slaves and wage-earners engaged in cultivation became a regular feature in the age of the Buddha. The *Arthashastra* of Kautilya shows that during the Maurya period they worked on large state farms. However, by and large, slaves in ancient India were meant to undertake domestic work. Generally the small peasant, occasionally aided by slaves and hired labourers, played the dominant role in production.

With the new techniques, peasants, artisans, hired labourers, and agricultural slaves produced much more than they needed for subsistence. A substantial part of this produce was collected from them by princes and priests. For regular collection, administrative and religious methods were devised. The king appointed tax collectors to assess and collect taxes, but it was also important to convince people of the necessity of obeying the raja, paying him taxes, and offering gifts to the priests. For this purpose, the varna system was devised. According to it, members of the three higher varnas or social orders were distinguished ritually from those of the fourth varna. The twice-born were entitled to Vedic studies and investiture with the sacred thread, and the fourth varna or the shudras and women were excluded from them. The shudras were meant to serve the higher orders, and some lawgivers reserved slavery only for the shudras. Thus the twice-born can be called citizens and the shudras non-citizens. However, there developed distinctions between citizen and citizen in the ranks of the twice-born. The brahmanas were not allowed to take to the plough and their contempt for manual work reached such limits that they developed a distaste and loathing for the hands that practised crafts, and began to regard some manual labourers as untouchables. The more a person withdrew from physical labour, the purer he was considered. The vaishyas, although members of the twice-born group, worked as peasants, herdsmen, and artisans, and later as traders. What is more important, they were the principal taxpayers whose contributions maintained the kshatriyas and brahmanas. The varna system authorized the kshatriya to collect taxes from the peasants and tolls from traders and artisans, and thus enabled him to pay his priests and employees in cash and kind.

The rate of payment and economic privileges differed according to the varna to which a person belonged. Thus, a brahmana was required to pay 2 per cent interest on loans, a kshatriya 3 per cent, a vaishya 4 per cent, and a shudra 5 per cent. Shudra guests could be fed only if they had done some work at the house of the host. These Dharmashastras rules were prescriptive and may not have been strictly observed, but they indicate the norms set by the dominant social orders.

As both priests and warriors lived on the taxes, tributes, tithes, and labour supplied by peasants and artisans, their relations were marked by occasional feuds over the sharing of social savings. The kshatriyas were also hurt by the vanity of the brahmanas, who claimed the highest status in society. However, both composed their differences in the face of opposition from the vaishyas and shudras. Ancient texts emphasize that kshatriyas cannot prosper without the support of the brahmanas, and the brahmanas cannot prosper without the support of the kshatriyas. Both can thrive and rule the world only if they cooperate with each other.

Social Crisis and the Rise of the Landed Classes

For several centuries, the system worked well in the Gangetic plains and the adjacent area, which saw a successive series of large states. In the first and second centuries AD it was characterized by booming trade and urbanism. In this phase, art flourished as never before. The old order reached its climax in about the third century and then its progressive role seems to have exhausted itself. Around the third century AD the old social formation was afflicted with a deep crisis. The crisis is clearly reflected in the description of the Kali age in the portions of the Puranas relating to the third and fourth centuries. The Kali age is characterized by *varnasankara*, that is, intermixture of varnas or social orders, which implies refusal of the vaishyas and the shudras (peasants, artisans, and labourers) to perform the producing functions assigned to them, that is, the vaishya peasants declined to pay taxes and the shudras refused to make their labour available. They did not respect the varna boundaries relating to marriage and other types of social intercourse. In the face of this situation, the epics emphasize the importance of *danda* or coercive measures, and Manu lays down that the vaishyas and shudras should not be allowed to deviate from their duties. The kings appear as upholders and restorers of the varna system.

However, coercive measures alone were not sufficient to make the peasants pay and labourers work. Rather than collecting taxes directly through its own agents and then distributing them among its priestly, military, and other employees and supporters, the state found it convenient to assign land revenues directly to priests, military chiefs, administrators, etc., for their maintenance. This development was in sharp contrast to the

Vedic practice. Formerly only the community had the right to give land to priests and possibly to its chiefs and princes. Now, however, the raja usurped this power and obliged the leading members of the community by granting land to them. These beneficiaries were also empowered to maintain law and order. This is how the fiscal and administrative problems were resolved. New and expanding kingdoms required more and more taxes to sustain themselves. These could be obtained from the backward tribal areas where the tribals adopted new methods of agriculture and were taught to be loyal. The problem was tackled by granting land in the tribal areas to enterprising brahmanas who could tame the inhabitants of the wild tracts, teach them better methods of agriculture, and make them amenable to discipline.

In the backward areas, land grants to brahmanas and others spread the agricultural calendar, diffused the knowledge of Ayurveda medicine, and thus contributed to an increase in overall cereal production. The beneficiaries also disseminated the art of writing and the use of Prakrit and Sanskrit. Through land grants, civilization spread in the deep south and far east, although earlier some spadework in this direction had been done by traders and by the Jainas and Buddhists. The grants brought to the brahmanical fold a large number of aboriginal peasants who came to be ranked as shudras. The shudras therefore began to be referred to as peasants and agriculturists in early medieval texts. However, the vaishyas, especially of the developed areas, lost the position of independent peasants, and therefore in post-Gupta times, economically and socially the gap between the the vaishya and the shudra was narrowed. The most significant consequence of land grants was the emergence of a class of landlords living on the produce of the peasants. Ancient Indian society cannot be called unchanging. By the fifth–sixth centuries this paved the way for a new type of social formation which can be termed feudal.

In the feudal set-up, the position of the women of the landed and fighting classes deteriorated. In early medieval times, sati became a common practice in Rajasthan. However, women from the lower orders were free to take to economic activities and remarry.

Summary

Considering the flux in social forces it is not possible to give a single label to society in ancient India, and we have to think of several stages in its evolution. The food gathering society of the Palaeolithic age was succeeded by the food producing societies of the Neolithic and Chalcolithic communities. Eventually the peasant communities developed into the Harappan urban societies. Then we have a break followed by a society of horse users and cattle-herders. The *Rig Veda* indicates a social formation that was largely pastoral and tribal. The pastoral society became agricultural in later Vedic times, but because of its primitive methods of agriculture, the rulers could not get much at the cost of the peasants. The class-divided society comes into full view in post-Vedic times which came to be known as the varna system. This social organization rested on the producing activities of the vaishyas supplemented by those of the shudras. By and large, the social system worked well from the age of the Buddha to Gupta times. Then it underwent a change due to internal upheavals. Priests and officials began to be granted lands for maintenance, and gradually there emerged a class of landlords between the peasants and the state. This undermined the position of the vaishyas and also modified the varna system.

Chronology

(BC)	
5 C	Iron tools in crafts and cultivation created conditions for the transformation of the egalitarian Vedic society into a fully agricultural and caste-divided social order.
500	Rise of many rural and urban settlements in the Gangetic basin.
(AD)	
1–2 C	Booming trade and urbanism, and the cultivation of art.
3–4 C	Society faced the Kali crisis. The Kali age marked by *varnasankara*, that is, intermixture of varnas or social orders leading to the vaishyas and shudras refusing to perform their producing functions.
5–6 C	The emergence of landlords living off the produce of peasants which led to the feudal system.

33

Legacy in Science and Civilization

Religion

Man's confrontation with nature gave rise to significant developments. People had to overcome the difficulties created by the jungles, hills, hard soils, droughts, floods, animals, etc., to earn their livelihood. In this process they developed technology and a scientific outlook. They began undertaking agriculture in the seventh millennium BC. But they were not able to effectively counter such natural hazards as fire, flood, and famine. They found these hazards insurmountable and inexplicable. On the other hand, people took advantage of the fertility of the soil, timely rain, and similar other gifts of nature. Therefore both the bounty advanced by nature and the scarcity caused by it led them to think of religion and supernatural forces.

Brahmanism or Hinduism developed as the dominant religion in early India and influenced the development of art, literature, and society as a whole. In addition to Brahmanism, India gave rise to Jainism and Buddhism. Although Christianity came here in about the first century AD, it did not make much headway in ancient times. Buddhism also disappeared from India in the course of time, though it had spread as far as Japan in the east and as far as Central Asia in the north-west. In the process of diffusion, Buddhism projected a great deal of Indian art, language, and literature in neighbouring countries. Jainism continued in India and helped the development of its art and literature. To this day it has a substantial number of adherents, especially amongst the trading communities in Rajasthan, Gujarat, and Karnataka.

The Varna System

Religion had a peculiar influence on the formation of social classes in India. In other ancient societies, the duties and functions of social classes were fixed by law which was largely enforced by the state. In India, however, varna laws enjoyed the sanction of both the state and religion. The functions of priests, warriors, peasants, and labourers were defined in law and were supposed to have been set out by divine agencies. Those who departed from their functions and were found guilty of offences were subjected to secular punishments. They had also to perform rituals and penances, according to their varna. Each varna was given not only social but also ritualistic recognition. In the course of time, varnas or social classes and jatis or castes were made hereditary by law and religion. All this was done to ensure that vaishyas produced and paid taxes and shudras served as labourers to enable brahmanas to act as priests and kshatriyas as rulers. Based on a division of labour and specialization of occupations, this peculiar institution, the caste or varna system, certainly helped the growth of society and economy at the initial stage and contributed to the development of the state. The producing and labouring classes were disarmed, and gradually each caste was so pitted against the other that those that were oppressed could not combine against the privileged orders.

The need to carry out their respective functions was so strongly ingrained in the minds of the various classes that ordinarily they would never think of deviating from their dharma. The *Bhagavadgita* taught that people should lay down their lives in defence of their own dharma rather than adopt the dharma of others which would prove dangerous. The lower orders worked hard in the firm belief that they would deserve a better life in the next world or birth. This belief lessened the intensity and frequency of tensions and conflicts between those who actually produced and those who lived off these producers as princes, priests, officials, soldiers, and big merchants. Hence, the necessity to coerce the lower orders was not very strong in ancient India. What was done by slaves and other producing sections in Greece and Rome under the threat of the ruler's whip was done by the vaishyas and shudras out of a conviction formed through brahmanical indoctrination and the varna system.

Philosophical Systems

The Indian thinkers viewed the world as an illusion and deliberated deeply on the relation between the soul and god. Indeed, philosophers of no other country delved so deeply into this problem as did the Indians. Ancient India is considered famous for its contribution to philosophy and spiritualism, but the Indians also developed a materialistic view of the world. In the six systems of philosophy that Indians created we find elements of materialistic philosophy in the Samkhya system of Kapila, who was born around 580 BC. He believed that the soul can attain liberation only through real knowledge, which can be acquired through perception, inference, and hearing. The Samkhya system does not recognize the existence of god. According to it, the world has been created not by god but by nature, and the world and human life are regulated by natural forces. The development of logic may have helped the Samkhya system. Prior to the fifth century, logic was not a well-established discipline. The *Nyaya Sutra* seems to have been compiled around AD 400. It mentions four proofs or *pramanas* comprising perception, inference, comparison, and testimony. We find detailed discussions regarding valid and invalid knowledge, and aspects of each kind of proof are treated in detail. Although debating devices were used in theological disputes, they could not have been developed in isolation from other disputes, including land disputes.

Materialistic philosophy received the greatest impetus from Charvaka, who lived in about the sixth century BC. The philosophy that he propounded is known as Lokayata. He argued that what is not experienced by man through his sensory organs does not really exist, which implies that gods do not exist. However, with the decline in trade, handicrafts, and urbanism, the idealist system of philosophy came to the fore. The idealist system taught that the world is an illusion. People were asked by the Upanishads to abandon the world and to strive for real knowledge. Western thinkers have taken to the teachings of the Upanishads because they are unable to solve the human problems created by modern technology. The famous German philosopher, Schopenhauer, found in his philosophy a place for the Vedas and the Upanishads. He used to say that the Upanishads consoled him in this life and would also console him after death.

Crafts and Technology

It would be wrong to think that Indians did not contribute to material culture. The first great contribution was made by the Harappan culture. During the Bronze Age culture, it covered an area larger than that of Egypt or of Mesopotamia. It produced the largest number of fired bricks and the best form of town-planning. There is no doubt that crafts, commerce, and agriculture made great strides and supported numerous cities.

In ancient times Indians attained proficiency in several fields of production. Indian craftsmen developed great expertise in dyeing and creating various kinds of colours. The basic colours made in India were so lustrous and lasting that the wonderful paintings of Ajanta are still intact.

Similarly, Indians developed great expertise in the art of making steel. This craft was first developed in India in 200 BC, and Indian steel was exported to many countries of the world from very early times and came to be called *wootz* in later times. No other country in the world could match the steel swords made by Indian craftsmen, and these were in great demand in the entire region from Asia to eastern Europe.

Polity

The *Arthashastra* of Kautilya leaves no doubt that Indians could run the administration of a large empire and tackle the problems of a complex society. India produced a great ruler in Ashoka who, in spite of his victory over Kalinga, adopted a policy of peace and non-aggression. Ashoka and several other Indian kings practised religious tolerance and stressed that the wishes of the followers of other religions should be respected. Also, besides Greece, India was the only other country to experiment with some form of democracy.

Science and Mathematics

India made an important contribution to science. In ancient times, religion and science were inextricably linked. Astronomy made great strides in India because the planets began to be regarded as gods, and their movements began to be closely observed. Their study became essential because of their connection to changes in the seasons and weather conditions which were important for agricultural activities. The science of grammar and linguistics arose because the ancient brahmanas stressed that every Vedic prayer and mantra should be recited with meticulous precision. In fact, the first result of the scientific outlook of Indians was the development of Sanskrit grammar. In the fifth century BC, Panini systematized the rules governing Sanskrit and produced a grammar called *Ashtadhyayi*.

By the third century BC, mathematics, astronomy, and medicine began to develop separately. In the field of mathematics, the ancient Indians made three distinct contributions: the notation system, the decimal system, and the use of zero. The earliest epigraphic evidence for the use of the decimal system is in the beginning of the fifth century AD. The Indian notational system was adopted by the Arabs who spread it in the Western world. The Indian numerals are called Arabic in English, but the Arabs themselves called their numerals *hinds*, and before they were adopted in the West they had been used in India for centuries. They are to be found in the inscriptions of Ashoka which were inscribed in the third century BC.

Indians were the first to use the decimal system. Aryabhata (AD 476–500) was acquainted with it. The Chinese learnt this system from the Buddhist missionaries, and the Western world borrowed it from the Arabs when the latter came into contact with India. The zero was discovered by Indians in about the second century BC. Indian mathematicians considered zero as a separate numeral, and it was used in this sense in sums of arithmetic. In Arabia, the earliest use of zero was in AD 873. The Arabs learnt and adopted it from India and spread it in Europe. Although both Indians and Greeks contributed to algebra, in Western Europe its knowledge was acquired not from Greece but from the Arabs who had acquired it from India.

The brick constructions of Harappa show that in north-western India, people had a substantial knowledge of measurement and geometry. Eventually the Vedic people may have benefited from this knowledge, which appears in the Sulvasutras of about the fifth century BC. In the second century BC, Apastamba produced a practical geometry for the construction of altars at which the kings could offer sacrifices. It describes the acute angle, obtuse angle, and right angle. Aryabhata formulated the method for calculating the area of a triangle, which led to the origin of trigonometry. The most famous work of this time is *Suryasiddhanta,* and no comparable work is to be found in the contemporary ancient East.

The most renowned scholars of astronomy were Aryabhata and Varahamihira. Aryabhata lived in the fifth century, and Varahamihira in the sixth. Aryabhata calculated the position of the planets in accordance with the Babylonian method. He discovered the cause of lunar and solar eclipses. The circumference of the earth, which he measured on the basis of speculation, is even today considered to be correct. He pointed out that the sun is stationary and the earth rotates. Aryabhata's work is entitled *Aryabhatiya* was a landmark in the development of mathematical and astronomical knowledge, and is a distinct contribution to trigonometry. On the basis of it, all the shapes and sizes of plots involved in gift making and property partition could be measured and assessed for fixation of rent or tax in early medieval times. This knowledge could also be used for the various measurements needed for the erection of temples and palaces, and other engineering work. The use of the zero and the decimal system finds a place in the *Aryabhatiya*, but it was not put to any significant use in India. Once it spread westward through the Arabs, it began to be used for bookkeeping by Italian traders in the tenth century. India's loss in trade between the sixth and the tenth centuries can perhaps be linked to the neglect of the zero and decimal system. More accurate knowledge relevant to measurement and also to agro-astronomical calculations was made available by the algebra developed by Brahmagupta during the first half of the seventh century.

Varahamihira's well-known work *Brihatsamhita* was written in the sixth century. He stated that the moon rotates around the earth and the earth rotates round the sun. He utilized several Greek works to explain the movement of the planets and some other astronomical problems. Although Greek knowledge influenced Indian astronomy, Indians doubtless pursued the subject further and made use of it in their observations of the planets.

Varahamihira's plant and animal classifications enriched agricultural knowledge. Although his predictions relate to numerous social matters, the instructions given by him regarding the selection of sites for building houses tie up with the founding of new villages. Similarly, Varahamihira's observations on the seasons and the weather could have been useful in planning the agricultural calendar. He emphasized that the calendar should be constantly updated to keep pace with the change in the seasons. Varahamihira acted as a kind of astronomer-cum-astrologer. The office of *jyotisi* began in early medieval times, as is indicated in many land charters. In the rural areas, the priest–*jyotisi* became an integral part of the *jajmani* system.

In the applied field, Indian craftsmen contributed much to the development of chemistry. Indian dyers invented lasting colours and they also discovered the blue colour. We may recall that Indian smiths were the first in the world to manufacture steel.

Medicine

The ancient Indian physicians studied anatomy. They devised methods to diagnose diseases and prescribed medicines for their cure. The earliest mention of medicines is to be found in the *Atharva Veda*, but, as in other ancient societies, the remedies recommended were replete with magical charms and spells, and medicine was not developed along scientific lines.

In the second century AD India produced two famous scholars of Ayurveda, Sushruta and Charaka. In the *Sushrutasamhita*, Sushruta describes the method of operating cataract, stone disease, and several other ailments. He mentions as many as 121 implements to be used for surgery. In the treatment of disease he lays special stress on diet and cleanliness. Charaka's *Charakasamhita* is like an encyclopaedia of Indian medicine. It describes various types of fever, leprosy, hysteria (*mirgi*), and tuberculosis. Possibly Charaka was not aware that some of these are infectious. His book contains the names of a large number of plants and herbs that could be used as medicines. The book is thus useful not only for the study of Indian medicine but also for that of ancient Indian flora and chemistry. In subsequent centuries Indian medicine developed on the lines set out by Charaka.

Geography

Ancient Indians also made some contribution to the study of geography. They had little knowledge of the geography of the lands outside India, but the rivers, mountain ranges, places of pilgrimage, and different regions of the country are described in the epics and Puranas. Although Indians were acquainted with China and Western countries, they neither had any clear idea of their location nor of their distances from India.

In early times Indians obtained some knowledge of navigation and contributed to the craft of shipbuilding. However, as the important political powers had their seats of power far away from the coast, and faced no threat from the sea, the ancient Indian princes did not pay any particular attention to navigation.

Art and Literature

The ancient Indian masons and craftsmen produced wonderful works of art, starting from Harappan times. In the historical period, the monolithic pillars erected by Ashoka are famous for their gloss and polish, which match the gloss on Northern Black Polished Ware. It is still a mystery how the craftsmen were able to achieve this kind of polish on pillars and pottery. The Maurya polished pillars were mounted on statues of animals, especially lions. The lion capital has been adopted as the national emblem of the Republic of India. We may also refer to the cave temples of Ajanta as well as the famous Ajanta paintings, which go back to the beginning of the Christian era. In a way Ajanta is the birthplace of Asian art and has as many as thirty cave temples constructed between the second century BC and the seventh century AD. The paintings started in the second century AD and most of them relate to the Gupta period. Their themes were borrowed from stories about previous incarnations of the Buddha and from other ancient literature. The achievement of the Indian painters of Ajanta has been justly and greatly lauded by all art connoisseurs. The lines and colours used at Ajanta display a proficiency that was unmatched in the world until the Renaissance in Europe. Indian art, moreover, was not limited to India but spread to Central Asia and China, at one end, and to Southeast Asia on the other. The focal point of the spread of Indian art into Afghanistan and the neighbouring parts of Central Asia was Gandhara. Elements of Indian art were fused with those of Central Asian and Hellenistic art giving rise to a new art style called the Gandhara style. The first statue of the Buddha was fashioned in this style. Although its features are Indian, the size and the presentation of the head and the drapery show Greek influence. Similarly, the temples constructed in south India served in some ways as models for the construction of temples in Southeast Asia. We may recall the temple at Ankor Vat in Cambodia and the temple at Borobudur in Java.

In the field of education, writing was first undertaken in the mid-third millennium BC in the Harappan culture, though this script has not so far been deciphered. In historical times we find provision for higher education in the huge monastic establishment of Nalanda which attracted students not only from different parts of India but also from Tibet and China. The standards of examination were stiff, and only those who could pass the test prescribed by the *dvarapandita* or the 'scholar at the gate' could be admitted to the university. Nalanda is one of the earliest examples of a residential-cum-teaching institution which housed thousands of monks devoted to learning, philosophy, and meditation.

In the field of literature, the Indians produced the *Rig Veda* which is the earliest specimen of the Indo-Aryan language and literature, and on its basis an attempt has been made to determine the nature of the Aryan culture. In Gupta times Kalidasa wrote his fine works, and his play *Abhijanashakuntalam* has been translated into all the important languages of the world.

Strength and Weakness

It is difficult to sum up the achievements of ancient India. Those of the Harappan culture are staggering and Harappan objects are displayed in the museums of India and Pakistan, though the contemporary Mesopotamian antiquities were largely lost or destroyed in the second Gulf War. In post-Harappan times, people contributed to various fields of science and civilization.

However, the caste system based on the brahmanical ideology persists to this day. In ancient times, the shudras, including the untouchables, were convinced of their inborn inferiority, and this was the case too with women who were considered items of property. Even now these relics have not completely disappeared. Similarly the common people continue to suffer from loss of land. The Satavahanas started the practice of land grants with administrative rights in the second century. Later rulers widely followed this practice which caused unequal distribution of land and the impoverishment of the cultivators. The people were required to respect the rights of the landlords, and it was decreed that the opponents of land grants would be punished. Thus appeared sharp inequalities in important fields. Although some ancient texts looked upon the world as a family (*vasudhaiva kutumbakam*), this ideal would not make any impact.

Chronology

(BC)

6 C	Charvaka's Lokayata or materialistic philosophy
580	Birth of Kapila, the founder of the Samkhya system.

5 C	The Sulvasutras set out the knowledge of measurement and geometry.
	Panini systematized the rules governing Sanskrit and composed *Ashtadhyayi*.
3 C	Independent development of astronomy and medicine. The Indian numerals, called Arabic in English, but called *hinds* by the Arabs, found in the inscriptions of Ashoka.
2 C	Discovery of zero. Apastamba's writings on practical geometry for the construction of altars. Invention of steel making.
2 C BC–AD 7 C	The Ajanta caves were built.
(AD)	
1 C	Arrival of Christianity.
2 C	Sushruta and Charaka.
400	The composition of the Ayurveda.
5 C	Epigraphic evidence for the use of the decimal.
476–540	Date of Aryabhata who wrote *Aryabhatiya*.
6 C	Varahamihira and his famous work *Brihatsamhita*.
873	The earliest use of zero in Arabia.

Chronology of Literary Sources

(BC)	
1500–1000	The *Rig Veda*
1400	The *Zend Avesta*
1000	Later strata of the *Rig Veda*
1000–800	The *Yajur Veda*, *Atharva Veda*, and *Sama Veda*
800–500	The *Brahmanas*, *Aranyakas*, and *Upanishads*
900–800	Homer's *Iliad* and *Odyssey*
600–300	The principal Shrautasutras and some Grihyasutras
6 C	Charavaka's Lokayata or materialistic philosophy
500–200	The Dharmasutras of Gautama, Apastamba, Baudhayana, and Vasishtha
5 C	The *Sulvasutras*
	The *Digha Nikaya*
450	Grammar of Panini (*Ashtadhyayi*)
4 C	*Indica* by Megasthenes (This work is lost. The fragments in quotations by later writers such as Strabo, Arrian, and Diodoros survive, and their collection translated into English by McCrindle.)
300	*Suttanipata*
300 BC–AD 100	*Arthashastra* of Kautilya (Inscriptional evidence shows insertions till early medieval times.)
300 BC–AD 600	The Sangam literature

2 C	Compilation of the *Brahmasutra* of Badarayana.
	Milinda Panho (Questions of Menander)
	The *Garland of Madurai* (A Tamil text tr. into English)
150	Patanjali's *Mahabhashya*
1 C	The *Mahavastu*
(AD)	
77	*Natural History* in Latin by Pliny
80–115	The *Periplus of the Erythrean Sea*
100–300	*Vishnudharmasutra* or *Vishnu Smriti*
2 C	Composition of some parts of the Sangam literature
150	Ptolemy's *Geography*
200–400	The Law-book of Manu (*Manu Smriti*)
3 C	The *Kamasutra* of Vatsyayana
300	13 plays of Bhasa including *Daridra Charudatta*, later refashioned as *Mrichchakatika*
300–600	Final composition of the *Sangam* literature and Puranas such as *Vayu*, *Vishnu*, *Markandeya*, and *Matsya*
400	The *Mahabharata* and the *Ramayana*
	Composition of the Ayurveda
5 C	*Narada Smriti*
	Aryabhatiya by Aryabhata
	Suryasiddhanta
5 C	Fa-hsien's *Travel-Accounts*
5–18 C	Commentaries in Sanskrit, Pali, and Prakrit
6 C	*The Christian Topography* by Kosmos Indikopleustes
	Composition of two Tamil epics, viz., *Silappadikaram* and *Manimekalai*
	The Prakrit Jaina texts, written in Ardhamagadhi, finally compiled in Valabhi in Gujarat
	Katyayana Smriti on Vyavahara

	Law-books recommending land grants for services
	Brihatsamhita by Varahamihira
Post-6 C	*Gathasattasai* (*Gathasaptasati*) finalized
7 C	Hsuan Tsang's *Travel-Accounts*
	Harshacharita by Banabhatta
	Travel-Accounts of I-tsing
	Buddhist writings from eastern India showing faint beginnings of Bengali, Assamese, Maithili, Oriya, and Hindi. Jaina Prakrit works showing the beginning of Gujarati and Rajasthani
8 C	Jaina works noticing the presence of eighteen major peoples or nationalities
9 C	Shankara's commentary on the *Brahmasutra*
	Vishakhadatta's work mentioning different regions of various religions, languages, and clothings
11 C	*Mushika Vamsha* by Atula
11–12 C	*Vikramankadevacharita* by Bilhana
12 C	*Ramacharita* by Sandhyakara Nandi
	Rajatarangini by Kalhana
	Ramanuja's commentary on the *Brahmasutra*

Bibliography

General and Survey Volumes

Aiyangar, K.V. Rangaswami, *Some Aspects of Ancient Indian Polity* (Patna: Eastern Book House, 1988).

Antonova, K., G. Bongard-Levin and G. Kotovsky, *A History of India*, 2 Books (Moscow: Progress Publishers, 1979).

Basham, A.L., *The Wonder That was India* (A survey of the history and culture of the Indian subcontinent before the coming of the Muslims), 3rd edn (Canberra: Sidgwick Jackson, 1967).

——— (ed.), *A Cultural History of India* (Oxford: Clarendon Press, 1975).

Bongard-Levin, G.M., *Ancient Indian Civilisation* (New Delhi: Arnold Associates, 1996).

Dhavalikar, M.K., *Historical Archaeology of India* (New Delhi: Books & Books, 1999).

Durant, Will, *The Story of Civilisation*, Vol. 1, Our Oriental Series (New York: Simon and Schuster, 1942).

Dutta, N.K., *Origin and Growth of Caste in India*, Vols 1 and 2, 1st combined rpt (Calcutta: K.L. Mukhopadhyaya, 1986).

Dutt, Romesh Chander, *A History of Civilisation in Ancient India*, 2 Vols (New Delhi: Cosmo Publication, 2000).

Filliozat, J., *Political History of India from the Earliest Times to the 7th Century A.D.* (Calcutta: Susil Gupta [India] Ltd, 1957).

Ghosh, A. (ed.), *An Encyclopaedia of Indian Archaeology*, 2 Vols (New Delhi: Munshiram Manoharlal, 1989).

Ghoshal, U.N., *A History of Indian Political Ideas* (Bombay: Oxford University Press, 1959).

Gluckman, M., *Politics, Law, and Ritual in Tribal Society* (Oxford: Basil Blackwell, 1971).

Godelier, M., *Perspectives in Marxist Anthropology* (Cambridge: Cambridge University Press, 1977).

Gonda, J., *Change and Continuity in Indian Religion* (New Delhi: Munshiram Manoharlal, 1997).

Goody, Jack, *The Oriental, the Ancient and the Primitive Systems of Marriage and the Family in the Pre-industrial Societies of Eurasia* (Cambridge: Cambridge University Press, 1990).

Heidrich, Joachim, Hiltrud Rustau, and Diathelm Weidemann (eds), *Indian Culture: Continuity and Discontinuity,* in Memory of Walter Ruben (1899–1982) (Berlin: Trafo verlag, 2002).

Herrmann, J. and E. Zürcher (eds), *History of Humanity, Scientific and Cultural Development,* Vol. 3, *From the Seventh Century BC to the Seventh Century AD* (Paris: UNESCO, 1996).

Hutton, J.H., *Caste in India,* 4th edn (London: Oxford University Press, 1963).

Jaiswal, Suvira, *Caste: Origin, Function and Dimensions of Change* (New Delhi: Manohar, 1998).

Jha, D.N. (ed.), *Society and Ideology in India: Essays in Honour of R.S. Sharma* (New Delhi: Munshiram Manoharlal, 1996).

_____, *Ancient India in Historical Outline* (New Delhi: Manohar, 1998).

Kapadia, K.M., *Marriage and Family in India,* 3rd edn (Calcutta: Oxford University Press, 1966).

Karve, Iravati, *Hindu Society: An Interpretation* (Pune: Deshmukh Prakashan, 1968).

Kosambi, D.D., *An Introduction to the Study of Indian History* (Bombay: Popular Prakashan, 1956).

_____, *The Culture and Civilisation of Ancient India in Historical Outline,* 4th Impression (New Delhi: Vikas, 1976).

_____, *Combined Method in Indology and Other Writings,* ed. B.D. Chattopadhyaya (New Delhi: Oxford University Press, 2002).

Kulke, Hermann and Dietmar Rothermund, *A History of India,* 3rd edn (London: Routledge, 1988).

Majumdar, R.C., H.C. Raychaudhuri and K.K. Datta, *An Advanced History of India,* 3rd edn (Delhi: Macmillan India, 1974).

Mauss, Marcel, *The Gift Forms and Functions of Exchange in Archaic Societies* (London: Cohen and West Ltd, 1970).

Morgan, L.H., *Ancient Society* (New York: Holt and Co., 1877).

Nilakanta Sastri, K.A., *History of India,* Part 1, *Ancient India* (Madras: S. Vishwanathan, 1950).

Rai, G.K., *Involuntary Labour in Ancient India* (Allahabad: Chaitanya Publishing House, 1981).

Rapson, E.J. (ed.), *The Cambridge History of India*, Vol. 1, *Ancient India* (Cambridge: Cambridge University Press, 1922; 1st Indian rpt, Delhi: S. Chand & Co., 1966).

Ray, Niharranjan, *An Approach to Indian Art* (Chandigarh: Panjab University, 1974).

Raychaudhuri, Hemachandra, *Political History of Ancient India* with a commentary by B.N. Mukherjee (New Delhi: Oxford University Press, 1996).

Renfrew, C. and P. Bahn, *Archaeology: Theory, Methods, and Practice* (London: Thames & Hudson, 1991).

Roberts, J. M., *The Penguin History of the World*, 3rd edn (Harmondsworth: Penguin, 1995).

Settar, S. and Ravi Korisettar (eds), *Indian Archaeology in Retrospect*, 4 Vols (New Delhi: Indian Council of Historical Research and Manohar, 2002).

Sharma, R.S., *Aspects of Political Ideas and Institutions in Ancient India*, 4th rev. edn (Delhi: Motilal Banarsidass, 1996).

——, *Sudras in Ancient India: A Social History of the Lower Order Down to circa AD 600* (Delhi: Motilal Banarsidass, 2002).

——, *Perspectives in Social and Economic History of Early India*, paperback edn (New Delhi: Munshiram Manoharlal, 2003).

——, 'Mode of Production in Ancient India', in D.N. Gupta (ed.), *Changing Modes of Production* (Delhi: Hindu College, 1995)

Sharma, R.S. and V. Jha (eds), *Indian Society: Historical Probings, D.D. Kosambi Volume* (New Delhi: People's Publishing House, 1974).

Sircar, D.C. (ed.), *Select Inscriptions Bearing on Indian History and Civilisation*, Vol.1, *From the Sixth Century B.C. to the Sixth Century A.D.*, 2nd edn (Calcutta: University of Calcutta, 1965); Vol.2, *From the Sixth Century to the Eighteenth Century A.D.* (Delhi: Motilal Banarsidass, 1983).

Subbarao, B., *The Personality of India*, 2nd edn (Baroda: The University of Baroda, 1958).

Thapar, B.K., *Recent Archaeological Discoveries in India* (Paris/Tokyo: UNESCO/ The Centre for East Asian Cultural Studies, 1985).

Thapar, Romila, *Ancient Indian Social History* (Hyderabad: Orient Longman, 1978).

—— (ed.), *Recent Perspectives of Early Indian History* (Bombay: Popular Prakashan, 1995).

——, *Cultural Past: Essays in Early Indian History* (New Delhi: Oxford University Press, 2000).

——, *Early India from the Origins to AD 1300* (New Delhi: Penguin, 2001).

Tripathi, R.S., *History of Ancient India* (Delhi: Motilal Banarsidass, 1967).

Von, Herausgegeben, Joachim Herrmann, and Jens Kohn (eds), *Familie, Staat una Gesellschaftsformation [Family, State, and the Formation of Society]* (Berlin: Akademie-Verlag, 1988).

CHAPTER 1 THE SIGNIFICANCE OF ANCIENT INDIAN HISTORY

CHAPTER 2 MODERN HISTORIANS OF ANCIENT INDIA

CHAPTER 3 NATURE OF SOURCES AND HISTORICAL CONSTRUCTION

Secondary

Agrawal, D.P., *The Archaeology of India* (New Delhi: Select Book Servicc, 1984).

Altekar, A.S., *State and Government in Ancient India* (Delhi: Motilal Banarsidass, 1996).

Basham, A.L., *The Wonder That Was India,* op. cit.

Beal, Samuel, *Si-Yu-Ki, Buddhist Records of the Western World,* trans. from the Chinese by Hieuen Tsang (AD 629) (London: Trubner & Co., 1884, rpt, Delhi: Oriental Books Reprint Corp., 1969).

Bentley, Michael (ed.), *Companion to Historiography,* 1st edn (London/New York: Routledge, 1997).

Bhandarkar, R.G., *Vaishnavism, Shaivism and Minor Religious Sects* (rpt, Varanasi: Indological Book House, 1965).

Binford, Lewis R., *An Archaeological Perspective* (New York: Seminar Press, 1972).

Binford, S.R. and L.R. Binford (eds), *New Perspectives in Archaeology* (Chicago: Aldine, 1968).

Bloch, Marc, *The Historian's Craft* (Manchester: Manchester University Press, 1954).

Bottomore, T.B., *Sociology: A Guide to Problems and Literature,* 2nd edn (London: George Allen & Unwin, 1971).

Braudel, Fernand, *On History,* tr. Sarah Mattews (London: Weidenfeld & Nicolson, Chicago: University of Chicago, 1980).

Bury, J.B., *Ancient Greek Historians* (New York: Dover Publications, 1958).

Butterfield, Herbert, *Man on His Past* (London: Cambridge University Press, 1955).

Carr, E.H., *What is History?* (Harmondsworth: Pelican Books, 1964).

Chattopadhyaya, Brajadulal, *Representing the Other? Sanskrit Sources and Muslims* (New Delhi: Manohar, 1998).

_____, *Studying Early India: Archaeology, Texts and Historical Issues* (New Delhi: Permanent Black, 2003).

Childe, V. Gordon, *History* (London: Cobbet Press, 1947).

Collingwood, R.G., *The Idea of History* (New York: Oxford University Press, 1966).

Crook, Nigel (ed.), *The Transmission of Knowledge in South Asia: Essays on Education, Religion, History, and Politics* (New Delhi: Oxford University Press, 1996).

Evans, John G., *An Introduction to Environmental Archaeology* (Ithaca, New York: Cornell University Press, 1975).

Farquhar, J.N., *An Outline of Hindu Religious Literature* (Oxford: Oxford University Press, 1919).

Filliozat, J., op. cit.

Finley, M.I., *The Use and Abuse of History* (London: Chatto & Windus, 1975).

Ghosh, A., op. cit.

Ghoshal, U.N., *Studies in Indian History and Culture*, 2nd rev. edn (New Delhi: Orient Longman, 1965).

———, *A History of Indian Public Life* (Bombay: Oxford University Press, 1966).

Giles, Herbert Allen (tr), *The Travels of Fa-hsien (399–414) or Record of the Buddhistic Kingdoms* (Cambridge: Cambridge University Press, 1923).

Gopal, Surendra, 'Foreign Visitors to India from Megasthenes to Manucci' in *Indica*, Vol. 40, no. 2, September 2003, pp. 103–38.

Gopal, S. and Romila Thapar, *Problems of Historical Writings in India* (New Delhi: India International Centre, 1963).

Gottlab, Michael (ed.), *Historical Thinking in South Asia* (New Delhi: Oxford University Press, 2003).

Goyal, Shankar, *Recent Historiography of Ancient India* (Jodhpur: Kusumanjali Prakashan, 1997).

———, *Contemporary Interpreters of Ancient India* (Jaipur: Book Enclave, 2003).

Gupta, Parmeshwari Lal, *Coins*, 2nd rev. edn (New Delhi: National Book Trust, India, 1979).

Habib, Irfan, *Essays in Indian History: Towards a Marxist Perception* (New Delhi: Tulika, 1995).

Herodotus, *The Histories* (Harmondsworth: Penguin Books, 1954).

Hodder, L., *Reading the Past* (Cambridge: Cambridge University Press, 1986).

Jain, Jyoti Prasad, *The Jaina Sources of the History of Ancient India* (New Delhi: Munshiram Manoharlal, 1964).

Jain, Rekha, *Ancient Indian Coinage: A Systematic Study of Money Economy from the Janapadas to the Early Medieval Period (600 BC to AD 1200)* (New Delhi: D.K. Print World, 1995).

Jayaswal, K.P., *Hindu Polity: A Constitutional History of India in Hindu Times*, Parts 1 and 2 (Patna: Eastern Book House, 1988).

Kane, P.V., *History of Dharmasastra*, 5 Vols, 2nd edn (Poona: Bhandarkar Oriental Research Institute, 1968–77).

Kosambi, D.D., *An Introduction to the Study of Indian History*, op. cit.

———, *Myth and Reality: Studies in the Formation of Indian Culture* (Bombay: Popular Prakashan, 1962).

———, *The Culture and Civilisation of Ancient India in Historical Outline*, op. cit.

Majumdar, R.C., *Classical Accounts of India* (Calcutta: Firma K.L. Mukhopadhyay, 1960).

McCrindle, J.W., *Ancient India as Described by Ptolemy* (rpt, New Delhi: Today and Tomorrow's Printers and Publishers, 1885).

_____, *Ancient India as Described in Classical Literature* (rpt, New Delhi: Oriental Books Reprint Co., 1979).

_____, *Ancient India as Described by the Commerce and Navigation of the Erythrean Sea and Ancient India as Described by Kteslas the Knidian* (Patna: Eastern Book House, 1987).

Muir, J., *Original Sanskrit Texts,* 5 Vols, 1872 (rpt, Delhi: Oriental Publishers, 1976).

Nilkanta Sastri, K.A., *History of India,* Part 1, *Ancient India,* op. cit.

_____, *Sources of Indian History with Special Reference to South India* (New Delhi: Asia Publishing House, 1964).

_____, *Aspects of India's History and Culture* (Delhi: Oriental Publishers, 1974).

Watters, T., *On Yuan Chwang's Travels in India,* eds T. Rhys Davids and S. Bushell (London, 1904–5; Indian rpt, New Delhi: Munshiram Manoharlal, 1974).

Pathak, V.S., *Ancient Historians of India: A Study in Historical Biographies* (Bombay: Asia Publishing House, 1966; 2nd Imp., Gorakhpur: Purva Sansthana, 1984).

Phillips, C.H. (ed.), *Historians of India, Pakistan and Ceylon* (London: Oxford University Press & SOAS, 1961).

Puri, B.N., *Ancient Indian Historiography* (Delhi: Atma Ram & Sons, 1994).

Rajwade, Vishwanath Kashinath, *Bharatiya Vivah Samstha ka Itihas* (New Delhi: Peoples Publishing House, 1986); tr. by Kamla Bhawe into Hindi from Marathi edn (Pune: Pragatik Pustak Prakashan, 1926).

Rapson, E.J. (ed.), *The Cambridge History of India,* Vol. 1, *Ancient India,* op. cit.

Rawlinson, H.G., *A Concise History of the Indian People,* 2nd edn (London: Oxford University Press, 1950).

Ray, Niharranjan et al. (eds), *A Sourcebook of Indian Civilisation* (Hyderabad: Orient Longman, 2000).

Raychaudhuri, Hemachandra, *Political History of Ancient India,* op. cit.

Schiffer, Michael B. (ed.), *Archaeological Method and Theory* (Tucson: University of Arizona Press, 1992).

Schoff, Wilfred H., *The Periplus of the Erythraean Sea: Travel and Trade in the Indian Ocean by a Merchant of the First Century,* 2nd edn (New Delhi: Oriental Books Reprint Corp., 1974; originally published New York: Longsman Green and Co., 1912).

Settar, S. and Ravi Korisettar (eds), *Indian Archaeology in Retrospect,* Vol. 4, *Archaeology and Historiography,* op. cit.

Sharma, R.S. (ed.), *A Survey of Research in the Social and Economic History of India* (New Delhi: ICHR and Ajanta Press, 1986).

R.S. Sharma, 'Exploiting History through Archaeology', *The Statesman Festival*, 1995, pp. 37–41.

Shrimali, K.M. (ed.), *Indian Archaeology since Independence* (Delhi: Association for the Study of History and Archaeology, 1996).

——— (ed.), *Reason and Archaeology* (Delhi: Association for the Study of History and Archaeology, 1998).

Spriggs, Mathew (ed.), *Marxist Perspectives in Archaeology* (Cambridge: Cambridge University Press, 1984).

Tewari, S.P., *Contributions of Sanskrit Inscriptions to Lexicograpy* (Delhi: Agam Kala Prakashan, 1987).

Thapar, Romila, *Time as a Metaphor of India: Early India* (New Delhi: Oxford University Press, 1996).

———, *Early India*, op. cit.

Warder, A.K., *An Introduction to Indian Historiography* (Bombay: Popular Prakashan, 1972).

Webster, John C.B., *An Introduction to History*, 2nd edn (Delhi: Macmillan, 1981).

Wells, Spencer, *The Journey of Man: A Genetic Odyssey* (New Delhi: Princeton and Oxford, 2002).

Wheeler, R.E.M., *Archaeology from the Earth* (Harmondsworth: Penguin Books, 1956).

Winternitz, Maurice, *A History of Indian Literature*, Vol. 1, 1905; tr. from the German by Srinivasa Sarma (Delhi: Motilal Banarsidass, 1981).

Winks, Robin W. (ed.), *The Historian as Detective: Essays on Evidence* (New York: Harper & Row, 1968).

CHAPTER 4 GEOGRAPHICAL SETTING

CHAPTER 5 ECOLOGY AND ENVIRONMENT

Secondary

Agrawal, D.P., *Man and Environment in India through the Ages* (New Delhi: Books & Books, 1992).

Allaby, Michael, *Oxford Dictionary of Ecology*, 2nd edn (Oxford: Oxford University Press, 1998).

Bennet, John W., *Human Ecology as Human Behaviour* (New Brunswick: Transaction Publishers, 1996).

Bharadwaj, O.P., *Studies in the Historical Geography of Ancient India* (Delhi: Sandeep Prakashan, 1986).

Bhattacharya, D.K., *Ecology and Social Formation in Ancient History* (Calcutta: K.P. Bagachi & Co., 1990).

Bultzer, Karl W., *Environment and Archaeology: An Ecological Approach to Prehistory* (Chicago: Aldine, 1971).

_____ , *Archaeology as Human Ecology* (Cambridge: Cambridge University Press, 1982).

Dalfes, H.N., G. Kukla and H. Weiss (eds), *Third Millennium BC Climate Change and Old World Collapse* (Berlin: Springer, 1997).

Dey, Nundo Lal, *The Geographical Dictionary of Ancient and Mediaeval India*, 3rd edn (New Delhi: Oriental Books Reprint Corp., 1971).

Dhavalikar, M.K., *Environment and Culture: A Historical Perspective* (Pune: Bhandarkar Oriental Research Institute, 2002).

Fairbridge, R.W. (ed.), *Encyclopaedia of Geomorphology* (New York: Reinhold Book Corp., 1968).

Gadgil, M. and R. Guha (eds), *The Fissured Land: An Ecological History of India* (New Delhi: Oxford University Press, 1992).

Grove, Richard H., Vinita Damodaran, and Satpal Sangwan, *Nature and the Orient* (New Delhi: Oxford University Press, 1998).

Hagget, Peter, *Geography: A Modern Synthesis*, rev. 3rd edn (New York: Harper & Row, 1979).

Hughes, J.D., *Ecology in Ancient Civilisations* (Albuquerque: University of New Mexico Press, 1975).

Lamb, H.H., *Climate: Past, Present, and Future*, Vol. 1 (London: Methuen, 1972).

_____ , *Climate: Past, Present, and Future*, Vol. 2 (London: Methuen, 1977).

Law, B.C., *Historical Geography of Ancient India* (rpt, New Delhi: Oriental Books Reprint Corp., 1984).

Mathur, S.M., *Physical Geology of India* (New Delhi: National Book Trust, India, 1986).

Schwartzberg, Joseph E., *A Historical Atlas of South Asia* (Chicago: University of Chicago Press, 1978).

Sinha, Rajiva Kumar, *Geographical Factors in Early Indian Economy* (Patna: Motilal Banarasidass, 2000).

Spate, O.H.K. and A.T.H. Learmonth, *India and Pakistan: A General and Regional Geography* (London: Methuen, 1967).

Wadia, M.D.N., *Geology of India* (New Delhi: Tata Mcgraw-Hill Publishing Co., 1978).

_____ , *Minerals of India*, 4th edn (New Delhi: National Book Trust, India, 1983).

Whyte, Ian D., *Climate Change and Human Society* (London: Arnold, 1995).

CHAPTER 6 THE LINGUISTIC BACKGROUND

Secondary

Andronov, M.S., *Dravidian Language* (Moscow: Nauka Publishing House, 1970).

——, *The Brahui Language* (Moscow: Nauka Publishing House, 1980).

Basham, A.L. (ed.), *A Cultural History of India*, op. cit.

Benveniste, Emile, *Indo-European Language and Society* (London: Faber & Faber, 1973).

Buck, C.D., *A Dictionary of Selected Synonyms in the Principal Indo-European Languages* (Chicago: University of Chicago Press, 1949).

Burrow, T., *The Sanskrit Language* (London: Faber & Faber, 1955).

Grierson, G.A., compiled and ed. *Linguistic Survey of India*, Introductory Vol. 1, Part 1 (Government of India, 1927; rpt, Delhi: Motilal Banarsidass, 1967).

Hoffmann, Rev John and Rev Arthur Van Emelen, *Encyclopaedia Mundarica* (Patna: Supdt, Govt Printing [Bihar], 1950).

Macdonell, A.A., *A History of Sanskrit Literature* (1899; rpt, New Delhi: Munshiram Manoharlal, 1972).

Mallory, J.P., *In Search of the Indo-Europeans Language Archaeology and Myth,* 1st edn (London: Thames & Hudson, 1991).

Singh, K.S. and S. Manoharan, *Language and Scripts, People of India*, Vol. 9 (New Delhi: Oxford University Press, 1993).

Turner, R.L., *A Comparative Dictionary of the Indo-Aryan Languages* (London: Oxford University Press, 1966).

Vidyarthi, L.P. and Binay Kumar Rai, *The Tribal Culture of India* (New Delhi: Concept Publishing Co., 1976).

Wells, Speneer, op. cit.

Zide, Norman H. (ed.), *Current Trends in Linguistics,* Vol. 5, *Linguistics in South Asia* (The Hague: Mouton, 1969).

CHAPTER 7 HUMAN EVOLUTION: THE OLD STONE AGE

CHAPTER 8 THE NEOLITHIC AGE: FIRST FOOD PRODUCERS AND ANIMAL KEEPERS

CHAPTER 9 CHALCOLITHIC CULTURES

Secondary

Allchin, Raymond and Bridget, *The Rise of Civilisation in India and Pakistan* (New Delhi: Cambridge University Press, 1982).

——, *Origins of a Civilisation: The Prehistory and Early Archaeology of South Asia,* 1st edn (New Delhi: Penguin, 1997).

Balasubramanian, D. and N. Appaji Rao, *The Indian Human Heritage* (Hyderabad: University Press [India] Ltd, 1998).

Bhan, Suraj, 'The Sequence and Spread of Prehistoric Cultures in the Upper Sarasvati Basin', in D.P. Agrawal and A. Ghosh (eds), *Radiocarbon and Indian Archaeology* (Bombay: Institute of Fundamental Research, 1973), 252–63.

Bhattacharya, D.K., *An Outline of Indian Prehistory*, 4th edn (New Delhi: Palaka Prakashan, 1994).

Chakrabarti, D.K., *India: An Archaeological History, Palaeolithic Beginnings to Early Historic Foundations* (New Delhi: Oxford University Press, 1999).

Childe, V. Gordon, *Man Makes Himself* (London: Watt, 1948).

DeLaet, S.J. (ed.), *History of Humanity*, Vol. 1, *Prehistory and the Beginning of Civilisation* (Paris: UNESCO, 1996).

Ember, Carol R. Melvin and Peter N. Peregine, *Anthropology*, 10th edn (New Delhi: Pearson Education Singapore, Indian Branch, 2002).

Farooqui, Amar, *Early Social Formations* (New Delhi: Manak, 2001).

Ghosh, A. (ed.), op. cit.

Gupta, S.P., *Archaeology of Soviet Central Asia and the Indian Borderlands*, Vol. 1 (Prehistory) and Vol. 2 (Protohistory) (Delhi: B.R. Publishing Corp., 1979).

Habib, Irfan, *Prehistory* (New Delhi: Aligarh Historians Society & Tulika, 2001).

Jain, K.C., *Prehistory and Protohistory of India*, 1st edn (New Delhi: Agam Kala Prakashan, 1979).

Jayaswal, Vidula, *Palaeohistory of India: A Study of the Prepared Core Technique* (New Delhi: Agam Kala Prakashan, 1978).

Joshi, R.V., *Stone Age Cultures of Central India* (Poona: Deccan College, 1979).

Narayan, Basudeo, *Prehistoric Archaeology of Bihar* (Patna: K.P. Jayaswal Research Institute, 1996).

Piggot, S., *Prehistoric India* (Harmondsworth: Penguin, 1950).

Raikes, Robert, *Water, Weather and Prehistory* (London: John Baker, 1968).

Ray, Reba, *Ancient Settlement Patterns of Eastern India: Prehistoric Period* (Calcutta: Pearl Publishers, 1987).

Roberts, J.M., *History of the World* (London: Penguin, 1995).

Sahu, B.P., *From Hunters to Breeders: Faunal Background of Early India* (New Delhi: Anamika Prakashan, 1988).

Sankalia, H.D., *Prehistory and Protohistory of India and Pakistan*, 2nd edn (Poona: Deccan College Postgraduate and Research Institute, 1974).

Settar, S. and Ravi Korisettar (eds), *Indian Archaeology in Retrospect*, Vol. 1, *Prehistory, Archaeology of South Asia;* Vol. 3, *Archaeology and Interactive Disciplines*, op. cit.

Sharma, G.R., V.D. Mishra, D. Mandal, B.B. Misra, and J.N. Pal, *Beginnings of Agriculture (Epi-Palaeolithic to Neolithic: Excavations at Chopani-Mando, Mahadaha and Mahagara)* (Allahabad: Abinash Prakashan, 1980).

Stacul, Giorgio, *Prehistoric and Protohistoric Swat, Pakistan (c. 3000–1400 BC)* (Rome: ISMEO, 1987).

Wells, Spencer, op. cit.

White, Leslie, *Evolution of Culture* (New York: McGraw-Hill, 1959).

Chapter 10 Harappan Culture: Bronze Age Urbanization in the Indus Valley

Original Archaeology and Inscriptions

Allchin, F.R. and J.P. Joshi, *Excavations at Malvan* (New Delhi: Archaeological Survey of India, 1995).

Bhan, Suraj, *Excavation at Mitathal (1968) and Other Explorations in the Sutlaj-Yamuna Divide* (Kurushetra: Kurushetra University, 1975).

Bisht, R.S., 'Dholavira: New Horizons of the Indus Civilisation', in *Puratattva,* no. 20, 1989–90, 71-82.

Joshi, J.P., *Excavation of Surkotada and Exploration in Kutch* (New Delhi: Archaeological Survey of India, 1990).

_____ , *Excavation at Bhagwanpura 1975–76 and Other Explorations 1975–81 in Haryana, Jammu & Kashmir and Punjab* (New Delhi: Archaeological Survey of India, 1993).

Marshall, J. (ed.), *Mohenjo-Daro and the Indus Civilisation,* 3 Vols (London: Arthur Probsthain, 1931).

Meadow, R.H. (ed.), *Harappa Excavation (1986–1990)* (Madison, Wisconsin: Prehistory Press, 1991).

Nath, Amarendra, 'Rakhigarhi: A Harappa Metropolis in the Saraswati–Drishadavati Divide', in *Puratattava,* no. 28, 1997–98, 39–45.

_____ , 'Further Excavations at Rakhigarhi', in *Puratattava,* no. 29, 1998–9, 46–9.

Parpola, Asko, *Corpus of Indus Seals and Inscriptions,* Vol. 1 *Collections in India* (with J.P. Joshi) and Vol. 2 *Collections in Pakistan* (with S.G.M. Shah) (Helsinki: Suomalainen Tiedeakatemia, 1987 and 1991).

Vats, Madho Sarup, *Excavations at Harappa,* Vol. 1 (New Delhi: Archaeological Survey of India, 1999).

Secondary

Allchin, Raymond and Bridget, *The Rise of Civilisations in India and Pakistan,* op. cit.

_____ , *The Birth of Indian Civilisation* (New Delhi: Penguin India, 1993).

Banerjee, Arundhati, *Early Indian Terracotta Art, circa 2000–300 BC: Northern and Western India* (New Delhi: Harman Publishing House, 1994).

Bisht, R.S., 'Secrets of the Water Port (Dholavira)', in *Down to Earth*, 15 May 1994, 25–31.

Chakrabarti, D.K., *The External Trade of the Harappans* (New Delhi: Munshiram Manoharlal, 1990).

DeLaet, S.J. (ed.), *History of Humanity*, Vol. 2, *From the Third Millennium to the Seventh Century BC* (Paris, UNESCO, 1996).

Dhavalikar, M.K., *Cultural Imperialism: Indus Civilisation in Western India*, 1st edn (New Delhi: Books & Books, 1995).

Fairservis (Jr.), A. Walter, *The Roots of Ancient India* (New York: George Allan & Unwin, 1971).

Farmer, Steve et al., 'The Collapse of the Indus-Script Thesis: The Myth of a Literate Harappan Civilization', *Electronic Journal of Vedic Studies*, Vol. 11, issue 2 (2004).

Ghosh, A. (ed.), op. cit.

Gupta, S.P. (ed.), *The 'Lost' Sarasvati and the Indus Civilisation* (Jodhpur: Kusumanjali Publishers, 1995).

Habib, Irfan, *The Indus Civilisation* (New Delhi: Aligarh Historians Society and Tulika, 2002).

Joshi, Jagat Pati and R.S. Bisht, *India and the Indus Civilisation* (New Delhi: National Museum Institute, 1994).

Kenoyer, Jonathan Mark, *Ancient Cities of the Indus Valley Civilisation* (New York: Oxford University Press, 1998).

Lal, B.B. and S.P. Gupta (eds), *Frontiers of Indus Civilisation: Mortimer Wheeler Commemoration Volume* (New Delhi: Books & Books, 1984).

Mackay, Ernest, *Early Indus Civilisation* (London: Clay & Sons, 1935); 2nd enlarged and rev. edn, ed. D. Mackay (London: Luzac, 1948; Delhi: Indological Book Corp., 1976).

Mahadevan, I., *The Indus Script: Text, Concordance and Tables* (New Delhi: ASI, MASI 77, 1977).

Mishra, Madhusudan, *From Indus to Sanskrit* (New Delhi: Yugank Publishers, 1996).

Mughal, M.R., 'Recent Archaeological Research in the Cholistan Desert', in G.L. Possehl (ed.), *Harappan Civilisation: A Comparative Perspective* (New Delhi: Oxford and IBH, 1982), 107–24.

Parpola, Asko, *Deciphering the Indus Script*, 1st edn (Cambridge: Cambridge University Press, 1994).

Possehl, Gregory L. (ed.), *Ancient Cities of the Indus* (New Delhi: Vikas Publishing House, 1979).

——, *Indus Valley Civilisation in Saurashtra* (New Delhi: B.R. Publishing Corp., 1980).

—— (ed.), *Harappan Civilization: A Comparative Perspective*, (New Delhi: Oxford & IBH, 1982).

Raikes, Robert, 'The Mohenjodaro Floods', in *Antiquity*, 39, 1965, 126–203.

——, 'Kalibangan: Death from Natural Causes', in *Antiquity*, 42, 1968, 286–91.

Rao, S.R., *Lothal and the Indus Civilisation* (New Delhi: Asia Publishing House, 1973).

——, *The Dawn and Devolution of the Indus Civilisation* (New Delhi: Aditya Prakashan, 1991).

Ratnagar, Shereen, *Encounters: The Westerly Trade of the Harappans* (New Delhi: Oxford University Press, 1981).

——, *Enquiries into the Political Organisation of Harappan Society* (Pune: Ravish, 1991).

——, *The End of the Great Harappan Tradition*, 1st edn (New Delhi: Manohar, 2000).

——, *Understanding Harappa* (New Delhi: Tulika, 2001).

Settar, S. and Ravi Korisettar (eds), *Indian Archaeology in Retrospect,* Vol. 2, *Protohistory, Archaeology of the Harappan Civilisation*, op. cit.

Sharma, R.S., 'Issues in the Identity of the Harappan Culture', in Joachim Heidrich, Hiltrud Rustau, and Diethelm Weidemann (eds), *Indian Culture: Continuity and Discontinuity*, op. cit., pp. 33–8.

——, 'Identity of the Indus Culture', *East and West*, Vol. 49, nos 1–4 (December 1999), pp. 35–45.

Subbarayappa, B.V., *Indus Script: Its Nature and Structure* (Chennai: New Era Publications, 1996).

Thakran, R.C., *Dynamics of Settlement Archaeology (Haryana)* (New Delhi: Gyan Publishing House, 2000).

Weber, S.A., *Plants and Harappan Subsistence* (New Delhi: Oxford and IBH, 1991).

Wheeler, R.E.M., *Early India and Pakistan* (London: Thames & Hudson, 1966).

——, *The Indus Civilisation*, 3rd edn (London: Cambridge University Press, 1968).

CHAPTER 11 IDENTITY OF ARYAN CULTURE

CHAPTER 12 THE AGE OF THE *RIG VEDA*

CHAPTER 13 THE LATER VEDIC PHASE: TRANSITION TO STATE AND SOCIAL ORDERS

Original Texts and Translations

Aitareya Aranyaka, ed. & tr. A.B. Keith, 1909 (London: Oxford University Press, 1969).

Aitareya Brahmana, ed. R.R. Agashe, 2 Parts (Poona: Anandashram, 1977–9).

The Atharvaveda, tr. R.T.H. Griffith, 2 Vols (rpt, Varanasi: Chawkhamba Sanskrit Series Office, 1968); ed. Vishva Bandhu (Hoshiarpur: Vishveshvaranand Vedic Research Institute, 1960–2).

Brhadaranyaka Upanisad, ed. & tr. S.C. Vasu (Allahabad: Panini Office, 1933).

Chandogya Upanisad, ed. & tr. Swami Gambhiranand (Calcutta: Advaita Ashrama, 1983).

Gopatha Brahmana, ed. Rajendra Lal Mitra (rpt, Delhi: Indological House, 1972).

Jaiminiya Brahmana, eds Raghu Vira and Lokesh Chandra (Nagpur: Sarasvati Vihar, 1954).

Kausitaki Brahmana, ed. B. Lindner (Jena: 1887); Eng. tr. A.B. Keith, *Rigveda Brahmanas: The Aitareya and Kausitaki Brahmanas of the Rigveda* (Harvard University Press; 1st Indian rpt, Delhi: Motilal Banarsidass, 1970).

Kathaka Samhita, ed. Leopold Von Schroder (Leipzig: F.A. Brockhaus, 1900–1910).

Mahabharata, Text as Constituted in its Critical Edition, ed. various hands (Poona: Bhandarkar Oriental Research Institute, 1927–66).

Maitrayani Samhita, ed. Leopold Von Schroder (Leipzig: Otto Harrassowitz, 1923).

Pancavimsa Brahmana (*Tandya Mahabrahmana*, Part I), ed. A.C. Sastri (Benaras: Chawkhamba Sanskrit Series Office, 1935); (Part II) (Benaras: Jay Krishna Das–Haridas Gupta, 1936).

Ramayana (Gorakhpur: Gita Press, VS 2023).

Rigveda Samhita, with the commentary of Sayana, 5 Vols (Pune: Vaidik Samshodhan Mandal, 1933–5); tr. Ralph T.H. Griffith, under the title *The Hymns of the Rgveda*, (rpt, Delhi: Motilal Banarsidass, 1986); tr. in German by R.F. Geldner as *Der Rigveda*, Harvard Oriental Series, nos. 33–5 (Cambridge, Mass.: Harvard University Press, 1951–7).

Samaveda, Hymns of the Samaveda, tr. R.T.H. Griffith (New Delhi: Munshiram Manoharlal, 1986).

Santi Parvan, in *The Mahabharata* as Constituted in its Critical Edition, Vol. 3 (Poona: Bhandarkar Oriental Research Institute, 1974).

Satapatha Brahmana, ed. Albrecht Weber, 1855 (rpt, Varanasi: Chawkhamba Sanskrit Series Office, 1964); tr. J. Eggeling, *Sacred Books of the East Series*. 12, 26, 41, 44 and 45 (rpt, Delhi: Motilal Banarsidass, 1963).

Srimadvalmikiya Ramayana, with Hindi tr., Janakinath Sharma (Gorakhpur: Gita Press, VS 2033).

Taittiriya Aranyaka, of the Black Yajur Veda with the Commentary of Sayanacarya, ed. R.L. Mitra (Calcutta: Bibliotheca Indica, 1872).

Taittiriya Brahmana, ed. A.N. Apte (Bombay: Anandashram Sankrit Series, No. 37, 1898).

Taittiriya Samhita, tr. A.B. Keith, 2 Vols (Cambridge: Harvard University Press, 1969); ed. T.N. Dharmadhikari, 2 Vols (Poona: Vaidika Samsodhana Mandala, 1981).

The Zend Avesta, Part 1, *The Vendidad,* tr. James Darmesteter; *Sacred Books of the East,* Vol. 4 (rpt, Delhi: Motilal Banarsidass, 1992); Part 2, *Sacred Books of the East,* Vol. 23 (rpt, Delhi: Motilal Banarsidass, 1988); Part 3, tr. L.H. Mills, *Sacred Books of the East,* Vol. 31 (rpt, Delhi: Motilal Banarsidass, 1988).

Archaeology

Lal, B.B., 'Excavations at Hastinapur and Other Explorations in the Upper Ganga and Satlej Basins 1950–52' in *Ancient India,* nos 10–11 (1954–5), 5–151.

Secondary

Altekar, A.S., *The Position of Women in Hindu Civilisation* (Delhi: Motilal Banarsidass, 1965).

Basu, Jogiraj, *India of the Age of the Brahmanas: Ancient Indian Culture and Civilisation as Revealed in the Brahmanas* (Calcutta: Sanskrit Pustak Bhandar, 1969).

Bhattacharji, Sukumari, *Literature in the Vedic Age,* Vol. 1, *The Samhitas* (Calcutta: K. P. Bagchi & Co., 1984).

——, *Literature in the Vedic Age,* Vol. 2, *Brahmanas, Aranyakas, Upanisadas and Sutras* (Calcutta: K.P. Bagchi & Co., 1986).

Bongard-Levin, G.M., *The Origin of Aryans from Scythis to India* (New Delhi: Arnold-Heinemann, 1980).

Bryant, Edwin, *The Quest for the Origins of Vedic Culture: The Indo-Aryan Migration Debate* (New Delhi: Oxford University Press, 2001).

Chattopadhyaya, Kshetresh Chandra, *Studies in Vedic and Indo-Iranian Literature,* Vol. 2 (Varanasi: Bharatiya Vidya Prakashan, 1978).

Chawla, Jyotsna, *The Rgvedic Deities and Their Iconic Forms* (New Delhi: Munshiram Manoharlal, 1990).

Choudhary, B.K., *From Kinship to Social Hierarchy: The Vedic Experience* (Patna: K.P. Jayaswal Research Institute, 1999).

Claessen, H.J.M. and P. Skalnik, *The Early State* (The Hague: Mouton, 1978).

Cohen, Ronald and Elman R. Service (eds), *Origins of the State: The Anthropology of Political Evolution* (Philadelphia: Institute for the Study of Human Issues, 1978).

Dandekar, R.N., *Vedic Bibliography,* Vol. 5 (Pune: Bhandarkar Oriental Research Institute, 1993).

Dange, S.A., *Cultural Sources from the Vedas* (Bombay: Bharatiya Vidya Bhawan, 1977).

Dani, A.H. and V.M. Masson (eds), *History of Civilisations of Central Asia,* Vol. 1 (Paris: UNESCO Publishing, 1992).

Deshpande, Madhav M. and Peter Edwin Hook (eds), *Aryan and Non-Aryan in India* (Ann Arbor: University of Michigan Press, 1979).

Drekmeir, C., *Kingship and Community in Early India* (Bombay: Oxford University Press, 1962).

Erdosy, George (ed.), *The Indo-Aryans of Ancient South Asia: Language, Material Culture and Ethnicity* (Berlin: Walter de Gruyter & Co., 1995); 1st Indian edn (New Delhi: Munshiram Manoharlal, 1997).

Gamkrelidge, T.V. and V.V. Ivanov, *Indo-European and the Indo-Europeans,* Part 1, The Text (New York: Mouton de Gruyter, 1995).

Ghosh, A. (ed.), op. cit.

Ghurye, G.S., *Vedic India* (Bombay: Popular Prakashan, 1979).

Habib, Irfan (ed.), *A Shared Heritage: The Growth of Civilisations in India and Iran* (New Delhi: Tulika Books, 2002).

Heesterman, J.C., *The Ancient Indian Royal Consecration* (The Hague: Mouton & Co., 1957).

Jha, D.N., *The Myth of the Holy Cow* (London/New York: Verso, 2002).

Jones, Grant D. and Robert R. Kautz (eds), *The Transition to Statehood in the New World* (Cambridge: Cambridge University Press, 1981).

Keith, A.B., *Religion and Philosophy of the Vedas* (London: Oxford University Press, 1925).

Kenoyer, J.M. (ed.), *Old Problems and New Perspectives of the Archaeology of South Asia,* Vol. 2 (Madison, Wisconsin: Archaeological Reports, 1989).

Kochhar, Rajesh, *The Vedic People: Their History and Geography* (Delhi: Orient Longman, 1999).

Kuiper, F.B.J., *Aryans in the Rigveda* (Amsterdam: Atlanta, GA, Rodopi B.V., 1991).

Lincoln, Bruce, *Priest, Warriors and Cattle* (Berkeley and Los Angeles: University of Calfornia Press, 1982).

Macdonell, A.A., *The Vedic Mythology* (rpt, Varanasi: Indological Book House, 1963).

Macdonell, A.A. and A.B. Keith, *Vedic Index of Names and Subjects,* 2 Vols (Delhi: Motilal Banarsidass, rpt, 1982).

Majumdar, R.C. (ed.), *The History and Culture of the Indian People,* Vol. 1, *The Vedic Age* (Bombay: Bharatiya Vidya Bhawan, 1951).

Mallory, J.P., op. cit.

Mauss, Marcel, op. cit.

Max Müller, F., *Biographies of the Words and the Home of the Aryans* (London: Longman, Green, 1888).

Nandi, Ramendra Nath, *Aryan Revisited*, (New Delhi: Munshiram Manoharlal, 2001).

Pandey, Rajbali, *Hindu Samskaras: Socio-Religious Study of the Hindu Sacraments* (Delhi: Motilal Banarsidass, 1987).

Parpola, Asko, 'The Coming of the Aryans to Iran and India and the Cultural and Ethnic Identity of the Dasas' in *International Journal of Dravidian Linguistics*, Vol. 17, no. 2, 1988, 85–229.

Radhakrishnan, S., *The Principal Upanisads*, Centenary edn (New Delhi: Oxford University Press, 1989).

Renou, Louis, *Vedic India, Classical India*, Vol. 3, tr. from the French by Philip Spratt (Calcutta: 1957).

Renfrew, C., *Archaeology and Language: The Puzzle of Indo-European Origins* (Harmondsworth, Penguin, 1989).

Richards, J.F. (ed.), *Kingship and Authority in South Asia* (New Delhi: Oxford University Press, 1998).

Roy, Brajdeo Prasad, *The Later Vedic Economy* (Patna: Janaki Prakashan, 1984).

Roy, K., *The Emergence of Monarchy in North India* (New Delhi: Oxford University Press, 1994).

—— (ed.), *Women in Early Indian Societies* (New Delhi: Manohar, 1999).

Sarkar, S.C., *Some Aspects of the Earliest Social History of India* (rpt, Patna: Janaki Prakashan, 1985).

Sastri, S.R., *Women in the Vedic Age* (Bombay: Bharatiya Vidya Bhawan, 1969).

Sethna, K.D., *The Problem of Aryan Origin from an Indian Perspective* (Calcutta: S. & S. Publishers, 1980).

Sharma, R.S., *Material Culture and Social Formations in Ancient India* (Delhi: Macmillan, 1983).

——, *Aspects of Political Ideas and Institutions in Ancient India*, op. cit.

——, *Sudras in Ancient India*, op. cit.

——, *Perspectives in Social and Economic History of India*, op. cit.

——, *Origin of the State of India*, D.D. Kosambi Memorial Lecture (1987) (Bombay Department of History, University of Bombay, 1989).

——, *Looking for the Aryans* (Madras: Orient Longman, 1995).

——, *Advent of the Aryans in India* (New Delhi: Manohar, 1999).

Shastri, Viswabandhu, *Vedic Padanukrama Kosa*, 5 Vols subdivided into 14 parts (Lahore: V.R.R. Institute, 1944).

Shende, N.J., *Religion and Philosophy of the Atharvaveda* (rpt, Poona: Bhandarkar Oriental Research Institute, 1985).

Singh, Sarva Daman, *Ancient Indian Warfare with Special Reference to the Vedic Period* (Leiden: E.J. Brill, 1965).

Thapar, Romila, *From Lineage to State* (New Delhi: Oxford University Press, 1984).

_____, *Early India*, op. cit.

Thite, G.U., *Sacrifice in the Brahmana Texts* (Poona: University of Poona, 1975).

Trautmann, Thomas R. (ed.), *Kinship and History in South Asia* (Michigen: Ann Arbor, 1974).

_____, *Aryans and British India* (New Delhi: Vistaar Publication, 1997).

Tripathi, Vibha, *The Painted Grey Ware: An Iron Age Culture of Northern India* (Delhi: Concept Publishing, 1976).

_____, *The Age of Iron in South Asia: Legacy and Tradition* (New Delhi: Aryan Book International, 2001).

Wells, Spencer, op. cit.

Witzel, Michael, 'Languages in Old Indo-Aryans (Rigvedic, Middle and Later Vedic)', in *Electronic Journal of Vedic Studies*, Vol. 5 (1999), issue 1 (Sept.); www.shore.net/~india/ejvs.

_____, 'Autochthonous Aryans? The Evidence from Old Indian and Iranian Texts', in *Electronic Journal of Vedic Studies*, Vol. 7 (2001), issue 3 (May 25); http://www.nautiles.shore.net/~india/ejvs.

CHAPTER 14 JAINISM AND BUDDHISM

CHAPTER 17 STATE STRUCTURE AND THE VARNA SYSTEM IN THE AGE OF THE BUDDHA

Original Texts and Translations

Anguttara Nikaya, ed. Bhikku J. Kashyap, 4 Vols, Devanagari–Pali Series (Nalanda: Pali Publication Board [Government of Bihar], 1960).

Apastamba Dharmasutra, ed. G. Bühler (Bombay, 1932); Eng. tr. G. Buhler, *Sacred Books of the East*, 2 (Oxford: Oxford University Press, 1879).

Asvalayana Grhyasutra, Anandasramasamskrtagranthavali, 105 (new edn, Poona, 1979); Eng. tr. H. Oldenberg, *Sacred Books of the East*, 29 (Oxford: Oxford University Press, 1886).

Asvalayana Srautasutra, Anandasramasamskrtagranthavali, 81 (Poona, 1917).

Avasyakacurni of Jinadasagani, 2 Vols (Ratlam: 1928).

Baudhayana Dharmasutra, ed. E. Hultzsch (Leipzig: 1884); Eng. tr. G. Buhler, *Sacred Books of the East*, 14 (Oxford: Oxford University Press, 1882).

Baudhayana Grhyasutra, ed. R. Shama Sastry, 2nd edn (Mysore: Oriental Library Publications, 1920).

Baudhayana Srautasutra, from the *Taittiriya Samhita*, ed. W. Caland, 3 Vols (Calcutta: Bibliotheca Indica, 1904–24).

Dhammapadam (with a gloss.), ed. Shri Satkari Sharma Vangiya and Hindi tr. Kancchedilal Gupta, 4th edn (Varanasi: Chowkhamba Vidyabhawan, 1960).

Digha Nikaya, eds T.W. Rhys Davids and J.E. Carpenter, 3 Vols (London: 1890–1911); tr. by T.W. Rhys Davids, 3 Vols (London: 1889–1921).

Gautama Dharmasutra, ed. Adolf Friedrich Stenzler (London: Sanskrit Text Society, 1876); Eng. tr. G. Buhler, *Sacred Books of the East* (Oxford: Oxford University Press, 1879).

Gobhila Grhyasutra, ed. Chintamani Bhattacharya (Calcutta: Calcutta Sanskrit Series no. 17, 1936); Eng. tr. H. Oldenberg, *Sacred Books of the East* (Oxford: Oxford University Press, 1886); text with Hindi tr., Thakur Udaya Narain Singh (Delhi: Chowkhamba Sanskrit Pratisthan, 1992).

Kalpa Sutra, Eng. tr. H. Jacobi, *Sacred Books of the East,* 22 (Oxford: Oxford University Press, 1884).

Mahaviracarita, ed. with Hindi tr. Rampratapa Tripathi Shastri (Allahabad: Lok Bharati Prakashan, 1973).

Majjhima Nikaya, ed. P.V. Bapat, Vol. 1; Rahul Sankrityayana, Vols 2–3, Devanagari–Pali Series (Nalanda: Pali Publication Board [Government of Bihar], 1958).

Nisitha Curni (Nisitha Visesa Curni) of Jinadasagani (with commentary), ed. Kavi Amar Mani Upadhyaya and Muni Kanhaiyalal (Agra: 1957–60).

Samyutta Nikaya, ed. Bhikku Jagdish Kashyap, Devanagari–Pali Series, 4 Vols (Nalanda: Pali Publication Board [Government of Bihar], 1959).

Sankhayayana Srautasutra, ed. Alfred Hillerbrandt (Calcutta: Bibliotheca Indica, 1888).

Srautakosa, Vols 1 and 2 (English Section) (Poona: Vaidik Samsodhana Mandala, 1962).

Sutta Nipata, Text and Hindi tr. Bhikku Dharmaratna (Varanasi: Mahabodhi Sabha, 1960).

Vaikhanasa Grhyasutra, ed. W. Caland (Calcutta: Bibliotheca Indica, 1927); text and tr. (Calcutta: Asiatic Society, 1927–9).

Vasistha Dharmasutra (Srivasisthadharmasastram), ed. Alois Anton Fuhrer (Bombay: Bombay Sanskrit and Prakrit Series 23, 1883); Eng. tr. G. Buhler, *Sacred Books of the East,* 14 (Oxford: Oxford University Press, 1882).

Vinaya Pitaka, Eng. tr. T.W. Rhys Davids and H. Oldenberg, *Vinaya Texts, Sacred Books of the East,* 13, 17 and 20 (Oxford: Oxford University Press, 1822–5); Hindi tr. Rahul Sankrityayana (Sarnath [Benaras]: Mahabodhi Sabha, 1935).

Archaeology

Altekar, A.S. and V.K. Mishra, *Report on Kumrahar Excavations (1951–53)* (Patna: K.P. Jayaswal Research Institute, 1959).

Lal, B.B., *Excavations at Sringaverapura (1977–86)*, Vol. 1 (New Delhi: Archaeological Survey of India, 1993).

Narain, A.K. and T.N. Roy, *Excavations at Rajghat*, Part 2 (Varanasi: Banaras Hindu University, 1977).

Sharma, G.R., *The Excavations at Kausambi (1957–59)* (Allahabad: Department of Ancient Indian History, Culture and Archaeology, University of Allahabad, 1960).

Sinha, B.P. and S.R. Roy, *Vaisali Excavations, 1958–62* (Patna: Directorate of Archaeology and Museums [Bihar], 1969).

Sinha, K.K., *Excavations at Sravasti: 1959* (Varanasi: Banaras Hindu University, 1967).

Srivastava, K.M., *Excavations at Piprahwa and Ganwaria* (New Delhi: Archaeological Survey of India, 1996).

Secondary

Adams, R.M., *The Evolution of Urban Society* (Chicago: University of Chicago Press, 1966).

Agrawala, V.S., *Paninikalin Bharatavarsha*, 2nd edn (Varanasi: Chaukhamba Vidya Bhawan, 1969).

Allchin, F.R., *The Archaeology of Early Historic South Asia: The Emergence of Cities and States*, 1st edn (Cambridge: Cambridge University Press, 1995).

Banerjee, N.R., *The Iron Age in India* (New Delhi: Munshiram Manoharlal, 1965).

Basham, A.L., *History and Doctrines of the Ajivikas: A Vanished Indian Religion* (London: Luzac & Co. Ltd, 1951).

Bechert, H., *The Date of the Historical Buddha: Symposium Zur Buddhismus forschung*, 2 Vols (Gottingen: Vandenhoek and Ruprecht, 1991).

_____ (ed.), *When did the Buddha Live? The Commentary on the Dating of Historical Buddha* (Delhi: Sri Satguru Publications, 1995).

Bhaskar, Bhagchandra Jain, *Jainism in Buddhist Literature* (Nagpur: Alok Prakashan, 1972).

Bhattacharyya, D.C., *Buddhist Shrines* (New Delhi: Publications Division, Ministry of Information and Broadcasting, Govt of India, 1987).

Bose, A.N., *Social and Rural Economy of Northern India*, 2 Vols (Calcutta: K.L. Mukhopadhyay, 1942–5).

Chakravarti, Uma, *The Social Dimensions of Early Buddhism* (New Delhi: Oxford University Press, 1987).

Chanana, D.R., *Slavery in Ancient India* (Delhi: People's Publishing House, 1960).

Cowell, E.B. (tr), *Buddhist Mahayana Texts, Sacred Books of the East*, 49 (rpt, Delhi: Motilal Banarsidass, 1978).

Davids, Rhys, *Buddhist India* (rpt, Delhi: Motilal Banarsidass, 1971).

——, *Buddhist Sutras, Sacred Books of the East*, 2 (rpt, Delhi: Motilal Banarsidass, 1980).

Dumont, Louis, *Homo Hierarchicus: The Caste System and its Implications* (New Delhi: Vikas, 1970).

Erdosy, George, *Urbanisation in Early Historic India* (Oxford: BAR International Service, 430, 1988).

Fick, Richard, *The Social Organisation in North-West India in Buddha's Time* (Calcutta: 1920; rpt, Delhi: Indological Book House, 1972).

Ghosh, A., *The City in Early Historical India* (Simla: Indian Institute of Advanced Study, 1973).

—— (ed.), op. cit.

Gopal, Ram, *India of Vedic Kalpasutra* (Delhi: National Publishing House, 1959).

Jain, Jagdish Chandra, *Life in Ancient India as Depicted in Jain Canon and Commentaries*, 2nd edn (New Delhi: Munshiram Manoharlal, 1984).

Jaiswal, Suvira, *Caste: Origin, Function and Dimensions of Change*, op. cit.

Jha, Satyendra Kumar, *Beginnings of Urbanization in Early Historic India: A Study of the Gangetic Plains* (Patna: Novelty & Co., 1998).

Kane, P.V., op. cit.

Lal, M., *Settlement History and the Rise of Civilisation in the Ganga–Yamuna Doab from 1500 BC–300 AD* (Delhi: B.R. Publishing Corp., 1984).

Law, B.C., *A Study of the Mahavastu* (Delhi: Bharatiya Publishing House, 1978).

Lewellen, Ted C., *Political Anthropology: An Introduction* (Massachusetts: Bergin & Garvey Publishers, Inc., 1983).

Narain, A.K. (ed.), *Studies in Pali and Buddhism* (Delhi: B.R. Publishing Corp., 1979).

Nath, Vijay, *Dana: Gift System in Ancient India* (New Delhi: Munshiram Manoharlal, 1987).

Raychaudhuri, Hemachandra, *Political History of Ancient India*, op. cit.

Rockhill, W.W., *The Life of the Buddha* (London: Trubner Oriental Series, 1907).

Roy, T.N., *The Ganges Civilisation* (Delhi: Ramanand Vidya Bhawan, 1983).

Sarao, K.T.S., *The Origin and Nature of Ancient Indian Buddhism* (Delhi: Eastern Book Linkers, 1989).

——, *Urban Centres and Urbanisation as Reflected in the Pali Vinaya and Sutta Pitakas* (Delhi: Vidyanidhi, 1990).

Sen, B.C., *Studies in the Buddhist Jatakas* (Calcutta: Saraswat Library, 1974).

Sen, Madhu, *A Critical Study of the Nisitha Curni* (Amritsar: Sohanlal Jain Dharma Pracharak Samiti, 1975).

Sharma, J.P., *Republics in Ancient India (c. 1500 B.C.–500 B.C.)* (Leiden: E.J. Brill, 1968).

Sharma, R.S., *Material Culture and Social Formation in Ancient India*, op. cit.

——, *The State and Varna Formations in the Mid-Ganga Plains: An Ethnoarchaeological View* (New Delhi, Manohar, 1996).

Singh, Madan Mohan, *Life in North-Eastern India in Pre-Mauryan India with Special Reference to c. 600 B.C.–325 B.C.* (Delhi: Motilal Banarsidass, 1967).

Singh, R.B.P., *Jainism in Early Medieval Karnataka* (Delhi: Motilal Banarsidass, 1975).

Sinha, B.P. (ed.), *Potteries in Ancient India* (Patna: Patna University, 1969).

Sircar, D.C. (ed.), *Religion and Culture of the Jains* (Calcutta: University of Calcutta, 1973).

Srivastava, K.M., *Discovery of Kapilavastu* (New Delhi: Books & Books, 1986).

Stevenson, Mrs Sinclair, *The Heart of Jainism* (London: Oxford University Press, 1915; New Delhi: Munshiram Manoharlal, 1970).

Thakur, Vijai Kumar, *Urbanisation in Ancient India* (New Delhi: Abhinav, 1981).

Thapar, Romila, *Ancient Indian Social History*, op. cit.

——, *Early India*, op. cit.

Tripathi, Vibha, *The Age of Iron in South Asia*, op. cit.

Upreti, G.B., *The Early Buddhist World Outlook in Historical Perspective* (New Delhi: Manohar, 1997).

Wagle, Narendra, *Society at the Time of the Buddha* (Bombay: Popular Prakashan, 1966).

Ward, C.H.S., *Buddhism*, Vol. 1, *Hinayana*, rev. edn (London: Epworth Press, 1947).

——, *Buddhism*, Vol. 2, *Mahayana* (London: Epworth Press, 1952).

Warder, A.K., *Pali Metre: A Contribution to the History of Indian Literature* (London: Luzac & Co. Ltd, 1967).

——, *Indian Buddhism* (Delhi: Motilal Banarsidass, 1970).

Chapter 15 Territorial States and the Rise of Magadha

Chapter 16 Iranian and Macedonian Invasions

Original Texts and Translations

Alexandri Anabasis, A.G. Roos (Leipzig: 1907); tr. J.W. McCrindle, *The Invasion of India by Alexander the Great*, 2nd edn (Westminster, 1896).

Anguttara Nikaya, ed. op. cit.

Bhagvati Sutra, ed. with Abhayadeva's Commentary (Bombay: Agamodaya Samiti, 1921).

Firdausi, *Shah-namah*, eds J.A. Vullers and S. Landauer (Leiden: 1877–84); Eng. tr. G. and E. Warner (London: 1905–15).

McCrindle, J.W., *Ancient India as Described by Megasthenes and Arrian*, ed. R.C. Jain (New Delhi: International Books & Periodicals Supply Service, 1972).

Strabo, *Geographica*, ed. A. Meineke (Leipzig, 1854–57); Eng. tr. H.C. Hamilton and W. Falconer (London: 1854–7).

Inscriptions

Sircar, Dinesh Chandra (ed.), *Select Inscriptions Bearing on Indian History and Civilization*, Vol. 1, op. cit.

Secondary

Basham, A.L., *The Wonder That Was India*, op. cit.

Bosworth, A.B., *A Historical Commentary on Arrian's History of Alexander* (Oxford: 1995).

Ghirshman, R., *Iran from the Earliest Times to the Islamic Conquest* (Harmondsworth: Penguin, 1954).

Ghosh, A. (ed.), op. cit.

Filliozat, J., op. cit.

Habib, Irfan (ed.), *A Shared Heritage: The Growth of Civilizations in India and Iran*, op. cit.

Jha, D.N., *Ancient India in Historical Outline*, op. cit.

Kosambi, D.D., *The Culture and Civilisation of Ancient India in Historical Outline*, op. cit.

Majumdar, R.C. (ed.), *The History and Culture of the Indian People*, Vol. 2, *The Age of the Imperial Unity* (Bombay: Bharatiya Vidya Bhawan, 1951).

Mehta, R.N., *Pre-Buddhist India* (Bombay: Examiner Press, 1939).

Narain, A.K., *From Alexander to Kanishka* (Varanasi: Banaras Hindu University, 1967).

Nilakanta Sastri, K.A. (ed.), *Age of the Nanda and Mauryas*, 2nd edn (Delhi: Motilal Banarsidass, 1967).

Rapson, E.J. (ed.), *The Cambridge History of India*, Vol. 1, *Ancient India*, op. cit.

Raychaudhuri, Hemachandra, *Political History of Ancient India*, op. cit.

Scharfe, H., *The State in Indian Tradition* (Leiden: Köln, 1992).

Sharma, R.S., *The State and Varna Formations in the Mid-Ganga Plains*, op. cit.

Shrimali, K.M., *History of Pancala to c. A.D. 500*, Vols 1 and 2 (New Delhi: Munshiram Manoharlal, 1985).

Smith, V.A., *The Early History of India from 600 B.C. to the Muhammadan Conquest*, 4th edn (Oxford: Clarendon Press, 1957).

Thapar, Romila, *Early India*, op. cit.

CHAPTER 18 THE MAURYA AGE

CHAPTER 19 THE SIGNIFICANCE OF MAURYA RULE

Original Texts and Translations

Mudraraksasa by Visakhadatta, ed. Alfred Hillebrandt, Part 1, Text (Breslau: M. and H. Marcus, 1912).

Divyavadana, eds E.B. Cowell and R. A. Neil (Cambridge: Cambridge University Press, 1886).

Gatha Saptasati of Hala (Leipzig, 1881).

Kautilya Arthasastra, 3 Parts, ed., tr. and a study, R.P. Kangle (Bombay: University of Bombay, 1960–5).

Mahabhasya of Patanjali, ed. F. Keilhorn, 3 Vols, Sanskrit and Prakrit Series, nos. 28–30 (Bombay: The Department of Public Instruction, 1892–1909).

McCrindle, J.W., *Ancient India as Described by Megasthenes and Arrian* (Calcutta: Chukerverity, Chatterjee Co., 1926).

Milindapanho, ed. V. Trenckner (London: 1928); Eng. tr. T.W. Rhys Davids, *The Questions of King Milinda* (New Delhi: Atlantic Publishers and Distributors, 1990).

Panini-Sutra-Patha and *Parisista*, with Word Index, comp. by S. Pathak and S. Chitrao (Poona: Bhandarkar Oriental Research Institute, 1935).

Archaeology and Inscriptions

Altekar, A.S. and V.K. Mishra, op. cit.

Hultzsch, E., *Corpus Inscriptionum Indicarum*, Vol. 1, *Inscriptions of Asoka* (Oxford: 1925).

Sinha, B.P. and L.A. Narain, *Pataliputra Excavation: 1955–56* (Patna: Directorate of Archaeology and Museums, 1970).

Sircar, D.C. (ed.), *Select Inscriptions bearing on Indian History and Civilization*, Vol. 1, op. cit.

Waddel, L.A., *Report on the Excavations at Pataliputra (Patna)* (Calcutta: Bengal Secretariat Press, 1903).

Secondary

Agrawala, V.S., *Indian Art* (Varanasi: Prithivi Prakashan, 1965).

Altekar, A.S., *The Position of Women in Hindu Civilisation*, op. cit.

Barua, B.M., *Asoka and His Inscriptions*, Parts 1 and 2 (Calcutta: New Age Publishers, 1955).

Basak, Radhagovinda (ed.), *Asokan Inscriptions* (Calcutta: Progressive Publishers, 1959).

Bhandarkar, D.R., *Ashoka* (Delhi: S. Chand & Co., 1964).

Bongard-Levin, G.M., *Mauryan India* (New Delhi: Sterling Publishers, 1985).

Chakrabarti, D.K., *The Archaeology of Ancient Indian Cities* (New Delhi: Oxford University Press, 1995).

Dikshitar, V.R. Ramchandra, *The Mauryan Polity* (Delhi: Motilal Banarsidass, 1993).

Ghosh, A. (ed.), op. cit.

Ghoshal, U.N., *Contributions to the History of the Hindu Revenue System,* 2nd edn (Calcutta: Saraswat Library, 1972).

Gupta, Chitrarekha, *The Brahmanas of India: A Study Based on Inscriptions* (New Delhi: Sundeep Prakashan, 1993).

Gupta, Parmeshwari Lal, *Coins*, op. cit.

Gupta, S.P., *The Roots of Indian Art: A Detailed Study of the Formative Period of Indian Art and Architecture: Third and Second Centuries B.C.—Mauryan and Late Mauryan* (Delhi: B.R. Publishing Corp., 1980).

Jain, Rekha, op. cit.

Jolly, Julius, *Hindu Law and Custom* (Varanasi/Delhi: Bhartiya Publishing House, 1975).

Kher, N.N., *Agrarian and Fiscal Economy in the Mauryan and Post-Mauryan Age* (New Delhi: Munshiram Manoharlal, 1973).

Majumdar, R.C. (ed.), *The History and Culture of the Indian People,* Vol. 2, op. cit.

Mishra, S.C., *Evolution of Kautilya's Arthasastra: An Inscriptional Approach* (Delhi: Anamika, 1997).

Misra, Yogendra, *Ashoka* (in Hindi) (Patna: Granthamala-Karyalaya, 1965).

Mookherji, Radhakumud, *Asoka* (Delhi: Motilal Banarsidass, 1995).

Nilakanta Sastri, K.A. (ed.), *Age of the Nanda and Mauryas*, op. cit.

——— (ed.), *A Comprehensive History of India,* Vol. 2, *The Mauryas and Satavahanas, 325 B.C.–A.D. 300* (New Delhi: People's Publishing House, 1987).

Parasher, Aloka, *Mlecchas in Early India: A Study in Attitudes towards Outsiders up to A.D. 600* (New Delhi: Munshiram Manoharlal, 1991).

Rangrajan, L.N., *Kautilya: The Arthasastra* (New Delhi: Penguin India, 1992).

Ray, Niharranjan, *Maurya and Post-Maurya Art: A Study in Social and Formal Contrasts* (New Delhi: Indian Council of Historical Research, 1975).

Raychaudhuri, Hemachandra, *Political History of Ancient India*, op. cit.

Rowland, Benjamin, *The Art and Architecture of India: Buddhist, Hindu, Jain,* 3rd edn (Harmondsworth: Penguin Books, 1967).

Sarkar, H.B., *Studies in Early Buddhist Architecture* (New Delhi: Munshiram Manoharlal, 1966).

Sarasvati, S.K., *A Survey of Indian Sculpture,* 2nd edn (New Delhi: Munshiram Manoharlal, 1975).

Sircar, D.C., *Inscriptions of Asoka,* 3rd edn (New Delhi: Publications Division, Ministry of Information and Broadcasting, Govt of India, 1975).

Smith, Vincent A., *Emperor Ashok* (Indian edn) (Bulandshahr [UP]: Wisdom Publications, 1981).

Thakur, Upendra, *Mints and Minting in Ancient India* (Varanasi: Chowkhamba Sanskrit Series Office, 1972).

Thapar, Romila, *Ancient Indian Social History,* op. cit.

_____, *Asoka and the Decline of the Mauryas* (New Delhi: Oxford University Press, 2000).

_____, *Early India,* op. cit.

CHAPTER 20 CENTRAL ASIAN CONTACT AND MUTUAL IMPACT

CHAPTER 23 CRAFTS, COMMERCE, AND URBAN GROWTH

Original Texts and Translations

Ancient India as Described by Ptolemy, ed. S.N. Majumdar (Calcutta: 1927).

Anguttara Nikaya, op. cit.

Buddhacarita of Asvaghosa, ed. and tr. by Johnson (Calcutta: Punjab University and Oriental Publications, 1935–6).

Charaka Samhita, ed. A.C. Kaviratna & P. S. Kavibhushan (Calcutta: 1890–1911).

Digha Nikaya, eds T.W. Rhys Davids and J.E. Carpenter, op. cit., tr. T.W. Rhys Davids, op. cit.

Divyavadana, eds E.B. Cowell and R.A. Neil (Cambridge: 1886).

Gotha Saptasati of Hala, (Leipzig: 1881).

Horasastra of Prthuyasas (Son of Varahamihira), ed. and tr. P.V. Subraihmanya Sastri (Bangalore: 1949).

Huntingford, G.W.B., ed. and tr., *The Periplus of the Erythraean Sea* (London: Hakluyt Society, 1980).

Kamasutra of Vatsyayana (with Commentary of *Jayamangala* of Yasodhara), ed. Goswami Damodar Shastri, (Banaras, 1929); tr. Sir Richard Burton (New Delhi: Penguin India, 1993).

Lankavatarasutra, ed. Bunyiu Nanjio (Kyoto: 1923); tr. D.T. Suzuki (Routledge: 1932).

Mahabhasya of Patanjali, op. cit.

Mahavastu, ed. E. Senart, 3 Vols (Paris: A.L. Impremerie National [Societe Asiatique Series, no. 2], 1882–97).

Malavikagnimitra of Kalidasa (Bombay: 1907).

Manu Smriti or *Manava Dharmasastra*, ed. S.N. Mandlik (Bombay: Ganpat Krishnaji's Press, 1886); tr. G. Buhler, *Sacred Books of the East*, 33 (Oxford: Oxford University Press: 1886).

Milindapanho, op. cit.

Saundarananda of Asvaghosa, Critical ed. with notes and tr., E.H. Johnston, 2 Vols (London: 1932); ed. H.P. Sastri (Calcutta: Bibliotheca Indica, 1910).

Silappadikaram with Commentary of Adiyarkkunattar, ed. V.S. Iyer (Madras: 1920); Eng. tr. V.R.R. Dikshitar (Oxford: 1939).

Sumangala Vilasini: Commentary to Digha Nikaya, eds T.W. Rhys Davids and others, 3 Vols (London: Pali Text Society, 1886–1932).

Sushruta Samhita, 30, 4 Vols (Varanasi: Chaukhamba Sanskrit Series, 1963–4).

Sutta Nipata, ed. V. Fausboll, 2 Vols (London: Pali Text Society. 1885–94).

Vinaya Pitaka, ed. H. Oldenberg, 5 Vols (London: Pali Text Society, 1879–83); *The Book of Discipline*, tr. I.B. Horner, 5 Parts, *Sacred Books of the Buddhists* (London: 1938–52).

Archaeology, Coins, and Inscriptions

Gardner, P., *The Coins of the Greek and Scythian Kings of India of Bactria and India in the British Museum* (rpt, Chicago: Argonaut, 1970).

Hartel, H., 'Some Results of the Excavation at Sonkh', in *German Scholars on India*, 2 (New Delhi: 1976).

Konow, Sten, *Corpus Inscriptionum Indicarum*, Vol. 2, Part 1, *Kharosthi Inscriptions with the Exception of those of Asoka* (Calcutta: Central Publication Branch, Government of India, 1929).

Lahiri, A.N., *Corpus of Indo-Greek Coins* (Calcutta: Poddar Publications, 1965).

Luders, H., *Mathura Inscriptions*, ed. K.L. Janert (Gottingeri: 1961).

Marshall, J.H., *Taxila: An Illustrated Account of Archaeological Excavations* (Cambridge: Cambridge University Press, 1951.).

Sharma, G.R., *The Excavations at Kausambi (1957–59)*, op. cit.

Sircar, D.C. (ed.), *Select Inscriptions Bearing on Indian History and Civilization*, Vol. 1, op. cit.

Wheeler, R.E.M., *Charsada: A Metropolis of the North-West Frontier* (Oxford: Oxford University Press, 1962).

Secondary

Adhya, G.L., *Early Indian Economics—Studies in the Economic Life of Northern and Western India (c. 200 B.C.–300 A.D.)* (New Delhi: Asia Publishing House, 1966).

Bagchi, P.C., *India and Central Asia* (Calcutta: National Council of Education Research, 1955).

Basham, A.L. (ed.), *A Cultural History of India*, op. cit.

Boulnois, L., *The Silk Road* (London: George Allen & Unwin, 1966).

Chakraberti, Kanchan, *Society, Religion and Art of the Kushana India* (Calcutta: K.P. Bagchi and Co., 1981).

Charlesworth, Martin P., *Trade-Routes and Commerce of the Roman Empire* (Cambridge: Cambridge University Press, 1926).

Chattopadhyay, Bhaskar, *The Age of the Kushans: A Numismatic Study* (Calcutta: Punthi Pustak, 1967).

_____, *Kushana State and Indian Society: A Study in Post-Mauryan Polity and Society* (Calcutta: Punthi Pustak, 1975).

Chattopadhyaya, Sudhakar, *The Sakas in India*, 2nd edn (Santiniketan: Visva Bharati, 1967).

_____, *Early History of North India: From the Fall of the Mauryas to the Death of Harsha*, 3rd edn (Delhi: Motilal Banarsidass, 1976).

Ghosh, A. (ed.), op. cit.

Guha, Amalendu (ed.), *Central Asia: Movement of People and Ideas from Times Prehistoric to Modern* (New Delhi: Indian Council for Cultural Relations, 1970).

Gupta, P.L., *Roman Coins from Andhra Pradesh* (Hyderabad: Govt of Andhra Pradesh, 1965).

Habib, Irfan (ed.), *A Shared Heritage: The Growth of Civilizations in India and Iran*, op. cit.

Jain, Rekha, op. cit.

Jayaswal, Vidula, *Kushana Clay Art of Ganga Plains* (Delhi: Agam Kala Prakashan, 1991).

Joshi, N.P., *Life in Ancient Uttarapatha: Material Civilisation of Northern India from c. 200 B.C. to c. 300 A.D. as Revealed by the Sculptures, Terracottas and Coins* (Varanasi: Banaras Hindu University, 1967).

Lahiri, A.N., *The Archaeology of Indian Trade Routes up to c. 200 B.C.* (New Delhi: Oxford University Press, 1992).

Liu, Xinru, *Ancient India and Ancient China: Trade and Religious Exchanges A.D. 1–600* (New Delhi: Oxford University Press, 1988).

Lohuizen-de Leeu, J.E. Van, *The 'Scythian' Period: An Approach to the History, Art, Epigraphy and Palaeography of North India from the First Century to the Third Century AD* (Leiden: E.J. Brill, 1949).

Motichandra, *Trade and Trade Routes in Ancient India* (New Delhi: Abhinav Publications, 1977).

Mukherjee, B.N., *The Disintegration of the Kushana Empire* (Varanasi: Banaras Hindu University, 1976).

——, *Kushana Silver Coinage* (Calcutta: Indian Museum, 1982).

——, *The Rise and Fall of the Kushan Empire* (Calcutta: Firma KLM Pvt. Ltd, 1989).

Narain, A.K., *The Indo-Greeks* (London: Oxford University Press, 1957).

——, *From Alexander to Kanishka*, op. cit.

Nilakanta Sastri, K.A. (ed.), *A Comprehensive History of India*, Vol. 2, op. cit.

Prasad, Kameshwar, *Cities, Crafts and Commerce under the Kushanas* (Delhi: Agam Kala Prakashan, 1984).

Puri, B.N., *India under the Kushans* (Bombay: Bharatiya Vidya Bhawan, 1965).

——, *India in the Time of Patanjali*, 2nd edn (Bombay: Bharatiya Vidya Bhawan, 1968).

——, *Kusana Bibliography* (Calcutta: Naya Prokash, 1977).

Ray, Himanshu Prabha and Jean-Francois Salles (eds), *Tradition and Archaeology: Early Maritime Contacts in the Indian Ocean* (New Delhi: Manohar, 1996).

Raychaudhuri, Hemachandra, *Political History of Ancient India*, op. cit.

Romani, F. De and A. Tchernia (eds), *Crossings: Early Mediterranean Contacts with India* (New Delhi: Manohar, 1997).

Rosenfield, John M., *The Dynastic Arts of the Kushans* (California: University of California Press, 1967).

Rydh, Hanna, *Rang Mahal: The Swedish Archaeological Expedition to India (1952–54)* (Lund: 1959).

Sagar, Krishna Chandra, *Foreign Influence on Ancient India* (New Delhi: Northern Book Centre, 1992).

Sahay, Sachidanand, *Indian Costume, Coiffure and Ornament* (New Delhi: Munshiram Manoharlal, 1975).

Sharma, G.R. (ed.), *Kushana Studies* (Allahabad: University of Allahabad, 1968).

Shastri, Ajay Mitra, *Mitra Coins and Early Indian Economy* (Varanasi: Numismatic Society of India, 1976).

Singh, Ajoy Kumar, *Indo-Roman Trade: An Archaeological Perspective* (Patna/New Delhi: Janaki Prakashan, 1988).

Singh, Ravindra, *Ancient Indian Glass Archaeology and Technology* (Delhi: Parimal Publications, 1989).

Tam, W.W., *The Greeks in Bactria and India*, 2nd edn (Cambridge: Cambridge University Press, 1951).

Thakur, Upendra, op. cit.

Thakur, Vijay Kumar, *Urbanisation in Ancient India*, op. cit.

Thapar, Romila, *Early India*, op. cit.

Turner, Paula J., *Roman Coins from India* (London: Royal Numismatic Society, 1989).

Warmington, E.H., *The Commerce between the Roman Empire and India,* 2nd rev. and enlarged edn (Indian edn, Delhi: Vikas Publishing House Ltd, 1974).

CHAPTER 21 THE SATAVAHANA PHASE

CHAPTER 22 THE DAWN OF HISTORY IN THE DEEP SOUTH

CHAPTER 28 BRAHMANIZATION, RURAL EXPANSION, AND PEASANT PROTEST IN THE PENINSULA

Original Texts and Translations

Silappadikaram, op. cit.

Gathasaptasati of Hala, op. cit.

Manimekalai, ed. U.V. Caminata Iyer, 5th edn (1956).

Tirukkural or *Tiruvalluvar*, Tamil Text and Eng. tr. with Notes and Comments by K.M. Balasubramaniam Tiruvachakamani (Madras: 1962).

Archaeology and Inscriptions

Mirashi, V.V., *Corpus Inscriptionum Indicarum,* Vol. 5, *Inscriptions of Vakatakas* (Ootacamund: Department of Archaeology [India], 1955).

Sircar, D.C. (ed.), *Select Inscriptions Bearing on Indian History and Civilization,* Vols 1 and 2, op. cit.

Wheeler, R.E.M. 'Arikamedu: An Indo-Roman Trading Station on the East Coast of India', in *Ancient India,* no. 2, 1946, 17–124.

Secondary

Aiyangar, P.T.S., *History of the Tamils to 600 A.D.* (Madras: 1929).

Aravamuthan, T.G., *The Kaveri, the Maukharis and the Sangam Age* (Madras: 1925).

Ayyar, C.V.N., *Origin and Early History of Saivism in South India,* (Madras: 1936).

Champakalakshmi, R., *Trade, Ideology and Urbanization in South India 300 BC to AD 1300* (New Delhi: Oxford University Press, 1996).

Champakalakshmi, R., Kesavan Veluthat, and T.R. Venugopalan, *State and Society in Pre-Modern South India* (Thrissur [Kerala]: Cosmobooks, 2002).

Chattopadhyay, B.D., *Coins and Currency System in South India* (New Delhi: Munshiram Manoharlal, 1977).

Desai, P.B., *Jainism in South India* (Sholapur: 1957).

Desikachari, T., *South Indian Coins* (Trichirapally: 1933).

Dikshitar, V.R.R., *Studies in Tamil Literature and History* (Madras: 1936).

Ganguly, D.C., *The Eastern Chalukyas* (Benares: 1937).

Ghosh, A. (ed.), op. cit.

Gupta, Chitrarekha, *The Brahmanas of India*, op. cit.

Gopalan, B., *History of the Pallavas of Kanchi* (Madras: 1928).

Hultzch, E., *South Indian Inscriptions* (Mysore: Archaeological Survey of India; rpt, Varanasi: Indological Book House, 1972).

Jha, D.N., *Revenue System in the Post-Maurya and Gupta Times*, (Calcutta: Punthi Pustak, 1967).

Jonveau-Dubreuil, G., *Ancient History of the Deccan*, tr. from the French by V.S. Swaminathan Dikshitar (Pondicherry: 1920).

Kramrisch, Stella, *A Survey of Painting in the Deccan* (London: 1937).

Kuppuswami, T.V., *Sangam Chieftains and Their Times* (Thanjavur: T.V.K. Felicitation Committee, 1984).

Margabhandu, C., *Archaeology of the Satavahana-Kshatrapa Times* (New Delhi: Sundeep Prakashan, 1985).

Majumdar, R.C. and A.S. Altekar (eds), *The Vakataka-Gupta Age* (Delhi: Motilal Banarsidass, 1946).

Majumdar, R.C. (ed.), *A Comprehensive History of India*, Vol. 3, *A.D. 300–985*, Parts 1 and 2 (New Delhi: People's Publishing House, 1981 and 1982).

Moraes, G.M., *The Kadamba Kula* (Bombay: 1931).

Nandi, Ramendra Nath, *Social Roots of Religion in Ancient India* (Calcutta: K.P. Bagchi & Co., 1986).

Narayanan, M.G.S., *Foundations of South Indian Society and Culture* (Delhi: Bharatiya Book Corp., 1994).

Nilakanta Sastri, K.A., *The Pandyan Kingdom* (London: Luzac & Co., 1929).

_____, *The Cholas*, 2 Vols, 2nd edn (Madras: University of Madras, 1955).

_____, *A History of South India: From the Earliest Times to Vijayanagar*, 4th edn (Madras: Oxford University Press, 1976).

_____ (ed.), *A Comprehensive History of India*, Vol. 2, op. cit.

Pillay, K.K., *A Social History of Tamils* (Madras: University of Madras, 1975).

Parashar-Sen, Aloka (ed.), *Social and Economic History of Early Deccan: Some Interpretations* (New Delhi: Manohar, 1993).

Prakash, V., *Coinage of South India: An Introductory Survey* (Varanasi: 1968).

Raychaudhuri, Hemachandra, *Political History of Ancient India*, op. cit.

Prasad, O.P., *Decay and Revival of Urban Centres in Medieval South India* (New Delhi: Commonwealth, 1986).

Ramkrishna, G., Gayathri, and Debiprasad Chattopadhyaya, *An Encyclopaedia of South Indian Culture* (Delhi: K.P. Bagchi & Co., 1983).

Rao, M.V.K., *The Gangas of Talkad* (Madras: 1936).

Rao, B.V.K., *Early Dynasties of Andhradesa (200–625 A.D.)* (Madras: 1942).

Roy, Sita Ram, *Suvarnavarnavadana* (Patna: K.P. Jayaswal Research Institute, 1976).

Sarkar, H. and S.P. Nainar, *Amaravati* (New Delhi: 1972).

Sarkar, H. and B.N. Misra, *Nagarjunakonda* (New Delhi: 1972).

Settar, S. and G.D. Sontheimer, *Memorial Stones: A Study of their Origin, Significance and Variety* (Dharwad: Karnataka University, 1982).

Sharma, R.S., *Urban Decay in India (c. 300–c. 1000)* (New Delhi: Munshiram Manoharlal, 1987).

_____, *Aspects of Political Ideas and Institutions in Ancient India*, op. cit.

Shastri, A.M., *Early History of the Deccan: Problems and Perspectives* (Delhi: Sundeep Prakashan, 1987).

_____ (ed.), *The Age of the Vakatakas* (New Delhi: Harman Publishing House, 1992).

Shrimali, K.M. (ed.), *Agrarian Structure in Central India and the Northern Deccan: A Study in Vakataka Inscriptions* (New Delhi: Munshiram Manoharlal, 1987).

Sircar, D.C., *The Early Pallavas* (Lahore: 1935).

_____, *The Successors of the Satavahanas in the Lower Deccan* (Calcutta: 1939).

Srinivasan, K.R., *Cave Temples of the Pallavas* (New Delhi: 1964).

_____, *Temples of South India*, 3rd edn (New Delhi: National Book Trust, India, 1985).

Thapar, Romila, *Early India*, op. cit.

Varadarajan, Mu, *A History of Tamil Literature*, tr. from Tamil by E. Sa. Viswanathan (Delhi: Sahitya Akademi, 1988).

Venkataramanayya, N., *The Eastern Chalukyas of Vengi* (Madras: 1950).

Yazdani, G. (ed.), *The Early History of the Deccan* (London: Oxford University Press, 1960).

Chapter 24 Rise and Growth of the Gupta Empire

Chapter 25 Life in the Gupta Age

Original Texts and Translations

Abhijnanasakuntalam, ed. and tr. C.R. Devadhar (Delhi: 1966).

Amarakosa, eds H.D. Sharma and N.G. Sardesai (Poona: Oriental Book Agency, 1941).

Aryabhatiya of Aryabhata, Critical ed. with tr. and notes by K.S. Shukla and K.V. Sharma (New Delhi: Indian National Science Academy, 1976).

Beal, Samuel, tr. *Travels of Fa-hien and Sung-Yun* (London: 1869; Indian rpt, New Delhi: Oriental Publication, 1971).

Bhagvadgita, Sanskrit text with English tr. Annie Besant and Bhagvan Das (Benaras: 1905).

Bhagavata Purana, ed. J.L. Shastri (Delhi: Motilal Banarsidass, 1983).

Brahmanda Purana, ed. J.L. Shastri (Delhi: Motilal Banarsidass, 1973).

Brhaspati Smrti, ed. K.V. Rangasvami Aiyangar, 85 (Baroda: Gaekvad Oriental Series, 1941).

Brhat Samhita of Varahamihira, ed. with Hindi tr. Achyutanand Jha Sharma (Varanasi: Chowkhamba Vidyabhavan, 1917).

Giles, Herbert Alen, tr. *The Travels of Fa-hsien (399–414)*, op. cit.

Kamandaka Nitisara (Trivandrum: Trivandrum Sanskrit Series, 1912).

Katyayana Smrti on *Vyavahara* (Law and Procedure), ed. with reconstituted text, trans. notes and introduction by P.V. Kane (Bombay: 1933).

Mahabharata, op. cit.

Manu Smrti or *Manava Dharmasastra*, with the commentary of Kulluka Bhatta, ed. Pandit Kesava Prasad Sharma Dvivedi (Bombay: Venkatesvara Steam Press, Saka Samvat, 1826).

Mrcchakatika of Sudraka, ed. and tr. R.D. Karmakar (Poona: 1937); tr. R.P. Oliver (Illinois: 1938).

Narada Smriti, ed., tr. and commentary by Richard W. Lariviere, Part 1 (text), Part 2 (trans.) (Philadelphia: University of Pennysylvania, 1989).

Ramayana, op. cit.

Vayu Purana, ed. R.L. Mitra, 2 Vols (Calcutta: Bibliotheca Indica, 1880). *Visnu Purana* (Gorakhpur: Gita Press edn); tr. H.H. Wilson, 5 Vols (London: 1864–70).

Visnu Smrti or *Vaisnava Dharmasastra* with extracts from the Commentary of Nanda Pandita, ed. J. Jolly (Calcutta: Bibliotheca Indica, 1881).

Coins and Inscriptions

Altekar, Anant Sadashiv, *The Coinage of the Gupta Empire,* Vol. 4, *Corpus of Indian Coins* (Varanasi: Numismatic Society of India, 1957).

Diskalkar, D.B., *Selections from Sanskrit Inscriptions (2nd cent. to 8th cent. A.D.)* (New Delhi: Classical Publishers, 1977).

Fleet, J.F., *Corpus Inscriptionum Indicarum,* Vol. 3, *Inscriptions of the Early Gupta Kings and their Successors* (Calcutta: Government of India, 1888); revised by D.R. Bhandarkar (New Delhi: Archaeological Survey of India, 1981).

Secondary

Agrawala, V.S., *Indian Art*, op. cit.

Agrawala, Prithvi Kumar, *Gupta Temple Architecture* (Varanasi: Prithivi Prakashan, 1981).

Altekar, A.S., *The Position of Women in Hindu Civilisation*, op. cit.

Asher, F.M., *The Art of Eastern India (300–800),* edn for South Asia (New Delhi: Oxford University Press, 1980).

Banerjea, Jitendra Nath, *The Development of Hindu Iconography,* 4th edn (New Delhi: Munshiram Manoharlal, 1985).

Banerji, Rakhal Das, *The Age of the Imperial Guptas* (Varanasi: Banaras Hindu University, 1933).

Basak, Radhagovinda, *The History of North-Eastern India Extending from the Foundation of the Gupta Empire to the Rise of the Pala Dynasty of Bengal (c. 320–760 AD)* (London: Kegan Paul, Trench, Trubner & Co. Ltd, 1934).

Basham, A.L., *The Origins and Developments of Classical Hinduism* (New Delhi: Oxford University Press, 1990).

Charkrabarti, D.K., *The Archaeology of Ancient Indian Cities,* op. cit.

Chakraborti, Haripada, *India as Reflected in the Inscriptions of the Gupta Period* (New Delhi: Munshiram Manoharlal, 1978).

Chattopadhyaya, Sudhakar, *Early History of North India,* op. cit.

Dasgupta, Kalyan Kumar, *A Tribal History of Ancient India: A Numismatic Approach* (Calcutta: Nababharat Publishers, 1974).

Deva, Krishna, *Temples of North India,* 3rd edn (New Delhi: National Book Trust, India, 1997).

Dutt, Nalinaksha, *Early Monastic Buddhism* (Calcutta: Firma K.L. Mukhopadhyay, 1971).

Eliot, Charles N.E., *Hinduism and Buddhism* (rpt, London: Routledge & Kegan Paul Ltd, 1962).

Ghosh, A. (ed.), op. cit.

Ghoshal, U.N., *Contributions to the History of the Hindu Revenue System,* op. cit.

Goyal, S.R., *A History of the Imperial Guptas* (Allahabad: Central Book Depot, 1967).

Goyal, S.R. and Shankar Goyal (eds), *Indian Art of the Gupta Age from Pre-Classical Roots to the Emergence of Medieval Trends* (Jodhpur: Kusamanjali Book World, 2000).

Gupta, Chitrarekha, *The Brahmanas of India,* op. cit.

_____, *The Kayasthas: A Study in the Formation and Early History of a Caste* (Calcutta: K.P. Bagchi, 1996).

Gupta, P.L., *The Imperial Guptas,* 2 Vols (Varanasi: Vishwavidyalaya Prakashan, 1974–9).

Harle, J.C., *Gupta Sculpture: Indian Sculpture from the Fourth to the Sixth Centuries A.D.* (Oxford: Oxford University Press, 1974).

Hazara, R.C., *Studies in Upapuranas,* 2 (Calcutta: Sanskrit College, 1971).

_____, *Studies in the Puranic Records on Hindu Rites and Customs,* 1st edn (Dacca: Dacca University, 1940); 2nd edn (Delhi: Motilal Banarsidass, 1975)

Jain, K.C., *Kalidasa and His Times* (Delhi: Agam Kala Prakashan, 1990).

Jaiswal, Suvira, *Origin and Development of Vaisnavism,* 2nd edn (New Delhi: Munshiram Manoharlal, 1981).

Jha, D.N., *Revenue System in the Post-Maurya and Gupta Times,* op. cit.

Lingat, Robert, *The Classical Law of India,* tr. and with additions by J. Duncan M. Derrett (California: University of California Press, 1973).

Maity, S.K., *Economic Life of Northern India in the Gupta Period, c. AD 300–550* (Calcutta: The World Press, 1957).

——, *The Imperial Guptas and their Times (c. A.D. 300–550)* (New Delhi: Munshiram Manoharlal, 1975).

Majumdar, R.C. and A.S. Altekar (eds), *The Vakataka-Gupta Age,* op. cit.

Majumdar, R.C. (ed.), *The History and Culture of the Indian People,* Vol. 3, *The Classical Age* (Bombay: Bharatiya Vidya Bhawan, 1954).

—— (ed.), *A Comprehensive History of India,* Vol. 3, op. cit.

Mookerji, R.K., *Ancient Indian Education: Brahmanical and Buddhist,* 3rd edn (Delhi: Motilal Banarsidass, 1960).

Motichandra, op. cit.

Nath, Vijay, *Dana: Gift System in Ancient India,* op. cit.

Nigam, Shyamsunder, *Economic Organisation in Ancient India* (New Delhi: Munshiram Manoharlal, 1975).

Parasher, Aloka, *Mlecchas in Early India: A Study in Attitudes towards Outsiders up to A.D. 600,* op. cit.

Pargiter, F.E., *The Purana Text of the Dynasties of the Kali Age* (Oxford: 1913; Indian rpt, Benaras: Chowkhamba Sanskrit Series, 1962).

Rai, Jaimal, *The Rural–Urban Economy and Social Changes in Ancient India* (300 B.C. to A.D. 600) (Varanasi/Delhi: Bharatiya Vidya Prakashan, 1974).

Raychaudhuri, Hemachandra, *Political History of Ancient India,* op. cit.

Rowland, Benjamin, *The Art and Architecture of India: Buddhist, Hindu, Jain,* op. cit.

Roy, S.N., *Historical and Cultural Studies in the Puranas* (Allahabad: Puranic Publications, 1978).

Sarasvati, S.K., op. cit.

Sharma, R.S., *Urban Decay in India,* op. cit.

——, *Sudras in Ancient India,* op. cit.

Shrimali, K.M., *History of Pancala to c. A.D. 500,* op. cit.

——, *Agrarian Structure in Central India and the Northern Deccan: A Study in Vakataka Inscriptions* (New Delhi: Munshiram Manoharlal, 1987).

Sinha, B.P., *The Decline of the Kingdom of Magadha* (Patna: Motilal Banarsidass, 1954).

Thakur, Upendra, op. cit.

Thapar, Romila, *Early India*, op. cit.

Vettam, Mani, *Puranic Encyclopaedia* (rpt, Delhi: Motilal Banarsidass, 1984).

CHAPTER 26 SPREAD OF CIVILIZATION IN EASTERN INDIA

CHAPTER 31 FROM ANCIENT TO MEDIEVAL

Original Texts and Translations

Beal, Samuel, tr. *Travels of Fa-hien and Sung-Yun*, op. cit.

_____ , *Si-Yu-Ki*, op. cit.

Lingat, Robert, *The Classical Law of India*, op. cit.

Mudraraksasa by Visakhadatta, op. cit.

Narada Smriti, op. cit.

Subhasitaratnakosa by Vidyakara, eds D.D. Kosambi and V.V. Gokhale (Mass.: Harvard University Press, 1957).

Visnudharmottara Purana (Bombay: Venkatesvara Press, 1912).

Vyavaharamayukha of Bhatta Nilakantha, ed. P.V. Kane (Poona: Bhandarkar Oriental Research Institute, 1926).

Inscriptions

Mirashi, V.V., *Corpus Inscriptionum Indicarum, Inscriptions of Kalachuri Cedi Era*, Vol. 4, 2 Parts (Ootacamund: Department of Archaeology [India], 1929 and 1955).

_____ , *Corpus Inscriptionum Indicarum*, Vol. 5, *Inscriptions of Vakatakas*, op. cit.

Mukherjee, R. and S.K. Maity, *Corpus of Bengal Inscriptions Bearing on the History and Civilization of Bengal* (Calcutta: Firma K.L. Mukhopadhyaya, 1967).

Sarma, Dimbeswar (ed.), *Kamarupasasanavali* (Gauhati: Publication Board, 1981).

Sircar, D.C. (ed.), *Select Inscriptions bearing on Indian History and Civilization*, 2 Vols, op. cit.

Tripathi, Snigdha, *Inscriptions of Orissa (circa Fifth-Eighth Centuries AD)*, Vol. 1 (Delhi: Motilal Banarsidass, 1977).

Secondary

Anderson, Perry, *Passages from Antiquity to Feudalism* (London: New Left Books, 1974).

Bagchi, P.C., *Studies in the Tantras*, Part 1 (Calcutta: University of Calcutta, 1939).

Banerjea, J.N., *Puranic and Tantric Religion* (Calcutta: University of Calcutta, 1966).

Banerjee, R.D., *History of Orissa*, 2 Vols (Calcutta: 1930–1).

Barua, K.L., *Early History of Kamarupa*, Vol. 1 (Shillong: 1933).

Basham, A.L. (ed.), *A Cultural History of India*, op. cit.

Bhattacharya, Batuknath, *The Kalivarjyas* (Calcutta: University of Calcutta, 1943).

Bhattacharya, N.N., *History of the Tantric Religion* (New Delhi: Manohar, 1982).

Chakrabarti, Kumud, *Religious Process: The Puranas and the Making of Regional Tradition* (New Delhi: Oxford University Press, 2001).

Chakravarty, Chintaharan, *The Tantras: Studies on their Religion and Literature* (Calcutta: Punthi Pustak, 1963).

Chand, Mohan, *Jain Sanskrit Mahakavyon Mein Bhartiya Samaj* (New Delhi: Eastern Book Linkers, 1989).

Chattopadhyaya, Annapurna, *The People and Culture of Bengal: A Study in Origins*, Vol. 1, Parts 1 and 2 (Kolkata: Firma KLM Pvt. Ltd, 2002).

Chattopadhyaya, Brajadulal, *Aspects of Rural Settlements and Rural Society in Early Medieval India* (Calcutta/New Delhi: K.P. Bagchi, 1990).

——, *The Making of Early Medieval India* (New Delhi: Oxford University Press, 1994).

Chattopadhya, K.P., *The Ancient Indian Culture, Contacts and Migrations* (Calcutta, Firma K.L.M., 1970).

Choudhury, P.C., *History of Civilization of the People of Assam to the 12th Century A.D.* (Gauhati: 1959).

Chowdhari, T., 'Paryayamuktavali', in *Journal of the Bihar Research Society*, Vol. 31, 1945, App., 1–53; 'Index to Paryayamuktavali', Vol. 32, 1946, App., 54–134.

Datta, Swati, *Migrant Brahmanas in Northern India: Their Settlements and General Impact, c. AD 475–1030* (Delhi: Motilal Banarsidass, 1989).

Desai, Devangana, *Erotic Sculptures of India: A Socio-Cultural Study*, 2nd edn (New Delhi: Munshiram Manoharlal, 1985).

Deyell, J.S., *Living without Silver: The Monetary History of Early Medieval North India* (New Delhi: Oxford University Press, 1990).

Gopal, Lallanji, *The Economic Life of Northern India (c. A.D. 700–1200)* (Delhi: Motilal Banarsidass, 1965).

Hindess, Barry and Paul Q. Hirst, *Pre-Capitalist Modes of Production* (London: Macmillan, 1975).

Jha, D.N. (ed.), *Feudal Order State, Society and Ideology in Early Medieval India* (New Delhi: Manohar, 2000).

Jha, Vishwa Mohan, 'The Artless Pirennion', in *Indian Historical Review*, Vol. 18, nos. 1–2, July 1991–Jan. 1992, 92–103.

——, 'Settlement, Society and Polity in Early Medieval Rural India', in *Social Science Probings*, Vols 11 and 12, Special Issue, March 1994–Dec. 1995, 35–65.

Jain, K.C., *Madhya Pradesh through the Ages (From the Earliest Times to 1305 A.D.: A Study of Culture and Civilization)*, Vol. 1 (New Delhi: D.K. Publishers, 1997).

Krader, Lawrence, *The Asiatic Mode of Production* (The Netherlands: B.V. Assen Van Gorcum & Co., 1975).

Leach, Edmund, S. N. Mukherjee, and John Ward (eds), *Feudalism: Comparative Studies*, no. 2 (Sydney: The Sydney Association for Studies in Society and Culture, 1985).

Mahtab, H., *The History of Orissa* (Lucknow: 1949).

Majumdar, R.C., *History of Ancient Bengal* (Calcutta: G. Bhardwaj & Co., 1971).

Nandi, Ramendra Nath, *Religious Institutions and Cults in the Deccan (c. A.D. 600–A.D. 1000)* (Delhi: Motilal Banarsidass, 1973).

_____, *State Formation, Agrarian Growth and Social Changes in Feudal South India c. A.D. 600–1200* (New Delhi: Manohar, 2000).

Nath, Vijay, *Puranas* and *Acculturation: A Historico-Anthropological Perspective* (New Delhi: Munshiram Manoharlal, 2001).

O'Leary, Brendan, *The Asiatic Mode of Production: Oriental Despotism, Historical Materialism and Indian History* (Oxford: Basil Blackwell, 1989).

Ray, Niharranjan, *History of the Bengali People (Ancient Period)*, tr. from the Bengali, John H. Hood (Calcutta: Orient Longman, 1994).

Sah, Ayodhya Prasad, *Life in Medieval Orissa (c. AD 600–1200)* (Varanasi: Chaukhamba Orientalia, 1978).

Sahu, B.P. (ed.), *Land System and Rural Society in Early India: Readings in Early Indian History* (New Delhi: Manohar, 1997).

Sen, Madhu, op. cit.

Sengupta, Gautama and Sheena Panja, *Archaeology of Eastern India: New Perspectives* (Kolkata: Centre for Archaeological Studies and Training, Eastern India, 2002).

Sharma, A.K., *Evidence for Early Cultures in Northeast India* (Delhi: Aryan Books International, 1995).

Sharma, B.N., *Social Life in Northern India (AD 600–1000)* (New Delhi: Munshiram Manoharlal, 1966).

Sharma, R.S., *Indian Feudalism*, 2nd edn (Delhi: Macmillan, 1980).

_____, *Early Medieval Indian Society: A Study in Feudalisation* (Hyderabad: Orient Longman, 2001).

Shrimali, K.M., 'Money, Market and Indian Feudalism AD 600–1200', in A.K. Bagchi (ed.), *Money and Credit in Indian History from Early Medieval Times* (New Delhi: Tulika Books, 2002), pp. 1–39.

Sircar, D.C., *Land System and Feudalism in Ancient India* (Calcutta: University of Calcutta, 1966).

——, *The Sakti Cult and Tara* (Calcutta: University of Calcutta, 1967).

——, *Landlordism and Tenancy in Ancient and Medieval India as Revealed in Epigraphical Records* (Lucknow: University of Lucknow, 1969).

——, *Studies in the Political and Administrative Systems in Ancient and Mediev India* (Delhi: Motilal Banarsidass, 1974).

——, *Studies in the Religious Life of Ancient and Medieval India* (Delhi: Motilal Banarsidass, 1971).

Tambiah, S.J., 'From Varna to Caste through Mixed Unions', in Jack Goody (ed.), *The Character of Kinship* (Cambridge: Cambridge University Press, 1973), pp. 191–229.

Thakur, V.K., *Historiography of Indian Feudalism, Towards a Model of Medieval Economy, c. A.D. 600–1000* (Patna/New Delhi: Janaki Prakashan, 1989).

Veluthat, Kesavan, *The Political Structure of Early Medieval South India* (New Delhi: Orient Longman, 1993).

Warder, A.K., *Indian Kavya Literature,* Vol. 3, *The Early Medieval Period (Sudraka to Visakhadatta)*, 2nd revised edn (Delhi: Motilal Banarsidass, 1990); Vol. 4, *The Ways of Originality (Bana to Domodaragupta)* (Delhi: Motilal Banarsidass, 1983).

White (Jr), Lynn, *Medieval Religion and Technology* (London: University of California Press, 1978).

Woodroffe, Sir John, *Principles of Tantras* (Madras: 1952).

Yadava, B.N.S., 'The Accounts of the Kali Age and the Social Transition from Antiquity to the Middle Ages', in *Indian Historical Review*, Vol. 5, nos. 1 and 2, 1978, 31–63.

CHAPTER 27 HARSHA AND HIS TIMES

Original Texts and Translations

Beal, Samuel, *Si-Yu-Ki*, op. cit.

Harsacarita (with the commentary of Sankara), ed. K.P. Parab, 5th edn (Bombay: Nirnaya Sagar Press, 1925).

Parasara Smrti, with the commentary of Manohara (Benaras: Sanskrit Series, 1907).

Takakusu, T., tr. *A Record of the Buddhist Religion as Practised in India and the Malay by I-tsing* (Oxford: Oxford University Press, 1886).

Inscriptions

Sircar, D.C. (ed.), *Select Inscriptions Bearing on Indian History and Civilization,* Vol. 2, op. cit.

Thaplyal, Kiran Kumar, *Inscriptions of the Maukharis, Later Guptas, Puspabhutis and Yasovarman of Kanauj* (Delhi/New Delhi: Agam Prakashan/Indian Council of Historical Research, 1985).

Secondary

Chattopadhyaya, Sudhakar, *Early History of North India*, op. cit.

Devahuti, D., *Harsha: A Political Study*, 2nd edn (New Delhi: Oxford University Press, 1980).

Ghosh, A. (ed.), op. cit.

Majumdar, R.C. (ed.), *The History and Culture of the Indian People*, Vol. 4, *The Age of Imperial Kanauj* (Bombay: Bharatiya Vidya Bhawan, 1955).

Pires, Edward A., *The Maukharis* (Madras: B.G. Paul, 1934).

Ray, H.C., *Dynastic History of Northern India*, Vol. 1, 2nd edn (New Delhi: Munshiram Manoharlal, 1973).

Sharma, Baijnath, *Harsa and His Times* (Varanasi: Sushma Prakashan, 1970).

Srivastava, B.N., 'History of the Maukharis of Kanauj during the Seventh Century A.D.', in *Bulletin of the U.P. Historical Society*, no. 1 (Lucknow: U.P. Historical Society, 1958).

_____ , 'Sasanka, King of Gauda', in *Bulletin of the U.P. Historical Society*, no. 3 (Lucknow: U.P. Historical Society, 1965).

Thapar, Romila, *Early India*, op. cit.

Tripathi, R.S., *History of Kanauj* (Delhi: Motilal Banarsidass, 1964).

CHAPTER 29 DEVELOPMENTS IN PHILOSOPHY

CHAPTER 33 LEGACY IN SCIENCE AND CIVILIZATION

Secondary

Bag, A.K. (ed.), *History of Technology in India*, Vol. 1, *From Antiquity to c. 1200 A.D.* (New Delhi: Indian National Science Academy, 1997).

Belvalkar, S.K. and R.K. Ranade, *History of Indian Philosophy: The Creative Period* (Poona: Bilva-Kunja Publishing House, 1927).

Bhishagacarya, G.M., *History of Indian Medicine*, 2 Vols (Calcutta: 1923–6).

Bose, D.M., S.N. Sen, and B.V. Subbrayappa (eds), *A Concise History of Science in India* (New Delhi: National Science Academy, 1971).

Chattopadhyaya, D.P., *Lokayata: A Study in Ancient Indian Materialism* (New Delhi: People's Publishing House, 1959).

_____, *What is Living and What is Dead in Indian Philosophy* (New Delhi: People's Publishing House, 1976).

_____ (ed.), *Studies in the History of Indian Philosophy*, 3 Vols (Calcutta: K.P. Bagchi & Co., 1978).

——, *Science and Society in Ancient India* (Calcutta: Research India Publishing, 1977).

——, *History of Science and Technology in Ancient India: The Beginnings* (Calcutta: Firma KLM Pvt. Ltd, 1986).

—— (ed.), *Studies in the History of Science in India,* 2 Vols (New Delhi: Editorial Enterpriscs, 1982).

Dasgupta, Surendra Nath, *A History of Indian Philosophy,* 5 Vols (Cambridge: Cambridge University Press, 1923–49); rpt, (Delhi: Motilal Banarsidass, 1975).

Datta, B. and A.N. Singh, *History of Hindu Mathematics,* 2 Parts in one Vol. (Bombay and London: 1962).

Datta, D.M., *Six Ways of Knowing,* 2nd edn (Calcutta: 1960).

Ghosh, A. (ed.), op. cit.

Hegde, K.T.M., *An Introduction to Indian Metallurgy* (Bangalore: Geological Survey of India, 1991).

Hiriyanna, M., *Outlines of Indian Philosophy* (London: 1970).

Keith, A.B., *Indian Logic and Atomism* (Oxford: 1921).

Max Müller, F., *Six Systems of Indian Philosophy* (rpt, London: 1919).

Menon, C.P.S., *Ancient Astronomy and Cosmology* (London: 1931).

Radhakrishnan, S., *Indian Philosophy,* 2 Vols (London: 1958).

Radhakrishnan, S. and C.A. More, *A Source Book of Indian Philosophy* (Princeton: 1957).

Singerist, H.E., *History of Medicine,* Vol. 2, *Early Greek, Hindu and Persian Medicine* (Oxford: 1962).

Takakusu, J., *Essentials of Buddhist Philosophy* (Honolulu: 1947).

Thakur, V.K. and K.K. Mandal (eds), *Science, Technology and Medicine in Indian History* (Patna/New Delhi: Janaki Prakashan, 2000).

Zimmer, H., *Philosophies of India,* ed. by J. Campbeu (London: 1953).

Chapter 30 Cultural Interaction with Asian Countries

Secondary

Basham, A.L. (ed.), *A Cultural History of India,* op. cit.

Coedes, George, *The Indianized States of South East Asia* (Honolulu: East–West Centre Press, 1968).

Gombrich, Richard, *Theravada Buddhism: A Social History from Ancient Benares to Modern Colombo* (London and New York: Routledge & Kegan Paul, 1988).

Hall, D.G.E., *A History of South East Asia,* 3rd edn (London: 1968).

Le May, R., *The Culture of South-East Asia* (London: 1954).

Majumdar, R.C., *Ancient Indian Colonies in the Far East,* Vol. 1, *Champa* (Lahore: 1927); Vol. 2, *Suvarnadvipa,* 2 Parts (Dacca: 1937–38).

_____, *Kambujadesa* (Madras: 1944).

_____, *Hindu Colonies in the Far East* (Calcutta: 1963).

_____, *History of the Hindu Colonization and Hindu Culture in South-East Asia* (Jabalpur: University of Jabalpur, 1970).

Mendis, G.C., *Early History of Ceylon* (London: 1883).

Nilakanta Sastri, K.A., *South Indian Influences in the Far East* (Bombay: 1949).

Sarkar, H.B., *Indian Influences on the Literature of Java and Bali* (Calcutta: 1934).

Wales, H.G.Q., *The Making of Greater India* (London: 1951).

Dictionaries

Allen, Robert (ed.), *Encarta World English Dictionary* (Special Indian edn, Chennai: Macmillan India, 1999).

Bottomore, T.B. (ed.), *A Dictionary of Marxist Thought,* Blackwell Reference (Oxford: Basil Blackwell, 1983).

Bray, Warwick and David Trump, *Dictionary of Archaeology,* 2nd edn (Harmondsworth: Penguin Books, 1982).

Crystal, David (ed.), *The Cambridge Paperback Encyclopedia* (New Delhi: Foundation Books, 2000).

Dikshitar, V.R.R., *Puranic Index* (incomplete) (Madras: 1952).

Ehrich, Robert W., *Chronologies in Old World Archaeology,* 3rd edn, Vol. 1 (Chicago: University of Chicago Press, 1992).

Ghosh, A. (ed.) *An Encyclopaedia of Indian Archaeology,* 2 Vols (New Delhi: Munshiram Manoharlal, 1989).

Hoffmann, Rev John and Rev Arthur Van Emelen, *Encyclopaedia Mundarica* (Patna: Supdt, Govt Printing [Bihar], 1950).

Joshi, Laxmanshastri (ed.), *Dharmakosa,* Parts 1–3, (Wai, Satara Dist: Prajna Pathasala Mandala, 1937–41).

Macdonnel, A.A. and A.B. Keith, *Vedic Index of Names and Subjects,* 2 Vols (London: Indian Text Series, 1922).

Malalasekere, G.P., *Dictionary of Pali Proper Names* (London: John Murray, 1937).

Monier-Williams, Monier, *A Sanskrit–English Dictionary* (Oxford University Press, 1899); Indian rpt, (Delhi: Motilal Banarsidass, 1986).

Pearsall, Judy and Bill Trumble (eds), *The Oxford English Reference Dictionary* (Oxford: Oxford University Press, 1995).

Rhys Davids, T.W. and W. Stede, *Pali-English Dictionary* (London: Pali Text Society, 1921).

Robinson, Mairi and George Robinson, *Chambers 21st Century Dictionary* (New Delhi: Allied Chambers [India] Ltd, 1997).

Shastri, Visvabandhu, *Vedic Padanukrama Kosa,* in 5 Vols subdivided into 14 parts (Lahore: V.R.R. Institute, 1944).

Shaw, Ian and Rombert Jameson, *A Dictionary of Archaeology* (Kundli: Blackwell Publishing Co., 2002).

Sircar, D.C., *Indian Epigraphical Glossary* (Delhi: Motilal Banarsidass, 1966).

Turner, R.L., *A Comparative Dictionary of the Indo-Aryan Languages* (London: Oxford University Press, 1966).

Journals and Periodical Publications

Annals of the Bhandarkar Oriental Research Institute, Pune.

Antiquity, Avenel, New Jersey, United States of America.

Electronic Journal of Vedic Studies, Harvard.

Epigraphia Indica, New Delhi.

Indian Archaeology: A Review up to 1997–8, New Delhi.

Indian Epigraphy, New Delhi.

Indian Historical Review, New Delhi.

Journal of the American Oriental Society, Baltimore.

Journal of the Asiatic Society, Kolkata.

Journal of the Bihar and Orissa Research Society, Patna.

Journal of the Bombay Asiatic Society, Mumbai.

Journal of Indian History, Trivandrum.

Journal of the Numismatic Society of India, Varanasi.

Journal of Peasant Studies, London.

Journal of the Royal Asiatic Society of Great Britain and Ireland, London.

Journal of the Social and Economic History of the Orient, Leiden.

Proceedings of the Indian History Congress, New Delhi.

Puratattava, New Delhi.

Social Science Probings, New Delhi.

Social Scientist, New Delhi.

South Asian Archaeology, Toronto.

Index